*The People of the Dead Sea Scrolls*

D1566802

FLORENTINO GARCÍA MARTÍNEZ
& JULIO TREBOLLE BARRERA

# The People of the Dead Sea Scrolls

*translated by Wilfred G. E. Watson*

*E. J. Brill   Leiden   New York   Cologne*

This book has been translated with the financial assistance of the Dirección General del Libro y Bibliotecas of the Ministerio de Cultura, Madrid, Spain.

Cover illustration: Qumran caves 4 and 5. Photograph by Garo Nalbandian, Jerusalem. Reproduced with permission from the Biblical Archaeology Society, Washington, D.C.

Original title: *Los Hombres de Qumrán*
Copyright © 1993 by Editorial Trotta SA, Madrid, Spain

Library of Congress Cataloging-in-Publication Data

García Martínez, Florentino.
[Hombres de Qumrán. English]
The People of the Dead Sea Scrolls / Florentino García Martínez and Julio Trebolle Barrera ; translated by Wilfred G.E. Watson.
p. cm.
Includes bibliographical references and index.

ISBN 90 04 10085 7 (pbk.: alk. paper)

I. Dead Sea Scrolls - - Criticism. interpretation, etc. 2. Qumran community, 3. Essenes. 4. Christianity - - Origin. I. Trebolle Barrera, Julio C. II. Title.
BM487.G32413 1995
296. 1'55 - - dc20

95-24822 CIP

Copyright © 1995 by E.J. Brill, Leiden, the Netherlands

Die Deutsche Bibliothek – CIP-Einheitsaufnahme

García Martínez, Florentino :
The People of the Dead Sea Scrolls : their writings, beliefs and practices / Florentino García Martínez and Julio Trebolle Barrera. Transl. by Wilfred G.E. Watson. – Leiden ; New York ; Köln : Brill, 1995

ISBN 90-04-10085-7
NE: Trebolle Barrera, Julio:; hombres de Qumrán, Los , <engl.>

Printed in the Netherlands

# Contents

# *Foreword*

The present book offers a collection of studies of very differing character and content. They provide complete and up to date information concerning the content of this literature and the social structure and religious concepts of the Qumran community.

A series of articles provides the basic information of interest to the reader who has seen headlines in the media which raise questions such as: Have there been unjustified delays in the publication of the manuscripts? Have texts been found which call into question the «canonical» form of the Bible? Is it true that in the beginning Christianity was a form of Essenism? What is known about the Essenes and other Jewish and Christian groups of the period? Is it true that the texts from Qumran challenge significant aspects of Jewish and Christian tradition?, etc.

Another set of articles attempts to bring the reader into the kitchen of Qumran research. The cooked dish is accompanied by the recipe. These articles deal with some of the most recent and most debated questions in the study of the Qumran texts: the origins of the Essene movement and of the Qumran sect, the borderlines between biblical and extra-canonical books, the boundaries between pure and impure, the messianic hopes of the Qumran group and one example, from many other possible examples, of a very striking agreement between a Qumran text and a New Testament text, with differences between them that are no less important.

The studies collected here which make up the various chapters of the present work appeared originally in various recent academic publications and three of them have been specially written for this volume.

* Note that quotations are from F. García Martínez, *The Dead Sea Scrolls Translated. The Qumran Texts in English*, Leiden 1994, here referred to as *DSST*.

1 *The Men and the Community of Qumran*

The Dead Sea Scrolls[1]

Florentino García Martínez

1  Bedouin, Monks and Treasure

Legends sometimes become a pale reflection of real events and this actually
happened in Palestine between 1946 and 1956. 1946 is one of those years in
which millennialist dreams and unshaped events rush unthinking into the por-
tals of history. The political scene in Palestine was dominated by birth pangs
which were to result in the birth of the State of Israel. Yet, the life of the bedouin Taᶜamireh tribe followed its own unchanging pattern of transhumance
through its ancestral territories in the Judaean desert on the margins of the
convulsions disturbing the country.

The legend of «the shepherd, the goat and the treasure» belongs to universal
folklore and is a favourite theme in the long family gatherings under the starry
desert sky. However, it is very uncertain that Muhammad Adh-Dhib, the
young shepherd who, following a lost she-goat, penetrated the inside of what
later would be known as Cave 1, attracted by the noise of broken debris caused
by the stone thrown into it, would think he had found a great treasure. If the
sight of a series of large jars deposited in that inaccessible place could have
made him believe for a moment that he was the main character of the legend
favoured with the find of a hidden treasure, disappointment was not long in
coming. In that cave, situated to the North East of the Dead Sea and close to
the ruins known by the name of Qumran, there was neither gold nor jewels, or
anything like that. All he was able to recover from inside it were some old skins
wrapped in rags and stored in large jars. The strange signs visible on the skins
had no meaning for him; like most members of his tribe, he was illiterate. The
signs had no meaning, either, for Khalil Iskander, better known as Kando. He
was the Bethlehem dealer in whose tent the Taᶜamireh bedouin bought provi-
sions, and was also a carpenter and a cobbler. Although the skins were rather
fragile and in such a bad state that they could not be used for repairs, they
might at least be worth something, since they seemed to be ancient. Kando kept
the first scrolls. In his tent also would be kept part of the result of a second
visit by the bedouin to the Cave in the middle of 1947. In all, Kando thus retrieved four of the scrolls found. Another three ended up in the hands of Faidi
Salahi, an antiques dealer of Bethlehem[2].

Towards the end of 1947, the very days of the birth of the State of Israel,
Salahi succeeded in making contact with Professor E. L. Sukenik of the Hebrew
University of Jerusalem, in spite of the difficulties of communication between
the Arab and Jewish zones. Sukenik immediately recognised the antiquity and
interest of the three manuscripts in Salahi's possession (the *War Scroll* [1QM],

the *Hymns* scroll [1QH] and a fragmentary copy of the text of Isaiah [1QIs[ab]])
and managed to acquire them for the University Library[3].

Kando was a Syrian Christian, and after some time decided to consult the
wiser members of his community, the monks of the Syrian monastery of St
Mark in Jerusalem. In the end, he sold them the four scrolls in his possession
(a complete copy of Isaiah [1QIsa[a]], the *Community Rule* [1QS], the *Habakkuk
Pesher* [1QpHab] and the *Genesis Apocryphon* [1QapGen]). The superior of the
convent, the archimandrite Athanasius Yeshue Samuel, then embarked on a
series of consultations intended to determine the contents of the manuscripts
and their antiquity. In one way or another, representatives of the Library of the
Hebrew University and of the École Biblique et Archéologique Française were
able to inspect the manuscripts in the Monastery of St Mark. Sukenik himself
also took the opportunity to examine them. However, either they did not realise
the value of the texts or their attempts at buying them failed[4].

In February 1948, an emissary from the archimandrite Samuel took the four
manuscripts to the American Schools of Oriental Research, where they were
examined by J. C. Trever. Subsequently, he was convinced of their importance
and their antiquity and obtained permission to photograph three of them in
their entirety, with a view to publication[5]. The originals were immediately
transferred to the United States, where the archimandrite Samuel hoped to
find a buyer prepared to pay the price wanted for them. This was only to happen much later, in 1954, when the son of Professor Sukenik, Y. Yadin, with the
help of a broker, succeeded in buying them for the State of Israel and transferred them to the Hebrew University[6].

Meanwhile, the Palestinian scene had changed completely. In May 1948 the
British Mandate had ended and the war began which was to end up dividing
the country into two halves. The rest of this story was to unfold in the Jordanian sector of the country.

In April 1948 the first news appeared in the press, about the manuscripts
studied by the members of the American School and about the manuscripts in
the possession of the Hebrew University[7]. With the arrival of this first news
began the frenzied activity of searching and recovery of material which was to
end by forming the different collections known as «the Dead Sea Scrolls».

Unknowingly, the shepherd Adh-Dhib had unleashed the search for and
recovery of a treasure even greater than those described in *The Thousand and
One Nights*.

The importance of the first texts (and their resulting monetary worth) stimulated the search for new manuscripts. First Kando, then the Syrian monks, and
last, an archaeological team from the Jordanian Department of Antiquities (in
1949) excavated Cave 1, each of them collecting part of the booty[8]. The cave
had contained more than seventy manuscripts, although for the most part only
minute fragments have been recovered. Those found by the archaeologists were

in the safe hands of the Palestine Archaeological Museum, but the remainder had to be recovered. In this process, Kando was to become the indispensable go-between. Through his hands were to pass most of the manuscripts acquired by the Museum, each time at a higher price.

The discovery of Cave 1, its excavation and the recovery of the manuscripts found there does not comprise the end of the epic of the Dead Sea Scrolls, but rather its beginning. In 1952, the Ta꞊amireh bedouin discovered Cave 2 in the vicinity of the first cave. To ascertain whether other caves in the same area had also been used to store manuscripts, a large-scale archaeological operation was organised, with the assistance of the Jordanian Arab Legion, which explored all the caves of the region. In this way, the archaeologists found Cave 3, and later Caves 5, 7, 8, 9 and 10, which contained remains of manuscripts[9], as well as many other caves with pottery and other traces of human habitation. However, the Ta꞊amireh bedouin succeeded in being much quicker and more skilful than the archaeologists. In the summer of 1952, during the excavations of the ruins of Qumran where they had been employed as labourers and at a stone's throw from the archaeologists' camp, they succeeded in emptying a large part of the contents of Cave 4 in one night. On the following morning, the team of archaeologists still succeeded in finding the remains of more than 100 manuscripts in the Cave. However, thousands and thousands of fragments from more than 400 other manuscripts had already been «excavated» by the bedouin and moved to a safe place. A little later on, they also found Cave 6 and in 1956, the last cave with manuscripts, Cave 11. In it, as in Cave 1, were found a large number of complete manuscripts in a good state of preservation.

Little by little, all these texts were appearing and could be acquired by the Palestine Archaeological Museum. However, before the avalanche of material, the funds of the Museum were quickly exhausted, as were the contributions of the Jordanian government. Accordingly, the Museum was forced to appeal to international assistance to be able to buy the manuscripts which continued to be offered in increasing numbers. As compensation for their economic contributions, various international institutions (such as the Royal Dutch Academy of Sciences) acquired the exclusive right to study and publish part of the finds in proportion to the aid provided to acquire the manuscripts. At the same time, Father de Vaux, director of the École Biblique and of the excavations of Qumran, organised an international and interdenominational team to complete the enormous task of classifying the thousands of fragments, repair the manuscripts from which they came and prepare them for publication. The team included representatives of the various institutions which had contributed to the acquisition of the manuscripts. whether from the various caves in the Qumran region or those found in other places in the desert of Judah.

In fact, Qumran is not the only place in which ancient manuscripts were found during those years. The Ta꞊amireh bedouin have never felt themselves constrained by the political frontiers which cut their ancestral territory in two. In spite of controls by the Jordanian army and the Israeli army, they continued to explore the rocky ravines on both sides of the frontiers. Their perseverance and their patience were to be rewarded with rich finds. They found the caves of Wadi Murabbaᶜat in the Jordanian sector. And they found Nahal Hever in the Israeli sector, which contained impressive testimony to the period of the second revolt against Rome led by Bar Kochba in the years 132-135 of the first century. The whole corpus of these separate collections of manuscripts is what is usually known as «the Dead Sea Scrolls». However, all these other finds come from a period some two centuries later than the time when the manuscripts found in the caves of the vicinity of the ruins of Qumran were written. It is better, therefore, to separate those texts from the collection we are dealing with here, the collection comprising the manuscripts found in those caves and known as the «manuscripts from Qumran»[10].

## II The Most Important Manuscripts Found in Modern Times

The richness and variety of the material which forms the collection of manuscripts from Qumran can only be suitably appreciated when they have all been published. However, with the publication of the first texts from Cave 1 it was already apparent that this material offered us something very different from the other great manuscript finds with which our century has been favoured. This was because their contents connected them directly with the book which has made the deepest impression on Western religious experience, the Bible.

The first texts published were an almost complete copy of the book of Isaiah, a commentary on the book of Habakkuk and a collection of the regulations which governed the life of a religious community attempting to live in accordance with all the prescriptions of the biblical text. Later publications made available a wider range of material, but always remaining within the confines of religious literature, either biblical or para-biblical, which the first texts portended. In total, more than 800 manuscripts have been recovered. Of these, a quarter comprises copies of various books of the Old Testament, more or less complete and differing more or less from the known text. The sole exception is the book of Esther, of which no fragment has been found. The other 600 manuscripts represent a good selection from the religious literature of the period. There are many apocryphal compositions, very similar in style and content to the books of the Old Testament, but which did not succeed in forming part of the canon of the Bible. Some of them, such as the Books of Enoch or the Book of Jubilees, were known to us through having been transmitted (in translation) by one of the later Christian Churches. Many more were completely unknown previously. Among them we find all the literary forms which occur in the various books of the Old Testament: narratives which retell sacred history, poetic compositions and hymns, wisdom compositions, edifying tales, liturgical compositions, various apocalypses, etc. Even odder and more interesting is a whole range of compositions which reflect the thought, polemics, biblical interpretation, religious observances, social organization and way of life of a Jewish group (or of several Jewish groups) located on the margins of official Judaism. These provide us with a view of Judaism which is very different from what we knew through later rabbinic writings[11].

In addition, all these texts, which had been written and preserved in the actual land of the Bible, reached us directly from their hiding-place in the desert. They were, therefore, completely free from any later interference. This means either the interference of rabbinic censorship (which destroyed all earlier Jewish religious literature which did not conform to the new orthodoxy) or the interference of Christian censorship (which had included or preserved some of the works now recovered, but adapting them to their own requirements).

Preliminary palaeographic study and Carbon 14 analysis quickly established that all the manuscripts had been copied between the 3rd cent. BCE and the first half of the 1st cent. CE[12]. Archaeological excavation of the various caves and of the ruins of Qumran[13] made it equally clear that all the manuscripts had been deposited in the caves before the destruction brought about by the Roman army during the first Jewish war against Rome in 66-74 of the first century. All the texts, therefore, come from a specially important period in the evolution and development of religious ideas. This is a period prior to the definitive canonization of the text of the Hebrew bible, and above all prior to the formation of rabbinic judaism and the birth of Christianity.

The initial scepticism regarding the unlikelihood of such a discovery soon gave way to the highest expectations. Since the biblical manuscripts recovered were earlier than the canonization of the Hebrew Bible, study of the differences from the official text which they provide will allow the formation process of the various books and the progressive fixation of the sacred text to be understood. These texts were preserved in their original language (in Hebrew, in Aramaic and a few in Greek). Studying them will help to fill large gaps in our knowledge of exactly how Hebrew and Aramaic were written and spoken in Palestine during the Hellenistic and Roman periods. Since they are religious texts which come directly from a Jewish group, analysing them will allow us to understand what the Jewish world was really like before the great catastrophe of 70 CE. And since this group had been contemporary with the birth of the Christian group, their texts promise to provide us a privileged observation point for understanding the genesis of Christianity within the Judaism of the period. In the words of a great specialist, the manuscripts from Qumran were «a dream that has come true»[14].

## III  Library or Genizah?

The extremely dry climate and the constant temperature within the caves had succeeded in preserving part of this treasure during two thousand years. But where did all these manuscripts come from? The question is anything but idle if one thinks about the price and the scarcity of manuscript scrolls at that time and about the size of other contemporary collections.

It is not at all surprising that the first interpretation proposed in reply to this question should fall back on a well known fact in later Jewish tradition: the existence of «genizahs» in which unusable sacred books are abandoned to natural destruction without human intervention. The example of the genizah of the Ezra synagogue of Old Cairo in which at the beginning of this century, S. Schechter recovered a large quantity of manuscripts that have transformed our knowledge of mediaeval Judaism, seemed to provide a good precedent. However, the existence of genizahs in such an early period is unattested. And apart from this fact, the care with which some of the manuscripts had been deposited (wrapped in cloths and placed within large jars) does not allow the thought that they had been deposited in the caves to be destroyed by natural causes. In addition, the inaccessibility of the site, in the heart of the desert, makes it hard to imagine that anyone would take the trouble to carry the scrolls there so that they could be destroyed by time. The Qumran caves are not genizahs like the one of the synagogue of Old Cairo.

Nor are they the deposit from the various libraries of Jerusalem, hidden in the desert as a precautionary measure against imminent Roman attack, and containing the literary output of all of Judaism of that period, as N. Golb supposes. The American scholar tries to explain in this way the amount and variety of the Qumran manuscripts. He also tries to explain the fact that apart from these manuscripts no other Jewish literary text of the period has reached us directly. The manuscripts certainly come from the library of a group (the presence of several copies of the same work excludes it being an individual's library). And they were deposited in the caves to protect them from the imminent Roman attack. These two factors, which Golb's hypothesis has in common with traditional interpretation, are correct, but his own two explanations are false. Nothing in the manuscripts indicates that the texts come from Jerusalem or from the Temple library or from other unspecified libraries, or still less that they represent the literary output of the whole of Judaism of the period.

All the manuscripts found come from the library of the community which lived in what today are the ruins of Qumran. This community we know, for lack of another name, as the «Qumran community». That this is the correct reply to the question, has been demonstrated in two ways: through analysis of all the texts found, and thanks to the results of the archaeological excavation in the ruins of Qumran.

Excavation of the ruins has shown that they belong to a centre of communal activity: large buildings for ritual baths, meeting rooms, a large refectory, a *scriptorium*, kitchens, workshops and various cemeteries in the vicinity, with more than 1,200 tombs. The members of this community lived in the caves round about (the archaeologists have identified about 40 of these caves) and in tents and huts of which no trace at all has been left. It is not a fortress or a farm centre but the meeting place of a true community. In addition, excavation of the ruins and of the caves in which the manuscripts were found, has shown that there is an organic relationship between them. Both were occupied during the same period and in both is found the same unusual type of pottery which comes from the potter's workshop found in the ruins.

The manuscripts, for their part, prove that the texts found in the various caves come from the same library. The same typically sectarian works turn up in different caves. In fact, biblical books as well as sectarian works which come from various caves have been copied by the same scribe. In addition, the manuscripts reveal to us the life of a tightly structured community, with religious assemblies, sessions for study, ritual baths, communal meals, etc. In particular, they show us that it is an exclusive community, a community which has broken with the rest of Judaism and forbids all contact with non-members. And in fact, in spite of the large variety and range of material, no writing has been found which contradicts the basic ideas of this community or represents the ideas of a group opposed to it. To be precise, the characteristic elements of the Pharisees, the most influential group of the Judaism of the period, do not appear in any manuscript.

Evidently, not all the manuscripts transmit to us works which are this community's own product. The large quantity of biblical texts and other compositions which are earlier than the birth of the community comprise the best proof that not all the works present in the community library were their own typical compositions. However, the exclusive nature of the community which the texts reveal assures us that all the works contained there, in spite of their variety, were considered as compatible with the special ideology of this community and with their peculiar interpretation of legal regulations. Also that they all formed part of its history or its prehistory, its most precious legacy, the safeguarding of which was worth any effort.

The precious treasure of the Qumran manuscripts is nothing but shreds, mangled and fragmented remains of what used to be the impressive library of the Qumran community.

## IV  A Sectarian Community

It is not easy to describe this community in brief. Still less to attach an identification label to it which allows us to classify it conveniently, equating it with one or other of the known communities of the period. The information which the manuscripts provide is too fragmentary for that, on the one hand and on the other, too plentiful and not always consistent. None of the manuscripts presents us in a complete and systematic way with the constitutions and laws of the community. One of the documents specifies the reasons for which its members separated themselves from the rest of the people of Israel. In another, some typical theological ideas are developed. From other texts can be deduced some elements of its internal organization or of the penitential system by means of which the loyalty of its members is maintained, or the stages followed in the formation and admission of candidates. Other texts project current practices of the community into the future of the messianic age. We can characterise this community as a peculiar community thanks to its special religious concepts, such as dualism or determinism, on account of its legal rigour, because of its estrangement from the Temple, which it considered temporarily defiled, thanks to the substitution of the sacrificial cult, etc. And, what is even more important, we can define it as a properly sectarian community, because of its use of a different calendar from the rest of Judaism, its elitism and its hierarchical structure. And especially because of the awareness its members had of having separated from the rest of the people. But it is impossible to reduce all these different elements to the characteristics of one or other of the communities and groups of antiquity.

The manuscripts do not even provide us with a name with which we could conveniently call this community, beyond such generic ones as «community», «congregation», «session of the many», etc. Its members are known as the elect, the men of the new covenant, the sons of light, the many, the poor, the dwellers in camps, the devout, or simply as the men of the community, the men of the congregation, etc. And all the texts where concrete allusions are more frequent, and could lead to an exact identification of the protagonists, use nicknames to refer both to enemies and to their own members. For the authors of the texts, «The angry lion», «the Wicked Priest», «the house of Absalom», «Ephraim» or «Manasseh», must have been expressions as transparent as «Teacher of Righteousness» or «House of Judah». However, to us right now they do not convey much to identify the community or its members.

It is not surprising, then, especially in the early stages, that the most varied identifications were proposed for the community. They were thought to be a Pharisee, Sadducee, zealot or even Christian group. Little by little, though, the conviction prevailed that the manuscripts came from an Essene community. In fact, it reached the point where the Essenes were simply equated with the Qumran community.

The Essenes were known to us thanks to a certain number of descriptions by ancient authors, the most important of which are those provided by Pliny, Philo and above all Flavius Josephus. And of the various Jewish groups previously known it is certainly with the group of the Essenes that the manuscripts present the greatest affinity. Some of their key ideas are determinism, a strictly hierarchical organic structure, a gradual «novitiate» to prepare new members for admission, communal life, common wealth, strict observance of the prescriptions for ritual purity, communal meals and possibly celibacy of the members. These are some of the most significant elements which, according to the manuscripts, the community had in common with what the classical narratives describe to us as characteristics of the Essenes.

However, many other elements present in the manuscripts are hard to reconcile with a simple identification of the Qumran community with a Essene community. Attempts have been made to explain these differences, either by attributing them to the result of a development of Essenism or as the result of the esoteric character of Qumran Essenism. However, these explanations (valid up to a certain point) cannot disregard one basic fact. Essenism is a widespread national movement which covers the whole country and its members do not at all consider themselves separate from the rest of the people of Israel. The Qumran community, instead, is a marginal phenomenon, a closed and isolated group, which deliberately lives apart from the rest of Judaism.

I think that the best explanation for these common elements and of these differences is provided by the hypothesis known among specialists as the «Groningen hypothesis». In this hypothesis, the ideological roots of the Qumran community are located within the Palestinian apocalyptic tradition. Also, its actual origins are found in a split which occurred within the Essene movement during the reign of John Hyrcanus (134-104 BCE). A handful of Essene priests, grouped around the «Teacher of Righteousness», separated from the mother movement and made their way to the desert. There they established their own sectarian community. The most important reasons for this break are as follows: the problem of the calendar and the organization of the cycle of feasts; a particular way of understanding the biblical prescriptions relating to the Temple, the cult and the purity of people and of things, which is founded in the revelation received by the Teacher of Righteousness; and the conviction of the imminence of the end of days. The result is the creation of the Qumran community. For a couple of centuries this community was to remain faithful to the directives of the Teacher of Righteousness, living in the tense eschatological expectation which marked its origins. To its zeal for the study and interpretation of the Law we owe this rich library, part of which the discoveries of Qumran have enabled us to recover.

v  The Qumran Manuscripts and the Old Testament

Although a large part of the biblical manuscripts which come from Qumran have not been published officially, the material known already has completely altered the way of perceiving the development of the text of the Old Testament[15].

## VI The Qumran Manuscripts and Christianity

The contribution of the Qumran manuscripts to knowledge of Christianity is, if possible, even more spectacular than their contribution to the study of the Old Testament.

However, this contribution is not exactly what appears with such regularity as first page headlines in certain newspapers or sensationalist magazines.

Not long ago the Italian magazine *30 Giorni* began a long *dossier* dedicated to the gospel of Mark as follows:

> A tiny fragment of papyrus, ochre in colour, 3.9 centimetres by 2.7, with the remains of some Greek words, twenty letters in all, written in black ink. Precisely this tiny remain of an ancient scroll, called 7Q5, was provoking an underground earthquake in the Church. For scholars it is a time-bomb which so far is defused and enclosed in the tight circle of «experts». But it seems that the moment of «explosion» has already arrived and there are many who fear the consequences[16].

This «bomb» is a discovery made in 1972 by the great Spanish papyrologist, the Jesuit José O'Callaghan (professor of the Biblical Institute of Rome and director of the Institute of papyrology of Barcelona). The discovery is that certain fragments of papyrus found in Cave 7 of Qumran could contain remains of what had been the oldest copies of several books of the New Testament. Fragments of the gospel of Mark, of the Acts of the Apostles, the Epistle to the Romans, 1 Timothy and even 2 Peter and the Epistle of James. These fragments would provide the proof that towards the year 50 CE in Palestine the Gospels and the whole New Testament had already acquired the form we know. The opinions of scholars, who assumed a long process of oral transmission before the texts were put into written form and a much later dating for the first Christian texts, had to collapse before the new evidence from Cave 7. This is why for twenty years the «experts» had been stubborn in discrediting the discovery and in hiding or denying evidence which spoiled commonly accepted progressive ideas.

The facts, however, are very different. The «experts» can be blamed for many things, but if there is anything of which they cannot be accused, it is precisely of having attempted to hide a discovery which, to be honest, would certainly be sensational. O'Callaghan published his findings in 1972, in a short article in the periodical *Biblica* of the Pontifical Biblical Institute, Rome[17]. He disclosed them at the same time in a public lecture which I remember well. It is strongly etched on my memory and on the memories of all of us who had the luck to be actual witnesses of the announcement and passionate followers of the polemics which ensued in the years succeeding this announcement. O'Callaghan's article was immediately translated into English and came out that same year as a supplement to the *Journal of Biblical Literature*[18]. The academic publications devoted to examining the pros and cons of O'Callaghan's hypothesis were so numerous that the list of books and articles devoted to the topic already fill five pages of Fitzmyer's Bibliography, published in 1975[19]. It cannot be said, then, that attempts have been made to hide the discovery. In fact, it is the one hypothesis which has received the most attention since its launch. As the years have passed, the hypothesis has fallen into oblivion, like so many others which failed to succeed. In recent years it has been retrieved and launched anew, though restricted to identifying fragment 7Q5 with the gospel of Mark, especially through Thiede's book[20]. There has even been a whole congress dedicated to the subject[21].

Nor can the «experts» be blamed for rejecting *a priori* the identification of a text because its contents seem incompatible with the archaeological context in which it was found. The same «experts» have, without difficulty, accepted the identification of a fragment found in the fortress of Masada as a passage from Virgil's *Aeneid*, in spite of its presence appearing unlikely in a such a zealot group as that which occupied Masada until its destruction.

Nor can the first publishers of the Greek papyri from Cave 7 be accused (as in the article in question) of refusing to accept O'Callaghan's hypothesis due to «the reticence of an editor who does not admit that another has succeeded where he has failed»[22]. After close scrutiny of O'Callaghan's arguments, the editors rejected them as inconclusive. The same editors have had no difficulty at all in accepting identifications made later by other scholars for other fragments which they had not succeeded in identifying, and even (as has happened repeatedly) for fragments which they had identified wrongly[23].

The problem with the hypothesis (of identification) proposed by O'Callaghan, and the reason why the vast majority of «experts» have not accepted it, does not lie in the historical or theological conclusions which would derive from the identification of these fragments with various texts from the New Testament. The difficulties are, instead, at the purely technical level. First come transcription problems: the readings of certain letters made by O'Callaghan in the different fragments are very debatable. In view of the minute size of the fragments, all the weight of identification lies in the exact agreement of the remains preserved with the presumed texts. Of the 20 letters preserved on 7Q5, only 14 are certain. To identify the fragment with the gospel of Mark, O'Callaghan is forced to read the other 6 in a different way from the editors. As a result, the «experts» conclude that O'Callaghan makes the evidence suit his own identification.

In addition, and staying with 7Q5, even reading the fragment as O'Callaghan would like, it can only be made to agree with Mark 6:52-53 by supposing a textual variant (the omission of three letters) not witnessed by any manuscript. However, the strongest argument of those who oppose the identification is that other identifications (such as various texts of the Old Testament or apocryphal literature, which are also more plausible) are equally possible and even more probable, since they involve none of the changes of letters required by O'Callaghan[24]. And if several identifications are possible, none of them can be considered as conclusively established[25]. And still less can it comprise the starting point from which one can claim to alter the course of exegesis. In other words, although the hypothesis of identification is in itself interesting, it has such a meagre foundation and implies so many questionable factors that nothing solid can be built upon it.

O'Callaghan, as a good scholar, presented his identification cautiously as a mere possibility, taking great care not to draw hasty conclusions from it about the gospels or about the Qumran community. Others, less wary and no doubt less competent, have not hesitated to do so, presenting the «experts» with the minute remains of 7Q5 as a key element in a process. They forget, unfortunately, that a dispassionate examination of the evidence does not allow the identification proposed by O'Callaghan to be confirmed. The contribution of the manuscripts from Qumran to knowledge of the New Testament does not include having provided us with the oldest copy of Mark's gospel or of any other writing from the New Testament.

Nor are these contributions located on the level of an «esoteric» reading of the Qumran texts. This kind of «reading» assumes that the manuscripts were written in code. The manuscripts do not intend to say what apparently they do say, but under the laconic surface of the words a hidden meaning is found, accessible only to those who have discovered this key to a secret reading. The «Teacher of Righteousness» would be Jesus Christ, or Paul, or James or John the Baptist (all these codes and very many others have been suggested) and his enemies and the conflicts in which he and his community saw themselves involved would be those we know through the New Testament. Read in this way, the manuscripts from Qumran would be nothing more than the other face of the New Testament, the true one, the one which later history had intentionally marred and hidden. The result of this «reading» is that the manuscripts from Qumran would allow us to know the true face of an Essene Jesus Christ and that of a Christian community earlier than Jesus Christ. In this «esoteric» interpretation, the manuscripts from Qumran would reveal to us a series of doctrines and secret or forgotten practices in which are shown the true nature of Christianity. Unfortunately, this «reading» does not withstand the slightest scrutiny either, and proper analysis of the facts shows that they are pure speculation. Not only is this «reading» speculative and unfounded, it is even contradicted by what the texts say and by the concrete historical and chronological context to which they refer.

The real contribution of the manuscripts to knowledge of primitive Christianity and of the New Testament lies at another level and is much more important than these lucubrations. It affects all levels of New Testament study: linguistic, literary, legal, historical and theological[26]. Thanks to the manuscripts from Qumran we can now discover the real meaning of enigmatic sentences and expressions in the New Testament, previously unintelligible in a Greek context and now documented in a contemporary Jewish milieu. Thanks to these same manuscripts we can now trace the origin of certain insertions we find incorporated in various New Testament writings. Thanks to them we now have available precise literary parallels to some pericopes as important as the Beatitudes. These manuscripts reveal to us for the first time the legal prescriptions in force in marginal Jewish groups and thanks to them we can understand certain New Testament prescriptions, such as brotherly rebuke or the arguments over sabbath observance. The same Qumran manuscripts make the theological thinking of the recipients of certain New Testament writings, such as the Letter to the Hebrews, less bewildering to us. They also prove that certain theological ideas about the priestly character of the expected Messiah, about the vicarious atonement of a saviour of heavenly origin, about justification by faith, about the omnipresence of the action of an angelic enemy, etc., are not inventions of the primitive Christian community. Instead, they are the development of certain Old Testament ideas already present in certain Jewish circles. Even the awareness of living in the last times, the intense feeling that the prophecies have already begun to be fulfilled within the community are profusely attested in the manuscripts from Qumran.

However, perhaps the most important contribution of the manuscripts from Qumran to knowledge of primitive Christianity and of the New Testament consists, paradoxically, in the knowledge they have provided of Palestinian Judaism in the 1st century. Thanks to these manuscripts, and for the first time, we can really know the Jewish background in which primitive Christianity and the New Testament were born, against which they stood out and from which they began to develop. Before the Qumran discoveries, the only form of Judaism which we really knew and with which we could compare nascent Christianity was rabbinic Judaism. We knew that this form of Judaism was the result of a long process of reorganisation due to the two disasters which the wars against Rome had been. Yet, ignorance of the preceding phases forced us to resort to it in order to understand the Christian phenomenon. Compared with rabbinic Judaism, Christianity appeared as an isolated phenomenon, strange and incomprehensible in 1st century Palestine. The manuscripts from Qumran have proved to us that the Judaism of this 1st century (and of the previous centuries) was very different from later rabbinic Judaism. They also proved that Palestinian Judaism was very diverse, very much richer and more complex than we suspected. We now see rabbinic Judaism as the victory of one of the movements current in earlier Judaism, as one of several forms of Judaism, not simply as Judaism. And in the face of this pluralistic Judaism, nascent Christianity appears to us as what in fact it was: a new Jewish sect among many others. Thanks to the manuscripts from Qumran, we can now compare this new sect, its origins, its contribution, its development, with that other sect, which vanished two thousand years ago but which has gained new life with the discovery of the remains of its library.

VII  An Unexplored Treasure

The effort invested in the recovery, publication and study of the manuscripts from Qumran is huge. The results already gained amply justify their description as «the greatest manuscript find of modern times». And yet, the task of retrieving completely this treasure accidentally discovered by a young bedouin more than forty years ago is still far from being finished.

Not all the texts recovered have been published. The debate reflected in the American newspapers of recent years clearly shows that part of the manuscripts from Cave 4 still remain unpublished. A considerable part of the biblical texts still awaits its definitive publication and a good number of apocryphal and sectarian texts are only known through provisional, partial or incomplete descriptions. The reasons for this situation are quite varied: first, the war followed by a tangled political situation, the premature disappearance of the directors of the editorial project and of several of the editors before they had finished their work and above all the appalling condition of the as yet unpublished fragments. These are some of the causes which if they do not justify this delay, they at least explain it. In any case, this situation is certainly deplorable and all of us editors have our share of the blame. Every scrap of text which turns up helps extend our knowledge of this key period in the religious history of the West.

However, this fact (and the clamour of a certain type of newspaper around it) cannot make us forget that the complete publication of all the texts is not the end of the task of recovery, but only its beginning. The study and understanding of the material already available years ago is very far from being finished. Up to now, study has been focused on a few texts, naturally the longest and most complete. These texts, though, do not comprise even ten percent of the total material retrieved and duly published. The task still outstanding is enormous and requires the combined efforts of several generations of scholars. Are not the fruits already gained the best proof that these efforts are worthwhile?

# The Qumran Finds Without a Hint of Scandal

## Julio Trebolle Barrera

The history of the Qumran finds always begins with the story of a bedouin shepherd who goes in search of a stray ewe. As is his habit, he throws a stone which this time slips through a hole in the rock. He enters through the narrow opening and on the bottom of the cave he finds some pottery jars which contain several rolls of parchment. The account is certainly apocryphal. The only truth is the chance nature of the find and also the fact that shepherds and farmers have always preceded academics in the discovery of ancient treasure. This founding legend, indispensable in every famous discovery, would not be worth repeating here. Unless, that is, the history of Qumran could be completed and could find the final key to its secrets by going back to count the sheep and goats of the flock belonging to the settlers of Qumran.

DNA analysis of the goatskin or sheepskin from which the parchments of Qumran are made can show what fragments of skin or parchment belong to the same animal. In this way, it is possible to match some fragments with others and, as a result, some texts with others. Fragments from the same skin correspond, in principle, to the same text. It is not necessary to imagine that the scribe ordered an animal to be sacrificed for every strip of parchment in order to write a column of text on it, taking into account that a text could cover 50 or more columns. Study of the DNA of the parchments will allow checking of the results already obtained through palaeographic study of the manuscripts. Loose fragments with unidentified text can be assigned to a group of fragments which come from the same skin and correspond to the same literary work.

Cool research will turn into frenzy and delirium if it succeeds in determining the degree of parentage and the genealogical tree of every skin and of the corresponding animal. Especially if identity cards in the form of DNA can be assigned to every sheep and goat, so that the complete Qumran flock is known and sheep and goats can be identified as possible intruders or imports from other herds. This tracking through the caprine genealogy of Qumran will allow one to determine which manuscripts were written in Qumran using skins from native sheep and which manuscripts were written in other places, such as Jerusalem, as N. Golb demands, using skins from foreign animals. These writings were later transferred to Qumran to be deposited in the nearby caves.

Let us return to the foundation history of the original ewe so as not to anticipate the Qumranic eschatology of the separation of the sheep and goats at the end of times.

## 1  The First Manuscripts

In the winter of 1947, a few months before the proclamation of the State of
Israel and the outbreak of the war between the Jews and the Arabs in 1948, a
bedouin from the Ta<sup>c</sup>amireh tribe, called Mohammed Adh-Dhib, made a discovery, however it might have happened: seven rolled up manuscripts deposited in a couple of jars inside a cave in the vicinity of Qumran, on the North-
west shore of the Dead Sea. The history which followed this discovery is a
veritable detective story, of which the principal characters in real life were bedouin and Arab merchants, archimandrites, university professors (Jews, Christians of various faiths and others with no religious affiliation or openly opposed
to religion), officials of the defunct British Mandate in Palestine, wily diplo-
mats, naive American patrons, and so on. If money is a measure of the value
of things, four of the manuscripts from Qumran to fetch £24 (sterling) in 1947
were sold in 1954 for the much rounder figure of $250,000. The cultural and
religious value of the manuscripts is incalculable. The controversies of recent
years in the media, especially in the United States, show that these manuscripts
touch a very sensitive chord in the history of man and in the history of his
cultural past and of his religious beliefs.

The story of the finds has been told a thousand and one times by the various
principal characters who took part in it, in versions which do not always coincide. The account which follows focuses attention on the history of the discovery, study and publication of the texts[27]. It focuses less on the history of the
excavations and of the archaeological finds. In recent years, doubts have been
cast on the publication process of the manuscripts and accusations made against
those responsible for it. We will try to present an objective and sober account,
without wishing to be controversial or sensational. The fact of having lived
close to this history over the last years, knowing and enjoying the friendship of
many of the leading characters, forces me to greater respect, which on many
occasions becomes deep admiration, for those who have dedicated their intelligence and years of enthusiastic work to the study of «the greatest manuscript
find of modern times» as the great Semitist W. F. Albright defined it from the
beginning.

The bedouin who in the spring of 1947 had discovered the first manuscripts
in what was later to be called Cave 1, attempted to sell the scrolls to some antique dealers in Bethlehem. Right from that moment, one of them, Khalil
Iskander Shahin, better known as Kando, was to become an agent between the
bedouin and the scholars interested in acquiring and studying the manuscripts.
In July 1947, Kando sold four of those seven manuscripts to the metropolitan Athanasius Y. Samuel of the Syrian-Orthodox monastery of Saint Mark in
the Old City of Jerusalem. They were: the first Isaiah scroll (1QIs<sup>a</sup>), the *Habakkuk Pesher* (1QpHab). the *Community Rule* (1QS) and the *Genesis Apocryphon*

(1QapGn). The price agreed was the £24 (sterling) already mentioned. At the end of that same year, Eleazar L. Sukenik, a professor of the Hebrew University of Jerusalem, bought the three remaining manuscripts from the lot of seven found so far, in Bethlehem, probably from Kando. These were the Hymns scroll (1QHª), the War Scroll (1QM) and the second manuscript of Isaiah (1QIsᵇ).

At the beginning of the following year, 1948, Mar Athanasius, wishing to know the scientific and monetary value of the four copies which he owned, had them taken to Professor Sukenik. After lengthy examination, he showed himself prepared to acquire them. The Syrian-Orthodox metropolitan wanted to get other opinions and sent three of the manuscripts (1QIsª, 1QpHab and 1QS) to the American School of Oriental Research. In the absence of the director of the institute, it was John C. Trever who took the opportunity of examining the manuscripts. After recognising their authenticity, he requested the owner for permission to photograph them. This he proceeded to do over several weeks, in black and white and in colour.

The research completed independently by Professor Sukenik and by John C. Trever confirmed the authenticity and antiquity of the manuscripts. The fact that they had remained deposited in well-sealed jars explained their good state of preservation. At the same time, it showed that the manuscripts were a precious treasure to those who had kept them with such care.

The seven manuscripts discovered represented a very varied set of works. Apart from the two copies of a biblical book – the book of the prophet Isaiah (1QIsª; 1QIsᵇ) – the other manuscripts were copies of the text of previously unknown works. These were: an exegetical commentary of a type characteristic of the Qumran community, the *pesher* on the book of Habakkuk; a book of the «re-write» genre of the bible, called the *Genesis Apocryphon*; a text which contained the *Community Rule* or *Serek* (1QS); an eschatological work with a very typical title, *War Rule (of the sons of light against the sons of darkness)*(1QM) and lastly, a book of *Hymns* of the Qumran community (*Hodayot*, 1QHª).

The finding of this rich lot of manuscripts could not fail to arouse enough interest to complete archaeological excavation in the area of the discovery. Circumstances arising from the war between Jews and Arabs in 1948 forced archaeological exploration to be delayed until January–March 1949. The excavation of Cave 1, in which the first manuscripts had been found, took place under G. Lankaster Harding and Roland de Vaux. Work on the edition of the new texts began very quickly and on a regular basis. In the spring of 1950, the American School of Oriental Research (ASOR) published the first Isaiah scroll (1QIsª) and the *Habakkuk Pesher* (1QpHab) in an edition under the supervision of M. Burrows[28]. A year later, the second volume appeared with the edition of the *Community Rule* (1QS). Towards the end of the same year, 1951, the first excavations were begun in the actual site of Qumran, under both R. de Vaux and G. L. Harding. The coins and pottery found confirmed the connection between the site and the cave in which the manuscripts had been discovered.

At the same time, new manuscripts did not stop appearing. At that time, the Ta‘amireh bedouin found the first fragments which came from the caves of Wadi Murabba‘at and took them to the Palestine Archaeological Museum, the Rockefeller Museum, located in the Arabic Eastern quarter of the city of Jerusalem, which was divided between Arabs and Jews after the 1948 war. A little later, Kando brought new fragments from the same source to de Vaux. As a result the excavations at the site of Qumran were completely suspended from the beginning of 1952 and exploration in the Wadi Murabba‘at caves began. In February, the bedouin located a new cave in the Qumran area, in which manuscript material was also found. In March, de Vaux and William Reed, director of the American School of Oriental Research, excavated this cave (Cave 2), and completed exploration of the rocky area of the mountain to a distance of 4 kilometres North and South of Qumran. In the summer, the bedouin, always ahead of the scholars, found more manuscripts, first in Khirbet Mird and then in Nahal Hever, in the so-called «Cave of Horrors» and «Cave of Letters». In the first fortnight of September, the bedouin discovered the cave which was to provide the biggest surprises (Cave 4), as well as Cave 6. In the same month, September, De Vaux and Harding proceeded to excavate Cave 4. Only 30 metres away from the cave, J. T. Milik found Cave 5. By then, the discovery of manuscripts had already supplied fat profits to the bedouin. The Jordanian government paid the bedouin the amount of 15,000 dinars, the equivalent of 42,000 dollars, for approximately 15,000 fragments which came from Cave 4.

## II  The Manuscripts from the «Qumran Library»

The most important cave, Cave 4, contained what can possibly be called the «library of the community» of Qumran. In 1956, four additional caves were found, which also contained the remains of manuscripts. All the manuscripts were stored in the Palestine Archaeological Museum or Rockefeller Museum. The custody and conservation of the manuscripts, therefore, belonged to the Jordanian Department of Antiquities. At that time and although the British mandate over Palestine had ended in 1948, the Department was still under the direction of a British person, the archaeologist G. Lankaster Harding mentioned already.

The huge accumulation of manuscripts and other objects throughout 1952 which had to be studied and published, led Harding to seek cooperation from the archaeological and biblical institutes of the Jordanian part of Jerusalem. These are the famous «École Biblique et Archéologique Française», the American Institute already mentioned, today called the «Albright Institute of Archeology», and the British and German Institutes. The team needed to be international and interconfessional in character. It was made up of four representatives from or connected with the «École Biblique»: Roland de Vaux in the position of director, D. Barthélemy and J. T. Milik, a little later joined by M. Baillet. The first two were Dominicans. Milik, of Polish origin and a refugee in the West, was later to become a member of the «Centre National de la Recherche Scientifique» (CNRS) in Paris. In 1953 and 1954, the group was gradually joined by the Americans F. M. Cross (Jr.) and P. W. Skehan, John M. Allegro and John Strugnell, both British, and the German C.-H. Hunzinger, who later left the research team. Until 1960, this group worked with exclusive commitment and total efficiency, thanks to the funds administered through the Rockefeller Foundation.

Towards the end of 1952, Milik began the work of classifying the material from Cave 4. Cross took on the task of publishing the biblical scrolls (4Q1-10, 13-21, 23-43, 47-54, 70-81, 99-100, 104-118). Milik's lot was the most extensive and most mixed. It included the non-biblical texts from Cave 1, the Hebrew and Aramaic texts from the Murabbaʿat caves and the manuscripts from Cave 5. In addition, the texts of phylacteries, *mezuzôt* and *targumim* (4Q128-157, cf. DJD VI) and many non-biblical texts of every kind, all from Cave 4 (4Q195-363). J. M. Allegro took charge of editing the parabiblical texts, commentaries and paraphrases (4Q158-186 = DJD V). The Frenchman, Jean Starcky, a specialist in Palmyrene Aramaic texts, joined the group in January 1954, taking charge of the study of non-biblical Aramaic texts and several Hebrew texts (4Q521-575). P. W. Skehan undertook the edition of part of the biblical texts, including palaeo-Hebrew and Greek texts, corresponding to the books of Isaiah, Psalms, Proverbs, as well as a manuscript of Deuteronomy and another of the Minor Prophets (4Q11-12, 22, 44-46, 55-69, 82-98, 101-103, 119-127). J. Strugnell took charge of editing a whole series of non-biblical Hebrew texts previously unknown: a paraphrase of the Pentateuch, pseudo-prophetic, liturgical and wisdom texts, hymns and various others (4Q364-48). To Hunzinger was entrusted the edition of the *War Scroll* and of several liturgical texts. After his resignation, this lot was assigned to Baillet (4Q482-520 = DJD VI) who already had the task of editing the manuscripts from Caves 2, 3 and 6-10 (DJD 3).

The ceaseless arrival of new material exceeded the acquisition budget of the Jordanian government and the Rockefeller Museum. They sought to avoid at any cost a situation where, due to the impossibility of buying all the material and collecting it for study in the Museum, it would begin to enter the trade circuit of antique dealers and be scattered among chance buyers from America and Europe, making the systematic study of it in its entirety impossible. Scattering the material would make the reconstruction of the manuscripts even more difficult. It was decided, therefore, to invite certain academic institutes to make a financial contribution to the editing of the manuscripts in exchange for certain rights. The Universities of McGill in Canada, Manchester and Hei-

delberg, the Vatican Library, the «McCormick Theological Seminary of Chi-
cago», the Royal Dutch Academy of Sciences, the Biblical School of Jerusalem,
«The All Souls' Church» of New York and the University of Oxford gradually
answered the invitation.

III  The Last Caves to be Discovered.<br>The Research still Required

Meanwhile, excavation work and the editing of the texts continued. Between
February and April, 1954, the third campaign of excavation in the site of
Qumran was completed, bringing to light the so-called «refectory» and the
buildings with the pottery ovens. The fourth campaign was carried out between
February and April, 1955. At the beginning of the year, 1QIs[b], 1QH[a] and 1QM
were published under the direction of E. L. Sukenik[29]. Also, the first volume
of the series *Discoveries in the Judaean Desert* (DJD) appeared. Once J. Beiber-
kraut had succeeded in unrolling the *Genesis Apocryphon* scroll from Cave 1, Y.
Yadin and N. Avigad published it in 1956[30].

In March 1955, professors M. Avi-Yonah, N. Avigad, Y. Aharoni, I. Duna-
yevsky and S. Gutman, commissioned by the Hebrew University of Jerusalem,
the «Israel Exploration Society» and the Department of Antiquities, completed
the first campaign of archaeological exploration in Masada, paying special attention to the palace situated in the Northern area. One year afterwards, Y.
Aharoni and Gutman conducted a second campaign. A year later, Yadin directed two excavation campaigns, from October to April in 1963-64 and from
December to March in 1964-65, with the intention of uncovering the whole
site. In the first campaign, several biblical manuscripts and others of varied
content were discovered as well as coins, ostraca and non-religious papyrus
documents.

More than seven years had passed since the first discoveries and they showed
no signs of abating. In March 1965, the bedouin found a new cave in Wadi
Murabba[c]at, in the vicinity of the other four found earlier. In January 1966, it
was again the bedouin who discovered Cave 11, where there was an important
lot of manuscripts, among them 11QtgJob, 11QpaleoLev[a] and 11QPs[a]. The Cave
was immediately excavated by de Vaux, who continued the fifth campaign of
excavations at Qumran. Cave 11 was the last to provide manuscripts. It should
not be forgotten, though, that in 1962 the bedouin found a quantity of papyri
in Wadi ed-Daliyeh, which were also passed on to the Rockefeller Museum.

From 1955 onwards, the research team had in front of them a real jigsaw
puzzle made up of some 40,000 manuscript fragments. To put it back together
they allowed themselves ten or twelve years. This reckoning turned out be
over-optimistic. More than forty years have passed, and the jigsaw continues
to engage the 55 members who at present form the international team entrusted

with the official publication of the manuscripts. The first task requiring completion consisted in unfolding and cleaning the fragments rescued from the dust of the caves and classifying them in groups based on the features and colouring of the leather or papyrus used, the ink, type of writing, etc. Once classified, they were then photographed, in many cases using the infra-red method. This was in order to achieve greater contrast and so make easier the reading of some texts which over time had become blackened to the point where in some cases reading them became almost hopeless. The work of classifying the manuscripts entailed identifying the texts, that is, determining to which work the fragments found belonged. Once a text had been successfully identified, it became much easier to connect some fragments with others and even join them, little by little completing the preserved text of the work in question. If they were biblical texts, identification did not turn out to be too difficult. Reference to «Concordances» of the Hebrew text of the Old Testament (complete lists of all the words used in the Bible, which were already available) enabled a word or group of words to be identified. From there, the remaining material preserved of that manuscript could be reconstructed and identified. Nor did it prove to be very difficult to identify fragments which belonged to a lost Hebrew work, if ancient versions of it in other languages such as Greek, Latin, Syriac, Ethiopic etc., had been preserved. Identification was very difficult and it still is when it is a matter of texts of which no other copy or translation is known and of which only tiny and disconnected fragments are preserved.

Publication of the manuscripts proceeded at a reasonably rapid rate in the first few years (DJD I 1955, II 1961, III 1962, IV 1965, V 1967). The editors also supplied «preliminary» or provisional information about the rest of the material at a shattering rate. The identification of the manuscripts from Cave 4 also progressed at a good pace. In August 1955 it had been possible to identify 330 manuscripts from Cave 4, in a set of 420 photographs. In the summer of 1956, 381 manuscripts had been identified in 471 photographs. The fragments assembled on another 29 plates could not be identified and 13 other plates with papyrus fragments have still not been studied. In June 1961, the total number of manuscripts identified was 511 on 620 photographic plates. Fragments on 25 plates still defy identification. In 1957, J. Fitzmyer began work on preparing a «Concordance» of the manuscripts, which R. Brown and W. G. Oxtoby continued. A Spaniard, Xavier Teixidor, currently a research scholar in the «Centre National de la Recherche Scientifique» in Paris, also took part in this work, inserting the texts from the so-called «small caves» (2, 3 and 5-10) into the concordance.

This short survey would be incomplete if it made no reference to the research completed while they were working on the preparations for publishing the texts. Some of this research was absolutely essential for progress in the

process of publication. Other research presents syntheses or conclusions derived from study of the manuscripts. From the first type of research it is necessary to cite the article in which F. M. Cross sketched the history of the palaeography of Qumran, «The Development of the Jewish Scripts»[31]. From the
second type must be singled out the work in which D. Barthélemy discovered
the existence of early recensions or revisions of the text of the Greek version
of the LXX[32].

From the end of the sixties, the process of editing the manuscripts was becoming considerably slower. Until 1976 and 1977 lengthy publications had
ceased to appear. In 1976, Milik edited texts 4Q201-212 under the title *The
Books of Enoch: Aramaic Fragments of Qumran Cave IV*; in 1976 Y. Yadin published the edition of the *Temple Scroll*; the same year, volume VII of DJD also
appeared, with the publication of the archaeological excavation of Cave 4 and
part of Milik's allocation[33]. Years later, in 1982, volume VI of the series DJD
appeared, edited by M. Baillet: *Qumrân Cave 4 III* (4Q482-4Q520). In 1985, D.
N. Freedman and K. A. Mathews published one of the great manuscripts of
Qumran[34].

In 1984, professor John Strugnell of the University of Harvard was appointed editor-in-chief of the international team, succeeding Father Benoit of
the École Biblique; he had previously succeeded de Vaux (in 1971), who had
died.

IV  Grounds for a Scandal and the Reasons for a Delay
or is it the Other Way Round?

In the last few years, the press and the general public have been hit by what
Geza Vermes, a professor of Oxford University, has defined as «the academic
scandal *par excellence* of the twentieth century»[35]. The fact that more than forty
years have passed without the whole of the manuscripts found in the caves of
the Dead Sea being published has given rise to suspicions which in some cases
have gone beyond what is reasonable. The real scandal is the scandal itself. How
can a wide spectrum of the well-read and well-informed public, and the communication media which supply its reading-material and images, grant complete credibility to «suspicions» and minority theories, and yet distrust the judgment of the expert majority? The scandal of Qumran is more a social than an
academic phenomenon. The scandal is that a satisfactory mix of firsthand scientific information and a small dose of sensationalism and scandal makes up a
type of journalism and of literature which has a guaranteed success. Two British journalists, M. Baigent and R. Leigh, published an archetypal book of this
hybrid of information and disinformation. The very title of the book draws
attention to the scandal of the Dead Sea Scrolls, revelations about which make
even the Vatican tremble. I saw the book for the first time at an exhibition in

the United States. I could not avoid making quite negative comments in front of the publisher's representative, there at the sales stand. My comments did not seem to surprise him in the least. In professional tones he stated: «The publisher is not responsible for the opinions of the authors».

The fact that American magazines and newspapers with large circulations had echoed a great deal of information and comments about the inexcusable delay in the publication of the manuscripts roused suspicions about the existence of a real «conspiracy of silence». At the same time, the opinions of two professors, R. Eisenman and Barbara E. Thiering, were made known to the public in general. They claimed that the Qumran manuscripts, and more specifically the *pesharim*, came from a Judaeo-Christian sect or from a Jewish group with Zealot tendencies; they were written in the years of the Jewish revolt against Rome (68-70 CE) and contain information which alters the history of Christian origins. The two authors, however, make very vague and conflicting proposals. According to Eisenman, the Teacher of Righteousness mentioned in the manuscripts from Qumran could be Jesus of Nazareth himself, or perhaps John the Baptist or Saint James. For Barbara Thiering, the person called the Wicked Priest could have been Paul or Jesus of Nazareth himself, and so on.

At the International Congress on the Dead Sea Scrolls organised by the Complutense University and held in the El Escorial in March 1991, results of some Carbon-14 tests were presented for the first time. The tests had been applied to a series of manuscripts from different periods, four of them with a well-known date, so as to be able to check in this way the results of the scientific tests. The result was a resounding confirmation of the dating of the manuscripts which had been proposed previously by palaeographers, especially by Professor F. M. Cross of Harvard University. In his paper at this Congress, Professor H. Stegemann resolves the discussion concerning Eisenman's proposal with these words:

«Therefore one may dismiss Dr. Eisenman's ideas in this field. At least they can no longer trouble the common Qumran Essene hypothesis»[36].

The thesis that the Qumran manuscripts reflect Judaeo-Christian origins rests on incorrect dating of those manuscripts.

The supposition is that the most important manuscripts from Qumran are of Judaeo-Christian origin and therefore provide important information about the origins of Christianity. In addition, there is the suspicion that this information contradicts the traditional interpretation held by the Christian Churches. Furthermore, the rumour seems to be going round that a large part of the manuscripts remains hidden since their discovery. These factors make it understandable that many apprentices to «masters of suspicion» have rushed to make the accusation that religious authorities have been attempting to hide something sensational and compromising.

The scandal collapses under its own weight, or else, as is already happening it is watered down in disputes, in court if necessary. But for the general public, unless other scandals occur, these disputes will not cease to be mere discussions about authors' or publishers' rights, or Byzantine debates between scholars. My instinct as the son of a provincial printer has made me «suspect» right from the first moment that in all this scandal there is more involved than the content of the actual manuscripts which provokes great popular outcry. Namely, questions about the rights of authors and right to publication of the manuscripts, which carry great academic prestige and prestige in publishing and journalism, for those who hold them.

The recent scandal does no more than repeat another similar scandal of forty years ago. Today, as then, the reason for the scandal was the suspicion that religious authorities could be hiding as yet unpublished manuscripts which could change the traditional and official interpretation about Jewish and Christian origins. It must be clearly stated that Judaism and Christianity have nothing to fear from study of the Qumran manuscripts. The best proof of that is provided by the placard which a fundamentalist organization paraded in front of the building where a Qumran congress was being held (Kansas City, 1991). The placard read as follows: «Qumran Yes, JEDP No». The abbreviation JEDP (Yahwist–Elohist-Deuteronomist–Priest or priestly) refers to the four literary sources which, according to modern criticism, make up the Pentateuch. The very conservative have always viewed modern criticism with great suspicion. Qumran, on the contrary, does not alarm them, perhaps because they perceive a certain affinity with the Qumran community, which in the end was converted into a fundamentalist Jewish sect of the period.

At the moment of judging the delay in publication it is necessary to take into account the present state of the manuscripts and the circumstances in which their study has been achieved. I would like to start with a remark which has nothing to do with the delay in publication of the manuscripts, but a great deal with recent haste to speed up the publication process. The complaints about the delay have coincided with the beginning of a general use of computers in research work. The invention and spread of the computer, like the invention of the alphabet 1500 years before Christ and of the printing-press 1500 years after Christ, have brought with them a radical change in procedures of scientific work. The processes of collecting, studying and transmission of data are carried out today with a speed unbelievable only a few years ago. Speed is possible today because we have the technical means available not only to allow but even to demand speed, which in research work can be very dangerous.

One must not forget what the situation was only a few years ago. In the summer of 1988, I went down for the first time into the basements of the Rocke-feller Museum where the manuscripts from Cave 4 were kept, waiting to be studied. After the first emotions of feeling between my fingers the mystery of the writing on the tiny fragments which I had to prepare for publication, I set to work. I had two tools available there. The catalogue of manuscripts on type-written sheets with many handwritten corrections, and the «Concordance», mentioned above, on handwritten cards. The yellow colour of the cards re-vealed that the «Concordances» had been made years ago. The catalogue and the concordances, prepared by different hands over a very long period as studies progressed, could only contain mistakes, inaccuracies, gaps, etc. Accordingly, several members of the international team decided to augment the team of researchers responsible for the publication of the manuscripts in their charge. In 1988, to make the work of the researchers easier, a very abbreviated form of the «Concordances» was made. One of the copies is to be found in the library of the Department of Hebrew and Aramaic Studies of the Complutense Uni-versity. Another copy of the «Concordances» was used to make the computer edition completed in 1991 by Ben Zion Wacholder and Martin G. Abbeg.

Nor should we forget that the longest manuscripts from Qumran had already been published years ago. Many times a certain confusion between manuscripts and fragments from manuscripts has been played on. When the criticism was made repeatedly that most of the manuscripts from Qumran have not yet been published, it has been ignored or it has not been mentioned that the lengthy manuscripts were already published. And there has been a wish to ignore that what awaits publication comprises chiefly fragments and, according to Flo-rentino García Martínez, «A large part of the unpublished manuscripts – like a good part of the manuscripts published already, comprises such fragmentary remains that to translate them would be of absolutely no value to the reader»[37]. In a world where English becomes more dominant each day as the only lan-guage for academic communication, there are still some who consider as «un-published» anything which is not in English. They even present as unpublished, material which was already known in other languages years ago.

There have been many and various factors which influenced the process of study of the manuscripts and the delay in their publication. One of the most decisive has been determined by the political situation in the Middle East, criti-cal on many occasions since the beginning of the discoveries. The first finds took place in the situation which ensured the war between Arabs and Jews in 1948. In 1956, the Suez crisis and the occupation by Israel of the Sinai penin-sula created such a climate of tension in the Arab part of Jerusalem that it forced foreign scholars to leave the city for a while. For reasons of security the manuscripts of Cave 4 were moved to the Ottoman Bank in Amman, the Jorda-nian capital. The following year they were returned to the Rockefeller Museum in Jerusalem, but some manuscripts came back in a hopeless condition.

The vicissitudes of Middle Eastern politics also affected the publication process by the Clarendon Press in Oxford. The official series of publication was called *Discoveries in the Judaean Desert* (= DJD). From 1962 it changed to *Discoveries in the Judaean Desert of Jordan*, with express reference to the Hashemite kingdom of Jordan, whose Department of Antiquities then supervised the safekeeping and publication of the manuscripts. Volumes IV and V of the series appeared under this title. From 1967, when Israel took the Eastern part of Jerusalem and the Rockefeller Museum came under Israeli jurisdiction, the new authorities insisted that the series should change its name to «Discoveries in the Desert of Judah of Israel». This one factor helped delay publication of the volume which P. W. Skehan had prepared, beyond the death of its author. This volume actually appeared in 1993 under the responsibility of another editor, E. C. Ulrich of the University of Notre-Dame, to whom P. W. Skehan had entrusted the definitive edition[38].

Another reason for the delay has been in some measure due to the type of edition chosen by those responsible for it. They could have confined themselves to publishing the photographs of the manuscripts, presenting a transcription of the text in Hebrew characters and adding the corresponding translation in a modern language. Those responsible for editing the manuscripts opted for an edition accompanied by extensive studies and commentaries. With the increase in the number of the texts needing comparison – both from Qumran literature and from Jewish and non-Jewish literature from the Persian, Hellenistic and Roman period – the task acquired immeasurable proportions. J. T. Milik in particular has been criticised for withholding important unpublished texts in the hope of completing detailed studies on them and on other texts. With time Milik should be granted the admiration and respect he deserved. He was the one who published the most with the greatest speed (DJD I, 1955 and II, 1961). Through his unceasing work directly with the manuscripts right from the start of the research, he possesses an overall view of the manuscripts, the fruit of his vast knowledge of the languages and literatures of the period.

The economic factor should not be forgotten. Until 1960, the international team could use the funds of the Rockefeller Foundation for its work. In that year the group dispersed and they returned to their respective universities or research centres, where they had to do the work on Qumran and at the same time teach and carry out many other duties in very different areas.

The criticism has been made that some of the editors entrusted their students with the edition of manuscripts in their charge. In fact, this helped to give a new impetus to the editorial process and involved the first widening of the initial group of editors. It is true that this circumstance created an attitude of resentment towards the privileged position of the students of a particular professor or of a university such as Harvard. Professors and doctoral candidates who had no access to the study of the manuscripts felt themselves to be in inferior conditions with the risk that the conclusions of their work appeared as disproved by data from the Qumran manuscripts to which they had no access.

In the United States, the *Biblical Archaeology Review* and *Bible Review*, two journals with a large circulation, carried out a campaign for freedom of access to the photographs of the manuscripts. In their pages there appeared a flood of articles and letters to the editor with harsh, sometimes excessive criticism against the members of the editorial team. From this side of the Atlantic, I followed the successive instalments of the public trial against the so-called syndicate or cartel formed by the official editors of the Qumran texts. Sporadically, I attended international meetings, such as that held jointly by the «Society of Biblical Literature» and the «American Schools of Oriental Research» in Kansas City in November, 1991. At this meeting a statement was approved about the preservation, distribution and publication of manuscripts and other ancient material. One did not know what to think. Should I admire the pioneer struggle of the North Americans for freedom, in this case freedom of access for all scholars to material conserved in museums? Or should I think that through the mass media I was witnessing yet another case of a bitter or ordinary struggle for the rights due respectively to museums, libraries, editorial teams, publishing houses, scholarly journals, general reader, etc.

A statement made public through those attending the colloquium on Qumran in Cracow («The Mogilany Resolution 1989»[39] requested the rapid publication by the Clarendon Press of the photographs of the manuscripts still unpublished, without waiting for the critical edition of these manuscripts. It also requested a rapid «preliminary edition» of all the texts from Qumran in *Revue de Qumran*», the publication of «Concordances», as well as the preparation of bibliographies about Qumran and a dictionary of Qumran. It is surprising to verify how this series of *desiderata* is being fulfilled or becoming on-going projects.

The Huntingdon Library of San Marino in California announced its decision to place at the disposal of scholars in general the collection of photographs of the manuscripts which it possessed in store. After that, in October 1991 the Israel Antiquities Authority also decided to place at the disposal of scholars the complete collection of all the photographs of all the manuscripts in the museums of Jerusalem. I could immediately verify that the vast majority of unpublished texts consisted of small fragments from which often it is impossible to reconstruct even one sentence with any sense at all

The recent publication of all the manuscripts in microfiche format and the expansion of the group of editors to 54 will no doubt speed up the editing process, but the new editors and those who have access to the microfiche edition will also need time for their studies.

The Men of the Dead Sea[40]

Florentino García Martínez

In *The Dead Sea Scrolls Translated* I attempted to offer a faithful and respectful translation of the most important texts or fragments of the collection of manuscripts from Qumran. Here, starting with these same fragments, I would like to meet the men behind these texts, the men of the Dead Sea. By means of a selection of quotations from different manuscripts I intend to present a kaleidoscopic image of these people, as fragmented and incomplete as the texts themselves. The people who wrote them, read them, copied and recopied them, considered them as their most precious treasure and in this way caused them to reach our hands.

For this we must embark on an imaginary journey which will allow us to cross the frontiers of space and time and also those other frontiers, subtle but no less real, of a language which to us is alien and a culture which to us is foreign.

This journey takes us across the desert of Judaea, makes us walk on scorched near-white lands and forces us to cross gullies of a rusty iron ochre. It compels us to descend through deep and rocky ravines and to follow the tortuous course of parched torrents which seek out the deepest rift in the earth: the Jordan Valley and its extension, which the ancients called «Lake Asphalt», and we know by the name of «The Dead Sea», which is just as appropriate. In its still waters, fringed with saline deposits and about 300 metres below the level of the Mediterranean are reflected the mountains of Moab on one side and the gullies of the Judaean Desert on the other. Halfway between these two peaks and the Dead Sea, there is a wide marl terrace, the conclusion of our journey. On it the ruins of Qumran are still visible. And in the rocky walls of the desert or in the gullies carved out by the waters in the terrace itself among many other cavities, are to be found the caves in which our texts were found. And in this same terrace we can find the men of the Dead Sea in their hundreds.

Do not worry. I am not going to describe them with their white one-piece robes moving silently to the communal meal in the great hall, or modelling vases or baking them in the potter's oven still visible among the ruins. Nor am I going to describe them building or repairing the aqueduct which conveys the water from the basin in the nearby wadi towards the cisterns, or purifying themselves in the ritual baths, or even bent over the tables of the scriptorium while they copy or compose the texts which have reached us.

We can meet the men of the Dead Sea in a much more concrete and real way, and the meeting occurs even before we have been able to penetrate within the ruins of Qumran. Outside the Khirbet, in fact, about fifty metres away, are located the three cemeteries where their remains repose[41]. A large cemetery, with more than a thousand tombs, in which only the remains of males have been found. And two small cemeteries, in which tombs of women and children have also been found.

There are no gravestones or names on the surface. Only small oval mounds of stones mark the tombs set out in rows. Each tomb is a simple ditch, one or two metres in depth, with the niche containing the corpse dug out of one of the sides and sealed with slabs or sun-dried bricks. Within them there are no other remains except those of the corpses, each lying on its back, with the hands crossed over the pelvis, and the head facing South.

For the last two thousand years the men of the Dead Sea are here in their tombs waiting to be rewarded for their faithfulness. A delightful text transforms the promise of national restoration of the prophet Ezekiel's vision of the dry bones into a promise of individual resurrection:

> *1* [And they shall know that I am YHWH,] who rescued my people, giving them the covenant. *Blank 2* [And I said: «YHWH,] I have seen many in Israel who have loved your name and have walked *3* on the paths of [justice.] When will these things happen? And how will they be rewarded for their loyalty?». And YHWH said to me: *4* «I will make the children of Israel see and they will know that I am YHWH». *Blank 5* [And he said:] «Son of man, prophesy over the bones and say: May a bone [connect] with its bone and a joint *6* [with its joint».] And so it happened. And he said a second time: «Prophesy, and sinews will grow on them and they will be covered with skin *7* [all over».] And so it happened. And again he said: «Prophesy over the four winds of the sky and the winds *8* [of the sky] will blow [upon them and they will live] and a large crowd of men will rise and bless YHWH Sebaoth who [caused them to live.»] (4Q385 frag. 2; DSST, 286)[42].

Evidently, they are the ones who loved the name of the Lord and walked on the paths of justice. This great multitude, the men of the Dead Sea, are waiting in these tombs in silence for the reward of their faithfulness in a new life. Why and when did they retire to the desert? How did they live? What did they think? Who were they? The very texts which they wrote two thousand years ago, which by chance have reached our hands for us to read towards the end of this twentieth century, will give us the answers to these queries.

## 1 Why and When did they Withdraw to the Desert?

One of these texts, 4QMMT, states clearly *why* they separated themselves from all their brothers: out of a desire for absolute faithfulness to the revealed word, of which only they possessed the correct understanding:

[And you know that] we have segregated ourselves from the rest of the peop[le and (that) we avoid] *93* mingling in these affairs and associating with them in these things. And you k[now that there is not] *94* to be found in our actions deceit or betrayal or evil, for concerning [these things w]e give [... and further] *95* to you we have wr[itten] that you must understand the book of Moses [and the words of the pro]phets and of David [and the annals] *96* [of eac]h generation. And in the book it is written [...] (4QMMT 92-96; DSST, 79)[43].

«These things» is a long list of instances where the others, the rest of the people, have turned aside from the correct interpretation of the Law: the calendar, the sacrifices of the gentiles, the transmission of impurity by flowing liquids, defilement brought into the holy city by animal skins, dogs, the blind, the deaf, lepers, corpses, unlawful unions, marriages of priests with the laity, tithes, etc.

How is it possible to take part in the worship of a temple whose festival cycle does not correspond to the fixed and immutable rhythm which God revealed? A temple into which the wheat of the gentiles is brought, a temple whose peace offerings are not consumed on the same day, or in which a cow and her calf are immolated on the same day? How is it possible to live within the walls of a city which must be as holy as the desert camp, where the divine presence dwells, with those who have a different idea of what is required to preserve this holiness? With those who not only make vessels with the skins and bones of unclean animals, but even bring those skins into the temple, or allow dogs to roam the city? How co-exist in this holy city with the blind, the deaf or lepers, or with someone who has not purified himself after sacrificing the red heifer? How share a roof with those who yoke together animals of different species, or mix wool and linen in their clothes, or sow different seeds on their fields or vineyards? How live together with those who do not worry about contact with corpses, or think that liquids do not transmit impurity? How live together with those who believe that a son of Aaron can be joined with impunity to someone not of priestly lineage?

When it is divine precepts which are in question, peaceful co-existence is impossible. If the city is unclean through the fault of its inhabitants, to remain in it is to be contaminated. If the temple is profaned, if the festivals are celebrated out of season, if the sacrifices have been made unclean, there is no sense in taking part in worship. And if, in spite of the zeal displayed, they do not have the means to restore order and impose observance, all that remains is to maintain the purity of the remnant by withdrawing and waiting for the moment when divine intervention allows restoration of the order which has been destroyed.

But why to the desert? In these conditions, flight to the desert can be a real alternative, in spite of the difficulties. For the men of the Dead Sea, steeped in the Bible, the desert is the place of the Exodus. Therefore, it is not difficult for them to transform it from a place of exile into a dwelling, a temporary residence or a stage on the path. From there, these «exiles of the desert» will one day leave for the great battle which will make possible the return to a new Jerusalem and a new temple. Accordingly, in their texts, the desert is a place of meetings, of visions, of voices. Above all, it is the remembrance of the Exodus of the historical Israel en route to the land and, therefore, a metaphor of the sons of light travelling towards the true homeland. The *Community Rule* (reusing the text of Isaiah) describes for us the plan of being transformed into a group, of forming a community, of which these «separated ones» dream:

> And when these exist /as a community/ in Israel *13* /in compliance with these arrangements/ they are to be segregated from within the dwelling of the men of sin to walk to the desert in order to open there His path. *14* As it is written: «In the desert, prepare the way of \*\*\*\*, straighten in the steppe a roadway for our God». *15* This is the study of the law which he commanded through the hand of Moses, in order to act in compliance with all that has been revealed from age to age, *16* and according to what the prophets have revealed through his holy spirit (1QS VIII 12-16; DSST, 12)[44].

In this way the same *Rule* explains to us the *purpose* of this segregation, in order to form a community in the desert, a community of possessions and of law, under the authority of lawful priests:

> *1* This is the rule for the men of the Community who freely volunteer to convert from all evil and to keep themselves steadfast in all he prescribes in compliance with his will. They should keep apart from *2* men of sin in order to constitute a Community in law and possessions, and acquiesce to the authority of the sons of Zadok, the priests who safeguard the covenant and to the authority of the multitude of the men *3* of the Community, those who persevere steadfastly in the covenant. By its authority, decision by lot shall be made in every affair involving the law, property and judgment, to achieve together truth and humility, *4* justice and uprightness, compassionate love and seemly behaviour in all their paths. No-one should walk in the stubbornness of his heart in order to go astray following his heart *5* and his eyes and the musings of his inclination. Instead he should circumcise in the Community the foreskin of his tendency and of his stiff neck in order to lay a foundation of truth for Israel, for the Community of the eternal *6* covenant. They should make atonement for all who freely volunteer for holiness in Aaron and for the house of truth in Israel and for those being entered together for the Community for the lawsuit and for the judgment. *7* They should proclaim as guilty all those who sabotage the decree (1QS V 1-7; DSST, 9).

We are unable to know precisely *when*. Our texts are not concerned with history. At best they are concerned with «salvation history» for which it is difficult to give exact dates. A famous passage of the *Damascus Document* pinpoints its origins as follows:

> For when they were unfaithful in forsaking him, he hid his face from Israel and from his sanctuary *4* and delivered them up to the sword. However, when he remembered the covenant of the very first, he saved a remnant *5* for Israel and did not deliver them up to destruction. And at the moment of wrath, three hundred and *6* ninety years after having delivered them up into the hands of Nebuchadnezzar, king of Babylon, *7* he visited them and caused to sprout from Israel and from Aaron a shoot of the planting, in order to possess *8* his land and to become fat with the good things of his soil. And they realised their sin and knew that *9* they were guilty men; but they were like blind persons and like those who grope for the path *10* over twenty years. And God appraised their deeds, because they sought him with a perfect heart *11* and raised up for them a Teacher of Righteousness, in order to direct them in the path of his heart. *Blank* And he made known *12* to the last generations what he had done for the last generation, the congregation of traitors (CD-A I 3-12, DSST, 33)[45].

The date of Israel's exile is known, and the addition of the 390 years, plus the 20 years when the group walks like a blind man who looks for his path by groping, is not particularly difficult. This would provide us with a date at the beginning of the 2nd century B.C.E. It would all be easy if the prophet Ezekiel had not used exactly the same number, 390, to indicate the days in which, lying on his left side, he would himself bear the sin of the house of Israel, one day for every year. To these add another 40 days, lying on his right side, to remove iniquity from the house of Judah, alluding in his turn to the 430 years of slavery in Egypt mentioned in Ex 12:40. Whatever can be made of this play on symbols and allusions, it is certain that in the second half of this 2nd century before the Christian era, our men of the Dead Sea had already broken with «the rest of the people». They had settled in the surroundings of the ruins of Qumran to realise this dream of community life in conformity with the Law.

## II How did the Men of the Dead Sea Live?

Perhaps the easiest way to describe their life is to define it as a life completely dedicated to the observance of the Law. From the moment of entry up to the moment of final repose in the cemeteries in which we have met them, their whole life was ruled by observance. Observance of the divine decrees and of all those other precepts derived from the revealed regulations, and whose purpose is to create a protective barrier around the Law which prevents any of its commandments being infringed.

To enter this community is, of course, a free act, though it is anything but easy. Certain qualifications were required. Also, joining was regulated by a process with separate stages, at each of which a progressively higher level had to be reached, with its appropriate rites of passage:

> And to any in Israel who freely volunteers *14* to enrol in the council of the Community, the Instructor who is at the head of the Many shall test him with regard to his insight and his deeds. If he suits the discipline he shall introduce him *15* into the covenant so that he can revert to the truth and shun all sin, and he shall teach him all the precepts of the Community. And then, when he comes in to stand in front of the Many, they shall be questioned, *16* all of them, concerning his duties. And depending on the outcome of the lot in the council of the Many he shall be included or excluded. If he is included in the Community council, he must not touch the pure food of *17* the Many while they test him about his spirit and about his deeds until he has completed a full year; neither should he share in the possession of the Many. *18* When he has completed a year within the Community, the Many will be questioned about his duties, concerning his insight and his deeds in connection with the law. And if the lot results in him *19* joining the foundations of the Community according to the priests and the majority of the men of the covenant, his wealth and his belongings will also be included at the hands of the *20* Inspector of the belongings of the Many. And they shall be entered into the ledger in his hand but they shall not use them for the Many. He must not touch the drink of the Many until *21* he completes a second year among the men of the Community. And when this second year is complete he will be examined by command of the Many. And if *22* the lot results in him joining the Community, they shall enter him in the Rule according to his rank among his brothers for the law, for the judgment, for purity and for the placing of his possessions in common. And his advice will be *23* for the Community as will his judgment (1QS VI 13-23; DSST, 10).

At each one of these stages the candidate must give proof of his progress in the knowledge and perfect observance of all the precepts. This would not have been at all easy. It is enough to compare the decrees concerning the observance of the sabbath which we find in the *Damascus Document* with the biblical decrees in this regard, or with the usual practice of other groups of the period:

> *14* Concerning the sabbath, to observe it in accordance with its regulation...
> And on the day of the sabbath, no-one should say a *18* useless or stupid

word. He is not to lend anything to his fellow. He is not to discuss riches or gain. *19* He is not to speak about matters of work or of the task to be carried out on the following day. *20 Blank* No-one is to walk in the field to do the work which he wishes *21* (on) the sabbath. He is not to walk more than one thousand cubits outside the city. *22 Blank* No-one is to eat on the sabbath day except what has been prepared; and from what is lost *23* in the field, he should not eat. And he should not drink except of what there is in the camp... (*Col.* XI) *3* No-one is to wear dirty clothes or (clothes) which are in the chest, unless *4* they have been washed with water or rubbed with incense. *Blank* No-one should fast voluntarily *5* on the sabbath... *9* He is not to open a sealed vessel on the sabbath. *Blank* No-one should wear *10* perfumes on the sabbath, to go out or come in. *Blank* In his dwelling no-one should lift *11* a stone or dust. *Blank* The wet-nurse should not lift the baby to go out or come in on the sabbath. *12 Blank* No-one should press his servant or his maidservant or his employee on the sabbath. *Blank* No-one should help an animal give birth on the sabbath day. *Blank* And if he makes it fall into a well *14* or a pit, he should not take it out on the sabbath. *Blank* No-one should stay in a place close *15* to gentiles on the sabbath. *Blank* No-one should profane the sabbath by riches or gain on the sabbath. *16 Blank* And any living man who falls into a place of water or into a place <...>, *17* no-one should take him out with a ladder or a rope or a utensil... (CD-A X 14- XI 17; DSST, 41-42).

However, not only must he gives proofs of knowledge and perfect observance; his «lot» must be among the sons of light. For our men of the Dead Sea, the line which divides light from darkness is not limited to the world of the angels and the whole universe. It also runs through the being of every man. What ultimately determines that one can succeed in being a perfect member of the community of «the sons of light» is the fact that from the beginning he has received more parts of light than of darkness. That is, his destiny has fallen among the lot of light:

Until now the spirits of truth and of injustice feud in the heart of man *24* and they walk in wisdom or in folly. In agreement with man's birthright in justice and in truth, so he abhors injustice; and according to his share in the lot of injustice he acts irreverently in it and so *25* abhors the truth. For God has sorted them into equal parts until the appointed end and the new creation. He knows the result of his deeds for all times *26* [everlas]ting and has given them as a legacy to the sons of men so that they know good [and evil], so they decide the lot of every living being in compliance with the spirit there is in him [at the time of] the visitation (1QS IV 23-26; DSST, 7-8).

This is why the Inspector and the Many must resort to all means possible to determine the parts of light and of darkness of each candidate. Even an examination of his physical characteristics, of his horoscope, of birth sign, etc., can provide important information in this truly decisive matter. One of the most surprising texts, preserved in Hebrew and Aramaic fragments, describes two types of people as follows: (4Q186 and 4Q561):

> And his teeth are of differing lengths (?). The fingers of *4* his hand are stumpy. His thighs are fat and each one covered in hair. His spirit has *6* eight (parts) in the house [of darkness] and one in the house of light.

> His eyes are of a colour between black and striated. His beard is *2* ... [...] and frizzy. The sound of his voice is simple. His *3* teeth are sharp and even. He is neither tall *4* nor short, and like that from his birth. Then the fingers of his hands are slender *5* and long. His thighs are smooth and the soles of his feet *6* [...] are even. His spirit has *7* eight (parts) [in the house of light] in second rank, *8* and one [in the house of darkness] (CDSST, 456)[46].

The candidate who has passed these different tests, knows all the precepts of the community and observes them, and in the mystery of divine choice has received as his lot more parts of light than of darkness, is finally considered suitable to be a member with full rights of the community. He can enter to become part of the new covenant. This enrolment takes place with solemnity in a feast at which the blessings and curses of the covenant are proclaimed:

> *16* And all those who enter in the Community Rule shall establish a covenant before God in order to carry out *17* all that he commands and in order not to stray from following him for any fear, dread or grief *18* that might occur during the dominion of Belial. When they enter the covenant, the priests *19* and the levites will bless the God of salvation and all the works of his faithfulness and all *20* those who enter the covenant shall repeat after them: «Amen, Amen». *Blank* (1QS I 16-20; DSST, 3).

Immediately afterwards, the priests and levites proclaim the blessings and curses of the covenant. And all the candidates respond in chorus, so sealing their promise and being enrolled in this way into this «eternal society» formed by the members of the «new covenant». From this moment onwards they are members with full rights in the community and can take part in the sacred banquet for which the highest level of purity is required. We find the best description of this banquet projected into the future, in the messianic age. But it will serve us perfectly well as an illustration, since this future is presented as a reflection of the present, as an ideal image of everyday life:

And [when] they gather at the table of community [or to drink] the new wine, and the table of *18* community is prepared [and] the new wine [is mixed] for drinking, [no-one should stretch out] his hand to the first-fruit of the bread *19* and of the [new wine] before the priest, for [he is the one who bl]esses the first-fruit of bread *20* and of the new wine [and stretches out] his hand towards the bread before them. Afterwards, the Messiah of Israel shall stretch out his hand *21* towards the bread. [And after, he shall] bless all the congregation of the community, each [one according to] his dignity. And in accordance with this regulation they shall *22* act at each me[al, when] at least ten m[en are gat]hered (1QSa [1Q28a] II 17-22; DSST, 127-128)⁴⁷.

This meal, this taking part in the «purity», in the pure food of the Many, which we see here projected as a messianic banquet, is, in fact, the community meal of each day. The members take part in it only when they find themselves in such a state of ritual purity as to be considered like angels:

No man, defiled by any of the impurities *4* of a man, shall enter the assembly of these; and everyone who is defiled by them should not be *5* established in his office amongst the congregation. And everyone who is defiled in his flesh, paralysed in his feet or *6* in his hands, lame, blind, deaf, dumb or defiled in his flesh with a blemish *7* visible to the eyes, or the tottering old man who cannot keep upright in the midst of the assembly, *8* these shall not enter to take their place among the congregation of famous men, for the angels *9* of holiness are among their congre[gation] (1QSa [1Q28a] II 3-9; DSST, 127).

However, it is not only these temporary or permanent «defilements» which can prevent a member from taking part in the «purity». Daily life is full of risks. Since the requirement of faithfulness is absolute, and the regulations established to safeguard the total observance of the precepts of the Law are many and various, any member runs the risk of breaking one or other of them. The seriousness of the transgression in the eyes of the community determines how long the deprivation of sharing in the «purity» lasts, which is imposed on the one who is guilty. Here are some examples:

And if he has spoken angrily against one of the priests enrolled in the book, he will be punished *3* for a year and shall be excluded, under sentence of death, from the pure food of the Many. However, if he had spoken unintentionally, he will be punished for six months. And whoever lies knowingly *4* shall be punished for six months. Whoever knowingly and for no reason insults his fellow will be punished for a year *5* and will be excluded.

And whoever speaks to his fellow with deception or knowingly deceives him, will be punished for six months. And if *6 Blank* he is /negligent/ to his fellow he will be punished for three months. However, if he is negligent with the possessions of the Community achieving a loss, he shall replace them {...} *7* in full. *Blank 8 Blank 9 Blank 10* And if he does not manage to replace them, he will be punished for /sixty days/. And whoever feels animosity towards his fellow for no cause will be punished for {six months} /a year/. *11* And likewise for anyone retaliating for any reason. Whoever utters with his mouth futile words, three months; and for talking in the middle of the words of his fellow, *12* ten days. And whoever lies down and goes to sleep in the session of the Many, thirty days. And the same applies to whoever leaves the session of the Many *13* without cause, or falls asleep up to three times during a session shall be punished ten days; however, if ... *Blank 14* and he withdraws, he shall be punished for thirty days. And whoever walks about naked in front of his fellow, without needing to, shall be punished for three months. *15* And the person who spits in the course of a meeting of the Many shall be punished thirty days. And whoever takes out his 'hand' from under his clothes, or if these are rags *16* which allow his nakedness to be seen, he will be punished thirty days. And whoever giggles inanely causing his voice to be heard shall be sentenced to thirty *17* days. And whoever takes out his left hand to gesticulate with it shall be punished ten days. And whoever goes round defaming his fellow *18* shall be excluded for one year from the pure food of the Many and shall be punished; however, whoever goes round defaming the Many shall be expelled from their midst *19* and will never return. And whoever complains against the foundation of the Community they shall expel and he will never return (1QS VII 2-19; DSST, 11).

As a consequence, the deprivation can be permanent. This is equivalent to expulsion of the offending member. The community does not hesitate to cut off dry branches or those whose fruits are not as expected. As with admission, expulsion takes place officially, at the feast of the renewal of the covenant which is celebrated in the third month and includes the curses upon those who have been unfaithful to the new covenant: «The sons of Levi and the men of the camps shall assemble in the third month and shall curse whoever bends to the right or to the left of the Law», as the end of one of the copies of the *Damascus Document* from Cave 4 (4Q267 18 V 17-18) tells us:

And so is the judgment of everyone who enters the congregation of the men of perfect holiness and is slack in the fulfilment of the instructions of the upright. *3* This is the man who is melted in the crucible. When his deeds are evident, he shall be expelled from the congregation, *4* like one whose lot did not fall among the disciples of God. In accordance with his misdeed, all the men *5* of knowledge shall rebuke him, until the day when he returns to take his place in the session of the men of perfect holiness. But when his deeds are evident, according to the exact interpretation of the law in which *7* the men of perfect holiness walked, no-one should associate with him in wealth or work, *8* for all the holy ones of the Most High have cursed him. And (proceed) according to this judgment, with all those who despise, among the first *9* as among the last, for they have placed idols in their heart and have walked in the stubbornness of *10* their heart. For them there shall be no part in the house of the law (CD-B XX 1-10; DSST, 46).

### III What did the Men of the Dead Sea Think?

To give a simple sketch of the thought of the men of the Dead Sea would take much too long. The library which they bequeathed us is too large and too varied for that. To attempt to outline even what they felt would take even longer. A perusal of the *Hymns* allows us to compile the most varied echoes of a human experience utterly ablaze, passionate, rich, indefinable. I will restrict myself, then, to indicating only one of the elements which seem typical: their dualistic thought which is expressed in metaphors and images: light and darkness, opposing paths, good and evil. A cosmic dualism which only stops short of the basic principle of monotheism, the uniqueness of God and the covenant, the primordial source of all that exists, whether light or darkness, good or evil. A dualism which divides heavenly beings into two categories: angels and demons of every plumage. A dualism which divides history between «the good» and «the bad», the sons of light and those of darkness. A dualism which penetrates the heart of man and finds in each one the presence of that part of light and of darkness, of sin and of grace, which forms the root of man's being. A treatise incorporated into the beginning of the *Community Rule* expresses this thought as follows:

> From the God of knowledge stems all there is and all there shall be. Before they existed he made all their plans *16* and when they came into being they will execute all their works in compliance with his instructions, according to his glorious design without altering anything. In his hand are *17* the laws of all things and he supports them in all their needs. He created man to rule *18* the world and placed within him two spirits so that he would walk with them until the moment of his visitation: they are the spirits of truth and of deceit. *20* In the hand of the Prince of Lights is dominion over all the sons of justice; they walk on paths of light. And in the hand of the Angel *21* of Darkness is total dominion over the sons of deceit; they walk on paths of darkness. Due to the Angel of Darkness *22* all the sons of justice

stray, and all their sins, their iniquities, their failings and their mutinous deeds are under his dominion *23* in compliance with the mysteries of God, until his moment; and all their punishments and their periods of grief are caused by the dominion of his enmity; *24* and all the spirits of their lot cause the sons of light to fall. However, the God of Israel and the angel of his truth assist all *25* the sons of light. He created the spirits of light and of darkness and on them established all his deeds *26* [on their p]aths all his labours. God loved one of them for all eternal ages and in all his deeds he takes pleasure for ever; of the other one he detests his advice and hates all his paths forever. *Blank* (1QS III 15- IV 1; DSST, 6).

Other texts convey to us the actual names of these two heavenly princes, the chiefs of the armies of light and of darkness: Prince of Light, Michael, Melki-zedek; Prince of Darkness, Belial, Melki-resha$^c$. They also show them quarrelling over possession of man's heart:

> *10* in my vision, the vision of my dream. And behold, two were quarrelling over me and they said: [...] *11* and they entered into a great debate over me. And I asked them: You, why are you [...] thus [over me? And they replied and said to me: We] *12* [have received] the dominion and we rule over the sons of Adam. They said to me: Which of us do you [choose ...?] I lifted my eyes and saw] *13* [that one] of them had a dreadful appearance [...] and his clothing was coloured and obscured by darkness [...] *14* [And I looked at the other, and behold [...] in his appearance and his face was smiling and he was covered with [...] (4Q544 I 1-10; DSST, 273)[48].

In this fight without quarter, the men of the Dead Sea are not defenceless. As we have already said, their lot has been predestined and they belong to the forces of good, the armies of the «sons of light». Their whole life is spent in communion with the angels. In the silence of the desert «the noise of divine silence»[49] echoes continually. And the vision of the angelic liturgy accompanies the prayer of those who have made the «offering of the lips», a temporary substitute for the sacrifices of the defiled temple. Although the forces of evil continue to operate, «the sons of light» are able to protect themselves from the attacks of darkness and exorcise the influence of the angels of destruction. One of the *Songs of the Sage* shows us the Instructor exercising these functions of an exorcist:

> And I, the Instructor,
> declare the grandeur of his radiance
> in order to frighten and terr[ify]
> *5* all the spirits of the ravaging angels

and the bastard spirits,
demons, Liliths, owls and [jackals…]
6 and those who strike unexpectedly
to lead astray the spirit of knowledge,
to make their hearts forlorn and …
in the era of the rule of wickedness
7 and in the periods of humiliation of the sons of light,
in the guilty periods of those defiled by sins
(4Q510 I 4-7; DSST, 371)[50].

This hermeneutic framework, where the human and the heavenly mingle, and all light comes from the perpetual spring but co-exists with surrounding shadows even in the heart of «the sons of light», enables them to discover the root of man's being in the ceaseless conflict between this sinful being and saving grace. A conflict which for them, «the chosen ones», will end by being resolved in a trusting abandon in the embrace of a God:

These things I know through your knowledge,
for you opened my ears to wondrous mysteries
although I am a creature of clay, fashioned with water,
22 foundation of shame, source of impurity,
oven of iniquity, building of sin,
spirit of mistake, astray, without knowledge,
23 terrified at your just judgments.
What shall I be able to say which is not known?
What will I be able to declare which has not been told.
24 Everything has been engraved in your presence
with the stylus of remembrance
for all the incessant periods
in the eras of the number of everlasting years
in all their predetermined times.
25 How will a man tell his sin?
How will he defend his infringements?
26 How will he answer every just judgment?
To you, God of knowledge,
belong all the works of justice
27 and the foundation of truth;
to the sons of man,
the service of sin and the deeds of deception (1QH IX 21-27; DSST, 327).

What is flesh compared to this?
What creature of clay can do wonders?

He is in sin from his maternal womb,
*30* and in guilty iniquity right to old age.
But I know that justice does not belong to man
nor the perfect path to the son of man.
*31* To God Most High belong all the acts of justice,
and the path of man is not secure
except by the spirit which God creates for him
*32* to perfect the path of the sons of man
so that all his creatures come to know the strength of his power
and the extent of his compassion
with all the sons of his approval.
*33* And dread and dismay have gripped me,
all my /bones/ have fractured,
my heart has melted like wax in front of the fire,
my knees give way like water which flows down a slope,
*34* for I have remembered my faults
with the disloyalty of my ancestors,
when the wicked rose up against your covenant
*35* and the doomed against your word –
I said «For my sin I have been barred from your covenant».
But when I remembered the strength of your hand
*36* and the abundance of your compassion
I remained resolute and stood up;
my spirit kept firmly in place
in the face of my distress.
*37* For you have supported me by your kindnesses
and by your abundant compassion (1QH XII 29-37; DSST, 336).


For you have known me since my father,
*30* from the vitals [you have established me,]
[from the womb of] my mother you have filled me,
from the breasts of her who conceived me
your compassion has always been upon me,
*31* from the lap of my wet-nurse [you have looked after me,]
from my youth you have shown yourself to me in the intelligence of your
judgment,
*32* and with certain truth you have supported me.
You have delighted me with your holy spirit,
and until this very day you have guided me.
*33* Your just rebuke escorts my path,
your peace watches over the salvation of my soul,
with my steps there is bountiful forgiveness

*34* and great compassion when you judge me,
   until old age you support me.
*35* For my mother did not know me,
   and my father abandoned me to you.
   Because you are father to all the sons of your truth.
*36* In them you rejoice,
   like one full of gentleness for her child,
   and like a wet-nurse,
   you clutch to your chest all your creatures (1QH XVII 29-36; DSST, 349-350)[51].

This confidence in a tenderness which even portrays a God with motherly features cannot allow us to forget the fighting spirit of these men of the Dead Sea. If the elect can confidently leave himself in God's hands, he must at the same time fight with all his strength to destroy evil. All life is a fight, and the desert is a place of practice, of preparation for the battle which will finally conclude dualism through the victory of light. This battle will involve all the forces of good, heavenly and earthly, and will mark the ultimate triumph of the «sons of light»:

   You are a God, awesome in the splendour of your majesty,
   and the congregation of your holy ones is amongst us
   for everlasting assistance.
   [We will] treat kings with contempt,
*8* the powerful with jeers and mockery,
   for the Lord is holy
   and the King of glory is with us
   together with his holy ones.
   The heroes of the army of his angels
   are enlisted with us;
*9* the war hero is in our congregation;
   the army of his spirits, with our infantry and our cavalry.
   They are like clouds and dew to cover the earth.
*10* like torrential rain which pours justice on all that grows.
   Get up, hero,
   take your prisoners, glorious one,
*11* collect your spoil, worker of heroic deeds!
   Place your hand on the neck of your foes
   and your foot on the piles of the dead!
   Strike the nations, your foes,
*12* and may your sword consume guilty flesh! (1QM XII 7-12; DSST, 106)[52].

The great battle that was expected never happened. The Romans arrived in the 68th year of that exceptional century from which we number our days. And before the might of their legions, the men of the Dead Sea only succeeded in hastily protecting their texts in the caves. One thing is certain: the men of Qumran tried to defend themselves. The ruins of Qumran are mute witness, first to destruction and then to re-use as temporary quarters for a small Roman garrison. Whether the men of the Dead Sea had considered the arrival of the legions as a phase of the final and long-awaited battle is something we can never know. The battle surely ended in rout. Or is it merely one of the skirmishes marking a combat which will only be resolved ultimately «in the seventh lot» on a day that has not yet arrived?:

> And on the day on which the Kittim fall, there will be a battle, and savage destruction before the God of *10* Israel, for this will be the day determined by him since ancient times for the war of extermination against the sons of darkness. On this (day), the assembly of the gods and the congregation of men shall confront each other for great destruction. *11* The sons of light and the lot of darkness shall battle together for God's might, between the roar of a huge multitude and the shout of gods and of men, on the day of the calamity. It will be a time of *12* suffering fo[r al]l the people redeemed by God. Of all their sufferings, none will be like this, from its haste (?) until eternal redemption is fulfilled. And on the day of their war against the Kittim, *13* they [shall go out to destr]uction. In the war, the sons of light will be the strongest during three lots, in order to strike down wickedness; and in three (others), the army of Belial will gird themselves in order to force the lot of *14* [...] to retreat. There will be infantry battalions to melt the heart, but God's might will strengthen the hea[rt of the sons of light.] And in the seventh lot, God's great hand will subdue *15* [Belial, and a]ll the angels of his dominion and all the men of [his lot.] (1QM I 9-15; DSST, 95).

Whatever might have happened, after the year 68 CE the men of the Dead Sea did not return to what today are the ruins of Qumran. The echoes of their voices, their texts, were to remain silent over many centuries. And in more than a thousand tombs in the cemeteries, the men of the Dead Sea continue to wait for the reward for their faithfulness. Here they remain, in the hope that sinews, flesh and skin will again cover their blackened bones, that bones will be joined to bones and they will arise like a numerous people to whom the Lord will give life once more:

> From no-one shall the fruit [of] good [deeds] be delayed, *11* and the Lord will perform marvellous acts such as have not existed, just as he sa[id] *12* for he will heal the badly wounded and will make the dead live (4Q521 frag. 2 II 10-12; DSST, 394)[53].

## IV  Who Were the Men of the Dead Sea?

If, at the end of this journey, the men of the Dead Sea, «the Many», «the sons of light», the «men of the new covenant», «the poor» ... are rather more tangible, I will have reached my goal. The men of the Dead Sea, though, continue to be anonymous persons to us, figures without a face. We cannot even give them names. At most they are titles, functions: Mebaqqer, Paqid, Interpreter, Teacher of Righteousness... The real persons who lived, suffered, hoped, and whose mortal remains are found in rows in the three cemeteries around Qumran, reach us merely as voices. Two hundred years of life have been converted into text, shreds of words which reach us like an echo, hardly distinguishable from the desert wind.

Only one tiny fragment from among the many thousands allows us to lift this veil a little from such anonymity and give a concrete name to some of these voices. And with it I conclude. However, in order to understand this fragmentary text, which was not included in the first edition of *Textos de Qumrán*, it is necessary to listen first to another text, one which specifies how brotherly correction was carried out in the community[54]. The *Damascus Document* specifies the procedure which the members must follow when they are witnesses to a transgression of the Law committed by any of their brothers (CD IX 17-20):

> Any matter in which a man sins against the law, and his fellow sees him and he is alone; if it is a capital matter, he shall denounce him *18* in his presence, with rebuke, to the Inspector, and the Inspector shall write with his hand until he commits it *19* again in the presence of someone alone, and he denounces him to the Inspector; if he returns and is surprised in the presence of *20* someone alone, his judgment is complete (DSST, 40-41).

This procedure implies that within the community, the Inspector has to keep a list of infringements and of the corresponding corrections. The purpose was to be able to establish of a member's guilt and to apply the sanctions stipulated for his failing. Well, then, a small fragment, with the number 4Q477[55], seems to be precisely the remains of one of these lists in which were noted down the «rebukes» made to transgressing members. Separated by several short lines, each one of the phrases contains the name of one of the transgressors and of the failings for which he has been rebuked. Unfortunately, neither the names nor the failings have been preserved completely, but the gist of the text seems certain:

> And they rebuked] Johanan, son of Mata[thias because he ...] *4* and was quick to anger, [and ...] with him, and has the evil eye, and also has a boastful spirit. [...] *5* [...] ... to darkness. [...] *Blank* – And they rebuked

Hananiah Notos because he [...] *6* [...to] reduce the spirit of the
communi[ty..] and also to mortgage [...] *7* [...] And they rebuked [...] son
of Joseph, because he has the evil eye, and also because no-one [...] *8* [...]
and also he who loves the covering of his flesh [...] *9* [...] – And [they re-
buked] Hananiah, son of Sime[on..] *10* [...] And also he who loves the [...]
(DSST, 90).

Johanan ben Mattatias, Hananiah Notos, Hananiah ben Simeon and another
member whose surname alone has been preserved (ben Joseph). Scarcely four
names from among the hundreds of «sons of light». Four names, besides, of
sinners, of discordant voices, of members who, for one reason or another, did
not always succeed in maintaining the level demanded in the daily battle of
faithfulness to all the regulations of the Law. These four names, though, are the
most concrete example of those men of the Dead Sea, of those countless and
so very human voices hidden behind *The Dead Sea Scrolls Translated*.

# The Essenes of Qumran: Between Submission to the Law and Apocalyptic Flight

## Julio Trebolle Barrera

The interest aroused by the texts from Qumran is stimulated chiefly by the information these documents supply about the world surrounding the historical figure of Jesus of Nazareth and the writings of the early Christians. This point of view frequently leads to the distortion of the meaning of the Qumran texts themselves. These have to be studied for themselves and not so much in terms of a literary corpus of a somewhat later period and of a geographical horizon and ideas which are much wider than and differ from those of the Qumran texts. This does not mean to say that these manuscripts do not throw light, in many cases dazzling light, on the origins of Christianity[56].

Among the manuscripts from Qumran published recently there are some whose Jewish character is very marked. It must be acknowledged that «there is no Christian who understands them». Only a Jew, and not just any Jew, but someone brought up from infancy in a rabbinic environment of strict observance and later a student of all the mysteries of the Mishnah, the Talmud, and in some cases, perhaps, of the Kabbalah as well, is able not to feel strange before a «halakhic» or legal text, such as that published recently from what is called the «Halakhic Letter» (4QMMT).

The Dead Sea Scrolls are unequivocally important for knowing the origins of Judaism in the period midway between the Biblical age (basically up to the end of the Persian period), and classical and Rabbinic Judaism, represented by the Mishnah and the Talmud, the period between the 2nd century BCE and the 2nd century CE. These manuscripts have revealed that in this intermediate period, sometimes called the intertestamental period (between the Old and New Testaments), Judaism took on many different forms of various kinds, which contrast with the monolithic character of rabbinic Judaism of the last two thousand years. In this context Christianity was born, which initially did not appear to be more than one of the many Jewish groups of the period.

Until the appearance of the Dead Sea Scrolls, our information concerning the Persian and Hellenistic periods did not go much beyond what it was possible to extract from the Books of Maccabees and from the works of the Jewish historian Flavius Josephus. To obtain more data it was necessary to turn to Rabbinic literature of a later period, with the grave risk of being persistently anachronistic.

The manuscripts from Qumran bring us close to «failed forms of Judaism», forms of Judaism which could have existed but did not. Or, to use a less blunt expression, movements and groups of Judaism which could have developed further but chose to be on the fringes or were left there in the course of history.

Rabbinic Judaism succeeded in dominating the rest. This was because it faced the challenges of history head on and did not take flight towards an apocalyptic messianism as did the Essenes. Movements which did not acquire permanence in Judaism were developed in some way in the movements, trends and institutions of Christianity.

Among these forms of Judaism, the one represented by the «apocalyptic Essene community» stands out, as known by means of the manuscripts from Qumran. The definition of the three terms, «community»–«Essene»–«apocalyptic», presents great problems for academic research.

1. The Rules, the books of prayer and various others found at Qumran, appear to show that the members of the group which resided there lived in *community*, followed a way of life in common, shared their possessions, ate, prayed and worked together in a sort of «monastery» (if that is how to define the collection of buildings preserved in the archaeological site of Khirbet Qumran, which has been questioned by some scholars in recent publications).

2. It is an *Essene* community. This is the most common opinion among scholars. When it comes to saying exactly which type of «Essenes» is reflected in the manuscripts from Qumran, problems of interpretation and differences of opinion create a maze in which it is easy to get lost.

3. The most defining characteristic of the Essenes is certainly their *apocalypticism*. The meaning of the adjective «apocalyptic» and of the noun «apocalypse» and the application of these terms to the Qumran community and to the texts found there, does not cease to present problems (Stegemann, Carmignac). Apocalyptic does not only refer to the last days and to a Messianic age, the beginning of which is expected from one moment to the next. The term «apocalypse» means originally «unveil the hidden». Apocalypses refer, therefore, to visions and revelations of mysteries, whether mysteries of history or of the cosmos. There are, therefore, two types of apocalypse, some referring to revelations about history and the future, and others relating to visions of the cosmos and the stars.

On the other hand, in Judaism, and especially in Essenism, this revelation of mysteries is closely related to the study of the Law which contains all the mysteries of the godhead. It is necessary to be aware of this relationship between the two seemingly opposed worlds, of Law and of Mystery, and between two opposing tendencies, legalism and apocalyptic.

I do not believe it an exaggeration to say that herein lies the key to understanding Essenism, and indeed Judaism in general, which in the Bible itself is structured as Law and Prophets – as reality and utopia.

The sequence of terms («community»–«Essene»–«legalistic» and «apocalyptic») will form the outline of our approach to the literature, social structure and religious mentality of the group from Qumran[57].

## 1 The Qumran Community

We have firsthand information available concerning the way of life of the Qumran community through the writings of that community. The most important are the *Community Rule* (1Qserek) and the *Damascus Document* (CD), to which should be added the book of *Hymns* or prayers of the same community (1QH<sup>a</sup>).

### 1 The Writings of the Community

It is necessary to give a brief description of these writings so that later the information they can provide concerning the way of life of the group from Qumran can be extracted. When studying the texts it is necessary to differentiate clearly the dates when different manuscripts of the same work were copied. Also, but more difficult, the date of composition of each of the parts which make up a complete work. Highly sensational theories which pay no attention to these problems fall into no less sensational errors.

#### a  The Community Rule (1QS)

The oldest copy of the *Community Rule* (1QS) goes back to 100-75 BCE. This means that the Qumran community was already well established at this period. The *Rule* is not the work of a single author, but instead was composed in successive stages by different authors. It is not easy to reconstruct the process of literary composition of this text. Among the many proposals suggested by scholars (H. E. del Medico, A. R. C. Leaney, A.-M. Denis, P. von der Osten-Sacken, J. Duhaime, G. Klinzing) we select that of Murphy-O'Connor, who suggests that the edition of the *Rule* developed in four stages. The oldest corresponds to a kind of «manifesto» of the Teacher of Righteousness about the withdrawal to the desert (VIII 1-16; IX 3-X 8). Next to be edited was the penal code in VIII 18-IX 2, which seems to be intended for a community of fewer members. The third stage is to be found in two passages. The first (V 1-13) is related to the reform of the community's character, and the second (V 15-VII 25) to a more detailed legislation than that of the preceding stage. The fourth and last stage is composed of different sources, included in I 1- IV 26 and X 9-XI 22, which really comprise an exhortation on the spirit of strict observance. The text called the *Rule of the Congregation* (1Qsa) comprises an appendix to the *Community Rule* and is eschatological in content. Similarly, the *Collection of Blessings* (1Qsb) forms an appendix to the *Community Rule* and to the *Rule of the Congregation*.

## b  The Damascus Document (CD)

The text known as the *Damascus Document* (CD) had already been known since the end of the last century. In 1886-87 two manuscripts (A and B) of this work were found in the genizah of the El Cairo synagogue, dated to the 10th and 12th centuries. At Qumran, ten copies of this document came to light. This served to prove that it was not a composition from the mediaeval period but a work which was already known in about 100 BCE, since the oldest copy found at Qumran goes back to 75-50 BCE.

The work is divided into two parts: an exhortation and a body of laws. Many texts of ancient Near Eastern literature follow this pattern, which within biblical literature has its best counterpart in the structure of the book of Deuteronomy.

The first part of the *Damascus Document* includes an important historical reference. It mentions a period of 390 years (I 5-6) which, it seems, runs from the destruction of Jerusalem by Nebuchadnezzar in the year 587 BCE. This puts the origin of the Qumran community at the beginning of the 2nd century BCE. On the other hand, according to this text (I 10), the arrival of the «Teacher of Righteousness» on the scene happens 20 years after the appearance of the «root of the plant». During these 20 years the group went wandering «like blind men and like people who seek their path by groping». This is a symbolic way of referring to the period between 175 and 152 BCE, during which the legitimate succession of the high priest was broken until the nomination of Jonathan Maccabeus as high priest. Jonathan is very probably the «wicked priest» against whom the «Teacher of Righteousness» arises. The «Teacher» then founds the Qumran community and breaks with the priesthood of Jerusalem.

The second part of the *Damascus Document* is legal in character and is divided into five sections: XV 1- XVI 16 (entry into the covenant), IX 1- X 10a (internal code of conduct), X 10b-XII 18 (ritual), XII 19-XIV 19 (organization), XIV 20-22 (penal code).

The first part of the *Document* was composed in successive stages, but it is not easy to determine what is original and what was added later at the various stages. The metrical criterion followed by such authors as R. H. Charles, I. Ravinowitz and R. A. Soloff turns out to be incorrect. Nor does the approach of considering the «midrashic» parts as later additions lead to satisfactory conclusions. (K. G. Kuhn, J. Becker). A.-M. Denis distinguishes three sources. The oldest, I 4-IV 6a, presents a vocabulary close to that of Daniel and reflects a «movement» more than an organised community. The following source, IV 6b-VI 11, already corresponds to the moment when the movement has become institutionalised. The third is in turn divided into three sources, the last of which is already a reflection of a community which has a long experience of life behind it. For Murphy-O'Connor there are four sources of this work, all of them independent from each other and prior to the occupation of Qumran by the Essenes. They are the missionary exhortation (II 14-VI 1), the memorandum (VI 11-VIII 3), the critique of the princes of Judah (VIII 3-18) and the call to faithfulness (XIX 33-XX 1b.8b-13). The *Damascus Document* was basically a work of missionary exhortation, whose aim was to strengthen the morale of the community and to bring its ideals and way of life into new surroundings.

### c The Hymns

The *Hymns* scroll is the most damaged of those found in Cave 1. Sukenik reconstructed 18 columns, leaving 66 fragments unidentified. H. Stegemann has succeeded in placing them in the corresponding position of the manuscript, after having reconstructed the original sequence of the columns in the scroll. According to Sukenik and Dupont-Sommer, the author of these *Hymns* can be no other than the «Teacher of Righteousness». This is virtually certain in respect of the passages II 2-19; IV 5-29; V 5-19; V 20-VI 36; VII 6-25; VIII 4-40 (H. W. Kuhn, Jeremias and Becker provide a somewhat longer list). The «I» who is speaking in these *Hymns* has a strong personality and is very much aware of his mission («bearer of revelation»). In the other hymns, the «I» appears much more watered down. The author of those could be a member of the community. These hymns created in the Qumran community correspond to an atmosphere of worship, either of prayer and daily liturgy (Becker) or, more probably, one of rites of initiation into the community or of yearly covenant renewal (Kuhn). More serious is the fact that research has not yet succeeded in assigning a date to these hymns.

### 2 Way of Life in the Qumran Community

Using passages from the writings mentioned we can now attempt to know the way of life of the Qumran community, the personality of its founder, the way it was run and the conditions of entry into the community, the ritual meals and dietary rules practised, the festival calendar, etc.

### a The «Teacher of Righteousness»

The «Teacher of Righteousnesss is the most prominent figure of the Qumran community. Possible connections of this figure with that of Jesus of Nazareth make it especially interesting. However, the parallels between these two characters which some have wished to establish cannot sustain serious critical analysis. This applies especially to all those referring to a supposed crucifixion of the «Teacher of Righteousness» and to the hope in his immediate return on the part of his followers.

The title «Teacher of Righteousness» corresponds to a historical figure with
very blurred outlines. It is certain he was a priest of Zadokite lineage, who was,
perhaps, the high priest in the time of Jonathan Maccabeus (162-142 BCE). The
texts describe him as a man appointed by God to lead the community of his
followers in the final days: «and he raised up for them a Teacher of Righteousness, in order to direct them in the path of his heart» (CD I 11; DSST, 33). They
also consider him as the recipient of a special revelation and understanding of
the Scriptures: «(the Teacher of Righteousness), to whom God has disclosed
all the mysteries of the words of his servants, the prophets» (1QpHab VII 4-5;
DSST, 200). As has been said, he was certainly the author of the *Hymns*
(1QHodayot) written in the first person.

It is possible that the Teacher of Righteousness will end his days by being
executed. In the *Habbakkuk Pesher* it says that the Wicked Priest «hunted down
the Teacher of Righteousness to consume him with the ferocity of his anger in
the place of his banishment, in festival time, during the rest of the day of
Atonement. He paraded in front of them, to consume them and make them fall
on the day of fasting, the sabbath of their rest» (1QpHab XI 5-8; DSST, 201-202).
Of course, the meaning of the term «to consume» is not clear, for first it refers
to the Teacher, but a little later on, it is applied to the whole community and
not just to a single individual.

It is possible to find another reference to the «Wicked Priest»'s intention of
killing the Teacher of Righteousness in a passage from the *Psalms Pesher*:

> *8* Its interpretation alludes to the [Wic]ked Priest, who spies on the just
> man [and wants] to kill him [...] and the law *9* which sent him; but [God
> will not desert him] or permit them to convict him when he is judged
> (4QpPs$^a$ IV 8-9; DSST, 205).

Here, the expression «just man» could refer to the Teacher of Righteousness,
but there is no certainty at all about that. Another text from the *Damascus Document* (I 20) speaks in general about enemies who make an alliance «against the
life of the just man», which could not refer to the Teacher but is a collective
reference to a threat against the whole community.

Another passage from the same *Psalms Pesher* makes it impossible to consider
the preceding texts as a reference to the execution of the Teacher of Righteousness:

> The wicked of Ephraim and Manasseh who will attempt to lay hands *19* on
> the Priest and the members of his council in the period of testing which
> will come upon to them. However, God will save them *20* from their hands
> and after they will be delivered into the hands of dreadful nations for judg-
> ment (4QpPs$^a$ II 18-20; DSST, 204).

Analysis of the texts from Qumran does not authorise anyone to state, (as Dupont-Sommer did), that the Teacher of Righteousness died crucified like a messiah. The texts which speak about death by crucifixion make no mention at all of that character. The first text is from the *Nahum Pesher* and runs as follows:

[And as for what he says: (Nah 2:13) «he fills] his cave [with prey] and his den with spoils», *Blank* Its interpretation concerns the Angry Lion *7* [who filled his den with a mass of corpses, carrying out rev]enge against those looking for easy interpretations, who hanged living men *8* [from the tree, committing an atrocity which had not been committed] in Israel since ancient times, for it is horrible for the one hanged alive from the tree. (Nah 2:14) Here am I against [you]! *9* Orac[le of the Lord of Hosts. I shall burn your throng in the fire] and the sword will consume your cubs. I will eradi[cate] the spoils [from the earth]. *Blank 10* and no [longer will the voice of your messengers be heard. Its inter]pretation: «Your throng» are his gangs of soldiers [...]; «his cubs» are *11* his nobles [and the members of his council, since...] and «his spoils» is the wealth which [the priests of Jerusalem accu]mulated ... (4QNahum Pesher Frags 3+4 col. I 6-11; DSST 195-196).

The second text alluding to the crucifixion is from the *Temple Scroll*:

And all the men of the city shall stone him *6* and he will die. Thus shall you eradicate the evil from your midst, and all the children of Israel shall hear it and fear. *Blank* If *7* there were to be a spy against his people who betrays his people to a foreign nation or causes evil against his people, *8* you shall hang him from a tree and he will die. On the evidence of two witnesses and on the evidence of three witnesses *9* shall he be executed and they shall hang him on the tree. If there were a man with a sin punishable by death and he escapes *10* amongst the nations and curses his people /and/ the children of Israel, him also you shall hang on the tree *11* and he will die. Their corpses shall not spend the night on the tree; instead you shall bury them that day because *12* they are cursed by God and man, those hanged on a tree; thus you shall not defile the land which I *13* give you for inheritance (11QTemple Scroll LXIV 5-13; DSST, 178).

### b System of Government

The information on the system of government by which the Qumran community was ruled is made obscure by the fact that the data provided by the *Community Rule* do not agree with those contributed by the *Damascus Document*. The text from the *Rule*, 1QS II 21-22 already quoted, distinguishes three orders in the community: priests, levites and laity. The laity are subdivided in turn into groups called «thousands», «hundreds», «fifties» and «tens». These classifications are symbolic in meaning rather than real (cf. CD XIII 1-2).

The texts mention a «council» of the community, which on some occasions seems to be the community itself and on others, a group within the community. The passage from 1QS VIII 1 speaks of «twelve men and three priests» in «the community council». Possibly it refers to the group of the founders of the community, or perhaps to a group given special authority within it.

Presidency corresponds to the *mebaqqer* or «Inspector». According to the *Damascus Document* it is possible to say that a *mebaqqer* presides over each of what are called «camps» under a common higher authority:

> 6 and the Inspector shall instruct him in the exact interpretation of the law. *Blank* Even if he is a simpleton, he is the one who shall intern him, for his is 7 the judgment. *Blank* And this is the rule of the Inspector of the camp. He shall instruct the Many in the deeds of 8 God, and shall teach them his mighty marvels, and recount to them the eternal events with their solutions. 9 He shall have pity on them like a father on his sons, and will make all the strays (?) return, like a shepherd with his flock. 10 He will undo all the chains which bind them, so that there will be neither harassed nor oppressed in his congregation. 11 *Blank* And everyone who joins his congregation, he should examine, concerning his actions, his intelligence, his strength, his courage and his wealth; 12 and they shall inscribe him in his place according to his condition in the lot of light. *Blank* No-one 13 of the members of camp should have authority to introduce anyone into the congregation against the de[cision] of the Inspector of the camp. 14 *Blank* And none of those who have entered the covenant of God «should either take anything from or give (anything) to» the sons of the pit, except for «from hand to hand». *Blank* And no-one should make a deed of purchase or of sale without informing 16 the Inspector of the camp ... (CD XIII 6-16; DSST, 43-44).

However, another passage from the same *Damascus Document* implies that the *mebaqqqer* is the one who presides over all the camps:

> And the Inspector who is 9 over all the camps will be between thirty years and sixty years of age, master of every secret 10 of men and of every language according to their families. On his authority, the members of the assembly shall enter, 11 each one in his turn; and every affair which any man needs to say to the Inspector, he should say it 12 in connection with any dispute or judgment (CD XIV 8-12; DSST, 44).

The texts also mention a *maskil*, «wise man», «learned man», whose office the *Community Rule* describes in the following terms:

> For the wise man, that he may inform and teach all the sons of light about the history of all the sons of man, concerning all the ranks of their spirits, in accordance with their signs, *14* concerning their deeds and their generations, and concerning the visitation of their punishment and the moment of their reward (1QS III 13-14; DSST, 6).

Possibly, the term *maskil* is only another title for the *mebaqqer*. The levites seem to be mentioned only in connection with the blessings and curses pronounced at the rite of initiation into the community (1QS I 19- II 20).

Among those set up in authority, the «judges» are also mentioned, without specifying the functions they could carry out:

> And this is the rule of the judges and of the congregation. Ten men in number, chosen *5* from among the congregation, for a period; four from the tribe of Levi and of Aaron and six from Israel; *6* learned in the book of HAGY and in the principles of the covenant; between *7* twenty-five and sixty years. And no-one *8* over sixty years should hold the office of judging the congregation (CD X 4-8; DSST, 41).

The «Prince of the whole congregation» is also mentioned (CD XV 4; 1QM V 1) without his functions being specified. In the *War Scroll* the most conspicuous figure is «the principal priest».

Each member of the community was assigned a specific position: «And if the lot results in him joining the Community, they shall enter him in the Rule according to his rank among his brothers» (1QS VI 21-22; DSST, 10). The Zadokite priests, among whom the *mebaqqer* was counted, occupied a higher position in relation to the rest of the group of the «Many» (*ᶜal harabbîm*). The «elders» also occupied a preeminent position, although their functions do not seem to be specified:

> This is the Rule for the session of the Many. Each one by his rank: the priests will sit down first, the elders next and the remainder of *9* all the people will sit down in order of rank. And following the same system they shall be questioned with regard to the judgment, the counsel and any matter referred to the Many, so that each can impart his wisdom *10* to the council of the Community. No-one should talk during the speech of his fellow before his brother has finished speaking. And neither should he speak before one whose rank is listed *11* before his own. Whoever is questioned should speak in his turn. And in the session of the Many no-one

should utter anything without the consent of the Many. And if the *12* Examiner of the Many prevents someone having something to say to the Many but he is not in the position of one who is asking questions to the Community council, *13* that man should stand up and say: "I have something to say to the Many". If they tell him to, he should speak. And to any in Israel who freely volunteers *14* to enrol in the council of the Community, the Instructor who is at the head of the Many shall test him with regard to his insight and his deeds (1QS VI 8-14; DSST, 10).

According to the *Damascus Document*, the members of the community lived «in camps»:

And if they reside in the camps in accordance with the rule of the land, and take *7* women and beget children, they shall walk in accordance with the law and according to the regulation *8* of the teachings, according to the rule of the law which says: «Between a man and his wife, and between a father and his son» (CD VII 6-8; DSST, 37).

From this text it seems to follow that the members of the community lived in cities and villages, surrounded by their relatives and servants, devoted to business, farming and herding, although separate from the rest of the Jews and gentiles (cf. *infra*).

## c  Conditions of Entry

The conditions of entry into the community are given in detail in several texts. There is no better illustration than a straight quotation from one of them, in spite of its length:

And to any in Israel who freely volunteers *14* to enrol in the council of the Community, the Instructor who is at the head of the Many shall test him with regard to his insight and his deeds. If he suits the discipline he shall introduce him *15* into the covenant so that he can revert to the truth and shun all sin, and he shall teach him all the precepts of the Community. And then, when he comes in to stand in front of the Many, they shall be questioned, *16* all of them, concerning his duties. And depending on the outcome of the lot in the council of the Many he shall be included or excluded. If he is included in the Community council, he must not touch the pure food of *17* the Many while they test him about his spirit and about his deeds until he has completed a full year; neither should he share in the possession of the Many. *18* When he has completed a year within the Community, the Many will be questioned about his duties, concerning his in-

sight and his deeds in connection with the law. And if the lot results in him
*19* joining the foundations of the Community according to the priests and
the majority of the men of the covenant, his wealth and his belongings will
also be included at the hands of the *20* Inspector of the belongings of the
Many. And they shall be entered into the ledger in his hand but they shall
not use them for the Many. He must not touch the drink of the Many until
*21* he completes a second year among the men of the Community. And
when this second year is complete he will be examined by command of the
Many. And if *22* the lot results in him joining the Community, they shall
enter him in the Rule according to his rank among his brothers for the law,
for the judgment, for purity and for the placing of his possessions in common. And his advice will be *23* for the Community as will his judgment
(1QS VI 13-23; DSST, 10).

Entry into the community was carried out by means of a rite described in the
passage 1QS I 18-26, cited below as well as in 1QS II 11-23, which ends with
these words:

> *18* And all those who enter the covenant shall begin speaking and shall say
> after them: «Amen, Amen». *Blank 19 Blank* They shall act in this way year
> after year, all the days of Belial's dominion. The priests shall enter *20* the
> Rule foremost, one behind the other, according to their spirits. And the
> levites shall enter after them. *21* In third place all the people shall enter the
> Rule, one after another, in thousands, hundreds, *22* fifties and tens, so that
> all the children of Israel may know their standing in God's Community *23*
> in conformity with the eternal plan. And no-one shall move down from his
> rank nor move up from the place of his lot (1QS II 18-23; DSST, 5).

This text seems to refer to an yearly renewal of the ceremony of entry into the
community, coinciding with the renewal of the Covenant, which could have
taken place in the Feast of Weeks (Pentecost). The life of the community was
punctuated by ceaseless purification rites and other ceremonies. It is enough
to recall the text already quoted, 1QS I 18-26:

> *16* And all those who enter in the Community Rule shall establish a cove-
> nant before God in order to carry out *17* all that he commands and in order
> not to stray from following him for any fear, dread or grief *18* that might
> occur during the dominion of Belial. When they enter the covenant, the
> priests *19* and the levites will bless the God of salvation and all the works
> of his faithfulness and all *20* those who enter the covenant shall repeat after
> them: «Amen, Amen» (1QS I 16-20; DSST, 3).

## d  Ritual Meals and Dietary Rules

Some texts from Qumran refer to a kind of communal meal which was presided over by a priest who blessed the bread and the new wine in the presence of the Messiah of Israel. These ritual Essene meals could have been a forerunner of the Christian eucharist. However, some essential elements of the eucharist are missing from them, in particular, those connected with the feast of the Passover. It is enough to quote two texts:

> They shall eat together, *3* together they shall bless and together they shall take counsel. In every place where there are ten men of the Community council, there should not be a priest missing amongst them. *4* And when they prepare the table to dine or the new wine *5* for drinking, the priest shall stretch out his hand as the first *6* to bless the first fruits of the bread {or the new wine for drinking, the priest shall stretch out his hand as the first to bless the first fruits of the bread} and of the new wine. And in the place in which the Ten assemble ...(1QS VI 2-6; DSST, 9).

The closing expressions of this passage establish the *quorum* needed for the celebration of a ritual meal as ten members. This is a *quorum* similar to the *minyan* required for the celebration of the synagogue liturgy, according to rabbinic sources.

Appendix A, copied after *The Rule of the Congregation* II 11-22 offers a more detailed description:

> *11* This is the assembly of famous men, [those summoned to] the gathering of the community council, when [God] begets *12* the Messiah with them. [The] chief [priest] of the all the congregation of Israel shall enter, and all *13* [his brothers, the sons] of Aaron, the priests [summoned] to the assembly, the famous men, and they shall sit *14* befo[re him, each one] according to his dignity. After, [the Me]ssiah of Israel shall ent[er] and before him shall sit the chiefs *15* [of the clans of Israel, each] one according to his dignity, according to their [positions] in their camps and in their marches. And all *16* the chiefs of the cl[ans of the congre]gation with the wise [men and the learned] shall sit before them, each one according *17* to his dignity. And [when] they gather at the table of community [or to drink] the new wine, and the table of *18* community is prepared [and] the new wine [is mixed] for drinking, [no-one should stretch out] his hand to the first-fruit of the bread *19* and of the [new wine] before the priest, for [he is the one who bl]esses the first-fruit of bread *20* and of the new wine [and stretches out] his hand towards the bread before them. Afterwards, the Messiah of Israel shall stretch out his hand *21* towards the bread. [And after, he shall] bless all the

congregation of the community, each [one according to] his dignity. And in accordance with this regulation they shall act *22* at each me[al, when] at least ten m[en are gat]hered (1QSa II 11-22; DSST, 127).

For the dietary rules cf. CD XII 11-14 (DSST, 42-43). For the regulations about the sabbath cf. CD X 14- XI 18 (DSST, 41-42).

e  Festival Calendar

Questions relating to the calendar of feasts and of the hours of liturgical celebration take on primary importance in the world of religions. There have been many schisms which arose out of disagreements over the calendar. The schism between the Latin Church and the Greek Church started right from the earliest period of Christianity through a dispute over the date of the celebration of Easter. The Qumran community broke with the Jerusalemite priesthood also over a question of the calendar:

> But with those who remained steadfast in God's precepts, *13* with those who were left from among them, God established his covenant with Israel for ever, revealing to them *14* hidden matters in which all Israel had gone astray: his holy sabbaths and his *15* glorious feasts (CD III 12-15; DSST, 35).

It could not take part in the cult of Jerusalem, which celebrated its feasts on incorrect dates:

> To separate unclean from clean and differentiate between *18* the holy and the common; to keep the sabbath day according to the exact interpretation, and the festivals *19* and the day of fasting, according to what they had discovered, those who entered the new covenant in the land of Damascus (CD VI 17-19; DSST, 37); complying with all revealed things concerning the regulated times (1QS I 8-9; DSST, 3); They shall not stray from any one *14* of all God's orders concerning their appointed times; they shall not advance their appointed times nor shall they retard *15* any one of their feasts (1QS I 13-15; DSST, 3).

The people of Qumran followed a different calendar from that by which the rest of the Jews were ruled and the one used for the celebrations in the Temple of Jerusalem. The Jews used a calendar with 354 days and 12 months of 29 and 30 days, with no regard at all for the cycles of the seasons (solstices and equinoxes). This meant that every three years a supplementary month had to be intercalated, the second month of Adar, which followed the first month of Adar (February/March). The Qumran calendar, of priestly origin, was governed by the sun; the months were counted through a sequence of numbers, with no names for each month. The year had 364 days and was divided, with utter regularity, into 52 weeks and into four seasons of three months of 30, 30 and 31 days (13 weeks). As a result, all the feasts fell on a fixed day of the week. Passover began on the eve of the 14th day of the first month, always on the fourth day of the week, a Wednesday. The Feast of Weeks was celebrated on the 15th day of the third month, on the first day of the week, a Sunday. The celebration of (Yom) Kippur fell on the 10th day of the eleventh month, on the sixth day of the week, a Friday. The Feast of Tabernacles was the 15th day of the seventh month, on the fourth day of the week, Wednesday. The *Community Rule* gives no information about how they resolved the problem that in this calendar 29 hours, 48 minutes and 48 seconds are missing for an exact match with the movement of the earth around the Sun.

The use of this type of calendar is attested in the numerous calendars found in Cave 4 and appears to be implied in the following two texts:

> And he (David) wrote psalms: *5* three thousand six hundred; and canticles to be sung before the altar over the perpetual *6* offering of every day, for all the days of the year: *three hundred and sixty-four...* (11QPsalms[a] XXVII 4-7; DSST, 309);

> ...fathers of the congregation, *fifty-two*. They shall arrange the chiefs of the priests behind the High Priest and of his second (in rank), twelve chiefs to serve *2* in perpetuity before God. And the twenty-six chiefs of the divisions shall serve in their divisions and after them the chiefs of the levites to serve always... (1QWar Scroll II 1-2; DSST, 96).

Forerunners and references to this calendar can be found in Ez 45:18-20; Jub 6:29-33; 1 Enoch 74:11-12; 82:6.11.15.18.

The *Temple Scroll* (XIII 8- XX 2) provides a list of feasts unique to Qumran, not celebrated by other Jews.

## II  The Qumran Essenes. Who were They and When did they Originate?

1. On several occasions, the historian Flavius Josephus mentions the «Essenes» (*Jewish War* 2.8.2, no. 119) or «Esaioi» (*Antiquities of the Jews* 15.10.4, no. 371). They made up one of the three Jewish «philosophies» or «sects» of the period, about which Josephus himself provides information (*Autobiography* 2, no. 10). He mentions the Essenes for the first time in connection with the events which took place in the time of Jonathan Maccabeus. According to Josephus, the Essenes followed «a path of life taught to the Greeks by Pythagoras», distinguished by communal life and religious asceticism (*Antiquities..* 15.10.4, no.

371). The comparison with the Pythagoraeans is not very apt, but the fact is that they lived in community and considered themselves as observing and privileged members of the New Covenant. Pliny the Elder (*Natural history* 5.17.4) and Philo of Alexandria (*Hypothetica* 11.14, no. 380) refer to the celibacy of the Essenes. And Josephus, too, speaks of the scorn they showed towards matrimony although he also alludes to «another order of Essenes» who, in the interests of propagating the species, practised matrimony and had children (*Jewish War* 2.2, no. 120; 2.8.13, no. 160). It is possible that the Essenes of Qumran remained celibate while those who lived in cities and villages were married. Perhaps these were the ones who lived in what were called «camps». The fact is that the regulations of the *Community Rule* are intended for and concern only males, with no reference at all to women and children. On the other hand, the cemetery located to the East of the site of Qumran contains about 1,100 tombs, arranged in rows. All the tombs excavated (31 in all) except one, distributed in different areas, contained bones of males only. In tombs of more distant areas, bones of women and children were also found.

Some scholars query this connection between the archaeological site and the presumed «monastic» nature of the community, which seems to be reflected in the manuscripts found there. The thesis is that the site of Qumran was a kind of «monastery» in which a group of celibates devoted themselves to copying out and interpreting the text of the Law and of the remaining sacred Scriptures while waiting for eschatological times. This thesis has been challenged by N. Golb in a congress organised by the New York Academy of Sciences (14-17 December 1992) on the theme «Methods of Investigation of the Dead Sea Scrolls and from the Khirbet Qumran Site: Present Realities and Future Prospects». According to N. Golb, Qumran was not an isolated settlement lost in the desert of Judah. Instead, it was a sort of village in the form of a military enclave: a strategic emplacement, a tower and siege walls and a sophisticated system for collecting water. On the other hand, Robert Donceel and Pauline Donceel think that Qumran was a centre for the production of luxury glass and of a kind of Nabataean pottery, for which it was equipped with a sophisticated system of ovens. It was also a centre for exploiting the resources of the Dead Sea (bitumen).

The information transmitted directly by the *Community Rule* agrees significantly with the data supplied by Josephus and Philo about the way of life, organization and doctrines of the Essenes. The agreement between this and other information provides the most substantial proof so far for identifying the group from Qumran as an Essene group or as a branch of the Essenes. The discrepancies in detail may be due to the process of development which the community underwent during the two centuries of its existence (Vermes, Beall).

2. In the first years of the study of the Dead Sea Scrolls there were many and

very varied theories concerning the origin and history of the group from Qumran. It was identified with the mediaeval sect of the Karaites (a false hypothesis proposed by Zeitlin), with a Judaeo-Christian group (Teicher), with a group of zealots connected with the events of the Jewish war of the year 70 CE (Roth, G. R. Driver) or a group from the period of Alexander Jannaeus, Aristobulus or Hyrcanus II (De Vaux, at first). The group from Qumran was also connected with one or other of the Jewish movements which existed at that time: the Pharisees (Rabin), the Sadducees (R. North) or the zealots (Roth, Driver).

The theory which has gained most acceptance is the one which locates the origin of the Qumran community in the period of the Maccabees and identifies its members as a group of Essenes, formed at the start of the *hasidim* movement (Sukenik, Dupont-Sommer, Milik, Cross, De Vaux, Yadin, Vermes, G. Jeremias, Hengel, Stegemann, etc.). N. Golb, L. Schiffman and R. H. Eisenman have declared themselves against the «Essene thesis».

Recent studies tend to set the remote origins of the group from Qumran in a period earlier than the period of the Maccabees, either in Palestine or in Babylonia.

The theory of the Babylonian origin supposes that the group of Essenes was set up in Babylonia. At the time of the Maccabaean revolt this group returned to Palestine, very quickly coming into conflict with the other groups and movements of Judaism. At the root of that conflict a small group was formed which, led by the Teacher of Righteousness, broke with the majority Essene movement. They took refuge in the desert, so giving rise to the community of Qumran (Murphy O'Connor).

The so-called «Groningen hypothesis» developed by F. García Martínez[58] assumes that the Essene movement had its origin in Palestine in the context and milieu of Palestinian apocalyptic tradition, prior to the antiochene crisis. In other words, towards the end of the 3rd century BCE or at the beginning of the 2nd century BCE. The Qumran group was born as a result of a split within the actual Essene movement. As a consequence, the group faithful to the Teacher of Righteousness abandoned Jerusalem and finally established itself in Qumran. This hypothesis starts from several suppositions. They are as follows: The title «wicked priest» does not apply to a single Hasmonaean ruler, either Jonathan or any other of the Maccabees, but to several successive rulers. There is a clear difference between the origins of the Qumran group and the origins of the Essene movement. The apocalyptic tradition from which this movement starts goes back to the 3rd century BCE.

The Qumran community arose from the Essene movement, like a branch torn away from it. It is not easy to determine the moment when this severance occurred. The fact is that in the period of John Hyrcanus' pontificate, the group of Essenes which had followed the Teacher of Righteousness was already installed in Qumran.

So then, the Qumran community was an «apocalyptic community» which originated in the milieu of apocalyptic movements, very widespread at the time. The Teacher of Righteousness and the «Man of Lies» were prophetic figures from the middle of the 2nd century BCE. Their concerns revolved round questions which were halakhic and apocalyptic at the same time (cf. *infra*). It is not possible to establish with certainty more definite conclusions. The thesis of the Babylonian origin of the Qumran community seems to contradict the most specific data of the *Damascus Document*. On the other hand, the hypothesis according to which the withdrawal of the sect was caused by a dispute over succession in the high priesthood lacks any support in the texts. Likewise, the hypothesis that the Teacher of Righteousness functioned as a high priest during a period of «sede vacante» is not very likely (Collins).

3. A social group gains awareness of its own character in relation to other social groups, kindred or opposed. It is necessary, therefore, to study the kind of relationship which the Essenes held with the Pharisees, Sadducees, Zealots and other groups or movements of Judaism. This is one of the most complex questions of current research. It is to be hoped that the study of such manuscripts as the *Halakhic Letter* (4QMMT) will help to elucidate the matter. Expressions such as the one which refers to the «seekers of easy interpretations» could allude to the Pharisees (4QpNah Frags. 3+4 I 2.7; DSST, 195). The texts of the Qumran community carry to extremes the severity of the laws practised by the Pharisees (along these lines cf. the *Temple Scroll*). In respect of the relationship to the Sadducees, the members of the community seem to be called the «sons of Zadok» (1QS V 2.9; 1QSa I 2.24; 1QSb III 22; 4QFlor 1-2 I 17; CD III 21; IV 3). However, this does not mean that these «sons of Zadok» have to be related precisely to the group of the Sadducees, the priestly party around the Temple of Jerusalem.

One of the most distinctive characteristics of the Qumran community is its opposition to the Temple of Jerusalem and the worship celebrated there. It should not be thought that Essenism represents a religious movement opposed to sacrifices and the cult. In fact they were members of the priesthood, who considered themselves to be legitimate successors of the priests who held official religious power. Their break with the Temple was due more to ritual than to theological matters. They accused the priests of Jerusalem of having altered the calendar of feasts, which has sparked off numerous schisms in the history of religions. They also accused them of having abandoned the traditional practices of the cult, especially those relating to the laws of purity[59].

The break with the priesthood of Jerusalem was the reason for the withdrawal to the desert. The intention was to start the history of Israel afresh, beginning with its roots in the desert and especially to prepare in the desert the path of the Lord by means of the study of the Law:

they are to be segregated from within the dwelling of the men of sin to walk to the desert in order to open there His path. *14* As it is written: «In the desert, prepare the way of \*\*\*\*, straighten in the steppe a roadway for our God». *15* This is the study of the law which he commanded through the hand of Moses, in order to act in compliance with all that has been revealed from age to age (1QS VIII 13-15; DSST, 12).

Having broken with the Temple of Jerusalem and with no means of offering sacrifices, the community still considered itself as «the temple of God»:

> as is written in the book of *3* [Moses: «A temple of the Lord] will you establish with your hands. YHWH shall reign for ever and ever». This (refers to) the house into which shall never enter *4* […] either the Ammonite, or the Moabite, or the Bastard, or the foreigner, or the proselyte, never, because there [he will reveal] to the holy ones; *5* eternal [glory] will appear over it for ever; foreigners shall not again lay it waste as they laid waste, at the beginning, *6* the tem[ple of Is]rael for its sins. And he commanded to build for himself a temple of man, to offer him in it, *7* before him, the works of the law (4QFlor Frags. 1-3 I 2-7; DSST, 136).

Comparison of the regulations concerning the law contained in the Dead Sea Scrolls with the legal traditions preserved in Rabbinic literature emphasises the extremely strict regulations of the *Halakhic Letter* as definitely anti-Pharisee and probably Sadducean. Therefore, the common hypothesis according to which the members of the Qumran sect were Essenes, must be adapted to the new information that the religious regulations of the sect were Sadducee. Y. Sussmann suggests that the Essenes, possibly the Bethusians mentioned in Rabbinic literature, followed a Sadducee halakhic tradition. The sect, therefore, fought on two fronts. They kept up an ethical, social and theological conflict with the Sadducees, to whom they gave the name «Manasseh». And they maintained a legal and theological conflict with the Pharisees, called «Ephraim».

All the Jewish groups considered strict religious observance to be fundamental. The Sadducees and Pharisees represented the main movements of Judaism. Their roots go back to the later biblical period, or possibly to an earlier period. The priestly group thought that the Temple cult comprised the core of religious life, which is why the requirement for strict observance of the law was tantamount to strictness in the performance of the cult regulations. The most liberal group sought to extend religious observance to the widest possible circle of Jews and to all levels of ordinary life. The Qumran group lay somewhere between these two groups, more limited and more pious and zealot in character. They followed Sadducean halakhic regulations but based upon theological and religious foundations of a different orientation.

4. If the Essenes from Qumran avoided association with the rest of the Jews, they shunned contact with the Gentiles even more. The term used for the pagans is *goyim* (1QM II 7; IV 12). The *pesharim* (1QpHab I 2; III 4.9; IV 5; VI 1.10; IX 7) and the *War Scroll* (1QM I 2.3.6.9.12, etc.) refer to the Romans by the term *kittim*. It is derived from Greek *Kition* (present-day Larnaka, to the S. E. of Cyprus). The *Damascus Document* includes precise regulations about dealing with the gentiles:

> He is not to stretch out his hand to shed the blood of one of the gentiles *7* for the sake of riches and gain. Neither should he take any of his riches, so that they do not *8* blaspheme, except on the advice of the company of Israel. No-one should sell an animal, *9* or a clean bird, to the gentiles lest they sacrifice them. *10* And he should not sell them anything from his granary or his press, at any price. And his servant and his maidservant: he should not sell them, *11* for they entered the covenant of Abraham with him (CD XII 6-11; DSST, 42).

III  The Essenes of Qumran: Between Legalism and Apocalyptic

The Qumran community lived in a state of high tension between two opposing tendencies. One was the eschatological hope for an end announced in the Scriptures, which would actually happen in their own community. The other, the strict fulfilment of the regulations or the community's own halakhah. In the *Damascus Document* (I 5-12) it says that « (God)...raised up for them a Teacher of Righteousness, in order to direct them in the path of his heart. And he made known to the last generations what he had done for the last generation» (DSST, 33). These two clauses express the twofold mission of the Teacher of Righteousness: eschatological revelation – the apocalyptic dimension – and halakhic interpretation – the legalistic dimension –. Likewise, they express the polarity between the two characteristics and tendencies evident in the Qumran community leading to conflicting interpretations concerning the meaning of the writings of this community.

The question of the calendar, the «touchstone of disagreement» among the different Jewish groups, makes quite clear the twofold viewpoint, eschatological and halakhic simultaneously, of the texts and the way of life of the Qumran community. The festival calendar has legal significance, as a basic presupposition of the ordering of the cult. It also has the function of dividing history into periods, on the one hand and as a calculation of the end of time, on the other. Both are typical themes of earlier apocalyptic tradition accepted by the Essenes of Qumran.

So, then, the Qumran group combines within itself the two poles which put a strain on the Judaism of the period: halakhic interpretation and apocalyptic revelation.

1  Qumranic Legalism. The Temple Scroll, a Second Torah

a  Strictness in the Observance of the Law

The Qumran group formed a community of observers of the Law or Torah.
Besides the texts already referred to in describing the conditions of the life of
the community, it is possible to add yet others, in order to capture in all its
depth the legalistic spirit which was dominant in Qumran:

> This is the rule for the men of the Community who freely volunteer to
> convert from all evil and to keep themselves steadfast in all he prescribes
> in compliance with his will. They should keep apart from *2* men of sin in
> order to constitute a Community in law and possessions, and acquiesce to
> the authority of the sons of Zadok, the priests who safeguard the covenant
> and to the authority of the multitude of the men *3* of the Community, those
> who persevere steadfastly in the covenant. By its authority, decision by lot
> shall be made in every affair involving the law, property and judgment, to
> achieve together truth and humility... (1QS V 1-3; DSST, 8).
> These are the regulations of behaviour concerning all these decrees when
> they are enrolled in the Community. Whoever enters the council of the
> Community *8* enters the covenant of God in the presence of all who freely
> volunteer. He shall swear with a binding oath to revert to the Law of Mo-
> ses with all that it decrees, with whole *9* heart and whole soul, in compli-
> ance with all that has been revealed concerning it to the sons of Zadok, the
> priests who keep the covenant and interpret his will and to the multitude
> of the men of their covenant ...(1QS V 7-9; DSST, 8).
> *15* This is the study of the law which he commanded through the hand of
> Moses, in order to act in compliance with all that has been revealed from
> age to age, *16* and according to what the prophets have revealed through his
> holy spirit (1QS VIII 15-16; DSST, 12).
> And in the place in which the Ten assemble there should not be missing a
> man to interpret the law day and night, *7* always, each man relieving his
> fellow. And the Many shall be on watch together for a third of each night
> of the year in order to read the book, explain the norm, *8* and bless togeth-
> er. This is the Rule for the session of the Many... (1QS VI 6-8; DSST, 9-10).
> See, similarly, CD VI 4-7 and VI 14-15; DSST, 36-38.

Besides the books of the Torah, the religious legacy common to all Judaism, the
men of Qumran had the so-called book of *Hagy* at their disposal:

> From his youth they shall edu]cate him in the book of HAGY, and according
> to his age, instruct him in the precepts of the covenant (1QSa I 7; DSST,

126); and in the place of ten, a priest learned in the book of HAGY should not be lacking; and by his authority all shall be governed (CD XIII 2-3; DSST, 43); and the priest who is named [at the he]ad of the Many will be between thirty and sixty years old, learned in the book of [HAGY] (CD XIV 7-8; DSST, 44).

According to Yadin, this book of Hagy could be the *Temple Scroll* itself, a kind of second Torah or new Deuteronomy.

### b The Temple Scroll, a Second Torah

The studies completed by A. Wilson and L. Wills have shown that the *Temple Scroll* is a work made up of very different parts. The basic document (II 1- XIII 8 + XXX 3- XLVII 18) contains laws related to the building of the temple, followed by legal material adapted from Dt 12-22 (LI 11- LVI 21 + LX 1- LXVI 17). An editor added the calendar of feasts (XIII 9- XXX 2) and the laws of purity (XLVIII 1- LI 10). All these parts, as well as the «Torah of the king» (LVII–LIX) comprise independent documents. The Torah of the king could have been incorporated into the basic document prior to the intervention of the editor. The date and the original milieu of the various documents which make up this text have not yet been determined. The composition could be the work of the Teacher of Righteousness. It comes from the formative period of the Qumran sect, possibly before they settled there. Its witness is important, for the same reason, to establish which were the causes which influenced the schism of the Qumran sect with respect to Essenism and Judaism in general.

Other problems still awaiting solution are the connection between the *Temple Scroll* and the book of *Jubilees*, and with the pre-Qumranic material contained in the *Damascus Document*, and whether the editing of the *Temple Scroll* was completed in Qumran or in another place or whether it goes back to a period very much earlier than its definitive composition. After comparing the *Temple Scroll* with the works mentioned and with the Book of Enoch and rabbinic *halakhah*, Wacholder thinks that the author of the *Temple Scroll* was not merely a compiler or editor, but in fact had in mind nothing less than «replacing» the Mosaic Torah with this Qumranic Torah. Assuming that the *Temple Scroll* is a book of the Torah (*Sefer Torah*), H. Stegemann doubts whether it is the actual and specific Torah of the Essene community of Qumran. In his opinion, the *Temple Scroll* comprises a very ancient development of the Torah, a sort of sixth book added to the Pentateuch. It was composed in reaction to the canonization of the Pentateuch by Ezra. In 458 BCE, Ezra established a «shortened» Pentateuch as the Torah of Sinai. This was imported from Mesopotamia, and excluded traditions and developments of «priestly» extraction from Palestine, which were collected precisely in the *Temple Scroll* (the language and style of the *Temple Scroll* are close to the work of Chronicler, of priestly origin). The editing of this sixth book of the Torah represents the final phase of the formation of Scripture in so far as the Torah is concerned. All during the period of the Second Temple, from the close of the 5th century BCE to the close of the 4th or even of the 3rd century BCE, some priestly families from Jerusalem at least conceded this book the value of «Torah from Sinai», communicated directly by Yahweh, and used its text to complete and interpret the Torah of the Pentateuch.

## 2 Qumran Apocalyptic

Essenism has its roots in apocalyptic tradition. In the study of this tradition it is necessary to distinguish clearly three different aspects: the literary form of the «apocalypses» and the works which belong to this genre; «apocalyptic» as a social movement, which provides a setting for Essenism and the Qumran community, and «apocalyptic» eschatology. This is the world of ideas and symbolism which came to be expressed in the apocalypses. Apocalyptic was something that was in the air generally in that period. It is nothing unusual for ideas and motifs of apocalyptic style to appear frequently in works which belong to other literary forms and were written by authors from religious circles which were not specifically apocalyptic (Koch, Hanson, Stone, Knibb).

### a The Literary Form of Apocalypses

Among the literary works of the apocalyptic genre or «apocalypse» we will concentrate particularly on the two oldest, *Jubilees* and *Enoch* and on another very typical work, the *War Scroll*.

1. The Book of *Jubilees* is the oldest work of the genre. It adapts and brings up to date the books of Genesis and Exodus (up to Ex 24:18) and uses expressions and information from several biblical books. It also refers to older Enochian writings such as the books of the Luminaries, of the Watchers, of Dreams, and possibly also to the Epistle of Enoch.

The importance which the book of *Jubilees* had in the Qumran community is shown by the number of copies found of this writing: twelve copies, the oldest from the years around 100 BCE. Study of these manuscripts proves that the book was written in Hebrew and the only complete copy preserved, of the Ethiopic version, made from a Greek translation, reproduces the original text with great accuracy (VanderKam).

2. The *Book of Enoch* comprises, in fact, several books. In 1976, J. T. Milik published the *editio princeps* from the fragments of eleven copies of *1 Enoch*,

dated between the beginnings of the 2nd century BCE and the first half of the 1st century CE.

– The «Astronomical Book» or «Book of the courses of the heavenly luminaries» (*1 Enoch* 78-82) is the oldest part of those comprising *1 Enoch*. It mixes astronomical and geographical elements with other elements both apocalyptic and moral. VanderKam's study concludes that the oldest part of the «Astronomical Book», which was already in circulation at least towards the end of the 3rd century BCE, is contained in chapters 72-78; 82:9-20 and 82:1-8. The astronomical and geographical elements of this book go back to traditions of Mesopotamian origin and are now found inserted within the narrative context of a revelation: Enoch transmits to his son Methuselah the revelations received from Uriel about the sun, the moon, the stars, the winds, the cardinal points and the celestial sphere. The oldest part of the book already includes a calendar of 364 days, the origin of which is earlier than the formation of the Qumran «sect». VanderKam thinks that it is impossible to determine whether the calendar mentioned is «sectarian» in character or not. Beckwith, on the other hand, thinks that it is a creation by the Essene or pre-Essene movement. In any case, this calendar will be one of the elements to be taken into account in every discussion about the split of the Qumran community from the more central movements of Judaism. The oldest and most original part of the «Astronomical Book» cannot be labelled a true apocalypse. Yet, it contains enough elements of an apocalyptic nature so that later on, due to the addition of the two chapters 80-81, it was to become a genuine apocalypse.

– The oldest part of the «Book of Watchers» (*1 Enoch* 1-36) is included in chapters 6-11, in which Enoch is not yet mentioned. These chapters were combined later in the following chapters (12-16) and in the Enochian *corpus*. Manuscripts 4QEn$^{ab}$, which, it seems, contained only the section corresponding to chapters 1-36, stem from the beginning of the 2nd century BCE. The fact that this book is quoted in the book of *Jubilees* also proves that the book of «Watchers» is earlier than the period around the mid-second century BCE. On the other hand, the spelling of this book requires setting the date of its composition towards the end of the 3rd century BCE (Milik). This fact is of tremendous importance for present day discussion about the origins of apocalyptic. It shows that apocalypses of cosmic character are earlier than those historical in type. It also shows that apocalyptic in general is earlier, for the same reason, irrespective of the Hellenistic crisis and even the Hellenisation of Palestine.

– The «Book of Dreams» is included in chapters 83-90 of *1 Enoch*. Manuscripts 4QEn$^{cde}$, which contain this section, date to 150-125 BCE. The book was composed in the period which comes between the beginning of the Maccabaean wars and the death of Judas Maccabaeus, in 164, shortly after the battle of Bathsur (Milik). The book originated among the *hasidim* who took part in the Maccabaean revolt. In the opinion of D. Dimant, it stems instead from the

Qumran group, to whose origin the passage 90:6-7 refers. The content of the
book consisted of two dreams or visions of Enoch. The first, which has not
been preserved, referred to the flood; the second develops the history of man-
kind from the first man up to the last times by means of an animal allego-
ry.
– The «Epistle of Enoch» is found included in *1 Enoch* 91-105. Two manuscripts from Qumran (4QEn$^{cg}$) preserve remains of this «Epistle». The history
which the Book of Dreams divided into 70 periods appears here divided into
a cycle of «ten weeks of years»: the first seven refer to human history and the
last three to eschatological time. This pattern combines two others, one of 70
times 7 and the other of 10 times 49, both known through other texts from
Qumran. This ensemble forms the «Apocalypse of weeks» (chapters 93.91), a
work of pre-Maccabaean origin to be added to those surveyed earlier.

3. The work entitled *For the sage, the rule of war*, is better known as the *War
Scroll*. The copy from Cave 1 does not preserve the complete text of this work.
In Cave 4 were found fragments from six other copies (DJD 7). The writing
proposes a plan of campaign intended for the 40 years of war which would
occur when God annihilated the forces of evil referred to by the term *Kittim*,
which in other Qumranic writings is used to denote the Romans. It uses terms
typical of Roman military strategy (Yadin). The war develops, no doubt, according to a theological concept rather than following a realistic military strategy. The forces of light are arranged in a quasi-liturgical order, corresponding
to the recommendations of Nm 2:1-5:4. The standards present legends which
ensure victory on God's side. The priests harangue the people and blow the
trumpets with the various battle calls. The angels Michael, Raphael and Sariel
lead the forces of good; Belial, those of darkness. The leadership falls to the
high priest; no clear hope at all is expressed in a davidic messiah. The work
could have a pre-Qumranic origin in connection with Persian dualism. Most
authors date the work between 50 BCE and 25 CE. For some it is the work of a
single author; for others, two different works which appear to be combined.

Scholars discuss the literary formation of this writing. The most detailed
theory is the one proposed by P. Davies, who supposes that this work used
three sources from an earlier period and two other incomplete texts. These are:
a collection of traditions which go back to the Maccabaean wars, which was
composed in the Hasmonaean period (cols. II-IX); the development of a Maccabaean writing about the laws of war (cols. XV-XIX); and a collection of hymns
and prayers, many of which correspond to the typical ambience of the Maccabaean period (cols. X-XII). The incomplete texts correspond to passages from
cols. XIII and XIV.

## b  Messianism and Eschatological Apocalyptic

The fact that over a period of more than 150 years many works were written in apocalyptic style and form can only mean that there did exist a movement and an «apocalyptic» social group which gave rise to these literary works. The same apocalypses contain references to groups with these characteristics (*1 Enoch* 1:1; 90:6; 93:5.9-10). The movements, ideas and literary forms of apocalyptic crystallised into the Essene movement and later became institutionalised in the Qumran community, separated from the mainstream Essenes.

Today, there is a tendency to look for the origins of the apocalyptic movement in the world of Mesopotamia (VanderKam), even though it cannot be forgotten that Graeco-Roman and Persian literature also provide writings of an apocalyptic nature. Apocalyptic, born in Mesopotamia not later than the 3rd century BCE, crystallised into the Essene movement whose most typical features are precisely of an apocalyptic nature. These are determinism, an interest in everything referring to the world of angels (*Angelic liturgy*, *War Scroll* 7,6), the idea of the eschatological Temple (resulting in rejection of the Temple of Jerusalem) and a type of biblical interpretation with certain specific features.

The idea of predestination and of a fixed end towards which the world was inexorably going is deeply entrenched in the texts:

> And now, listen, all those who know justice, and understand the actions of *2* God; for he has a dispute with all flesh and will carry out judgment on all those who spurn him. *3* For when they were unfaithful in forsaking him, he hid his face from Israel and from his sanctuary *4* and delivered them up to the sword. However, when he remembered the covenant of the very first, he saved a remnant *5* for Israel and did not deliver them up to destruction (CD I 1-5; DSST, 33).

The members of the Qumran community lived in an atmosphere of excessive eschatology. All biblical history was for them a «preparation» for what had to come, which was nothing else but the community of the New Covenant which they themselves comprised. This *praeparatio essenica* anticipates the very idea of a *praeparatio evangelica* developed by the Christians. Passages from the *Habakkuk Pesher* express the belief that everyone who is just is attached to the Essene community which is living out the final period, extended in accordance with the plan of divine mysteries:

> *1* Its interpretation concerns all observing the Law in the House of Judah, whom *2* God will free from punishment on account of their deeds and of their loyalty *3* to the Teacher of Righteousness (1QpHab VIII 1-3; DSST, 200).

It states that everyone who is just attaches himself to the community:

> *1* And God told Habakkuk to write what was going to happen *2* to the last
> generation, but he did not let him know the end of the age. *3* And as for
> what he says: (Hab 2:2) «So that the one who reads it /may run/». *4* Its in-
> terpretation concerns the Teacher of Righteousness, to whom God has
> disclosed *5* all the mysteries of the words of his servants, the prophets.
> (Hab 2:3) For the vision has an appointed time, it will have an end and not
> fail. *7* Its interpretation: the final age will be extended and go beyond all
> that *8* the prophets say, because the mysteries of God are wonderful
> (1QpHab VII 1-8; DSST, 200).

There is no need, however, to identify the Teacher of Righteousness with a
messiah or with the messiah of the Qumran community. The texts do not portray him like that. Nor is it possible to identify the Teacher of Righteousness
with the «Branch of David», a title used of the so-called «Messiah of justice,
Branch of David» in 4QGenesis Pesher V (DSST, 215) and of a successor on the
davidic throne in 4QFlorilegium I 11-12 «This (refers to the) «branch of David»
who will rise with the Interpreter of the law who [will arise] in Zi[on in] the last
days» (DSST, 136). Nor is this same title of «Interpreter of the Law» applicable
to the Teacher of Righteousness as Allegro thought. The «Interpreter of the
Law» is also mentioned in the *Damascus Document* (VI 7) and identified with the
«star» to which allusion is made in the oracle of Balaam: «And the star is the
Interpreter of the Law who will come to Damascus, as is written...» (CD VII 18).
In the Old Testament, the title «Interpreter of the Law» is too vague to be applied to an actual historical person (Ezr 7:10; 1 Mac 14:14; Sir 32:15). In
Qumran he is rather a hoped for figure, possibly a legitimate priest.

The men of Qumran were waiting for the coming of two Messiahs:[60] one of
priestly character, the Messiah of Aaron, the other political in character, the
Messiah of Israel. It is not likely, therefore, that they were awaiting a further
two different Messiahs, a «Branch of David» and an «Interpreter of the Law».
It is possible that the title «Branch of David» denoted the Messiah of David
and the title «Interpreter of the Law» corresponded to the Messiah of Aaron.

The messianic hope of the Essenes from Qumran became tangible in the
hope for the coming of a prophet and of two messiahs, one priestly, «from
Aaron» and the other political, «from Israel» (1QS IX 11; DSST, 14; cf. CD XII 23;
XIV 19; XX 1; DSST, 43.44.46). The prophet awaited is the one promised by Moses in compliance with the book of Deuteronomy (18:18). Sometimes the formula occurs in the singular, «the Messiah of Aaron and Israel», especially in the
text of mediaeval copies. This hope is also evident in an important text from
4QTestimonia, which combines four biblical quotations. It mentions a prophet
like Moses, a star which symbolises a priest, a sceptre, symbol of the davidic
Messiah and a blessing of Levi:

*1* And \*\*\*\* spoke to Moses saying: «You have heard the sound of the words *2* of this people, what they said to you: all they have said is right. *3* If (only) it were given to me (that) they had this heart to fear me and keep all *4* my precepts all the days, so that it might go well with them and their sons for ever! *5* I would raise up for them a prophet from among their brothers, like you, and place my words *6* in his mouth, and he would tell them all that I command them. And it will happen that the man *7* who does not listen to my words, that the prophet will speak in my name, I *8* shall require a reckoning from him.» *Blank 9* And he uttered his poem and said: «Oracle of Balaam, son of Beor, and oracle of the man *10* of penetrating eye, oracle of him who listens to the words of God and knows the knowledge of the Most High, of one who *11* sees the vision of Shaddai, who falls and opens the eye. I see him, but not now, *12* I espy him, but not close up. A star has departed from Jacob, /and/ a sceptre /has arisen/ from Israel. He shall crush *13* the temples of Moab, and cut to pieces all the sons of Sheth.» *Blank 14* And about Levi he says: «Give to Levi your *Thummim* and your *Urim*, to your pious man, whom *15* you tested at Massah, and with whom you quarrelled about the waters of Meribah, /he who/ said to his father {...} *16* {...} and to his mother "I have not known you", and did not acknowledge his brothers, and his son did not *17* know. For he observed your word and kept your covenant. /They have made/ your judgments /shine/ for Jacob, *18* our law for Israel, they have placed incense before your face and a holocaust upon your altar. *19* Bless, \*\*\*\*, his courage and accept with pleasure the work of his hand! Crush /the loins/ of his adversaries, and those who hate him, *20* may they not rise!» (4QTestimonia 1-20; DSST, 137).

In conclusion, whoever wishes to understand the messianism of Judaism and the birth of Christianity, starting with this apocalyptic matrix of Judaism, represented so radically by Qumranic Essenism is required to do several things. He will have to be able to think simultaneously of the two concepts of the Law and Apocalyptic. He will let himself be moved simultaneously by two seemingly opposite forces and movements, legalistic and messianic. And he will respond to the evil in the world and in history with an ethic made at the same time of fidelity to the reality governed by the Law and of the aspiration to a messianic utopia. Within the Pharisaic ethic there is room for apocalyptic hope and in apocalyptic Essenism, the Law is the path for speeding up the eschatological coming.

Apocalyptic hope, represented by Essenism, aspires to the fulfilment, by means of a sudden divine intervention, of an atemporal or metahistorical ethic, predetermined in the Law which foresaw the restoration of Israel. The legalistic movement, represented by Pharisaism, advocates meticulous and faithful fulfilment, on the part of the Jewish community, of a moral of intrahistorical reality, contained and directed through the Law or Torah.

There is no need to contrast these two poles utterly, for in Judaism in general and in the Essene texts from Qumran very much in particular, the principle of the Law and the principle of apocalyptic messianism go together and support each other.

Law (*halakhah*) and messianism represent two terms in tension, but they are fused together to form the expression «messianic *halakhah*» or «Torah of the Messiah». The Qumran texts outline a utopian Law for the moment of the Restoration of Israel. It has been possible to state that the Mishnah is the Law designed by the Rabbis for messianic times (Wacholder). The Essene apocalyptics turn out to be more legalistic than the Pharisees (cf. the «Halakhic Letter») and their hope in the restoration of Israel is not less than that of the Essenes.

In the utopian messianism there are latent anarchical and anti-legalistic trends. Similarly, the world of the Law and of the *halakhah* views with enormous suspicion speculations and false messianic upstarts. But apocalyptic and legalism are sunk in the same roots and try to converge to the same end. The two movements, *halakhah* and messianism, always try to find an agreement in theory. However, in reality they clash whenever one of the two movements destroys the balance by taking its own tendencies to extremes.

Every form of messianism, archetypal Jewish messianism in particular, comprises an «explosive mixture» of these two forces. Through that it has the invincible force which confers belief that the definitive time has come, that the utopia has become a reality and has become the Law, and that the strict fulfilment of this Law hastens the fulfilment of the Messianic era (Scholem, Schiffman for the Qumran period).

# The Origins of the Essene Movement and of the Qumran Sect[61]

## Florentino García Martínez

To present a new hypothesis to understand better one of the most extensively and abundantly discussed problems in Qumran research for more than thirty years and attempt to sketch a solution could seem presumptuous. In any case, it runs the risk of further increasing confusion in a field in which clarity is not exactly the commonest virtue. Nonetheless, we dare to question the certainties laboriously reached through the efforts of many researchers. This is due to the conviction that none of the syntheses commonly accepted allows an understanding of the all the data known when such syntheses were prepared. It is due to the conviction that new theories of understanding the same data enable artificial barriers to be removed. And above all, it is due to the conviction that texts, either recently published or in the process of publication, contribute new data, and to allow for them the interpretative framework needs to be modified.

In essence, this new hypothesis proposes locating the ideological origins of the Essene movement in Palestinian apocalyptic tradition before the antiochene crisis. In other words, before the Hellenisation of Palestine and the ensuing Maccabaean revolt. It derives the Qumran community from a schism within the Essene movement and it tries to determine the many factors which initiated the rift and culminated in the setting up of the Qumran community.

However, before moving on to the reasons which led us to formulate this hypothesis, we have to prove that currently accepted theories cannot incorporate all the known data and cannot adequately explain the origins of the Qumran community.

These theories can be grouped into two general approaches[62]. The first identifies the Qumran community with the Essene movement and places the origins of the Essene movement in the *Hasidim* group of the Maccabaean era. Qumran Essenism is, then, a Palestinian phenomenon, the outcome of the opposition to the progressive Hellenisation of the country and of the crystallisation of this opposition in the Maccabaean revolt.

The second approach makes a clear distinction between Essenism and the Qumran group, and postulates a Babylonian origin for Essenism. The conflict with Palestinian Judaism of a group of exiled Essenes on its return to the country and the influence of the Teacher of Righteousness caused a schism within the Essene movement. The result was the birth of the Qumran group, loyal to the Teacher of Righteousness.

## 1 Hasidic Origins

The first of these theories is so widespread and so universally accepted that it has almost lost its character of working hypothesis. It has become the normal way of understanding and interpreting the data supplied by the manuscripts[63]. The most detailed and reliably prepared explanation of this hypothesis is by H. Stegemann in his *Habilitationsschrift*[64]. The most widespread form of the theory is the summary provided by G. Vermes[65]. For Vermes, Essenism was born directly from the *Hasidim* movement. This movement had arisen «in the age of wrath», a cryptogram for the Hellenistic crisis. The group of *Hasidim* had supported the Maccabaean revolt up to the moment of Jonathan's acceptance of the supreme pontificate from the hands of Alexander Balas (in 152 BCE). The opposition to the Maccabees by some of the group right from this moment had caused a rift within the movement, provoking the exile of the Teacher of Righteousness and his partisans. Stegemann contributed further details to this general picture of Qumran origins. The Teacher of Righteousness had been the lawful High Priest, or at least the acting High Priest, during this period. Stripped of his office with the installation in office of Jonathan, he had joined the *Hasidim* group. His presence among them caused a schism. One part of the Essene movement had accepted his authority and his interpretation of the Law, and the boycott he advocated of the Temple and of the cult. For the majority of the *Hasidim*, taking part in the cult of the Temple was unquestionable. Led by the Man of Lies, they had opposed the authority of the Teacher of Righteousness, his pretensions to embody the divine covenant and his interpretation of the Law. The group loyal to the Teacher of Righteousness founded Essenism and settled themselves in Qumran. The majority remained loyal to the Man of Lies and ended by founding the Pharisee movement[66].

The many problems of detail which cannot be resolved in this theory will not be discussed. We will only mention two fundamental factors which rule out this approach as inadequate to explain the problem of Qumran origins:

– the first is that it reduces Essenism to the marginal phenomenon of Qumran;

– the second is that nothing in the preserved texts indicates that the period of the antiochene crisis had played an important role in the origins or development of either Essenism or the actual Qumran group.

The advocates of this approach are not unaware of the differences between the image of the Essenes provided by classical sources[67] outside Qumran, and the image or images which the Qumran writings reflect. However, they play down these differences. They explain them as the result of the inevitable difference between two types of information: information which actually comes from within the Essene movement and is intended for its own members and information acquired from outside the Essene movement and intended for a different audience. Or else, they explain the differences either as reflecting different phases within the evolution of Essenism or as the result of the esoteric nature of Qumran Essenism[68]. However, these considerations, to some extent valid, cannot make us overlook a basic fact. For both Philo and Flavius Josephus the Essenes represent a very widespread movement[69], national in character, whose members do not live apart from the rest of Judaism but are to be found established in the cities of the land: «they are not in one town only, but in every town several of them form a colony»[70], as we are told by Josephus, who boasts of having personally experienced their way of life[71].

The fact that neither Josephus nor Philo mentions the founding of Qumran in their descriptions of the Essenes must already have formed the first obstacle to a simple equation between the Essenes and Qumran. Josephus makes a series of references: to Judas the Essene teaching in the Jerusalem Temple in the period of Aristobulus I (115-104 BCE); to Menahem serving in the court of Herod (37-4 BCE); to Simon the Essene prophesying at the close of Archelaus's rule (4 BCE-6 CE); to John the Essene, who was entrusted with the governorship of the province of Zama together with Lydda, Joppa and Emmaus during the war against Rome, directed the first attack against Ashkelon and died in that battle in 66 CE[72]. These are so many other facts that prevent simply subsuming the isolated and secluded community in Qumran into the Essene movement which was active in Jerusalem and in other parts of Palestine at least during the 150 years which come between the offices of Judas and John.

On the other hand, the connections between the Essenism described in classical and extra-Qumran sources and the sect whose thought, institutions and life have been revealed to us in the manuscripts from Qumran are so close and so substantial that they force us to define this group, marginal and sectarian in the true sense, as an Essene group[73]. That is to say, Essenism could and can be understood, although incompletely, without Qumran, but Qumran is only comprehensible in the wider context of the Essene movement. Since Josephus himself, while dealing with the celibacy and marriage of the Essenes, alludes to another distinct class of Essenes and so acknowledges the co-existence of at least two kinds of Essenes[74], the question of the relations of the Qumran group with one or the other is inescapable. Every theory which reduces the whole to one of its parts, even if it is the best known part, is flawed and deficient. In our particular case, this first explanation of Qumran origins is inadequate. This is because to identify and equate the Qumran group with the Essene movement leaves non-Qumranic Essenism unexplained. And it was a much wider and more important phenomenon than the one represented by the Qumran sect.

The second general objection to this theory is also insuperable. Nothing in the classical descriptions of the Essenes connects their origins with the antiochene crisis. Nor does the information contained in the manuscripts from Qumran allow stating that this is the foundation period in which the sect put down its roots. In fact, the allusions to the antiochene crisis are virtually non-existent. The name Antiochus occurs in only one document:

> Its interpretation concerns Deme]trius, king of Yavan, who wanted to enter Jerusalem on the advice of the those looking for easy interpretations, *3* [but he did not go in because God did not deliver Jerusalem] into the hand of the kings of Yavan from Antiochus up to the appearance of the chiefs of the *Kittim*. But later, it will be trampled (4Q169 3-4 I 2-3; DSST, 195).

Contrary to the opinion of most scholars, I am convinced that the Antiochus referred to here is not Antiochus IV Epiphanes but Antiochus V Eupator[75]. Even admitting, however, that the text mentions the period of occupation of the city by Antiochus IV Epiphanes, one is forced to acknowledge that it tells us nothing either about the attempt at Hellenisation nor about the resistance this attempt provoked. Nothing in the text suggests that the period during which Jerusalem was delivered into Antiochus' hands had a seminal importance in the development of the sect.

The period of origins is called «the age of wrath» in the *Damascus Document* (CD). G. Vermes states unequivocally that the expression is a cryptogram used to denote the antiochene crisis specifically[76]. G. Jeremias goes even further. On the basis of the use of «wrath» in the books of Maccabees, he claims that in ancient Judaism in general the expression «age of wrath» was understood as a specific allusion to the period of persecution by Antiochus IV Epiphanes[77]. Without entering a discussion here about the use of «wrath» in Maccabees (but noting that in the texts he cites the only reference to an age uses the expression «time of calamity», 1 Mac 2:49) we point out that the use of the expression in the *plural*, «ages of wrath»[78], invalidates this claim. It is not a cryptogram for the antiochene crisis. As much is evident from the use of the expression to allude to the eschatological judgment in the only other use of the expression in the *singular* in Qumran (1QH III 28). This forces us to understand the expression in CD as meaning that with the birth of the community the period has begun which will end with the eschatological judgment. To me this interpretation seems proved by the fact that a later redactor has felt obliged to specify the chronological meaning of the expression by adding a prose insert to the poetic text which explains that this «age of wrath» is dated 390 years after God «had delivered them up into the hands of Nebuchadnezzar, king of Babylon».

The fact that this insert breaks the metrical structure of the present historical introduction to CD (which proves it to be secondary and belong to a different redactional stage[79]), and that the actual number belongs to a tradition of exegesis going back to Ezekiel, does not lessen its importance in any way[80]. In fact, this famous insert in CD shows us that the pre-existing text with its mention of the age of wrath has been re-interpreted within the Qumran community. The purpose was to confer on it a more precise and accurate expression of the group's origins, origins related to (but not identical with) the Essene movement and independent of (and earlier than) the antiochene crisis.

## II Babylonian Origins

The second of the two theories mentioned has taken these two objections seriously. It provides a reconstruction of the origins of Qumran which avoids both pitfalls, with better regard for the known facts. This theory is linked with the name J. Murphy-O'Connor, who, starting with his detailed analysis of the various redactional levels of 1QS and CD[81], provided a brilliant though not completely convincing summary of Qumran origins[82]. Murphy-O'Connor makes a clear distinction between the Essene movement and the Qumran group. The origins of the Essene movement have nothing to do with the group of the *Hasidim* or with the crisis of the Hellenisation of Palestine. Instead, they are to be found in Babylonia and at an earlier period than the antiochene crisis. At a certain moment, difficult to specify exactly (Murphy-O'Connor suggests as possible the wave of anti-Semitism generated by the victories of Judas Maccabaeus and the attraction which these victories presumably had for the Jews of the diaspora), a group of conservative Essenes returns to Israel from Babylon. However, it soon comes into conflict with the situation in Palestine. The Teacher of Righteousness was to join this group and was to propose a new exile in the desert as a solution to the problems of the group. Part of the Essene movement was to accept his proposal and follow him to Qumran, so starting the Qumran sect, while the rest was to remained scattered in the cities of the land, loyal to the ideals of the Essene movement.

The chief problem of this second theory is that the arguments he puts forward to prove the Babylonian origin of the Essene movement are not convincing. The central argument derives from the understanding of CD VI 5 which Murphy-O'Connor translates as follows: «the returnees of Israel who went out of the land Judah and were exiled in the land of Damascus»[83]. In this sentence, Murphy-O'Connor gives Damascus a symbolic meaning, as equivalent of Babylon and maintains a real geographical meaning for the «land of Judah». He also holds that *šĕvy yiśra'el* should not be understood in a religious sense: «the repenters of Israel» but in a geographical sense: «the returnees from Israel». The last element seems more difficult to accept, not only because the root *šûb* is used in the Old Testament and at Qumran chiefly in the sense of repentance but because the same expression elsewhere in CD has precisely this meaning of «repenters of Israel». CD II 5 and XX 17 use the parallel expression *šĕvy pešaʿ*, «those who have repented from sin», where the religious meaning of *šûb* is unquestionable. Murphy-O'Connor is aware of this, but explains it as a re-interpretation of the geographical meaning of «the returnees from Israel» since the expression occurs at a later redactional stage[84]. However, Murphy-O'Connor is then forced to admit that CD VIII 16 and XIX 29 use the same expression, *ševy yiśra'el*, this time in a religious sense[85]. As in the case of those «who have repented from sin», the reference to those «repented of Israel» is found at a different redactional stage. However, since it is the same phrase here, Murphy-O'Connor cannot resort to re-interpretation. In all, we find *šûb* used six times in CD, four of which have an obvious religious meaning (even for Murphy-O'Connor). To propose a different meaning for the other two seems uncalled for[86]. If the Qumran redactor who combined the different elements of our actual CD had noticed the difference in meaning of the expression in IV 2/VI 5 and in VIII 6/XIX 29, he would not have failed to specify the meaning or to avoid the contradiction by changing the expression. So then, the theory which locates Qumran origins in the «return» of a group of exiles is seen to be deprived of its support in the text.

It has to be added that a detailed analysis of the three texts in CD telling us of the origin of the group does not provide any new element which could point to its Babylonian origins, as M. Knibb has proved convincingly[87]. The only fact they contain is that the birth of the community is seen as the end of the exile. In this perspective it is not the return in the 6th century BCE which ends the exile. Rather, the situation of the exile is prolonged until the birth of the community. By belonging to the community, each one is allowed to go from the situation of exile to membership of the new covenant, with no geographical limits.

The other arguments of Murphy-O'Connor – the presence of foreign influences which would be explained in a Babylonian context[88] and legislation directed at a community living among pagans[89] – are not convincing either. The foreign influences are not typically Babylonian but belong to the common heritage of Hellenistic culture which were influential and prevailed in Palestine from the close of the 4th century BCE, at least. Two recent works by Schiffman[90] have proved that the legislation regulating relations with the gentiles is substantially in agreement with traditional *halakhah*.

Neither of these two theories, then, provides a satisfactory explanation for the origins of Qumran. Each of them, though, includes elements which are valid and must be retained in an overall explanation. The distinction between the Essene movement and the fact of Qumran, and the separation of the origins of the Essenes from the antiochene crisis in Murphy-O'Connor's hypothesis match the data of the manuscripts. The same applies to locating the origins of the Essenes in Palestine, as in Vermes' theory. These valid elements can also be found in our hypothesis. However, before going on to explaining it in detail, it is necessary to make clear some of the methodological assumptions which determine it.

### III  Methodological Assumptions

1) The first is that any theory which attempts to interpret the texts must respect the *physical* limits set by archaeology and palaeography. In our case, this means that the period of the origins of Qumran must be placed before the high priesthood of John Hyrcanus, a period when the sectarian group was established in Qumran. Certainly, common opinion, based on the presentation of the results of the excavations given by R. de Vaux in the *Schweich Lectures*[91], accepts that the first sectarian occupation of Qumran goes back to the high priesthood of Jonathan. However, this conclusion contradicts the results obtained and published previously by De Vaux[92], and the very arguments he puts forward to support it[93]. The fact is that De Vaux changed his opinion between the different *rapports préliminaires* and this presentation (which has become established as authoritative while waiting for the full publication of the material from the excavations, which has not happened yet). He was forced to, not by the archaeological evidence, but only with the aim of making room for the theories identifying a single Wicked Priest as Jonathan or Simon. In other words, so as not to close the door on the interpretation of the texts proposed by Milik and Cross[94]. De Vaux's own words, in which this purpose clearly appears[95], are very telling. So are those of Cross himself[96], based on the lack of Seleucid coins earlier than Hyrcanus, apart from 6 undated bronzes of Antiochus III, IV and V. It must be remembered that Hyrcanus probably only began to coin money from 119 BCE[97]. Thus, it is clearly seen that the argument contradicts not only the identification of the Wicked Priest as Jonathan, but the identification as Simon proposed by Cross, and that the half-dozen years conjectured by him it is nothing but an excuse to fit that person in[98].

However, this artificial widening of the archaeological time-frame is not necessary if the hypothesis of a *single* Wicked Priest is given up and the theory of Van der Woude is admitted (he assumes that «Wicked Priest» is a collective expression referring in chronological order to the various Hasmonaean High Priests[99]), if it is accepted that the Teacher of Righteousness came into into conflict only with three of these «Wicked Priests»: Jonathan, Simon and John Hyrcanus, and also, that the famous passage 1QpHab XI 4-8 (DSST, 201-202) refers expressly to Hyrcanus, the only «Wicked Priest» who persecutes the Teacher of Righteousness in the place of his exile, i.e., in Qumran. (This in turn implies that the installation at Qumran coincides with Hyrcanus' high priesthood). The forced widening of the chronological framework thus becomes unnecessary and it is possible to match the results of a literary analysis of the *Habakkuk Pesher* with the limits set by archaeology. The firm dates provided by the excavations are as follows. Period Ib is preceded by a *short-lived* period of sectarian occupation, period Ia. This means that the sectarian occupation of Qumran begins during the 30 year long high priesthood of Alexander Jannaeus' predecessor, John Hyrcanus. He is the High Priest during whose term of office the rift takes place within the Essene movement giving rise to the installation in Qumran of the Teacher of Righteousness and of his partisans. He is also the last Wicked Priest with whom the Teacher of Righteousness comes into conflict.

2) Another important methodological assumption is that the rift between the Qumran group and the Essene movement from which it comes must have been preceded by a longer or shorter period. In any case, a period which was long enough to allow the ideological development which set the Qumran group apart from the Essene mould from which it comes and which would end in schism. A large part of the problems which research into Qumran origins has come against derives from the false assumption that the admittance of the Teacher of Righteousness to the Essene movement marks the moment of settlement in Qumran. Hence the objection frequently made to the supporters of a literal interpretation of the known chronology of CD is that this would force them to put the settlement in Qumran at an impossibly high date, irreconcilable with the chronological evidence. Or the awkwardness of Murphy-O'Connor to incorporate into his theory the 20 years which precede the entrance of the Teacher of Righteousness on the scene, during which the members of the Essene movement were «like blind persons and like those who grope for the path». Murphy-O'Connor dates the Essene return to Palestine after 165 BCE, and the installation at Qumran to 152 BCE. He is thus forced to interpret the 20 years as denoting half a generation and to understand this half generation as lasting only 10 years[100]. These problems are eliminated if one acknowledges the importance and length of this pre-Qumran phase or formative period. It was an extraordinarily fertile period from which must come the writings which lay the ideological foundations of the split with the Essene movement. During it there occurred the conflicts which were resolved by the march to the desert of the sectarian group.

　　These two assumptions determine the chronological limits of our hypothesis about the origins and require a distinction between the question of Qumran origins and that of the origins of the Essene movement.

3) A third assumption of our hypothesis is that the non-biblical literature found in the various caves at Qumran is connected either with the Qumran sect or with the ideological movements in which the sect has its roots. Obviously, not all the non-biblical manuscripts found have a Qumran origin. Palaeographic dating of some manuscripts formally excludes them from having been composed or copied in Qumran. The long redactional history of several works also requires that the oldest stages were composed in a period earlier than the settlement of the community close to the Dead Sea. In view of the character of the

Qumran community, though, it seems unthinkable that it kept and used works which were incompatible with their own ideology. The library of the community should not be seen as a modern library, a kind of store of the knowledge of the period. The complete absence of «secular» works is revealing in this respect. In view of the restrictive character of the community and the repeated prohibitions of contact with non-members it does not even seem possible that the community kept religious literature from alien or obviously hostile groups. Quite apart from the long period necessary for an inevitable ideological evolution and accepting that there is nothing which could be considered as a Qumran «canon», a situation like that of the old-fashioned libraries of Catholic seminaries where works which the Church had included in the Index of Forbidden Books were locked in a special and inaccessible section, is unthinkable at Qumran.

This assumption implies that while the fact of having been found in Qumran does not guarantee a Qumran origin for a particular work, it does assure us that this work has been understood by the community as compatible with its own ideology (and with its *halakhah*, even more important than its ideology). In other words, it comes either from the Essene movement or from the apocalyptic tradition which inspires the Essene movement[101]. This is tantamount to saying that the non-biblical literature found as part of the Qumran library can be divided into:

– sectarian works, representing the thought and *halakhah* of Qumran in its most developed and typical form;

– works from the formation period, which present a vision not yet clearly distinct from the Essenism from which they derive; however, they lay the foundations for later development and present a *halakhah* which is already characteristic;

– works which reflect Essene thinking and agree with what classical sources tell us about non-Qumran Essenism or Essenism which can be attributed to this movement;

– works which belong to the apocalyptic tradition from which Essenism derives and have been considered as part of the common heritage.

This assumption will allow us to establish three stages in the development culminating in the settlement of the sect at Qumran in the period before John Hyrcanus' pontificate:

– *apocalyptic* stage.

– *Essene* stage

– *pre-Qumran* stage: formation of the sect

These three stages are successive and culminate in the settlement of the group at Qumran. However, this assumption does not automatically assume a sequence in chronological order of the four types of literature indicated, since ideological compatibility is independent of the date of origin.

4) A final assumption, although no less important, is that of the composite nature of the basic works and the evolutionary character of thought reflected in them. Both elements are the result of a non-static vision of a religious phenomenon which has developed over more than 200 years. This assumption implies the recognition that a large part of the best preserved writings incorporate elements from different periods or stages, re-interpreted in line with historical development. It also implies accepting that the central ideas within the community, such as determinism, messianism or eschatology, can appear in different guises in different documents of the community or in different redactions of a single document. To mention only the two best known examples: «The foundation manifesto» of 1QS from the pre-Qumran formative period has been incorporated and modified to suit a series of historical, theological and organizational developments of the community already installed at Qumran. The Essene nucleus of CD, completed with a series of halakhic prescriptions from the formative period, has clearly been re-interpreted once the community was set up and in a period certainly before the death of the Teacher of Righteousness[102].

On the other hand, this assumption acknowledges that the development of thought is not necessarily linear and straight and that it is possible that different concepts even co-existed for a time. This determines the kind of evidence which our hypothesis takes into consideration and the critical way in which this evidence is evaluated.

## IV  A New Hypothesis

The hypothesis which we set out here for understanding the origins of Qumran starts from these assumptions. It also makes a clear distinction between the problem of the origins of the Essene movement and the problem of the origins of the Qumran sect[103]. Information about the origins of the Essene movement must be sought in classical writings which mention the Essenes, in Essene works preserved in Qumran and in Essene documents incorporated in later Qumran works. Study of this material allows us to conclude that Essenism is a Palestinian phenomenon, prior to the antiochene crisis, which is rooted in apocalyptic tradition. Information about Qumran origins, instead, is to be found in the works of the pre-Qumran formative period, in the documents from this period incorporated in later sectarian works and in the actual sectarian works which refer explicitly to the period of its origins. By studying them we are able to understand the halakhic, ideological and political reasons which initiated the schism within the Essene movement which was to result in the settlement in Qumran.

## 1 Origins of the Essene Movement

Josephus, who has preserved the most information about the Essene movement, introduces the Essenes for the first time into the political scene of Palestine at the time of Jonathan together with the Sadducees and Pharisees[104]. This seems to imply that he understands the Essene movement, like the pharisee and sadducee movements, as a typically Palestinian phenomenon. These is even more evident in the description of the three sects in *Ant.* XVIII, 11, where he assures us that these three Hebrew «philosophies, which exist since the most ancient times» have their roots in their *own traditions*. In his *Apologia*, Philo will express this fact by saying that they go back to Moses. Certainly, Josephus (*Ant.* XV 371) states that the Essenes are a group «which employs the same daily regime as was revealed to the Greeks by Pythagoras», a statement which has been used to place the origins of the movement in neo-Pythagorean doctrines. However, as has often been noted[105], all that Josephus does in this case is to give a reference point to his pagan readers to enable them to understand the Palestinian phenomenon. In the same way, when speaking about the Pharisees (*Vita* 12), he will say that they resemble the Stoics[106]. In neither case can one speak of an origin outside Palestine. As Hengel notes[107], direct dependence of the Essenes on the Pythagoreans is unlikely given the Essenes' zeal in defending their Jewish heritage against foreign influences.

On the other hand, the fact that Josephus presents the Essenes, Pharisees and Sadducees in the times of Jonathan (*Ant.* XIII 171-172) has often been used as proof of a Maccabaean origin of the sects. If this were the correct interpretation of the text, the statement cited already from *Ant.* VIII 11 that they exist «since the most ancient times», or as Pliny says (*Natural History* V 73) that they exist *per saeculorum milia*, would be meaningless. The fact is, however, that Josephus[108] does not say that the sects arose in this period. He says that the Essenes, like the Pharisees and the Sadducees, are sects which «already exist» in the time of Jonathan, which presumes logically that their origins lie in an earlier period.

However, it is not only classical information about the Essenes that indicates their Palestinian origin. The actual pre-Qumran Essene texts contain information in this vein.

In discussing Murphy-O'Connor's interpretation, we rejected as unconvincing the arguments which he uses to postulate a Babylonian origin of the group reflected in the oldest layers of CD. Here we can add that a series of indications in these same pre-Qumran layers of CD point to a Palestinian origin. The same applies to a series of halakhic prescriptions referring specifically to the city of Jerusalem and agreeing completely with the *halakhoth* of 11QTemple[109]. It is most logical to assume a Palestinian context for them and for the *halakhoth* which determine the presentation of offerings in the Temple[110].

Even more obvious than these oblique indications is the summary of *1 En* 90. Within the historical panorama provided by the second vision in the *Book of Dreams* known as the *Apocalypse of the Animals* and in the description of the period which runs from Alexander the Great to the Maccabaean uprising, the author describes the birth of a group. This group marks the end of the third period and the beginning of the fourth period into which he divides history from the exile up to the eschatological age:

> Behold, lambs were born from those white sheep and they began to open their eyes, and to see and to cry to the sheep. But the sheep did not cry to them and did not listen to what they said to them, but were extremely deaf, and their eyes were extremely and excessively blinded.

This group arises when the first 58 periods of history have ended. The remaining 12 periods before the Messianic kingdom are occupied by the persecution of these lambs and the martyrdom of one of them, together with the later Maccabaean revolt and the battles of Judas. In other words, the author places the birth of the group to which he belongs in Palestine, and in a period before the antiochene crisis. In a series of articles, R. Beckwith[111] has attempted to prove that the exact date when these lambs rise up is 251 BCE. D. Dimant, using a different reckoning system, arrives at the date 199 BCE[112]. It is not necessary to go into detail here. It is important to note that the *Book of Dreams*, which is not a Qumranic work[113], but is certainly connected with the sect, testifies to the Palestinian and pre-Maccabaean origins of the group from which the Qumran community was to come[114]. This is like classical information about the Essenes.

However, the best proof lies in showing that characteristic and fundamental ideas of Essenism and of the Qumran sect are already to be found in one form or other within Palestinian apocalyptic tradition. In addition, that this tradition is independent of and earlier than the antiochene crisis.

This second element, generally accepted today, is inescapable, thanks to the discovery of the Aramaic fragments of Enoch from Cave 4 of Qumran. These have forced recognition that both the *Book of the Watchers* and *Astronomical Enoch* go back to at least the 3rd century BCE and thus there is no relation between the origin of the oldest apocalypses and the antiochene crisis.

The notion that certain typical elements of the Essene movement and of the Qumran sect go back to this apocalyptic tradition is gradually beginning to gain acceptance, as we will demonstrate with the help of some recent publications.

Thus, P. Sacchi has clearly shown that the characteristic *determinism* of the Essene movement according to classical sources[115], which is so prominent in the sectarian writings[116], comes from an idea of original sin prior to history, an essential idea in the oldest apocalyptic tradition[117]. The idea that the angel of darkness has been created as such directly by God appears at a certain moment within the evolution of Qumran dualism. While destroying one of the poles of apocalyptic thought[118], it does not prevent the origins of Essene determinism from having been conditioned by the thinking of the oldest apocalyptic reflected in the *Book of Watchers*. Furthermore, the clear dualism of the strictly sectarian period is conditioned by the historical determinism reflected in works from the second stage of apocalyptic, such as the *Book of Dreams* or *Jubilees*. As we have suggested, such works cannot be considered Qumranic. What sectarian thinking achieves is the application at the individual level of this historical determinism of the apocalypses, a historical determinism which also appears as such in the sectarian works.

Another characteristic element of the Essene movement and of Qumran thought whose origins lie in apocalyptic tradition is that of *interpretation*. Philo (*Quod omnis probus*, 80-82) reminds us that the Essenes, for whom neither physics nor logic was an important discipline, deduced their ethics «constantly utilizing the ancestral laws, laws which no human soul could have conceived without divine inspiration». Further on he explains the hermeneutic context in which the interpretation of these laws takes place:

> One of them takes up the books and reads, and another from among the more learned steps forward and explains whatever is not easy to understand, in these books. Most of the time, and in accordance with an ancient method of inquiry, instruction is given them by means of symbols.

J. Blenkinsopp[119] (who remains faithful to the traditional hypothesis concerning the origins of Essenism) has analysed interpretation as a key in the development of sectarianism. His analysis shows that the Essene type of interpretation, which in Qumran was to culminate in the development of their own conception of this interpretation as revealed[120], is only the result and the extension of the transformation of prophetic interpretation which takes place within apocalyptic tradition. It is in this tradition that we first find resorting to secret books or heavenly tablets as a hermeneutical procedure, a recourse which appears in the classical descriptions of the Essenes (*Bell.* II 136.142.159), in Essene works[121] and in truly sectarian works[122].

A third important element in the Essene movement and in the sectarian writings is the awareness of *communion with the world of angels*, one of the elements generally accepted as central to apocalyptic tradition[123]. The importance of this element in sectarian writings appears in compositions such as the *Angelic Liturgy*. It also appears in texts such as 1QM VII 6, which justifies the need for a ritual purity in the holy war «for the angels of holiness are together with their armies», or 1QS XI 7-8:

To those whom God has selected he has given them as everlasting possession (DSST, 18).

These texts reveal to us a familiarity with the world of angels[124] which continues the familiarity we find already in the oldest levels of the apocalyptic tradition. It allows us to understand the information about the Essenes given by
Josephus (*Bell.* II 142) according to whom «the names of the angels» form an
important part of their secret knowledge.

Another revealing element[125] is the concept of the *eschatological Temple*.
Classical descriptions tell us that the Essenes sent their offerings to the Temple,
but did not offer sacrifices there (Josephus, *Ant* XVIII 19), but sacrificed among
themselves. Or else that they completely rejected sacrifices, preferring instead
the sanctification of thought (Philo, *Quod omnis probus*, 75). These two statements are difficult to reconcile with each other, but they testify to the Essene
rejection of the Temple and of the worship carried out there. The Qumran
manuscripts show us this same rejection and also provide us with enough data
to understand the reasons for this stance and to find its origins in the concept
of the eschatological Temple of apocalyptic tradition.

The concept of the normative Temple of 11QTemple explains how radical
the sectarian opposition was and at the same time its transient nature in the
hope of being able to make the normative Temple a reality. It also explains to
us the vicarious and temporary nature of the substitution of the Community
considered as a Temple for the Temple and its sacrifices. However, 11QTemple
XXIX 9-10 proves that this normative Temple is not the definitive Temple but
that it must only last «until the day of creation, when I created my Temple,
establishing it for ever». In other words, that the final, eschatological Temple
will be created directly by God. This idea, which also appears in other sectarian
texts such as 1QM II 1-6 and especially in 4Q174, allows us to understand the
Essene position regarding the Temple. It also explains its ambiguity, since it
reveals the inadequacy of the existing Temple and its transient nature. Moreover, this idea of the eschatological Temple, as Hammerton-Kelly[126] has
proved, develops within apocalyptic tradition, beginning with Ezekiel's Temple
ideology. After the defeat of the compromise between this Temple ideology and
the concept of the Temple of priestly tradition represented by Haggai and
Zachariah, this concept disappears from the official scene during the Restoration period. We only find it in apocalyptic tradition where it constantly recurs,
since it appears in *1 Enoch*, *Jubilees* and in the *Testament of Levi* or in the *Assumption of Moses* and II *Baruch*, to cite only a few representative examples from
two different periods.

This rapid survey shows that the best way to understand a good number of
typical elements of Essene thought is to place them in the context of the apocalyptic tradition of the 3rd century BCE. It seems to be impossible to give the

exact date when the Essene movement rose as a separate entity from the apocalyptic matrix. The concrete result of our investigation only allows the confident statement that these origins lie in a period before the antiochene crisis. Also that the information from *1 Enoch* and CD concurs in indicating the close of the 3rd century BCE or the beginnings of the 2nd century BCE as the period of the origins of the Essene movement.

## 2 The Origins of the Qumran Sect

At the origin of the evolution within Essenism that was to result in the formation of the Qumran sect stands the powerful figure of the person who, for lack of an actual name, we call by the title given him in the sectarian writings: the Teacher of Righteousness. CD I 5-12 is categorical in this regard[127]: the «root of the planting» which God causes to grow from Israel and from Aaron in the time of wrath, the only ones in Israel who understand their sins and acknowledge their guilt, the members of the Essene movement:

> they were like blind persons and like those who grope for the path *10* over twenty years. And God appraised their deeds, because they sought him with a perfect heart *11* and raised up for them a Teacher of Righteousness, in order to direct them in the path of his heart. *Blank* And he made known *12* to the last generations what he had done for the last generation, the congregation of traitors (DSST, 33).

In this text, the function of the Teacher of Righteousness is twofold: to guide the faithful on the right path and to tell everyone about the imminence and effect of the divine judgment. The first element underlines his function of halakhic interpreter as characteristic[128]. The second element, the intensity of eschatological hope in his message.

Eschatology is precisely one of the elements which in classical descriptions of Essenism are not conspicuous, but it is prominent in the sectarian writings from Qumran and displays a clear development[129]. This element is also basic in apocalyptic tradition and has enormous importance in works such as *Jubilees* and the *Book of Dreams*. As we have said, these works exhibit close relationships with sectarian works, although a different origin must be ascribed to them. Also, both were written during the formative period of the community. This fact allows us to see in them the leading thread which marks the development of eschatological hope from the prophetic stages of the Old Testament through apocalyptic eschatology. It was to culminate in the eschatological hope which defines the Teacher of Righteousness and was to mark the community created by him[130]. From this description of CD it follows that the eschatological element comprised an important aspect in the dispute which gave rise to the sect.

However, I think that the first element indicated in the quotation from CD was even more important and of greater influence in connection with the group becoming a sect. In the pluralistic Judaism of the period, the path of sectarian formation is not marked by ideological differences or by eschatology. Instead, it falls back on the level of the *halakhah* which regulates real life. Therefore, it is in the *halakhah* that we must look for the reasons which motivated the split.

Fortunately, we now have at our disposal two documents which exhibit some of the halakhic problems in question. The first, chronologically, is the *Temple Scroll* (11QTemple, DSST, 154-184). The second, which is more explicit, is a halakhic letter known by the title *Miqsat maʿaśe torah* («Some of the precepts of the Torah» = 4QMMT; DSST, 77-85) which specifies the reasons for the separation of the Qumran sect.

The *Temple Scroll* is a work whose composition can be attributed to the Teacher of Righteousness. In any case, it comes from the formative period of the sect and is earlier than the establishment of the community at Qumran[131]. This makes it particularly suited to enlighten us about the important halakhic aspects during the formative phase. It can also show us where the Teacher of Righteousness could come into conflict with the rest of Essenism and with the other elements of the Judaism of that period. An analysis of its contents shows us that the principal elements it comprises are:

– prescriptions about festivals and about the sacrifices of each festival, following a sectarian calendar;

– prescriptions about the Temple and the city and about the regulations for purity concerning them

– the statute of the King;

– various *halakhoth* particularly connected with problems of purity, the tithe and marriage.

The other work (4QMMT) is slightly later, since it was written once the split of the Qumran group was complete[132]. Even so it is perfectly suited to explain the reasons which caused this split since the epilogue says expressly:

We have segregated ourselves from the rest of the peop[le ...] avoid mingling in these affairs and associating with (them) in these things.

This proves that the *halakhoth* included in the letter represent points on which the sectarians were not prepared to compromise. Instead, they considered them important enough to decide to segregate themselves from the rest of the people on their account. The programmatic nature of this halakhic letter also transpires from the formulaic way in which the various *halakhoth* are introduced: «And also concerning XXX we say ...».

An analysis of the twelve *halakhoth* published by Strugnell shows a surprising thematic agreement with 11QTemple[133]. According to 4QMMT, the sect's dis-agreement with its opponents centres on:

– the cultic calendar;
– prescriptions concerning the Temple and the city and the regulations for purity concerning them[134].
– *halakhoth* relating to tithes, impurity and matrimonial statute[135].

The only significant element of 11QTemple which does not seem to be re-flected in 4QMMT comprises the *halakhoth* forming the Torah of the King. This is easy to explain once one takes into account that the halakhic letter seems to be directed not at the political power of Jerusalem or at the Hasmonaean kings but at the religious group from which the sect detached itself[136].

Both texts, then, indicate that the fundamental disputes within the Essene movement during the formative period of the sect centred on the question of the calendar and the resulting arrangement of the festival cycle. They also centred on a certain way of understanding the biblical prescriptions relating to the Temple, the cult and the purity of persons and things.

It was recognised right from the beginning of research on the manuscripts that the first of these elements (the disputes about the calendar) had been a decisive factor in the formation of the sect and one of the causes which pro-voked the Qumran schism[137]. CD III 14-15 (DSST, 35) specifies that «his holy *sabbaths* and his glorious feasts» are the first of the hidden things in which all Israel has strayed and God has revealed to those with whom he has established his Covenant. Among the obligations taken on by those who entered the Cove-nant, CD VI 18-19 (DSST, 37) specifies: «to keep the *sabbath* day according to the exact interpretation, and the festivals and the day of fasting according to what they had discovered[138], those who entered the New Covenant». However, the problems of the calendar, like eschatology, do not seem to be reflected in the classical descriptions of the Essene movement[139]. The important exception is the Essene group of the Therapeutae, one of whose most striking characteris-tics, besides complete dedication to the contemplative life, is precisely the adoption of a pentecostal festival calendar similar to that used in Qumran[140]. This allows us to suppose that the Essene movement accepted the festival cal-endar of the rest of the Judaism of that period and the adoption of a different calendar was one of the determining factors which made both the Qumran group and the Therapeutae group into a sect within the Essene movement.

A. Jaubert suggested that the origins of the sectarian calendar lay in an an-cient priestly calendar[141]. However, R. Beckwith has proved that the real ori-gins of this calendar lie within apocalyptic tradition and reflect the typical con-cerns of that tradition[142].

As in the case of eschatology, *Jubilees* provides us with the link. Further-more, it proves that the calendar was used not only to regularise the cult; it was also used as the chronological foundation which allowed «the reckoning of the periods» and stimulates the division of history into periods and the calculation of the «end of times», elements which evidently had an influence on the development of eschatological hope characteristic of the Qumran sect.

Besides the debate about the calendar, both 11QTemple and 4QMMT mention a series of *halakhoth* relating to ritual purity, Temple worship and, to a lesser degree, marriage *halakhah*, as the central areas of debate with the movement within which the Qumran sect was to form and with the rest of Judaism. These areas are, of course, fundamental in all communal religious life and are regulated by the prescriptions of the biblical text. Accordingly, the problem of the origin of the sectarian *halakhah* is reduced, ultimately, to a problem of interpreting the biblical text.

How is it possible to explain the emergence within the Essene movement of this different way of interpreting the biblical prescriptions which is the basis of sectarian *halakhah*? The answer to this question is simply the awareness by the Teacher of Righteousness of having received the correct interpretation of the biblical text through divine revelation. This interpretation, therefore, is inspired and binding. The other factor is the acceptance by the members of the community of this interpretation as revealed. The rejection of this interpretation and of the *halakhoth* derived from it by the other members of the Essene movement would result in making it impossible for them to live together.

The sectarian texts show that the biblical text is seen as a mystery, the meaning of which is only intelligible through a revealed interpretation[143]. Hence the conviction that the Book of the Law remained sealed and that not even David could read it, i.e., that it remained «hidden and was not revealed until the coming of Zadok» (CD V 5; DSST, 36). Also, those wishing to enter the Covenant were obliged to be converted to the Law of Moses «in compliance with all that has been revealed concerning it to the sons of Zadok» (1QS V 9; DSST, 8). For the Teacher of Righteousness to be capable of re-writing part of the Pentateuch in 11QTemple, even daring to present this new Torah as God's Torah was only possible from the conviction that this interpretation of the biblical text was under the direct action of divine revelation.

Some of the hymns included in 1QH and attributed to the Teacher of Righteousness show us the existence and extent of this conviction:

> But you have set me like a flag
> for the elect of justice,
> like a wise sower of secret wonders. *Blank*
> *14* To put to the test [all the men of] truth,
> to refine those who love learning.
> (1QH II 13-14; DSST, 329).

Through me you have enlightened the face of the Many,
you have increased them, even making them uncountable,
for you have shown me your wondrous mysteries.
*28* By your wondrous advice you have strengthened my position
(1QH IV 27-28; DSST, 335-336).

This inner conviction is accepted as an objective fact by the group of his followers. They credit his interpretation of the biblical texts with the character of divine and so binding revelation:

> The interpretation (of Hab 2:2) concerns the Teacher of Righteousness, to whom God has disclosed *5* all the mysteries of the words of his servants, the prophets (1QpHab VII 4-5; DSST, 200).

Hence, those not accepting this interpretation are considered enemies:

> The interpretation of the word (of Hab 1:5) [concerns the trai]tors *6* in the last days. They shall be violators of [the coven]ant who will not believe *7* when they hear all that is going [to happen to] the final generation, from the mouth of the *8* Priest whom God has placed wi[thin the Community,] to foretell the fulfilment of all *9* the words of his servants, the prophets (1QpHab II 5-9; DSST, 198).

The sectarian texts which refer to this founding schism[144] invariably put it in the context of a dispute about the correct interpretation of the biblical text. Expressions used are «not believing in the words of the Teacher of Righteousness from the mouth of God» (1QpHab II 2-3) or «not listening to the Interpreter of Knowledge» (4Q171 I 27). A typical text is 1QpHab V 9-12. It is a *pesher* on Hab 1:13, a text which mentions some traitors, a wicked man and a just man. The Qumran interpretation is:

> Its interpretation concerns the House of Absalom *10* and the members of his council who kept silent at the time of the rebuke of the Teacher of Righteousness, *11* and did not help him against the Man of Lies who rejected *12* the Law in the midst of their whole Community (DSST, 199).

The basic elements of the *pesher* are as follows: the Man of Lies «rejects the Law» in the midst of the whole community to which both he and the Teacher of Righteousness belong; the rest of this community accepts the position of the Man of Lies, even though the just rebuke of the Teacher of Righteousness reduces them to silence. This text reflects, in a restrained and concise way, the outcome of the long period of tension marking the formative period of the

Qumran community. The awareness of the Teacher of Righteousness of having received through divine revelation the correct interpretation of the Law leads him to defend a series of ideological and legal positions (imminence of the end of times, the actual calendar of feasts, inadequacy of the Temple and of the present cult in respect of the normative temple and cult, etc.) Also, to defend practical *halakhoth* which determine daily life (4QMMT and 11QTemple) and to attempt to impose this version of the Law on the other members of the Essene movement. According to the sectarian texts, the failure of this attempt is due to the influence of the Man of Lies. He was the leader of the Essene movement «who misled many with deceptive words since they thought up absurdities and did not listen to the Interpreter of knowledge» (4Q171 I 26-27; DSST, 203). The result was to be the split between the group of followers of the Teacher of Righteousness and the rest of the Essene movement.

On the actual decision to withdraw to Qumran, other elements must have been influential, such as the need for physical separation from the rest of Judaism so as to be able to practice its own *halakhah* and the prophetic tradition of preparation for the coming of the Lord in the desert. However, the ideological roots of the schism within the Essene movement lie in the different interpretation of the Law which underlies the sectarian *halakhah*. The «foundation manifesto»[145] words it as follows:

> And when these exist /as a community/ in Israel *13* /in compliance with these arrangements/ they are to be segregated from within the dwelling of the men of sin to walk to the desert in order to open there His path. *14* As it is written: «In the desert, prepare the way of ****, straighten in the steppe a roadway for our God». *15* This is the study of the law which he commanded through the hand of Moses, in order to act in compliance with all that has been revealed from age to age, *16* and according to what the prophets have revealed through his holy spirit (1QS VIII 13-15; DSST, 12).

Once the roots of the schism which gave rise to the Qumran community have been explained, the actual circumstances in which the schism took place must be determined. However, about these circumstances the texts preserved do not say much and study of the indications which can be recovered must be left to another occasion[146]. One certain fact is that in the high priesthood of Hyrcanus, the schism was already complete and the group of Essenes faithful to the Teacher of Righteousness set themselves up on the shores of the Dead Sea. There, its evolution was to continue for a couple of centuries, practising the sectarian *halakhah* and creating in unforgettable texts the eschatological hope and the biblical interpretation which nourished its origins.

II  *The Bible, Purity and Messianic Hope*

# The Bible and Biblical Interpretation in Qumran

## Julio Trebolle Barrera

Yigael Yadin, son of Sukenik, the first editor of the Qumran texts, himself a famous archaeologist and editor of important texts from Qumran, vice-president of Israel at the close of a brilliant military and political career, enjoyed telling about his negotiations with a rich American patron, Samuel Gottesman, with a view to acquiring some manuscripts, the sale of which had been publicised by means of a small ad in the business section of the *Wall Street Journal* of New York (1st June 1954). Under the heading «Miscellaneous for sale. The Four Dead Sea Scrolls» the notice read as follows: «Biblical manuscripts dating back to at least 200 BC are for sale. This would be an ideal gift to an educational or religious institution by an individual or group». The only contact address was a box number, «Box F 206» in the same newspaper.

Among the manuscripts on sale was a scroll of the book of Isaiah. Yadin explained to his would-be patron that the text of this scroll was exactly the same as that of mediaeval Jewish manuscripts. Gottesman did not seem very eager to give a large sum of money for a scroll which was practically identical to those already known. However, Yadin had no difficulty in persuading the then prime minister of Israel, L. Eshkol, that the State of Israel endorse the purchase of that lot of manuscripts for 250,000 dollars. The manuscripts are now in the «Shrine of the Book», built by the Gottesman family in the precincts of the Israel Museum in Jerusalem. There the *Isaiah Scroll* is located in the centre of the exhibition, although it has been replaced by a copy so as not to damage the original.

The *Isaiah Scroll* provides irrefutable proof that the transmission of the biblical text through a period of more than one thousand years by the hands of Jewish copyists has been extremely faithful and careful. The text of Isaiah which today can be read in a Hebrew Bible and in the corresponding translations into any modern language is the same as that read by Christ's contemporaries. The transmission of the text of the Hebrew Bible is of extraordinary exactitude, without parallel in Greek and Latin classical literature. The Rabbinic scribes developed very exact methods so that, in spite of difficult conditions of transmitting the texts in ancient times, the copy of a manuscript of the Bible would be as exact as possible.

The American patron, who at first seemed very interested in manuscripts of more novel content, did not feel cheated by the manuscripts which appeared a short time later. The new texts differed, sometimes considerably, from the traditional biblical Hebrew text and agreed, instead, with the text of the LXX version, the Greek Bible used by Christians. Other texts published in recent years present even more notable differences.

The question of the biblical text is posed today in a much more complex form than in the early days of Qumran studies. Now it is not so much a matter of knowing whether the transmission of the Biblical text has occurred in conditions of trustworthiness, but of explaining the plurality of texts and textual forms in which the Bible was transmitted in the period before the formation of Christianity and Rabbinism. Ultimately, it goes back to the fundamental problem of the relationship between the Jewish bible and the Christian Old Testament.

Study of the biblical manuscripts from the Dead Sea has had ramifications in very different fields of study. It has enriched our knowledge of Hebrew and Aramaic in the intermediate period between the Hebrew of the Bible and the Hebrew of the Mishnah. It has made it possible to draw a history of the transmission of the biblical text prior to the Christian and Rabbinic period. It has explained several questions concerning the history of the LXX version and the revision process of this translation by the hands of Jewish and Christian recensionists. It has considerably developed the field of studies about the interpretation of the Bible in post-biblical Judaism and in early Christianity. It has contributed material for textual criticism of the Old Testament, a discipline which has experienced a rebirth after the Qumran discoveries. It has also influenced the studies of literary criticism which attempt to reconstruct the formation process of the biblical books.[147]

Research into the biblical manuscripts from Qumran has gone through four stages and has afforded just as many surprises.

### 1 Four Stages and Four Surprises in the Study of the Biblical Manuscripts from Qumran

What is surprising about the first biblical manuscripts found was their exact agreement with the text already known from mediaeval manuscripts. Those published later were surprising in their agreement with the Hebrew text reflected in the ancient versions of the Bible. Later other manuscripts became known agreeing with the Samaritan Pentateuch, which showed that this form of the Pentateuch also circulated among the Jews, although without the interpolations of a Samaritan type. The texts published most recently were surprising for their borderline character between biblical and non-biblical. On the other hand, it must not be forgotten that each one of the texts found also has its own characteristics. They can only be examined in terms of the three forms of the text known since ancient times: the masoretic text of the mediaeval rabbis, the Hebrew text translated into Greek by the LXX in the 3rd-2nd centuries BCE, and the so-called Samaritan Pentateuch.

## 1  Fidelity of Biblical Textual Transmission

The two great manuscripts of Isaiah (1QIsᵃ) marked the initial stage of research on the biblical manuscripts from Qumran. They confirmed the marvellous fidelity with which the Hebrew text has been preserved during the thousand years which intervene between the period of Qumran and the period in which the most ancient mediaeval manuscripts preserved were copied (9th and 10th centuries CE). Extrapolating the example of the book of Isaiah to the remaining books of the Old Testament, today we can know that the traditional text of the Hebrew Bible is practically identical with that used by the Jews in the 2nd century CE and no doubt in the previous period. The manuscripts from Wadi Murabbaᶜat and Nahal Hever, connected with the second Jewish revolt against the Romans (132–135 CE), already reflect the climax of a process of establishing the consonantal text which had been begun some time before.

The first Isaiah scroll, 1QIsᵃ, which was copied around the years 125–100 BCE, shows, as has been said, a surprising agreement with the consonantal text of masoretic tradition. It was even thought that it could help to gain access to an earlier stage of the textual transmission of the book, but the fact is that for the most part of the cases in which these texts differ, the text preserved in the mediaeval manuscripts proves to be better than the text of the Qumran manuscript. The second Isaiah scroll (1QIsᵇ), dates from 100–755 BCE. Its similarity with the MT has also been exaggerated, as in the case of 1QIsᵃ.

## 2  Plurality of Texts and Multiple Library Editions

The second stage and the second surprise coincide with the discovery and study of other manuscripts, especially of the books of Samuel and Jeremiah, which showed clear divergences in respect of the masoretic Hebrew text. They agree, instead, in large measure with the form of the text represented by the Greek version of the LXX. If the manuscripts discovered in the beginning confirmed the fidelity of the transmission of the rabbinic Hebrew text, the new manuscripts provide proof that the Greek version, the Old Testament adopted by the Christians, was no less faithful to its own Hebrew original. In the library of Qumran there occur copies of the two text-forms in which the Bible has been transmitted to us, the rabbinic form and that known by the Christians.

This gave rise to the idea that some biblical books underwent a kind of «second edition, corrected and enlarged». The traditional Hebrew text transmits, as is the case in the book of Jeremiah, the text of the second edition, while the shorter textual form corresponds to the first edition. This was used to implement the known version of the LXX. The Hebrew copies of this first edition were lost and only now has it been possible to recover fragments of these texts in Qumran.

Until the appearance of these Qumran texts it was always possible to suspect that in those cases where the Greek version was different from the known Hebrew text, the Greek translators had confused the letter or the spirit of the Hebrew text used for the translation. After the Qumran discoveries this explanation cannot be sustained. A large part of the textual variants of the versions, and especially the more important ones and the largest only reflect with great exactness the lost Hebrew originals, very similar to those found at Qumran.

The most significant examples of double edition correspond to the books of Samuel, Jeremiah, Ezekiel, Job, Esther, Daniel, Ben Sira and Tobit. The fact that quite a few biblical books went through a complex process of editing up to the point that it is possible to speak of double editions, has great significance It broaches questions as promising for discussion as which of the two editions is authentic and original, which of the two texts is canonical, and which of them has to be translated into modern versions, especially if it is a matter of establishing the official and authorised version of a particular Christian confession.

## 3  Texts Related to the Samaritan Pentateuch

The manuscripts published in the last two stages produced even greater surprises from the academic point of view, although their meaning and consequences for the evaluation of traditional texts, the Rabbinic and Greek of the Christians, are undoubtedly less. The manuscripts studied in the first two stages actually did no more than confirm the value of what was already known. The manuscripts published in the last two stages revealed something completely new. The Samaritan Pentateuch had been known since the Renaissance. Its text is, in general, longer than the rabbinic Pentateuch and that of the Greek version. It frequently adds phrases such as that which follows Gn 30:36, taken from 31:11-13. In Moses' discussion with the pharaoh it inserts speeches by God and Moses. It completes passages of Numbers with others from Deuteronomy and vice versa. It introduces explanations into the text, with continual additions and repetitions of words or phrases.

The most important side of the text is a series of readings which reflect the viewpoint and theology of the Samaritans. The most telling is that which refers to the place chosen by Yahweh. This is Mount Garizim of the Samaritans and not the Mount Zion of the Jews in Jerusalem. In the text of the tenth commandment of the Decalogue a gloss is inserted (after Ex 20:17) taken from Dt 27:28 and 11:29-30. In this way the divine commandment to build an altar in Garizim, the sacred mountain of the Samaritans, becomes one more commandment of the Decalogue and gains maximum legal status.

Until the discoveries of Qumran it was thought that the Samaritan Pentateuch was unique and exclusive to the Samaritans. Study of 4QpaleoEx$^m$ and of other manuscripts has shown that the Samaritan Pentateuch does not comprise, as was thought a «sectarian» Samaritan text but duplicates a type of text spread both among the Jews throughout Palestine in the 2nd century BCE, in a much later period than that in which the Samaritan schism was supposed to have taken place. The Samaritans did nothing more than add those readings which reflect the viewpoint peculiar to the Samaritans, such as replacing «Zion» with «Garizim».

The study of the new texts, related to the Samaritan text tradition, has thus forced the history of the Samaritan schism to be re-opened. To judge from the textual, palaeographic and orthographic data available, the redaction of the Samaritan Pentateuch is not earlier than the period of the Maccabees (2nd century BCE). Similarly, study of the Qumran manuscripts and of the papyri from Samaria and Wadi Daliyeh, as well as the excavations at Shechem (Tell Balatah) and in Mount Garizim (Tell er-Rash) have come to show that the formation of the Samaritan sect occurred in this same period, contrary to earlier opinions based on the testimony of Flavius Josephus.

In short, the Qumran texts related to the Samaritan tradition are one more proof of the textual pluralism of the Bible and of the social and religious pluralism of Judaism in the period prior to the birth of Christianity and the formation of classic Rabbinism.

### 4  Borderline Texts: Between Biblical and Non-Biblical

The manuscripts of the Pentateuch which have become known in recent years yield utterly unsuspected features. They contain additions taken from legal traditions not included in the canonical texts (4QDeut^m) or rewrite legal texts from other canonical books (4QNum^b). These phenomena are similar to those to be noted in non-biblical texts such as the *Temple Scroll*, as well as in anthological texts (4QFlorilegium, 4QTestimonia and 4QCatena^a) and other texts published recently (*Psalms of Joshua*, 4Q378-379; *Second Ezekiel*, 4Q385-390, *Pseudo-Moses*, 4Q375-376).

The most recent and important case is certainly the group comprising manuscripts 4Q364-367, denoted by the siglum 4QRP, «Reworked Pentateuch» (Tov, White). Manuscript 4Q158 is a copy of the preceding work. 4QRP has passages in a different order, omits whole segments of text and adds other «non-biblical»(?) texts. Tov describes this work as a «reworking or rephrasing of the biblical text», comparable to that exemplified by the *Temple Scroll*, but more emphasis must be placed on the biblical character of the text and of the added material.

These manuscripts raise new questions which cannot be addressed here. The new texts shift to a no man's land between the biblical and the non-biblical. This borderline was completely marked off in both Jewish and Christian tradition. Now this borderline has become much more vague and the transition from biblical to para-biblical forms seems to be more fluid. The para-biblical forms can go back to ancient lost texts, which never succeeded in becoming part of the authorised or canonical biblical text, or they can represent developments on the margin of the text which was authorised later. These textual forms could still be part of biblical manuscripts which were in circulation until the start of the Christian era.

## 11 The Most Important Biblical Manuscripts Found in Qumran

For the reader interested in knowing the content and features of the text of the biblical manuscripts found in Qumran, there follows a short description of the most significant of them. The two manuscripts of Isaiah from Cave 1 have been referred to previously[148].

EXODUS. 4QEx[a], from the Herodian period, contains the text of 6:25-37:15. Its most outstanding feature is the level of agreement with the non-masoretic text of the Pentateuch. In general, its readings are close to those of the LXX, for example in the reference to Jacob's 75 descendants.

4QpaleoEx[m], from the first half of the 1st century BCE, contains 6:25-37:16. It represents the text type of the Samaritan Pentateuch with typical additions taken from Ex or Dt, excluding those added from the «sectarian» Samaritan text. The Samaritans used a very evolved biblical text which circulated also among other Jewish groups from Palestine, to which they did no more than add the readings peculiar to the Samaritans (Judit E. Sanderson).

LEVITICUS. From Cave 11, 11QpaleoLev[a] is an important manuscript which contains remains of 4:10.11.13-14.16.18.20-21 and of chapters 22-27, with readings agreeing with the MT, the Samaritan Pentateuch and the LXX; it also offers a large number of idiosyncratic readings; it lies in a position intermediate between MT and Samaritan (D. N. Freedman-K. A. Mathews, 1985).

NUMBERS. 4QNum[b], from the Herodian period, offers a very developed type of text, in the manner of the Samaritan Pentateuch, but still close to the text of the LXX; it inserts Dt 3:21 after Nm 27:23 and Dt 3:23-24 after Nm 20:13 (Cross, Jastram).

DEUTERONOMY. 4QDeut[j] contains remains from chapters 4, 6, 8, 11 and 32 and portions of the text of Ex 12-13, which confers on the text of the manuscript a «borderline» character between biblical and non-biblical (Duncan). 4QDeut[n] presents a different order of chapters and offers a harmonising text in the passage of the Decalogue (White). 4QDeut[q] contains the Song of Moses (Dt 32).

JUDGES. See below.

SAMUEL. Three copies of Samuel have come to light in Cave 4. 4QSam<sup>a</sup> contains a very large portion of text. The frequent agreement with the text of LXX confirms the Hebrew origin of the numerous variants of the Greek version. 4QSam<sup>b</sup> is the oldest document from Qumran; Cross dates it towards the end of the 3rd century BCE. The text, characterised by defective spelling, corresponds to a primitive period in the development of the Palestinian text tradition (Cross, Ulrich).

JEREMIAH. 4QJer<sup>a</sup>, c. 200 BCE, agrees with the long text of the masoretic tradition. In contrast, 4QJer<sup>b</sup> from a later period, corresponds to the shorter text reflected by the Greek version. 4QJer<sup>c</sup>, from the close of the 1st century BCE, or the start of the 1st CE, contains the text of chapters 8; 19-22; 25-27; 30-33, in a form of text close to the masoretic text (Janzen, Bogaert, Tov).

EZEKIEL. Four fragments of 4QEz<sup>a</sup>, in late Hasmonaean or early Herodian script, preserve remains of 10:5-15; 10:17-11:11; 24:14-18.44-47 and 41:3-6. Five tiny fragments of 4QEz<sup>b</sup>, in Herodian script, contain remains of Ez 1:10.11-12.13.16-17.20-24. The text of the two manuscripts is very close to the masoretic text (Lust).

MINOR PROPHETS. Cave 4 has supplied seven manuscripts of this collection of books, although some only preserve parts of the text corresponding to one or two of the books which form the collection. The text is essentially that of MT (Fuller)

PSALMS. 11QPs<sup>a</sup>, from the beginning of the 1st century CE, contains passages from 41 psalms from books four and five of the psalter, in a different order from the Hebrew bible. At the end, seven non-biblical psalms («Plea for Deliverance», «Apostrophe to Zion», «Hymn to the Creator», etc. Sanders). According to Talmon and Goshen-Gottstein, these comprise a collection of psalms intended for the liturgy in Qumran, a kind of prayer-book. They do not admit the surmise, therefore, that it is a variant or open canon, as Sanders and Yadin do. Sanders sees confirmation of this in the fact that in column 27 it is stated that David wrote 3,600 psalms and 450 poems through the gift of «prophecy» granted by God. According to Skehan, one cannot speak of a canon at Qumran and the collection of psalms represented by 11QPs<sup>a</sup> is a secondary derivation in respect of the collection of 150 psalms which had already been established in the Persian period (Skehan, Cross).

11QPs<sup>b</sup>, from the same period as the foregoing, adds the same «Plea for Deliverance» as 11QPs<sup>a</sup>.

DANIEL. Eight manuscripts of this book have been found. 4QDanᵃ, from the mid-1st century BCE, preserves the change of the Aramaic text to Hebrew in 8:1 and the short form of the text, although, on the other hand, it has several additions to the MT (2:20.28.30.40; 5:7.12; 8:3.4...), variants which agree with the LXX or with papyrus 967 and other peculiar readings. In 2:28 4QDanᵃ and the original Vorlage of the LXX seem to go back to a different textual tradition from the one represented by MT and Theodotion. 4QDanᵇ witnesses Hebrew-Aramaic bilingualism, as does 4QDanᵃ. 4QDanᵇ is very interesting because it comes from the close of the 2nd century BCE, not more than fifty years after the composition of the book. 4QDanᵈ, in a bad state of preservation, does not include the text of the prayer present in the Greek text of chapter 3. 4QDanᵉ corresponds to the text of the prayer of chapter 9 so that it witnesses its existence in Hebrew.

III   The Bible Text in the Period before Christianity

The Dead Sea Scrolls reveal the stage in which the biblical text was transmitted between the 3rd century BCE and the 2nd century CE. Since a large part or perhaps most of the manuscripts were copied outside Qumran, in various places in Palestine, the textual panorama which the manuscripts reflect refers not only to the Qumran community but embraces the whole of Palestine as well. The manuscripts found in Masada, Nahal Hever and Wadi Murabbaᶜat were written in other places and deposited in the caves in which they were found. Some of those found at Masada could also have been copied there.

In the first stages quite varied biblical texts were in circulation. This situation gave way to a very different one towards the end of the 1st century CE. Then a uniform consonantal text was established which was to remain unchanged. It was based on a very old text-form which is also found witnessed in the Qumran manuscripts.

The history of the text of the Bible is the history of the transition, recurring several times, from a situation of textual fluidity to one of a uniform text

Prior to the Qumran discoveries, Paul de Lagarde (1863) had formulated a theory according to which the Hebrew manuscripts of the Old Testament go back to a single exemplar or «unique archetype». Similarly, the Greek manuscripts preserved go back to three basic recensions (Origen, Hesychius and Lucian) and from them it is possible to go back to the single exemplar of the original Greek version. Much later P. Kahle proposed the theory of «vulgar texts». According to this theory, the Hebrew and Greek archetypes posited by Lagarde are only the final precipitate of a long process through which a mass of vulgar texts was becoming united through the efforts of Jewish, Samaritan and Christian copyists, crystallising into the official texts of these three religious communities: the proto-masoretic text of the Jews, the Samaritan version of the Pentateuch and the Greek text of the LXX transmitted by the Christians.

After the Qumran finds F. M. Cross formulated the theory of «local texts». Between the 5th and 1st centuries BCE three types of text were gradually formed in each of the great centres of Judaism: in Palestine, in the Jewish diaspora of Babylonia and the diaspora of Egypt. The Palestinian type tends towards expansion; the Babylonian is short and conservative and the Egyptian tradition represents an intermediate text which has neither the expansions of the Palestinian nor the omissions of the Babylonian traditions.

The theory of local texts has received various criticisms (Goshen-Gottstein, Talmon, Barthélemy). Nothing is known about possible literary activity of the Jews in Babylonia during the period which comes between Esdras and Hillel. Little is known, either, about whether the Jews of Egypt used texts in Hebrew. On the other hand, the LXX version was not completely carried out in Egypt nor was it made from Hebrew texts which came exclusively from Egypt. Finally, it is not easy to explain the fact that a community so closed upon itself as that of the Essenes of Qumran had available over a period of two centuries texts coming from such widely different places (of the book of Jeremiah, for example) as presupposed in the theory of local texts.

In Talmon's opinion, the number of existing text traditions is much higher than that supposed by Cross, but they disappeared through not being adopted by any religious group, as the Synagogue did with the Masoretic Hebrew text, the Church with the text of the LXX and the Samaritan community with the textual form of the Pentateuch, which they adopted putting their own stamp on it.

E. Tov, principally on the basis of study of the manuscript 11QpaleoLev[a] published in 1985, insists that more attention should be paid to the discrepancies and not so much the agreements of the biblical manuscripts from Qumran with the MT, the text of the LXX or the Samaritan Pentateuch. Tov proposes that the distinctive character of each text should be acknowledged even to the point of questioning the concept of textual «type».

IV  Importance of the New Manuscripts. Three Examples

We refer to the importance of the manuscripts published most recently. It has already been said that the manuscripts published in the first two stages came to confirm the value of the two great textual traditions, Jewish and Christian (also Jewish in origin), represented by the Hebrew masoretic text (MT) and by the Greek version of the Septuagint (LXX). We will choose three examples. The first refers to a case of textual difference between those great textual traditions (MT and LXX). The second is an example of a longer text and the third, a shorter text. In all the cases the question is posed: which is the oldest text? The general criterion, according to which the shorter text is more original, applies in these last two cases. In the first the longer text became longer through fusing more ancient elements with some that are more recent.

1. Before the discovery of the Dead Sea Scrolls, it was possible to suspect that the Greek text of Dt 32:43 contained older elements than those present in the Hebrew Masoretic text. The manuscript 4QDeut^q has proved that the Greek text is not an alteration or an incorrect translation of the Hebrew text which has reached us. The Greek translation only transmits a Hebrew text similar to the one now discovered in Qumran (4QDeut^q).

The masoretic text of Dt 32:43 is shorter than the Greek version. The manuscript 4QDeut^q preserves the longer Hebrew text, reflected in the Greek version.

| *Masoretic Hebrew text* | LXX *and Qumran text* (4QDeut^q) |
|---|---|
| «Acclaim, *nations,*<br>his people, | «Acclaim, *heavens,*<br>his people<br>*and be prostrate*<br>*before him*<br>*all gods* |
| because he will avenge the blood<br>of his *servants,*<br>he will give back vengeance<br>against his foes... | because he will avenge the blood<br>of his *sons,*<br>he will give back vengeance<br>against his foes... |

The reading of the masoretic text «pagan nations» looks like being late in respect of the older reading «heavens», witnessed by the LXX and also transmitted in 4QDeut^q. The reading «pagan nations» demythologises a text which had obvious mythological and polytheistic overtones, for it linked in synonymous parallelism the «heavens» and the «gods». The reference to the «sons» of God shows the mythological character of the older text. If there were any doubt, in v.8 of the manuscript 4QDeut^q provides the reading «according to the number of the sons of El», agreeing with the reading of the Greek version (*kata arithmon aggelon theou*). The masoretic text has changed «sons» into «servants» of God. There is no doubt that vv. 5, 19 and 20 contain clear references to the «sons» of God, in agreement with what is undoubtedly the older reading.

2. The second example emphasises the harmonising character of the text of the Samaritan Pentateuch and of the manuscripts related to this proto-Samaritan text-form (4QDeut^n and 4QpaleoEx^m).

Manuscript 4QDeut^n and the Samaritan Pentateuch add the passage from Ex 20:11 after the corresponding passage from Dt 5:15. In this way they juxtapose

two parallel passages from the books of Deuteronomy and Exodus, both related
to the third commandment of the Decalogue:

> (Dt 5:12) You will observe the sabbath day *to make it holy* as Yahweh, your
> God has commanded you. (13) Six days shall you work and do all your
> work; (14) but the seventh is of rest, consecrated to Yahweh, your God. You
> shall do no work...(15) And you will remember that you were a slave in the
> land of Egypt, and Yahweh, your God, took you from there with a mighty
> hand and outstretched arm; therefore Yahweh, your God, has commanded
> to keep the sabbath day *to make it holy* (+ Ex 20:11:) because in six days
> Yahweh made the heavens and the earth, the sea and all that is in them, but
> on the seventh day he rested. Therefore Yahweh blessed the sabbath day *to*
> *make it holy*. (Dt 5:16:) Honour your father and your mother... (S. White).

The agreement between the Samaritan Pentateuch and the manuscript 4QDeut[n]
must be explained by the common dependence of both texts on another earlier
text. The editor of this text, the antecedent of those two, fused parallel passages
from Deuteronomy and Exodus, juxtaposing two passages which justify in
different ways the precept of the sabbath. The first provides a reason of a social
nature, with reference to the history of slavery in Egypt: the Israelites shall rest
and also make their servants rest to show that after the entry into the Land of
Israel they will never go back to being slaves and let themselves be enslaved.
This is the reason offered by the deuteronomistic source of the Pentateuch
(«D», 7th cent. BCE?). The second reason, more ritual in motive, given by the
priestly source («P», 6th-5th cents. BCE), refers to Yahweh's rest on the seventh
day of creation: the *homo faber*, tired from the work of the week, must rest and
celebrate the sabbath as a feast day, in imitation of Yahweh the creator.

3. The manuscript of 4QJudges[a] of the book of Judges provides unusual interest. I edited its text in an article presented at the Qumran Congress organised
in Groningen in 1989. It represents a unique case amongst the biblical manuscripts from Qumran. The manuscript completely omits the text of a literary
section (Jg 6:7-11) preserved in all the other texts known. Modern criticism had
always considered that this passage comprised an extraneous section inserted
in the Gideon narrative. The reader can judge for himself by simply reading
the text:

> When the Israelites had sown, the Amalekites and the Easterners came to
> harass them; they camped opposite them and destroyed all their crops, up
> to the entrance of Gaza. They left nothing alive in Israel, neither sheep nor
> ox nor ass; because they came with their flocks and their tents, numerous
> as locusts, men and camels without number, and invaded the region, laying

it waste. By this, Israel became impoverished through Midian's fault. * [7-10: Then the Israelites cried out to the Lord. And when the Israelites cried out to the Lord on account of Midian, the Lord sent a prophet to tell them: «Thus says the Lord, God of Israel: I made you come up from Egypt, I freed you from the house of bondage, I rescued you from the Egyptians and from all your oppressors, I drove them out before you to bestow their lands on you, and I said to you: I am the Lord, your God; do not worship the gods of the Amorites in whose land you are going to live. But you did not obey me».] * The angel of the Lord came and sat under the terebinth at Ophrah, property of Joash of Abiezer, while his son, Gideon, was beating out wheat with a flail in the press, to hide himself from the Midianites...

The passage 6:7-11 is an interpolation. A glossator has placed in the mouth of an anonymous prophet an oracle directed at the Israelites in a moralising tone and in stereotype language. At first, scholars ascribed this text to an Elohist source. Today it is rather ascribed to a deuteronomist redactor, possibly the most recent, the redactor called «nomist». In any case, this manuscript provides very tangible proof that the Bible went through a process of composition through which sections were being added to others at different stages. This does not mean to say that the Bible has to be torn apart to extract its meaning and that this only applies to sections and not to the whole work.

## V  The Canon of the Bible at Qumran:
### Canonical Books and Apocryphal Books

Research in recent decades has called into question positions held since ancient times in respect of the history of the formation of the Hebrew canon and the existence of the Alexandrian Greek canon. Until a couple of decades ago it was customary to differentiate three stages in the history of the canon of the Old Testament. For it the Samaritan schism, which supposedly had occurred in the 5th cent. BCE, was taken as a reference. It was said that the Pentateuch acquired canonical recognition before the schism of the Samaritans since they grant canonical status to this collection of five books. The collection of prophetical books, which was not accepted by the Samaritans, had developed and gained canonical status only after the schism, towards the 3rd cent. BCE. Finally, the collection of writings was composed and became part of the canon at a much later period. The final process ended at the close of the 1st cent. CE, on the occasion of the Synod of Yabneh, at which the canon of the Hebrew Bible was permanently closed.

On the other hand, it was also said that together with this «Palestine canon» there also existed another «Alexandrian canon», belonging to the Judaism of the diaspora. It was represented by the books collected in the Greek version of the LXX. Christianity made this canon its own before the rabbis of Yabneh finally closed the Hebrew canon towards the end of the 1st century CE, leaving «outside» the «external» or apocryphal books, some of which feature in the Greek Bible of the Christians.

The discovery from the Dead Sea and another series of studies have demolished this classic hypothesis, which can still be found in many books. Today it is accepted that the so-called Samaritan schism certainly took place towards the end of the 2nd century BCE, in other words, when the collection of prophetical books had already been formed for some time. The theory of the Alexandrian Jewish canon has also been abandoned, as there is no proof at all of its existence.

In the Persian and Hellenistic periods, from the 5th century BCE until the beginning of the 2nd century CE, the decisive steps in the history of the Bible occurred: the collections of books were established which later went on to form the canon, it began the process of transmission, diffusion and translation of its text, a rich hermeneutic was created from principles and methods of interpretation and am enormous tradition of oral and written interpretation of the Bible was accumulated. The history of the formation of the Biblical canon runs parallel with the development of Judaism in the Persian and Hellenistic period.

An important strand of modern interpretation tends to consider that the Hebrew canon was formed in the Maccabaean period, towards the middle of the 2nd century BCE. This explanation, however, leaves unresolved the question about the origin of the Christian canon of the Old Testament. If it can no longer be said that the Christians inherited from the Jewish diaspora a collection of books more extensive than that of the Hebrew Bible, an explanation must be sought which justifies the fact that the Christians did not feel themselves obliged to keep to the strict Hebrew canon. This fact can have antecedents in the Essene community of Qumran. Assuredly the Essenes of Qumran had no awareness or intention at all of re-opening a canon allegedly closed already. However, it gives the impression that they accorded certain writings, as may be the case of the book of *Jubilees*, a sacred character comparable to that of other books included in the canon.

VI  The Interpretation of the Old Testament in the Texts from Qumran

Besides the biblical manuscripts, in the Qumran caves were also found manuscripts of works whose intention and raison d'etre is the interpretation of Scripture. The exegesis represented by such works is in some cases faithful to the letter of the text, in others more or less a periphrastic. In every case they imitate expressions and literary forms of the Biblical books. Thus, the *Rule of*

*the Community* II 2-10 is modelled on the «Priestly blessing» of Nm 6:24-26.
The *Damascus Document* imitates the style and structure of the book of Deuteronomy in its two parts, the parenetic introduction (CD 1-8 1-11) and the central
legislative corpus (CD 9-16).

Qumran hermeneutics had a twofold aim: to explain the biblical text to make
it more intelligible and clear («pure exegesis»), and to apply the biblical text to
a new situation or to discover in it the reply to topical questions which the
Scripture had not yet posed («applied exegesis») (Vermes).

The Essene community of Qumran held study of Scripture as central to its
life. The Teacher of Righteousness, founder of the Qumran community, was
presented as an authorised interpreter of the mysteries hidden in the Scriptures
(1QpHab 2, 1-9). The community believed it formed a continuous link with
Moses and the prophets, so that it considered itself authorised to draft new
laws on a par with those of the Mosaic Law. The *Damascus Document*, the *Rule
of the Community* and the *Temple Scroll* are compilations of legal interpretations
which aspire to have an authority comparable to that of the canonical books.
While the *Damascus Document* interprets Scripture by referring directly to the
biblical text, the *Temple Scroll* introduces interpretative elements into the actual
text of the Torah, converting its interpretation into a new and real Torah.

The explicit verbatim quotations of biblical texts are numerous. For example, the *Rule of the Community* cites Is 2:22 in 16-20. Explicit allusions are also
common. The passage 6,13-23 in the same *Rule* alludes to Lv 25:299-30. The
implicit quotations of the Old Testament contained in the writings of the
Qumran community are very numerous. All the works of Qumran, even those
not exegetical in character, are impregnated with biblical language (*Rule of the
Community*, *Hymns*, *War Scroll*, etc.).

The biblical quotation in some cases follows the discussion on the topic to
which the quotation refers. In other cases, this precedes the commentary of the
text quoted. The commentary can take the form of a pseudepigraphical writing,
a *pesher*, an anthology or an explanation of midrashic type.

Generally, the interpreter respects the biblical text scrupulously, or the form
of the text that he knew. In many cases the biblical text followed in the Qumran commentaries supports a variant already known from some other source.
It leads one to suppose that all or nearly all the variants present in the commentaries witness different recensions or textual traditions.

There are also variants of an exegetical nature. These can affect the grammar
or the syntax of a sentence or a change of person, gender or number, and the
verb form. They can suppose an omission in the text or represent different
forms of paronomasia (metathesis, transposition of letters to form different
words, plays on words favoured by the ambiguity of the consonantal Hebrew
text, etc.).

It has to be asked whether the biblical text and the interpretation witnessed in Qumran reflect a plurality of texts and of interpretations or whether, instead, they correspond to a situation in which an authorised line of tradition and of exegesis dominated, which nevertheless permits some textual variants and a variety of interpretations.

## VII  Literary Forms of Biblical Interpretation at Qumran: The Pesher and the Testimonia

The literary forms of biblical interpretation practised in Qumran are quite varied. Two of them, the *pesher* and the *testimonia* have special importance since they also appear to be used in the texts of the New Testament.

1. «Rewritten Stories» or midrashic paraphrase. It can refer to large or small units of the biblical text. The *Genesis Apocryphon* (1QapGen) comprises a narrative development of a large part of the book of Genesis.

2. «Rewritten laws» or halakhic paraphrase (legal). The *Temple Scroll* juxtaposes and combines different laws, harmonises some with others, or inserts new legal interpretations. It presents itself ultimately as a new Torah.

3. The interpretation *pesher* is a type of non-literal exegesis of apocalyptic character. The same term *pesher* is also used to denote works of exegetical commentary which use this form of interpretation (the *Pesharim*). The commentary can be made verse by verse or section by section. The *Pesharim* found in Qumran only comment on prophetic books and some psalms. The most important are those relating to the books of Habakkuk, Nahum, Isaiah, Hosea and Psalm 37.

The word *pesher* introduces the commentary to the corresponding verse or lemma Among the usual formulas are found some such as «its interpretation (*pesher*) is...» or «the interpretation of the oracle refers to...». An example taken from 1QpHab 7:3-8 is enough:

> And as for what he says: *So that the one who reads it may run. 4 The interpretation of this refers to* the Teacher of Righteousness, to whom God has disclosed *5* all the mysteries (*raz*) of the words of his servants, the prophets: *For the vision still continues for a while; it will hasten to the end and not fail. Blank 7 The interpretation of this* is that the final age will be extended and go beyond all that *8* the prophets say, because the mysteries (*raz*) of God are wonderful, etc. (DSST, 200).

The interpretation that the New Testament makes of the Old has many points of contact with that of the Qumran *Pesharim*. So, for example, the *pesher* corresponding to Is 54:11-12 identifies the precious stones used in the rebuilding of Jerusalem with the members of the Qumran community. It brings to mind the passage from the Apocalypse (21:10-14) which refers to «twelve bases ... the twelve apostles of the Lamb».

The Qumran community considered that the promises and institutions of the Old Testament reached fulfilment in their own community. The Christians presented themselves a little later as the «true Israel». The New Testament uses two biblical prophecies which are also used in texts from Qumran in reference to their own community (1QH III 6-18, the Immanuel prophecy; 1QH VI 25-27; VII 8-9, the prophecy about the corner-stone of Is 28:16).

4. The literary form of the anthology of *testimonia* juxtaposes biblical passages which refer to the same topic. The best representative of this genre is 4QTest, an anthology of messianic texts which express the hope in a prophet of the last days and in the two expected Messiahs, one priestly and the other davidic («the coming of a prophet and of the Messiahs of Aaron and Israel», *Rule of the Community* IX 11). 4QTest assembles various biblical texts referring to the hoped for prophet (Dt 5:28-29; 18:18f), the priest (Dt 33:8-11) and the king (Nm 24:15-17):

> *5* I would raise up for them a prophet from among their brothers, like you, and place my words *6* in his mouth, and he would tell them all that I command them. And it will happen that the man *7* who does not listen to my words, that the prophet will speak in my name, I *8* shall require a reckoning from him.» (Dt 18:18-19) *Blank 9* And he uttered his poem and said: «Oracle of Balaam, son of Beor, and oracle of the man *10* of penetrating eye, oracle of him who listens to the words of God and knows the knowledge of the Most High, of one who *11* sees the vision of Shaddai, who falls and opens the eye. I see him, but not now, *12* I espy him, but not close up. A star has departed from Jacob, /and/ a sceptre /has arisen/ from Israel. He shall crush *13* the temples of Moab, and cut to pieces all the sons of Sheth.» (Nm 24:15-17) (DSST, 137).

Similar combinations of biblical texts are frequent in the *Rule of the Community*, in the *Hymns* and in the *War Scroll*.

5. The explanation of a text by association with others on a similar theme underwent a special development in the fields of halakhic and haggadic exegesis.

6. Examples of allegorical interpretation are also found. The passage 1QpHab XII 2-4, corresponding to Hab 2:17, interprets allegorically the term «Lebanon» as a symbol of the Council of the Qumran Community. The root *laban* («Lebanon») means «white». The members of that Council wore white in their sessions.

7. There are also many examples of typological interpretation,, especially in the *Pesher on Nahum*. The term *kittim* refers to the Romans, «Judah» to the members of the Qumran Community, «Manasseh» to the Sadducees, «those looking for easy interpretations» to the Pharisees and «the lion» to Alexander Jannaeus, etc.

Biblical interpretation in Qumran represents the shackle which ties the interpretation of the Bible contained in the actual biblical books and the interpretation of the Bible developed in early Christian literature and in rabbinic literature. It must be noted, finally, that the interpretation of Qumran is not esoteric, against the opinion expressed some years ago by Dupont-Sommer.

## VIII Affinities between Qumran Exegesis and the Exegesis of the New Testament

The interpretation of the Old Testament by the New falls within the exegetical tradition of the Judaism of the period. To understand the exegesis of the early Christians it is necessary to know the Old Testament interpretation of the Jewish writings of that period, and in particular, of the Essene writings from Qumran.

The critical approach represented by the «School of the history of religion» (*Religionsgeschichte*) tended to see Christianity as a syncretistic precipitate from Jewish elements and various types of paganism. Therefore it studied the New Testament in the framework of Graeco-Roman literature. However, the Graeco-Roman world does not provide a lot of help for understanding the reading which the Christians made of the Jewish Scriptures. After the Qumran discoveries, it is necessary to grant more weight to the Old Testament and Jewish substratum of the texts of the New Testament (J. Jeremias, B. Gerhardsson, M. Hengel, etc., and especially Jewish authors such as J. Klausner and H. J. Schoeps). The early Christians used the principles and methods of Jewish exegesis, with a single but decisive difference: the «christological» reading of all the passages cited from the Old Testament.

The books of the New Testament were written in a period when there was still great freedom to quote the text of the Old Testament. In it the New Testament is closer to the Judaism of the Qumran period than to later rabbinic Judaism. Many expressions or formulas used in the Old Testament quotations in the New Testament correspond to Jewish exegetical usage, especially in contexts with apocalyptic content. Thus, for example, the expression «faithful is the word...» (*pistos o logos*) (Tim 1:15; 4:9; 2 Tim 2:11, cf. 1 Cor 1:9; 2 Thess 3:3; Ap 2:6) has its roots in the expression «certain is the word which must happen (*nakon haddabar labo'*) and faithful (*'emet*) the oracle» (1Q27 I 8). Similarly, the formula «this is» (*housto estin*) (Rom 9:7-9; Acts 2:16f., cf. Mt 3:3; 11:10; Jn 6:31.50; Acts 4:11; Rom 10:6-8; Heb 7:5; 1 Pt 1:24) is also found in an eschatological context and has its antecedents in the *pesher* type of interpretation (cf. 1QpHab XII 6; CD VII 14f.; 4QFlor I 11-14).

The New Testament interpretation of the Old Testament has antecedents in the Jewish exegesis of Qumran. Jesus and the New Testament share with Qumran apocalyptic the idea of a division of history into two ages. For the Jew the final age has not yet become a reality. The Christian, instead, believes that it has already begun with the message and saving action of Jesus the Christ.

New Testament exegesis of the Old Testament develops all the methods of interpretation known in the Judaism of the period, especially two characteristics of Qumran exegesis, the *pesher* and the anthological form of the *testimonia*.

## 1  The Form Pesher in the New Testament

This genre of interpretation, typical of Qumran exegetical writings, is found both in the gospels and in the letters of Paul and other writings of the New Testament.

### a  Pesher in the Gospels

Striking parallels have been noticed between the biblical quotations of Matthew and the exegesis of the *Habakkuk Pesher* (Stendahl). However Matthew did not empty of its own meaning the prophetic text alluded to, while the *Habakkuk Pesher* only grants to the biblical text a meaning related to the present and eschatological situation (Bruce). The 11 biblical quotations of Matthew have certainly to be considered as interpretations of the *pesher* genre. The quotation by Mt 1:23 of Is 7:14 «the virgin will conceive and give birth to a son and he shall be named Immanuel» (Is 7:14) used an impersonal subject and understands the name Immanuel as a title. These are not exactly *ad hoc* creations, for such changes find textual support in 1QIs$^a$ (*wqr'*) (De Waard). The influence of the LXX makes itself felt in the use of the term *parthenos* as a translation of the Hebrew term *'almah*, «young girl».

The gospel of Matthew, like the Qumran *Pesharim* with respect to the Essene community, interprets the biblical passages as prophecies about the present and future of the Christian community. Characteristic of the midrash of the school of Matthew is that it develops a whole biography of Jesus as a framework in which it inserts biblical quotations interpreted in the light of the Christian event

A very cogent example of the use of *pesher* in the gospel of Luke is Lk 4:16-21. Jesus applies to himself the text of an Old Testament prophecy: «Today this scripture has been fulfilled» (Is 61:1f). The same kind of interpretation is in play in the quotation by Mk 12:10f (Mt 21:42; Lk 20:17) of Ps 118:22f («the stone which the builders rejected... the cornerstone...»)

The biblical quotations of the gospel of John follow the model of *pesher* interpretation, but not in such a developed form as presented by the quotations in Matthew. They are the following seven: Jn 2:17 (Ps 69:9); 12:15 (Zc 9:9); 1:38

(Is 53:1); 12:40 (Is 6:9f); 19:24 (Ps 22:18); 19:36 (Ps 34:20); 19:37 (Zc 12:10).

## b  Pesher in the Epistles of Paul

The exegesis of Jesus and of his disciples settled in Jerusalem seem to have a much closer relationship with the *pesher* type of interpretation than Paul's exegesis. This offers many points of contact with the type of exegesis practised later by pharisaic rabbinism. Paul uses midrashic methods more than *pesher*. This is the reason why Paul could be classified among the hillelites ( J. Jeremias). However, on three occasions Paul develops a *pesher* method of interpretation in relation to «the revelation of a mystery kept secret for time eternal, but now revealed» (Rom 16:25-27; also Col 1:26f; Eph 3:1-11). It is necessary to say that Pauline exegesis is rabbinic in form and Christocentric in content. A certain degree of opposition can be established between the eschatological stress which Jesus imprints on his preaching in harmony with the Essene movement and the emphasis which Paul gives to the topic of the Law in polemic with Pharisaic rabbinism.

In the period prior to the Qumran discoveries it was though that the textual variants provided by the Pauline quotations were due to adaptations made by Paul himself or by the Christian tradition which he represents. However, Paul's quotations are a very complex phenomenon, which brings into play a whole series of factors: Paul's interest in the Gentile world, the rabbinic formation of the apostle, the knowledge that he had of textual variants transmitted in the manuscripts and the inclusion in his writings of texts characterised by the type of interpretation of the *Pesharim*.

Paul's freedom in respect of the biblical text is not comparable, however, to that which writings such as the *Genesis apocryphon*, *Jubilees*, *Biblical antiquities* or the *Temple Scroll* exhibit. In these writings the author never tries, as Paul does, to support or develop a statement of his own making use of a biblical quotation. Nor does Paul develop his interpretation concerning a previously chosen text, as Philo does or as happens in the *Pesharim*. Rather than quoting or commenting on texts, Paul develops a new theological formulation from the ancient biblical traditions.

It is more suitable to compare the Pauline quotations with those found in the *Damascus Document* (CD), in the *Rule of the Community* (1QS) and in the *War Scroll* (1QM), and, secondarily with those present in 4QTest, 4QFlor and the *Pesharim*. A more precise analogy is provided by the *Damascus Document*, but Paul goes much further in the combination of texts and his exegesis. On the other hand, his exegesis is less academic.

The discovery of the texts from Qumran had enabled recognition that important ideas and concepts which were attributed to Paul's genius and originality have antecedents in the Judaism of the Hellenistic period (300 BCE-200 CE).

Examples are: the insistence that all men have sinned (Rom 2:23; 1QH 1:22); men cannot acquire God's forgiveness (Gal 2:16; 1QH 4:30); the Torah is not the means to gain justification before God; only God can justify man; God predestined for salvation only those chosen by him; the importance of the Spirit, etc.

It is not possible to state emphatically that Paul had been influenced by the Essenes, although his words show clear contacts with the Dead Sea Scrolls (Fitzmyer) It is more likely that Paul's followers, members of the pauline school, such as those who composed the epistle to the Ephesians, were directly influenced by the Essenes (Kuhn) or perhaps by Essene groups converted to Christianity.

### c  Pesher and the other New Testament Writings

The epistles of James, of Peter (two), of John (three), of Judah and the Apocalypse have features in common in their exegesis of the Old Testament. Peter's epistles, especially the first, and also the epistle of Judas use the *pesher* genre (cf. 1 Pe 1:10-12; 1:24f.) In this they differ from those of John and James and also from the Apocalypse. The passage 1 Pe 2:4-8, which develops the theme of Christ «living stone», combines images from the Old Testament (also collected in writings of the Qumran community, 1QS VIII 7f and 1QH VI 26) and makes the corresponding Christological application of them, grouping together in a midrashic technique several passages from the Old Testament (Ps 118:22; Is 28:16 and Is 8:14).

### 2  The Qumran Genre of Testimonia in Christian Writings

The New Testament reads the Old Testament selectively, its themes and its quoted passages. It uses the genre of *testimonia*, now known through the texts from Qumran. This type of exegesis consists in juxtaposing passages from the Old Testament which focus on a common theme. The passages 1 Pe 2:6; Eph 2:20; Mt 21:42; Acts 4:11 blend texts from Is 28:16; Ps 118:22 and Is 8:14 which are used to develop the theme of «Christ-Stone»:

> For it is included in Scripture: *See, I place in Zion a chosen, precious foundation stone; and he who believes in it will not end up ashamed* (Is 28:16). So that the honour is for you the believers, for those who do not believe, *the stone which the builders rejected, it became the corner-stone* (Ps 118:22) *and a stone of offence and a rock of stumbling* (Is 8:14); they collide with it...

It has been postulated that for anti-Jewish polemics the primitive Church had available a *Book of testimonies*, from which the biblical quotations contained in the New Testament were extracted (J. R. Harris). According to Dodd, the quotations of the New Testament must rather have been made starting with large blocks of texts from the Old Testament and not so much on the basis of isolated verses. These large blocks, which comprise the «infrastructure of all Christian theology», are grouped around three basic themes of the Christian *kerygma*: apocalyptic and eschatology (Jl 2-3; Zc 9-14; Dn 7 and 12), the New Israel (Hos; Is 6:1-9:7; 11:1-10; 40:1-11; Jer 31:31-34; Hb 2:3f.) and the Servant of God or the Suffering Just Man (Is 42:1-44:5; 49:1-13; 50:4-11; 52:13-53:12; Pss 22, 3, 69, 118). Some particular texts received a marked messianic meaning: Pss 2, 8, 110; Dt 18:15.18f; 2 Sm 7:14.

The quotations contained in the Epistle to the Hebrews have been explained as free paraphrases of the corresponding biblical passages, as the fruit of the use of liturgical formulas or of *testimonia* of those passages, or as *ad hoc* creations by the author of the epistle. However, the agreements noticed between the epistle to the Hebrews and the Dead Sea Scrolls point to the possibility that these quotations knew variants of a recension of the LXX based on lost Hebrew texts. The fact that Hb 1:1-5 and 4QFlor join the passages Ps 2 and 2 Sam 7:14, forming a kind of *testimonia* on the messianic theme is significant, as is that Heb 5-7 and 11QMelk show similar interest in the eschatological figure of Melchizedek.

Jewish-Christian exegesis of the first patristic period has as its identifying mark the use of the *testimonia* genre. The most important examples are the *testimonia* referring to the cross. The passage from the *Letter of Barnabas* 5:13 links three quotations from the Old Testament, applying them to Christ's passion:

> It was necessary, in fact, for him to suffer upon wood, for apropos of him the prophet says: «Free my soul from the sword» (Ps 21:21) and «pierce my flesh with nails» (Ps 118:120) for «a band of evildoers has encircled me» (Ps 22:17).

The second quotation follows the text of the LXX «pierce my flesh with your fear» against MT «my flesh trembles with your fear». Later, Irenaeus (*Demonstration of the apostolic teaching 79*) reproduces the same set of quotations, but as if it were a single quotation and already without being aware that it was a composite text:

> Free my soul from the sword and my body from the nails, for a band of evildoers has encircled me.

Another example of *testimonia* on the cross seems to have a Jewish origin:

> When one of you receives a bite, he should turn towards the serpent placed
> upon the *wood* (*xylon*) and wait, having faith that even without life it can
> give life and he will be saved (*Letter of Barnabas* 12:7).

It is a paraphrase of Nm 21:8-9; the reference to this text is achieved by means
of a slight change of the biblical text: the term «wood» (*xylon* = cross) replaces
the term «sign» (*semeion*) of the LXX, which in its turn alters the Hebrew term
«standard» (*nes*), agreeing with an interpretation already found in Sap 16:1-7
«symbol of salvation» (*symbolon soterias*). A new example associates the cross of
Christ with the figure of Moses with his arms outstretched, interceding for the
Israelites:

> The Spirit spoke to the heart of Moses, inspiring him to make the shape
> of the cross and of Him who had to suffer on it (*Letter of Barnabas* 1:2).

This combination is also found in the *Sibylline Oracles* (VIII 25-253) as well as
in Justin, Irenaeus, Tertullian and Cyprian.

Justin assembles various *testimonia* related to the tree in connection with the
cross: the tree of life in paradise; the rod of Moses which divides the Red Sea
and makes water gush in the desert; Jacob's stick; Aaron's rod which flowers;
the rod of Jesse; the oak of Mamre; the wood of the ark; Elisha's rod thrown
into the Jordan and retrieved from the water, etc.

The *Gospel of Peter* provides a passage in which «the Cross of glory» appears
in association with the glorification of Christ:

> And whilst they were relating what they had seen, they saw again three
> men come out from the sepulchre, and two of them sustaining the other,
> and a cross following them, and the heads of the two reaching to heaven,
> but that of him who was led of them by the hand overpassing the heavens.
> And they heard a voice out of the heavens crying, «Thou hast preached to
> them that sleep», and from the cross there was heard the answer, «Yea»
> (10:38-42).

Here are to be found together several basic themes of Jewish-Christian theology: the descent from the cross to hell, the ascension and the voice from
heaven. The cross which accompanies Christ to the heavens is the same one
which will go before him when he comes «from the East» in the Parousia. With
this idea was connected the custom of painting a cross on the East wall of
houses to pray towards the East seven times a day. Later this connection between the Cross and the East was forgotten and people start to paint or hang
a cross on any wall without bothering about the direction. The apparition of the
glorious cross is a common theme up to the 4th century. The most transcen-

dental act of this century could be the vision of the shining cross to the emperor Constantine on the Milvius Bridge in Rome.

In the same period were settled also the last and still unresolved questions in connection with the «canonical» nature of some of the biblical books. The Jewish apocryphal writings and the writings which then the (Jewish-)Christians began to spread remained absolutely excluded from the Jewish *canon* and so forbidden in rabbinic libraries. At the same time were initiated the compilations of the *legal* and *exegetical traditions*, which were to crystallise in the law code of the Mishnah and in the exegetical *corpus* of Midrashic literature.

Summarising, the manuscripts from Cave 1, and in a special way the second Isaiah scroll (1QIs$^a$) agree surprisingly well with the text which has reached us by means of manuscripts from the 9th-10th centuries CE. They confirm, therefore, the quality of textual transmission of the rabbinic Hebrew Bible. In contrast, the manuscripts from Cave 4, especially those of the book of Samuel (4QSam$^{abc}$) and the second of Jeremiah (4QJer$^b$) exhibit remarkable differences in respect of the masoretic text and provide important agreements with the text of the Greek translation of the LXX. They confirm, therefore, the value of the text of the Greek Bible of Christian tradition. Other manuscripts provide points of contact with the Samaritan Pentateuch or transmit text forms which are situated on the margins of the biblical tradition known through Jewish, Samaritan and Christian traditions.

The importance of the biblical manuscripts from Qumran is twofold: on the one hand, they confirm the antiquity of the textual traditions known previously and on the other hand they bear witness that in the centuries before the appearance of Christianity, the Old Testament was known in text forms more varied than the traditional and canonical sources which have reached us would allow us to suspect.

The process of fixing the text of the biblical books ran concurrently with the processes of establishing the canon of the Bible and of compiling a corpus of authorised legal and exegetical interpretations. Qumran exegesis, and especially the genre of eschatological interpretation called *pesher* and the anthological genre of the *testimonia* are clearly reflected in the exegesis of the New Testament, which uses these same methods and genres of interpretation.

Florentino García Martínez

During the «Madrid Qumran Congress» organised by the Department of Hebrew and Aramaic of the Universidad Complutense of Madrid, which took
place in the Escorial in March 1991[150], one of the topics most discussed was
that of «borderlines»: the borderline between «biblical text», and «biblical texts»
on one side, and on the other, the borderline between «biblical text» and «non-
biblical text». The debate is very far from being resolved. However, it is a very
important debate which, without any doubt at all, will determine the discussions of the next few years and will make itself heard in many publications.

My intention here is not to extend the discussions mentioned, nor, of course,
to resolve the serious problems which this debate poses for biblical research in
general. My purpose is much more modest: to present, in the simplest possible
way, the manuscript evidence which has given rise to the debate and to high-
light the most significant elements so that it is possible to understand the importance of the discussion in progress and form one's own opinion.

For this I will present some biblical and related material, more specifically:

– Some recently published biblical texts from Qumran (11QpaleoLev, 4Qpa-
leoEx$^m$ and 4QNum$^b$) which have altered the way we understand the development of the actual text of the Old Testament.

– A new text (4QRP = 4Q364-367) which is located at the borderline between
the biblical and the non-biblical.

– Some new texts which apparently are not biblical (4QprEsth$^{a,b,c,d,e,f}$ = 4QAra-
maic proto-Esther), but are important for the understanding of the only Old
Testament book of which not a single copy has been found in the Qumran
Library.

It is certain that our evidence concerning most of these phenomena is limited
to a single library, which belonged to the sectarians of Qumran. However, it
has to be considered that a large number of these biblical texts found in the
caves of the shore of the Dead Sea are earlier than the founding of the Qumran
Community in the middle of the second century B.C.E. Also, a large number
of them were not copied there but brought in from outside. It follows that the
general situation in the whole of Palestine cannot have been very different from
the situation we find reflected in the manuscripts, and that from the concrete
evidence preserved it is legitimate to draw more general conclusions of an historical nature.

## I Biblical Texts

We will begin, then, with a few manuscripts which affect the actual text of the
Old Testament[151].

Before the discovery of the manuscripts from Qumran (and thanks to the different versions known), the usual way of classifying the different types of biblical texts, presumed to have existed prior to the fixing of the text known as the Masoretic Text and to its later canonization, was made up of the famous trilogy of text types: Masoretic Text, the LXX and the Samaritan Text. Each one of these text types would have been the product of a gradual development through the different recensions, with additions and modifications intended to adapt the different texts to the standard of the Temple. In time, these three text types would have been transformed into the respective bibles of the Jewish, Christian and Samaritan religions.

The first publications in the fifties and sixties of biblical texts which came from the caves of Qumran had already revolutionised the discipline of textual criticism, but fundamentally, had not altered this view. Now, for the first time, we were in possession of Hebrew manuscripts from the 3rd or 2nd century BCE. This means, they were earlier than the fixing and canonizing of the known biblical text, so reducing our dependence on the great mediaeval codices of a thousand years later. In addition, it was no longer necessary to postulate the form of Hebrew text underlying the Greek translation, since texts such as 4QJeremiah[b152] provide us with the same Hebrew text as the LXX present us with in this book. It is shorter than the Masoretic Text and with a different sequence of verses and chapters. But the textual diversity which these manuscripts reflect could go back to the same basic trilogy and the new texts could be grouped into proto-Masoretic, proto-Septuagintal or proto-Samaritan. Or, to use the terminology of the theory of «local texts» (which was made famous by F. M. Cross and dominated textual criticism for the last twenty years[153]): Babylonian, Egyptian or Palestinian texts respectively, depending on which of the readings common to one of the three textual traditions were predominant. With the development of the three textual types by means of recensions to approach the standard of the Temple were contrasted three textual types with their own characteristics developed autonomously in different localities (or by different communities[154]) and without contact with each other.

But this way of understanding the evolution of the biblical text has been radically altered by the publication of 11QpaleoLev[a] (a relatively complete manuscript of the book of Leviticus copied in palaeo-Hebrew characters) in 1985[155], by the study of 4QpaleoEx[m] (a manuscript of the same length and also copied in palaeo-Hebrew characters), which appeared in 1985[156], and by the description and part publication in 1991 of 4QNum[b157].

11QpaleoLev[a] has proved that it is impossible to reduce the textual diversity found at Qumran to the three textual types mentioned. The text of the book of Leviticus contained in our manuscript agrees in part with the Masoretic Text, in part with the LXX and in part with the Samaritan Pentateuch. However, it also contains many readings of its own which are not found in any of the three traditions and these force us to consider it as a separate and independent text[158]. The publication of this text has made the hermeneutic value of the theory of local texts relative, since this text, which (according to the theory) ought to belong to «the Palestinian family» does not exhibit the characteristics typical of this «family», but instead is found to be closer to the Masoretic Text than to the Samaritan Pentateuch.

Instead of making the task of biblical research simpler, the unexpected wealth and the textual diversity implied by the manuscript have made it even more complex. Broadly speaking, the publication of 11QpaleoLev[a] seems to force us to acknowledge that in Palestine, between the 3rd century B.C.E. and the 1st century CE, there did not exist one biblical «text» but a multiplicity of different biblical «texts». Of these, due to the chances of transmission, only a part has reached us. This is the conclusion reached by Tov. Against the theories of local texts or of the sociological support of the three textual types he proposed his own theory of the multiplicity of texts[159]. Against current hermeneutical theories, Tov raised clearly the problem of «text» *versus* «texts» and ended by radically diluting the organic relationships among the different manuscripts, dissolving the very concept of textual type and reducing the manuscript evidence to a forest of texts, a plurality of witnesses not to one biblical «text» but to different biblical «texts»[160].

The consequences drawn from the publication of the second of the texts mentioned, 4QpaleoExod[m], are just as important. This fairly complete manuscript of the Book of Exodus (copied at Qumran in the first half of the 1st century BC) shows all the typological features characteristic of the Samaritan Pentateuch, such as additions derived from other parts of the Book of Exodus or Deuteronomy, or typical expansions, with the sole exception of the single truly sectarian addition: the precept of worship on Mount Garizim, which is why 4QpaleoExod[m] exhibits no sectarian character.

Its publication has made relative the general validity of Tov's conclusions about almost unlimited textual diversity. Unlike 11QpaleoLev[a], 4QpaleoExod[m] is not an independent text, but a text which in spite of having its own readings, clearly fits within the Samaritan textual type. This not only justifies the use of «text type» as an element of classification, but even allows the notion of an original *Urtext* for this biblical book to be defended[161]. It is even more evident that it has dealt a severe blow to the theory of sociological support of Talmon's textual types, since this text clearly shows us that there was no difference at all either of nature or of method between the sectarian addition of the Samaritan Pentateuch (the precept concerning worship on Mount Gerizim) and all the other additions common to the Samaritan Pentateuch and to 4QpaleoEx[m]. This clearly means that the Samaritan community, before its constitution as a sectarian group, used a biblical text of the same expansionist type as other groups of the period.

On the other hand, this text, of which the textual type seems to be clearly defined, suggests to us that behind the apparent textual multiplicity lie hidden two different attitudes towards the biblical text. One is a freer attitude, in which modern spelling, the contextual and grammatical changes, the alteration of sections of text under the influence of parallel passages, the various expansions and harmonisations, and even the very transformations of the text through the influence of a specific exegesis, are permitted. There is also an attitude which is more conservative and in which these same phenomena (which are present as well) are found on a reduced scale.

4QpaleoExod$^m$ seems to prove to us that the textual tradition underlying the Masoretic Text, the Samaritan Pentateuch and 4QpaleoExod$^m$ continued to develop during a certain period after the separation from the common stem of the ancestor of the Greek translation. The tradition underlying the Masoretic Text then entered a period of transmission of a conservative nature, while the tradition underlying the Qumranic text and the Samaritan text continued to incorporate a series of expansions. Finally, the Samaritan tradition entered a period of conservative transmission similar to that of the Masoretic Text, once it had received the «sectarian» addition of the precept concerning worship on Mount Gerizim. The interesting thing about 4QpaleoExod$^m$ is the proof it provides that, whereas in the Samaritan community the free attitude towards the biblical text leads to the constitution of the group as a sect, in Qumran, the same free attitude co-existed, without obvious difficulties, with the conservative attitude revealed by other biblical manuscripts found there. This forces us to pose afresh the problem of the *status* and the authority of a specific text within a specific community. In other words, the problem of the canon and the related problem of inspiration.

No less interesting are the problems posed by the third text mentioned: 4QNum$^b$. This manuscript, which has preserved for us about 10% of the total words of the Hebrew text, is typologically related to 4QpaleoExod$^m$ and to the Samaritan Pentateuch, and belongs to the same textual family. The manuscript displays a certain number of original readings supporting the longer text of the LXX. It also has a much larger number of secondary readings (the interpolations from Deuteronomy inserted into Numbers, which the manuscript shares with the Samaritan Pentateuch, showing that these interpolations were typical of a Palestinian textual tradition and are not to be attributed to the Samaritan tradition), and a high number of unique readings. However, the most interesting element it provides is an interpolation of 12 lines in the last column of the manuscript. In essence, it comprises the addition of 27:2-11 after 36:2. This interpolation proves that the process of growth of the text represented by 4QpaleoExod$^m$, and in a more advanced form by the Samaritan Pentateuch, continued up to the Herodian period, a date to which 4QNum$^b$ can be assigned. This implies that the liberal attitude towards the biblical text which these texts represent co-existed within the Qumran community with other more conservative attitudes reflected in other manuscripts during a very long period.

The combined and conflicting evidence of these new texts has made it clear that the three theories referred to, which struggle for supremacy in the field of textual criticism after the discoveries at Qumran, are not enough to give a complete explanation for all the phenomena that these texts present. Each one of these three theories focuses on one aspect of the problem, without being able to provide a global explanation. Cross's theory (the theory of local texts) clarifies the problem of the origins of the various textual types, but it is unable to explain that in a particular place such as the Qumran library, different textual groups co-exist, apparently with the same status and the same authority. Talmon's theory (the theory of the sociological origin of the three textual groups) explains the final result of the three textual types as the Bibles of the Jewish, Christian and Samaritan groups. However, not only is it incapable of bringing proofs that the different groups intentionally altered the text to achieve this result, it even conflicts with the evidence provided by 4QNum$^b$ and 4Qpaleo-Exod$^m$. Tov's theory (the theory of multiplicity of texts) can throw light on the process. However, although it accepts that certain texts from Qumran can be classified as Samaritan in type, it forgets that the great majority of the texts found reflect the Palestinian textual tradition. Also, it minimises the importance of the textual types and gives too much weight to spelling as a determinative factor.

If the new texts have still not provided an overall theory allowing the problem of «text» versus «texts» to be resolved, at least they have enabled us to pose the problem clearly. They have also revealed that even within the history of the biblical text there is a large area which is still *terra incognita*. These new texts, at least, have made it very clear that we must separate the contributions they can provide for an understanding of the history of the biblical text, from the contributions they make through the patient and tiring work of textual criticism[162]. The unique and ideological variants which they help recover must be placed in their cultural and historical context so that they can allow us to recover the different biblical «texts» and compare them with each other. The common variants will enable us, perhaps, to trace the lines of the different recensions to arrive at *one* «text», in spite of the diversity of «texts».

## 11 Borderline Texts

Some of the «biblical» manuscripts which come from Qumran present us with a sequence of pericopes which differs from what we know through the Masoretic Text or the Greek versions. Thus, 4QDeut$^j$, a manuscript which contains remains of chapters 5, 6, 8, 11 and 32 of Deuteronomy, together with parts of chapters 12-13 of Exodus, was edited as a «biblical» manuscript by J. Duncan[163]. Now, however, it is interpreted by the same editor as a «non-biblical» text, a text with extracts from biblical quotations intended for liturgical or devotional use, perhaps for grace after meals[164]. Or, 4QDeut$^n$, a manuscript which contains Deut 8:5-10, 5:1-6:21 and a harmonizing form of the decalogue, in that order. It, too was published as a «biblical» manuscript by S. A. White[165], and is now interpreted by its own editor as a text with extracts from biblical quotations intended to be used for devotional purposes or for study[166].

Other «non-biblical» Qumran manuscripts published over the last ten years (such as the *Temple Scroll* [11Q19][167]) or which are appearing now (such as *Psalms of Joshua* [4Q378-379][168], *Second Ezekiel* [4Q385-390][169] or the *Pseudo-Moses* [4Q375-376][170]) have shown us that the borderlines between what in Qumran was considered as «biblical» text and what was seen as «interpretation» of the biblical text were much more fluid than we had dared to imagine.

But in Qumran there had also appeared another series of texts, the character of which was not easy to determine[171] – for example, 4QFlorilegium [4Q174], 4QTestimonia [4Q175], 4QCatena$^a$ [4Q177], and especially 4Q154, «Biblical Paraphrase», now considered by Tov as another copy of the same work represented by 4Q364-367 – since in some way they are situated between the two types of texts mentioned. On the one hand they are basically made up of biblical quotations and could be considered «biblical» texts. On the other hand, these biblical quotations are not in the sequence of the Masoretic Text, and they also include some other elements of which the «interpretative» character seems clear.

The text we are going to deal with, contained in manuscripts 4Q364-367 and given the siglum 4QRP[172] [= 4QR(ewritten) P(entateuch)] combines all these problems in one. It seems to offer us a large part of the Pentateuch, although in a different sequence from that of the Masoretic Text, together with biblical «interpretations» and other previously unknown texts. Inevitably, 4QRP confronts us with the problem of «borderlines» at the level of the biblical text, since it is not easy to determine whether it is a more or less unconventional biblical text or a composition closely related to the biblical text but not possessing the character of «Scripture». 4QRP thus confronts us in the most searching way with the problem of setting the borderlines between the «biblical» and the «non-biblical», between «text» and «paraphrase».

This text from Cave 4, which forms part of J. Strugnell's lot, has not yet been published in full. Some photographs, however, have appeared in Y. Yadin's *editio princeps* of the *Temple Scroll*[173], and a few years ago I myself made public a description of its contents provided by J. Strugnell[174]. Now, though, we have available a fairly detailed description of each of the manuscripts in which the work is preserved, of their inter-relationships and of the nature of the work preserved in them, given by E. Tov during the Madrid Congress and published in the proceedings of the Congress[175].

Four or five copies of 4QRP have been preserved, though not all of the same length. The two longest manuscripts are 4Q364 and 4Q365. 4Q364 contains remains of chapters 2 and 25-48 of Genesis, chapters 16-26 of Exodus, chapters 14 and 33 of Numbers and numerous remains of Deuteronomy 1-14. 4Q365 has only provided a single fragment of Genesis (chapter 21), but contains numerous remains of Exodus 8-38, Leviticus 11-26, Numbers 1-38 and two fragments of Deuteronomy (chapters 2 and 19). The remains of the other manuscripts are more meagre: 4Q366 offers only one fragment of Exodus (chapters 21-22) together with remains of Numbers 29 and of Deuteronomy 14 and 16, and 4Q367 has only preserved for us remains of Leviticus (chapters 12, 15, 19, 23 and 27). Together with this biblical material 4QRP also contains other elements, both short and long, not attested in any other strictly biblical manuscript. A large part of these additions, though, does not differ either in length or in type from the expansions characteristic of proto-Samaritan type manuscripts.

For Tov, 4QRP is characterised by combining the biblical text with exegetical commentaries, by presenting the biblical text in a different order from usual and by freely adding or omitting various sections of different lengths. Tov describes the work as a «re-writing of the biblical text» whose exegetical intent appears in the juxtaposition of certain biblical texts which are not found together in the original. It is similar in many ways to the *Temple Scroll*, a work with which 4QRP has certain elements in common, such as adding exegetical commentaries and re-arranging the text in accordance with its own principles. In other words, for him there is no doubt that it is a text which is not strictly biblical (as shown by the title he has given the work: «Re-written Pentateuch» or «Paraphrase of the Pentatetuch»). So convinced is he of this, that he goes so far as to separate the longest and most typical «non-biblical» sections from 4QRP, fragments 25 and 28 of 4Q365, to make out of them another copy of the *Temple Scroll*. This copy of the *Temple Scroll*, in fact, would have been made by the same scribe who wrote 4QRP (and on the same scroll).

However, this decision by Tov seems incomprehensible to me in view of the description he himself gives of the work. The only argument that Tov puts forward is that of content (these two additions correspond to 11QTemple) and length (these additions are longer than the rest), arguments which it is hard to consider as convincing. They also leave unexplained the statement by the co-editor of the text, White[176]: «This material is not the only parallel our manuscript has with the Temple Scroll. In four fairly large fragments 4Q365 contains material concerning festivals and the architecture of the temple, which is very similar to that same material in the Temple Scroll».

In her lecture, White indicated some of the lesser additions within familiar passages of the biblical text (such as the addition to Genesiis 28:6 of 4Q364) but she concentrated on the large blocks of additional text, with no biblical parallel. She presented their contents, to be found in various fragments of 4Q365: fragment 7 (the beginning of the canticle of Moses, added to Exodus 15:16-20), fragment 6 II (a non-biblical hymn followed by Exodus 15:22-26), fragment 25 (Leviticus 23:42-24:2, plus new halakhic material concerning the feast of oil and wood) and fragment 28 II (with the names of the gates of the outer courtyard of the Temple). Unlike Tov, White considers all these additions to the biblical text as part of the same work, a composition which must have been one of the sources used by the author of the *Temple Scroll*.

As for the textual character of 4QRP, Tov concludes that 4Q364 shows clear affinities with the text type known as proto-Samaritan and represented by manuscripts such as 4QpaleoExod$^m$, 4QNum$^b$, 4QDeut$^n$ or 4QTestimonia. He also concludes that 4Q158, too, is very close to this text type. The evidence preserved in the other manuscripts is not conclusive, but it would be compatible with this assessment, especially in the case of 4Q365.

While the texts have not yet been published in full, the precise definition of their «biblical» or «non-biblical» character is an impossible task. However, their mere existence and the difficulties encountered by the editors in classifying them as «biblical» or «non-biblical» shows us the extent of the problem and its interest for a better knowledge of the history of the Old Testament text.

### III  An Aramaic Proto-Esther?

These problems of «borderlines» are raised to their highest index by the last of the texts I wish to present. Everything seems to indicate that we have before us a composition (a novel or tale about exiled Jews in the Persian court) the relationship of which to the biblical «text» seems, at best, marginal or accidental. And yet (even though the interpretation which the editor proposes is not accepted) its contributions to our knowledge of the «history of the text» (or of its «pre-history») are of immeasurable value.

In the *Mémorial Jean Starcky*, J. T. Milik edited for the first time a series of Aramaic texts from Starcky's lot, known since 1955 as «the remains of a pseudo-historical text located in the Persian period which recalls Esther or Daniel»[177]. It consists of seven different manuscripts containing, in the words of the editor, Milik, «"the models", "the archetypes", "the sources" of the versions of the book of Esther preserved in Hebrew, Greek, Latin (and even a passage in Armenian)»[178]. These seven manuscripts come from three different works in which the plot we know from the book of Esther gradually unfolds[179].

The first work is attested in three different copies according to Milik[180], although only a fragment of each copy has been preserved, manuscripts which he labels 4Qpr(oto-)Esth(er) ar(améen)$^{a,b,c}$ respectively. The second work, preserved in the fourth manuscript, 4QprEsthar$^d$, is represented by a single copy, of which at least the remains of three different columns have reached us. Milik considers the two tiny fragments which he labels 4QprEsthar$^e$ as one of the two witnesses (together with 4QprEsthar^f) of the third work, although he accepts that «the writing of the two fragments of the manuscript *e* is similar to that of manuscript *d*, but the hand seems to be different». The published plates do not allow this statement by the editor either to be contradicted or accepted, but the material which these two fragments provide contributes nothing new to what the other manuscripts reveal to us, so I do not think it necessary to persist with them.

The content of the other witness of this supposed third work (4QprEsthar^f) is very different from the rest. Of this copy only a fragment has been preserved, with remains of three lines. Apparently, these come from the end of the work and have some very pronounced and apocalyptic echoes, very different from those of the other fragments and without the onomastic indications which would allow one to state that the content is the same. Therefore, the very existence of this third composition does not seem very certain and the labelling of this fragment as «proto-Esther» is rather problematic. Accordingly, here I will restrict myself to presenting only the fragments of the first two compositions in which Milik finds the sources and antecedents of the canonical book of Esther.

Of this book (which in the two extant Greek versions differs considerably from the Hebrew text) absolutely nothing has been found among the mass of biblical manuscripts which come from the various caves. The explanations which have been suggested are very varied, but the fact itself (which by no means could be purely by chance) does not cease to be significant. Accordingly, the publication of these Aramaic fragments is itself particularly important. Their publication would be even more important if Milik's interpretation is accepted. He sees a genetic relationship between these Aramaic fragments and the canonical book of Esther. And he explains its absence from the Qumran library as due to the Hebrew book not yet existing in the period when the manuscripts were deposited in the Qumran caves, since it was only translated from Greek after the disaster of the war with Rome[181].

The principal portions preserved of the various manuscripts can be translated as follows[182]:

4QProto Esther^a (4QprEsthar^a)

> *1* [and they ob]eyed your father Patireza [...] *2* and among the attendants of the royal wardrobe [...] performing *3* the service of the King according to all that [...] ... At that time *4* the lengthening of the King's spirit... [...] the books of his father were to be read in front of him; and among *5* the books was found a scroll [sealed with] seven seals of the ring of Darius, his father. The matter *6* [...] ... [... of Da]rius the King to the attendants of the Empire of the whole earth, peace». I read the beginning and found writ-

ten in it: «Darius the King ₇ [...] will rule after me and the attendants of the Empire, peace. Know that every tyrant and deceitful person [...] (DSST, 291).

In spite of its fragmentary nature it is possible to follow the general sequence of the story related. In this fragment, which comes from the last column of a leaf, probably the first of the scroll, we are introduced to the person called Patireza, son of an official in charge of the royal wardrobe, who must have served at some time during the reign of Darius. Then comes the theme of the king who, because of his insomnia, has the royal annals read to him. From among them there emerges a document sealed with his father's seal of which only the beginning has not been preserved.

However. the final words allow the supposition that the story told serves as a model, since it states that no tyrant or deceitful person will remain without his deserved punishment. The following fragment, which comes from another manuscript, but, as shown by the names of the characters, belongs to the same composition, enables us to understand better what it is about.

4QProto Esther^b (4QprEsthar^b)

> ₁ a man; but the King knows whether there is [...] ₂ and his good name will not pass away, and his loyalty [...] ₃ of the King will be for Patireza, son of Ya'[ir...] ₄ there fell upon him the dread of the house of Safra [...] ₅ herald of the King. May it be said and it will be given [...] ₆ from my house and from my belongings and all that which [...] ₇ be measured; and you shall receive your father's service [...] (DSST, 291).

The text is even more fragmentary than the previous one[183], but here too we can follow the thread of the story. Patireza's father has done something which deserves a reward fom the king, as is evident from Darius' document, but this reward has not been granted to him. Instead, upon him has fallen the wrath of the «house of Safra», an expression which seems to refer to Patireza's sufferings under a clan or rival official. The result of reading these deeds is clear: the king orders Patireza's son to be given all that his father promised, to be installed in the office which his father held and even new gifts to be added from the king's wealth.

These two fragments present us with a clear and well known narrative frame in broad agreement with the narrative which provides the setting for the biblical story of Esther and Mordecai.

The next fragment describes a conflict in which a new female character appears in the story for the first time. She is «the princess», or «Sarah», if the traces of the letter preserved in the margin are understood as a correction, who together with her daughters is punished by banishment. From the subsequent mention of Hama, the second in the kingdom, it can be concluded that the punishment to fall on them forms part of the punishment which he receives and with which Patireza's reward is contrasted. The text can be translated as follows[184]:

4QProto Esther[c] (4QprEsthar[c])

> *1* [...] herald of the King. He must say to the princess [...] bani[shed ...] *2* [...] Patireza [your] father, of Hama who rose above the attendants of the [kingdom] before the King [...] *3* [...] he served with justice and with [...] before her [...] *4* [...] and the herald said [...] *5* [...] the purp[le ...] *6* [...] ... [...] (DSST, 291).

Although (according to Milik) they come from different manuscripts, these three fragments represent remains of the same work, as the identity of the characters named proves[185]. The following fragments all come from the same scroll, a tiny manuscript with only seven or eight lines of text per column. The story told there runs parallel to what is narrated in the fragments set out above[186], although the names given to the characters are obviously different. The rivals in this case are Bagashro, the «prophet of God» and Bagoshe, who will be punished, stripped of his possessions and executed. The remains of three columns have been preserved, one of which seems to contain the ending of the work. The first is the longest and in some ways the most interesting. Its heroine is obviously feminine and she presents the enmity between the two officials in the royal court in terms of ethnic conflict: Jews against Samaritans. The text is as follows[187]:

4QprEsthar[d] I

> *1* Look, you know [...] and for the failings of my fathers *2* who had sinned before you, and [...] peaceful [...] and left [... of his at]tendants, a *3* Jew, from the chiefs of Benjam[in...] one of the diaspora, stands up for an accusation and wishes [... a] good divi[ner], *4* a good man, [...] attendant. What can I do for you? You know [...] possible *5* to a Kutean man the return [...] of your kingdom, rising after you rise [...] *6* However, what you wish command it of me and when you die I will bury you in [...] *7* ravaging (?) everything. Is it possible that the rise of my service means [...] all that [...] (DSST, 291).

The next fragment, which is difficult to understand (according to Milik it is an account of a vision by a Jewish prophet), apparently assumes an alternation of good and bad periods, portrayed as the alternating flow of black and white or luminous water. The same theme recurs in the Syriac apocalypse of Baruch (chaps. 53-76) where the different periods of world history are symbolised by luminous and dark waters which alternate. In the fragment, this alternation seems to represent the different fates of the two heroes. The text can be translated as follows[188]:

4QprEsthar[d] II

*1* [...] the decision of [...And] the second ones will pass [...] *2* [..the plagues and the third ones will pa[ss..] in the [royal] wardrobe [...] *3* [...] the crown of g[old upon his h]ead, And five years will pass [...] *4* [...] alone and [... and the sixth] ones will pass, bl[ack] *5* [...] all silver and all gold and all the wea]lth which belongs to Bagoshe, doubled, [...] *6* and the seve[nth ones will pass...Th]en Bagashro entered in peace into the court of the King [...] *7* Bagosh[e retur]ned to [...] his judgment was judged [and the verdict] announced and he was executed. Then Bagashro entered the sev[enth] court of the King [...] 8 And he took his hand [...] on his head [...] and hugged him, answering him and saying: «In [...] Bagashro of [...] (DSST, 292).

The next fragment apparently contains the end of the work[189]. It includes the prescriptions for maintaining the royal decision, a written record of the deeds and suggestions to future readers. Ultimately, what this colophon deals with is not only a conflict between two groups but the meteoric rise of a «Jewish prophet» within the Persian court.

4QprEsthar[d] III

*1* [...] the Most High whom you revere and venerate, is the one who governs [the whole] earth. All that one who approaches should wish [...] *2* [...] every man who utters a bad word against Bagashro [...] will be killed, because he has nothing [...] *3* [...] a barrier for ever. [...all] that he had seen in the two [...]. And the King said to him: «Wri[te... ] *4* [...] Emp[ire...] they in the inner courtyard of the royal palace [...] *5* [...] they shall rise after Bagashro, the readers of this written text [...] *6* [..ev]il, evil has returned against his [head...] 7 [... his desce]ndants. *Blank* (DSST, 292).

From this simple translation with some commentary we can draw some conclusions, more restrained than those drawn by Milik, but no less important for that. For Milik it is clear that these Aramaic «sources» are at the origin of the later book of Esther, and he even reconstructs the name Esther in one of the manuscripts. Milik also identifies the patronymic of Mordechai and sees in the mention of the Cuthaean (Samaritan) the original from which through various transformations the name Bagoas would later be reached. Starting from this direct and genetic relationship between the Aramaic models and from the transformations of these models which he discovers in the Greek versions and in the *Vetus Latina*, Milik concludes that the Hebrew text we know not only represents a later stage of the literary tradition but is also dependent on the Greek text from which it was translated.

In my view, another interpretative model is possible without the need for a genetic relationship among the different versions. It seems certain that the Aramaic work (or works) have preserved for us a version in which the narrative frame and the two typical motifs we find in Esther are already present. One is the motif of the official whose action has not been rewarded and later is, with interest. The other is the motif of the rivalry and fight between two courtiers, a fight for influence and power, which the King resolves in favour of one of them with disastrous results for the other. The motif is interpreted as code for the rivalry between collective groups (Jews–Samaritans) and with a clear religious slant. But the presence of these literary motifs (which make up the story of the book of Esther, together with that of the beauty contest which hardly appears in our fragments) does not require a genetic continuity between the different traditions. The Aramaic model (or models) (with real characters who prove to us that, in spite of being works of the same literary type, the two Aramaic compositions are in fact different works) could have been «Estherised» already within what we know through the different Greek versions. This process could then have been continued until it reached its present form in the Hebrew text. Or else, these motifs of popular folklore could have been «Estherised» from the start by the redactor of the book of Esther, and extended and modified later by those responsible for the Greek versions, etc. The parallel of the *Sayings* or the *Wisdom of Ahiqar*[190] is very illuminating in this regard. It underwent transformations in the different forms, in which the original nucleus has been preserved for us in the different versions, right up to the references to Ahiqar in the book of Tobit.

However, ultimately, these discussions are not too important. What is important is the recovery of some lost works and their undoubted relationships, as literary works, with the Esther narrative which has reached us in different forms. These forms are the Hebrew text of Esther, and the different forms of the Greek text of the same work and in the *Vetus Latina*. The *Vetus Latina* is an exceptional witness when it comes to recovering the ancestors of development and transmission of the literary complex of which the oldest representative we now have, in part, is in Aramaic.

However, the most important thing, in the face of the problem we are now confronting is the very existence of these «models» or «sources» of a work which ended up being «biblical» and in a period undoubtedly earlier than that of the writing down of this «biblical text». Seen this way, for us the «additions» of the Greek versions of the Book of Esther pose a problem of definition very like that of 4QRP. It is the problem of «borderlines» between the «biblical» and the «non-biblical», between «text» and «paraphrase». The recovery of these Aramaic «models» or «sources» of the book of Esther gives the problem a new dimension: the organic growth of a literary text. With them we are very far from the problems of «authority» or «canon», but we are located right inside this organic fabric of traditions which emerge as «texts» and end up being «bible». The route between these stories about Jews in the Persian court and the «biblical text» of Esther is, of course, very long. And on this journey many things happen: changes of characters, insertion of new motifs, re-arrangement of the narrative to glorify a liberation which is perpetuated in a liturgical feast, etc. These new Aramaic texts, however, are prime illustrations of how the texts which come from the Qumran scriptorium have forced us to be aware of the problems of the «borderlines» of «the biblical». In this case it is not a matter of the borderline between «text and texts» or between «text» and «paraphrase». Instead it is the «borderline» as insecure and movable as in the other cases in which a developing text appears to us in a phase of its development when it is «not yet» or «no longer» a biblical text.

## IV  The Problems

At the start I indicated that my intention was simply to present part of the manuscript evidence which gave rise of the debate about «biblical borderlines». The facts are there. The hermeneutical framework into which these facts are finally fitted is still inexact and does not allow an overall and satisfactory explanation. What these facts allow us right now is to have a clear awareness of the problems.

First of all, these manuscripts clearly pose the problem of «text or texts». In short, thanks to these manuscripts from Qumran, we are only now beginning to understand that the *hebraica veritas*, which caused so much ink to flow in the period of St Jerome or so much blood during the Reformation, is simply the imposition of the «biblical text» of the Pharisees after the destruction of the Temple. They were the only group within Judaism with enough influence to impose their «text» and to them we owe our Hebrew bibles.

Closely connected to this problem of «text or texts», the new facts present us with the problem of explaining the position of the biblical text within the Qumran community, a problem of «authority», or if you like, of «canon». Only now are we beginning to understand how inadequate it is to transpose an obviously later concept to a phase before the evolution of the text. Or how this concept cannot be applied to a situation of harmonious co-existence of different text types over a long period. Or how our categories of classification turn out to be inadequate for texts still in a state of flux.

No less forcefully, they present us with the problem of defining the borderlines between the «biblical» and the «non-biblical». It has been amply shown that in the period to which the manuscripts belong, in some areas at least, the biblical text or one of its forms, tolerated a significant process of expansion without losing its character as biblical text. 4QNum$^b$ is a suitable example. The problem lies in determining the limits of tolerance. What criteria can we apply to decide whether a particular manuscript with expansions or additions is still biblical? No-one doubts that the Greek text of Samuel or Jeremiah is a «biblical» text. However, if these texts had not been preserved for us by Christian tradition and we were now faced with the underlying Hebrew originals, would we describe them as «biblical» texts? Or would we include the corresponding masoretic text in the «paraphrase» section?

Something similar happens with the sequence of pericopes. What are the limits of tolerance for determining whether a manuscript in which texts are «combined» or in a different sequence is «biblical» or not? The change of siglum of 4QDeut$^n$ and of 4QDeut$^j$ is indicative of the uncertainties which still exist. From biblical manuscripts they were reclassified as manuscripts with extracts of biblical quotations for purposes of study or devotion. 4QRP combines biblical texts in a different order from our Bibles and also includes additions of considerable length not found in any other «biblical» text. It presents us, then, with both problems in a new light and will force us to look for solutions.

In the Catholic world, heir to both the Hebrew and Greek biblical tradition, no-one would hesitate in assigning the character of «biblical text» either to the Hebrew text of Esther or to the texts of both Greek versions, in spite of their great differences and of their reflecting different stages in the development of the same work. The new Aramaic fragments of these compositions are labelled «proto-Esther» by their editor. Within the Qumran community they could have had a position similar to the one which *Megillat Esther* gained in Palestinian Judaism or which the book of Esther achieved in Alexandrian Judaism. These fragments clearly present us with the problem of the growth of a narrative and of determining when it is «biblical text» and when it is «not yet» or is so «no longer».

And so as not to end by simply indicating a calendar of pending problems, I wish to close with an undisputed statement and with a well-founded hope. Forty years after the first discoveries of the Qumran manuscripts, the contribution of these texts for understanding the history and evolution of the text of the Old Testament is very far from being exhausted. The fruits gathered are already many and valid. However, the harvest is not yet complete. These fruits have provided the initiative which has allowed the problem of «borderlines» to be posed with clarity. This initiative, however, is far from being finished. And from it will emerge also the hermeneutical frame which allows us to incorporate this mass of data into a better understanding of the «biblical text» and of its long history.

The Problem of Purity: The Qumran Solution[191]

Florentino García Martínez

In the preface to the published volume of his *Haskell Lecture* of 1973, J. Neusner relates how, during a series of lectures given in Europe in 1971, he found, to his great surprise, that «In all, it seemed that everyone I know was talking about purity»[192]. In the same preface Neusner notes that Y. Yadin was completing the preparation of the publication of the *Temple Scroll* and that J. Strugnell had shown him as yet unpublished fragments from Cave 4 related to the regulations of purity. He notes that both texts could alter the description he was going to give in his book of the conceptions about purity in the Qumran Community. Twenty years later, the *Temple Scroll* has been published definitively[193] and there is an extensive description of the *Halakhic Letter* of Strugnell's allocation to which Neusner seems to refer[194]. However, of the widespread interest concerning the problem of purity few traces appear to remain. A perusal of the bibliographies or of the lists of papers to congresses or symposia does not allow the conclusion that it is one of the trendy topics. It does not even allow one to state that this problem is seen as an important problem, much less as a problem central to the understanding of the Qumran Community, of phariseeism or of early Christianity.

And yet, I am convinced that the problem of purity comprises one of the central problems of the Jewish and Christian world from the 2nd century BCE to the 2nd century CE. It provides an important key for understanding the process of self-definition of the various Jewish groups of the Second Temple period, including the early Christian community. Further, in respect of the early Christian community, without understanding the problem of purity, it is not possible to understand the process of Christian self-awareness which was to culminate in overcoming the problem of purity by means of their own solutions. Nor is it possible to understand the persistence within certain Jewish-Christian groups in later centuries of a problem already solved in theory, unless the variety of solutions to the problem provided within certain Jewish groups is taken into account.

The solutions given to the problem of purity by rabbinic Judaism have been extensively studied in the 22 volumes by J. Neusner on the history of the regulations of purity[195]. Neusner has also studied the Pharisee positions prior to 70 CE, and has given us a synthesis in his *The Idea of Purity in Ancient Judaism*, mentioned already.

Nor is there any lack of studies of the Christian solutions. The positions which the gospels attribute to Jesus himself, Paul's expressions on the subject, its importance in the controversies between the Jewish-Christians and the Gentile Christians or even between the Apostles as reflected in the Acts of the

Apostles–all these have given rise to abundant literature[196]. Accordingly, there is no need to concern ourselves with them again.

Here I shall concentrate on one of the groups for whom the problem of purity became a central problem, a problem which determined their self-awareness and their separation from the rest of Judaism[197]: the group we know as the Qumran Community.

There is no need for us to spend time here in presenting the actual problem since Paolo Sacchi has already done so, in masterly fashion. He has studied the development of ideas concerning impure/pure and their relationship with the concept of sacred/profane in ancient Israel and in the post-exilic period[198]. The only matter, perhaps, which needs to be justified is the decision not to include in that study the positions of the Essene movement from which the Qumran group stems. The same applies to the solutions of apocalyptic tradition in which the Essene movement is rooted[199]. Recently an excellent study has been published of the information which Flavius Josephus transmits concerning the purifications of the Essenes[200]. Apart from that, the decision to concentrate our study on the specifically Qumran group comes from the conviction that in the Jewish world the problem of purity worsened as a result of the antiochene crisis during the Maccabaean period. This is the period in which Josephus locates the origins of the various sects and their re-interpretation of the regulations of purity[201]. This is the period in which the disputes between the Pharisees and the Sadducees took place concerning the regulation of purity recorded in later Rabbinic tradition[202]. This is the period in which the writings of the formative stage of Qumran Community were drawn up, when, as we shall see, the problem of purity was a central element. The traumatic experience of the desecration of the Temple, around which the system of purity had been centred, must undoubtedly have acted as a powerful reagent. In fact, the re-dedication of the Temple by Judas Maccabaeus is presented primarily as a purification of the Temple. The Maccabaean conquests of the various cities are also presented as a purification of the land. (1 Mc 13:48 ends the account of Simon's capture of Gaza as follows: «He removed every impurity from it and settled men in it who would keep the Law»). Further, only this renewed concern for purity, which began with the traumatic experience of the profanation of the Temple, explains (beyond military necessity) Maccabaean policy and its radicalism which supposes forced Judaisation of the vanquished peoples in the estates annexed by the Hasmonaean kings. Judas and Simon would confine themselves to transporting the Jewish population of Galad and Galilee to Jerusalem. Hyrcanus was to impose compulsory Judaisation on Idumaea, and Aristobulos I was to do the same to Galilee. Jannaeus did the same to several of the cities of the Decapolis, of Galad and of the Traconitis. They were all following a policy for which not only is it impossible to find a basis in scripture, it even contradicts the very principle of Yahwism as «the particular religion and the peculiar possession of the chosen people»[203].

Both M. Smith and J. Neusner have emphasised the importance of the problem of purity in the development of Jewish sectarianism[204]. The study of the solution given to the problem between the Maccabaean revolt and the destruction of the Temple within the Qumran group will show the width and depth of the problem in the religious consciousness of the period and its centrality in «Israel in search of her identity». The Qumran solution to the problem of purity will enable us to understand better several matters: the novelty of the solution which the Jesus of the gospels provides; the theological foundation with which Paul endows the Christian solution; and even the persistence of strong tensions in the early Christian community owing to this problem, tensions which were to continue tearing apart the Jewish-Christian sects of the centuries that followed[205].

My method consists in analyzing separately the various Qumran writings in which the problem of purity comes to the fore. This is in order to try to determine the development of thought and the theological system which, eventually, would end by distinguishing the Qumran group from all the other Jewish groups of the period.

## 1 Purity in 11QTemple XLV-LI 10

The first document in which we find a lengthy and uniform corpus of teaching in respect of the problem of purity is in the Temple Scroll. I am convinced, in spite of opinions to the contrary, that this text comes from the formative period of the Qumran sect and that it lays the foundations of later developments. I am also convinced that its origin goes back to the beginnings of the period which interests us. It has the additional advantage that an important section of the Scroll (columns XLV to LI 10) is specifically concerned with posing the problem of purity. Without going into the discussion here of whether or not the whole section or any of its parts comprises an earlier source used by the redactor of the final document[206], it is clear that the section comprises a complete thematic unit, with its closing formula in LI 5a–10.

The first part of this unit (XLV–XLVII) focuses on the problem of purity in the area of the Temple and of the city of the Temple. Column XLV deals with possible defilement during the change of turns of service in the Temple (lines 3-7), is concerned with someone affected by nocturnal emission (lines 7-10), forbids entry into the city during three days to those who have had sexual relations (lines 10-12), prescribes the period of purification for those who suffer gonorrhoea (lines 15-17) and regulates for defilement acquired as a result of contact with a corpse or because of leprosy (lines 17-18). The following column commands a series of structures to be built with no other purpose than to avoid contamination of the Temple or of the city of the Temple. XLVI 1-4 prescribes the construction on the Temple roofs of a system to prevent the flight of unclean birds over it; it provides a platform around the outer courtyard and a trench around the Temple to separate it from the city (lines 5-12); it decrees the construction of latrines 3000 cubits away from the city (lines 13-16) and of three buildings, also outside the city, for lepers, for those who suffer from gonorrhoea and for those who have had a pollution (lines 16-18). Column XLVII is completely devoted to preserving purity within the city of the Temple, distinguishing it clearly from the other cities of the land. Lines 3-7 establish the general principle, and lines 7-18 require the exclusive use of skins which come from animals sacrificed in the Temple for bringing victuals into the city and the Temple.

The second part of this thematic unit on purity collects together the regulations of purity of persons and of things. Column XLVIII specifies the animals which one is allowed or forbidden to eat (lines 3-7) and forbids gashing oneself for the dead (lines 8-10). It legislates for the construction of cemeteries (lines 11-13) and allots special places in all the cities for lepers, those suffering from gonorrhoea and menstruating women (lines 13-17). The next two columns concentrate on impurity deriving from a corpse. Impurity of the house and of what it contains, due to the presence of a dead person (lines 5-10) and purification of the house and of those who have come into contact with the dead person (lines 11-12), a topic continued in the next column (L 4). There follow impurity through contact with a corpse and its purification (lines 5-9) and the uncleanness caused by the dead foetus in the maternal womb (lines 11-18). The last topic of the section is defilement through contact with the corpses of unclean animals, and its purification (lines 20-LI 5).

The section ends with a solemn exhortation in which the concept of purity is connected with that of holiness:

> Forewarn *6* the children of Israel of every uncleanness. *Blank* They are not to be defiled by those things which *7* I tell you on this mountain. They are not to defile themselves. *Blank* Because I, YHWH, reside *8* among the children of Israel. You shall sanctify yourselves and they shall be holy. They shall not make *9* their souls odious with anything that I have separated from them as unclean and they shall be *10* holy (11QTemple LI 5-10; DSST, 170).

Although quite a few details of this block of laws concerning purity come directly from the biblical text (chiefly from Leviticus and Deuteronomy), many others are due to changes or innovations inserted by the author of the *Temple Scroll*. It is precisely these details which allow us to evaluate his position (and that of the group to which the text belongs) in connection with the problem of purity.

This sectarian *halakhah* reveals several clearly defined tendencies[207]:

*a*) A desire to extend the level of purity required in the Temple to the whole city.

*b*) A desire to extend the specifically priestly regulations of purity to the whole people.

*c*) Extending the field of defilement.

*a*) It is well known that in traditional *halakhah* (*t.Kelim, Baba Qama* 1:12) Jerusalem was divided into three areas of increasing purity: the city, the hill of the Temple and the Temple itself. Also, in the same *halakhah* there is a tendency to restrict the rules of purity to the most sacred area, the Temple, although this requires departing from the literal meaning of the biblical text. The tendency of the *Temple Scroll* is in the opposite direction: to extend the requirements of purity of the Tabernacle to the whole city. The general way this is expressed, as found in 11QTemple XLVII 3-6, is typical:

> The city *4* which I will sanctify, installing my name and my temple [within it] shall be holy and shall be clean *5* from all types of impurity which could defile it. Everything that there is in it shall be *6* pure and everything that goes into it shall be pure (DSST, 168).

A couple of examples will show us this tendency clearly.

> *11* Anyone who lies with his wife and has an ejaculation, for three days shall not enter *12* anywhere in the city of the temple in which I shall install my name (11QTemple XLV 11-12; DSST, 167).

The first element of this *halakhah*, which is also found in CD XI 1-2, is that it forbids sexual relations within the city. In the traditional interpretation (*m.Kelim* 1:8), anyone unclean due to an ejaculation was only excluded from the camp of the *Shekinah*, that is, from the Temple itself. In the *Temple Scroll*, however, he is excluded from the whole city. The second element is that this exclusion, the duration of the impurity contracted by the sex act, is extended to three days. In the biblical text from which the author draws inspiration, though, purification occurs on the same day: «If a man lies with his wife and has an ejaculation, both of them shall bathe and remain unclean until the evening» (Lv 15:18). On the contrary, the purification required by the *Temple Scroll* for entry into the city is the preparation required by the biblical for the theophany of Sinai[208]: abstention from sexual relations for three days and bathing for purification (Ex 19:10-15). Certainly, our text does not specify the need for a bath, but this is because the full procedure has been given in detail in the previous *halakhah* with which it is strictly parallel and closely related. This *halakhah* specifies for us:

Anyone who has had a nocturnal emission shall not enter *8* the temple at all until three days have passed. He shall wash his clothes and shall bathe *9* on the first day and on the third day he shall wash his clothes /and bathe/ at sunset. Afterwards *10* he shall enter the temple. But they shall not enter my temple with their soiled impurity to defile it (11QTemple XLV 7-10; DSST, 167).

For the author of the *Temple Scroll*, nocturnal emission and marital ejaculation have exactly the same degree of impurity and require the same purification. What in one case prohibits the defiled person from entering «the Temple at all» and in the other case from entering «in all the city of the Temple» is due, as Milgrom has explained[209] to the fact that nocturnal emission can occur within the city, whereas marital ejaculation can occur outside it. Both legal regulations testify to making the conditions of purity in respect of the holy city more extreme and wide-ranging, as the manuscript specifies a little further on:

You shall make *17* three zones, to the east of the city, separate from each other, where *18* lepers, those who suffer gonorrhoea and men who have an emission of semen will go (11QTemple XLVI 16-18; DSST, 168).

As with marital ejaculation, the man who has had a nocturnal emission and the man with gonorrhoea are placed in quarantine and kept away from the holy city. In the traditional interpretation, only the man with gonorrhoea was excluded from the camp of the Levites, that is, the Temple hill.

The second of these examples in which we find the same fundamental principle at work is the following:

In their cities they shall make *9* with these hides (that is, the hides of animals slaughtered in the cities, not sacrificed in the Temple) utensils for all their needs, but they shall not bring them into the city of my Temple.... With the skins (of the animals) which they sacrifice *12* in the Temple, with these very same they shall bring into the city of my Temple their wine, their oil and all *13* their food. They shall not defile my Temple with the skins of the sacrifices *14* of their abominations which they sacrifice in their land... *16* What you sacrifice in my Temple is pure for my Temple; what you sacrifice in your cities is pure *17* for your cities. All the victuals of the Temple you shall bring in the skins of the Temple and you shall not defile *18* my Temple and my city with the skins of your abominations, because I reside among you (11QTemple XLVII 8-18; DSST, 169).

According to the traditional *halakhah* (*m. Hullim* 9:2), «when the skins have been treated in order to be used they are pure, except for human skin». The *Temple Scroll* forbids the use of the skins of clean animals (except those sacrificed in the Temple) for the transport of merchandise intended not only for the Temple but also for the whole city[210]. What was translated «victuals of the Temple» is expressed by the phrase *tohorat hammiqdaš*, which can be translated as «all that which requires the purity of the Temple». All this has to be brought into the city in the hides of animals sacrificed in the Temple in order not to «defile the Temple and the city». In other words, the level of holiness of the city is such that it requires the level of purity of the Temple. This is why is not surprising that in the whole city the only meat that can be eaten is likewise that of the sacrifices of the Temple:

> Within my city, which I make holy by placing my name within it, you shall not eat the flesh of cow, sheep or he-goat *20* which has not come into my temple; they shall sacrifice it there, *21* they shall pour out its blood over the base of the altar of holocausts and they shall burn its fat (11QTemple LII 19-21; DSST, 171).

Even more revealing of this same tendency: the consumption of the flesh of clean but blemished animals is forbidden within a radius of 30 *ris* or stadia, and defaecation is only permitted 3000 cubits from the city[211], a *halakhah* which flatly contradicts traditional opinion that human excrement does not defile (*y. Pesahim* 7:11) and the statement of *m. Tamid* 1:1 that there were latrines in the Immersion Chamber in rooms under the Temple.

In parallel with this extension to all the city of the regulations of purity traditionally reserved for the Temple, the level of purity required to come into contact with the Temple itself has been increased in the *Temple Scroll*. There, a series of actions which in traditional *halakhah* could take place within the city can now only occur within the Temple. This requires a higher level of purification. Accordingly, the passover sacrifice cannot be eaten in any part of the city (as the Mishnah says, *m. Zebahim* 5:8), but «those twenty years old and over shall celebrate it, and they shall consume it at night in the courtyards of the sanctuary» (11QT XVII 8-9). The communion sacrifice «can no more be eaten in any part of the city, by anyone, prepared in any way, during two days» (*m. Zebahim* 5:7), it must be consumed, instead, on the same day and in the outer courtyard of the Temple, as the *Temple Scroll* specifies in respect of the sacrifice of the Feast of New Oil: «And they shall eat it throughout this day in the outer courtyard in front of YHWH» (11QTemple XXII 13-14). In the same way the priests must consume the first-fruits in the inner courtyard (XIX 5-6) and prepare the peace-sacrifices in the kitchens located there (XXXVII 8-9). This principle even had to be accommodated architecturally in the Temple:

*9* You shall make a trench around the temple, one hundred cubits in width, which *10* separates the Holy temple from the city so that they do not suddenly enter *11* my temple and defile it (11QTemple XLVI 9-11; DSST, 168).

*b*) The tendency to extend to all the people the priestly regulations of purity can be detected already in several of the regulations cited. However, it emerges even more clearly in the following text:

No blind person *13* shall enter it (the city of the Temple) throughout his whole life; he shall not defile the city in the centre of which I dwell *14* because I, YHWH, dwell in the midst of the children of Israel for ever and always (11QTemple XLV 12-13; DSST, 167).

Yadin considers correctly that here «blind person» is not used only as a term for the blind. It comes at the head of the list as the beginning of (and as the abbreviation for) the quotation which includes other imperfections that in Lv 21:17-20 bar the exercise of priestly functions. His comment is strengthened by the use of verbs and suffixes in the plural. It is well known that a series of Qumran texts denies to the same persons which Leviticus excludes from priestly office on account of bodily defects the possibility of belonging to the sect or the messianic congregation, or of taking part in the final war[212]. The fact that the *Temple Scroll* forbids them entry into the city shows that it considers all the people as subject to the same requirements of purity in respect of the city as the priests are in respect of the Temple. An Israelite with one of these defects would make the city unclean, just as a priest similarly affected would make the Temple unclean.

*c*) To demonstrate the tendency of extending the field of defilement, I will quote only two examples which come from the sphere of contact with a corpse, «the father of the father of impurity» in rabbinic terminology:

The day on which they remove the dead person from the house, they shall cleanse it of every *12* stain of oil, wine, dampness from water; they shall rub its floor, its walls and its doors; *13* with water they shall wash its hinges, its jambs its thresholds and its lintels (11QTemple XLIX 11-15; DSST, 169).

In accordance with the traditional *halakhah*, the objects with are encrusted on the wall and especially on the floor are incapable of being defiled and therefore do not need any purification. Our text, on the other hand, does consider them as needing purification. This includes not only the jambs, the hinges, the thresholds and the lintels but even the actual floor and the walls[213]. Even more blatant is the expansion of the field of defilement in the following example:

When a woman is pregnant and her son dies in her womb, all the days which *11* he is dead within her she shall be impure like a grave. Every house which she enters *12* with all its utensils shall stay unclean for seven days; everyone who touches it (the house) shall stay impure up to the evening; and if *13* he enters the house with her he will stay impure for seven days; he shall wash his clothes *14* and bathe on the first day; the third day he shall sprinkle, wash his clothes and shall bathe; *15* on the seventh day he shall sprinkle a second time, he shall wash his clothes, bathe *16* and he will become pure by sunset (11QTemple L 10-16; DSST, 170).

In the traditional *halakhah*, the mother is not considered impure in such a case. *m. Hullin* 4:3 says explicitly: «If the foetus dies in its mother's womb and the midwife places her hand and touches it, the midwife remains impure for seven days, but the mother remains pure until the foetus comes out of her»[214]. The *Temple Scroll*, instead, states roundly that «she shall be impure like a grave».

This same extension of the field of defilement occurs in respect of the impurity contracted through contact with the bones of animals. In rabbinic tradition these are not able to transmit the impurity of the corpse, nor do the skin, the claws, the horns, etc. (*m. Hullim* 9:1). The *Temple Scroll*, instead, specifies how to treat animals which creep along the ground:

*4* Whoever carries their bones or their corpse, the skin or the flesh or the claws, shall wash *5* his clothes and bathe in water at sunset, afterwards he will be pure (11QTemple LI 4-5; DSST, 170).

## II  Purity in 4QMMT

Another equally important and equally ancient text which discloses to us Qumran attitudes when faced with the problem of purity is the famous halakhic letter. It was written by the chief of the sect to his opponents to explain the reasons why the Qumran group has separated itself from the remainder of Israel: «We have segregated ourselves from the rest of the peop[le and (that) we avoid] mingling in these affairs and associating with them in these things» as the epilogue expressly says. This text, known as *Miqṣat maʿaśe ha-torah* («some of the deeds of the Law» = 4QMMT) has still not been fully published. However, enough of its contents has been disclosed to allow us to appreciate more correctly the attitudes of the sect in connection with purity[215]. In fact, the greater part of the twenty legal regulations discussed in the letter or treatise are related to problems of purity, especially in respect of the Temple and the cult. Perhaps it is useful to reproduce here the list of the twelve themes discussed, as revealed by Strugnell and Qimron:

1) Ban on accepting sacrifices from the gentiles.
2) Slaughter of pregnant animals.
3) Who is prohibited from entering the Congregation.
4) The law of the red heifer.
5) Ban on the blind and the deaf from approaching the Temple.
6) Purity of flowing liquids (*nisoq*).
7) Ban on bringing dogs into Jerusalem.
8) The fruit of the fourth year is to be given to the priests.
9) The tithe on flocks is to be given to the priests.
10) Regulations connected with the uncleanness of leprosy.
11) Impurity of human bones.
12) Ban on marriages between priests and Israelites.

Of course, until the full text of all the regulations preserved is published completely it is impossible to undertake a detailed study. However, the mere list of contents of the *halakhot* preserved is interesting. It already allows us:

– to know which were the fundamental problems for the Qumran group at the moment of its split from the rest of Judaism;
– to distinguish its *halakhah* and its attitudes in the face of the problem of purity from the Pharisaic attitudes which would later crystallise in rabbinic *halakhah*;
– to appreciate the development of the problem of purity within the community, by comparing these contents with the contents of later documents.

The three trends which we see reflected in the block of *halakhot* about purity in the *Temple Scroll* also occur in the *halakhot* of 4QMMT. In addition, this text allows to determine that the third trend, the extension of the field of defilement, occurred in agreement with the Sadducee *halakhah*, as Geiger had already guessed and as P. Sacchi had noted as possible even before the publication of 11QTemple and 4QMMT[216]. There are not many halakhic disputes between Sadducees and Pharisees preserved in rabbinic tradition. In addition, later censorship (which replaced the name «Sadducees» with «heretics» in several places, both in the printed editions and in part of the manuscript tradition) makes the task of determining exactly the Sadducee *halakhah* even more difficult. Nevertheless, in two problems in which the Sadducees and the Pharisees had certainly come into conflict (the *Tebul Yom* and the *Nisoq*), 4QMMT presents the sectarian position as in agreement with the known Sadducee position[217].

For the people of Qumran, flowing liquid (*nisoq*) transmits impurity. In other words, when any liquid is poured from a clean container into an unclean one, the uncleanness of the latter is transmitted by the flow and defiles the container which was clean originally.

And also concerning flowing liquids: we say that in these there is no
*59* purity. Even flowing liquids cannot separate unclean *60* from clean because the moisture of flowing liquids and their containers is *61* the same
moisture (4QMMT 58-61; DSST, 78).

This position was formally contradicted by the Pharisees (*m. Yadayim* 4:7) and
defended by the Sadducees.

Also, in the controversy over whether the *Tebul Yom* (one who has bathed
but has not waited until sunset, in rabbinic terminology) should consider himself clean or unclean, the sectarian *halakhah* agrees with that of the Sadducees
and is stricter than that of the Pharisees (*m.Parah* 3:7). For the Pharisees, bathing permitted recovery of the state of purity without waiting for sunset, which
made people's lives considerably easier. For the people of Qumran, though,
only at sunset is one considered pure again. This can be deduced from several
of the *halakhot* of the *Temple Scroll*, but it is even more evident in the regulations concerning the impurity of the leper in 4QMMT and is stated expressly in
the *halakhah* on the red heifer from this document:

And also in what pertains to the purity of the red heifer in the sin-offering:
*17* that whoever slaughters it and whoever burns it and whoever collects the
ash and whoever sprinkles the [water of] *18* purification, all these ought to
be pure at sunset, *19* so that whoever is pure sprinkles the impure (4QMMT
16-19; DSST, 77).

### III  Purity in CD IX-XII 20

The *Temple Scroll* and 4QMMT are two typical texts of the formative period of
the community of Qumran. Only the germ of what later on will seem to be
distinctive elements of the Qumran solution to the problem of purity is found
in these texts. It occurs as a trend towards their own solutions within what
must have been a general problem for Judaism in the mid 1st century BCE. This
problem changes appreciably when we begin to study the texts which correspond to a later period. They show us which were the important problems for
the community, once the bonds which joined it to Jerusalem and the Temple
were broken.

The second part of the *Damascus Document* contains a lengthy *halakhic* section
which suits our purpose perfectly (CD IX 1- XXII 20) and concludes with a kind
of colophon[218]:

*19* This is the Rule for the assembly of the cities of Israel. In accordance
with these regulations, to keep *20* the unclean apart from the clean, and

distinguish between holy and profane (CD XII 19-20; DSST, 43)[219].

This section is even provided with sub-headings which indicate the broad out-lines of its contents: concerning oaths (IX 8); concerning the judges of the Con-gregation (X 4); concerning purification with water (X 10); concerning the *sab-bath* (X 14).

Included too, of course, are *halakhot* connected with the topic which we have seen to be characteristic of 11QTemple and 4QMMT. Thus, CD XII 1 takes up the ban on coition in the city of the Temple so as not to make the city impure, and XII 16-18 is a reminder that the impurity of death is transmitted to wood and stone and even to the nails and walls of houses. Most of the rules, though, which are meant to separate «the impure from the pure» are adapted to the new situation and are directed to guaranteeing the purity of the community. This is shown by the *halakhah* indicating that whoever violates the *sabbath* (to the preservation of which the greater part of the section is dedicated, i.e., from CD X 4 to XI 18) can only be reinstated in the assembly after seven years of expul-sion and scrupulous observance. It is not surprising, then, to find statutes con-cerning the purity or impurity of certain foods especially suited to desert life (CD XII 12-15) or about the quality and amount of water needed to purify one-self (CD X 10-12). One incomplete *halakhah*, which is difficult to understand, seems to forbid entry into the «house of prostration(s)» with «impurity of wash-ing» (CD XI 22); another forbids sending sacrifices to the Temple by means of an impure courier (CD XI 19-21). To this same trend belongs the series of *halakhot* which regulate relations with the gentiles. They are all intended to safeguard the purity of the members of the community, who are forbidden to spend the *sabbath* close to the gentiles (CD XI 15) or to sell them beasts or clean birds, slaves or, of course, any product of their mills or presses (CD XII 6-11).

In his description of the as yet unpublished copies of CD, Milik indicates that in two manuscripts from Cave 4 the existing columns XV-XVI (which, like col-umn IX, deal with oaths and vows) come immediately before column IX. He also notes that in the original work both columns are preceded in turn by several other columns, partially preserved in the fragments from Cave 4. «These con-tain prescriptions concerning the cultic purity of priests and sacrifices; a more detailed treatment of the law of diseases (Lv 13:29ff.) and an expanded version of Lv 15 (fluxes of men and women), laws of marriage, prescriptions relating to agricultural life, the payment of tithes, relations with pagans, relations be-tween the sexes, a prohibition of magic, etc.»[220].

From this description by Milik, the enormous interest of these still unpub-lished fragments for our topic is obvious. It is possible that, once published, the picture of the laws of purity which we can deduce from the copy of CD from the Cairo Genizah must be changed in some way. However, the contents which Milik describes seem rather to confirm the conclusion we have already drawn.

It is that, for the most part, the rules are directed towards preserving the purity of the members in their new situation. All the more so since Milik also indicates that two other still unpublished fragments contain a Penal Code similar to the *Rule of the Community* which we will study next. In the original work it would have continued the existing columns IX-XIV, and it is precisely in this Penal Code of 1QS that we find the Qumran solutions to the problem of purity fully developed.

In the *halakhot* of the block from CD examined we can note that the three trends, mentioned above, persist. Also, the regulations of purity are adapted to the new situation of the community. However, the new and most interesting thing is that already in this block from CD one of the elements which will be characteristic of Qumran thought begins to appear. This is the transfer of the purity of the Temple sphere, its place of origin, to the community itself. The impurity which prevents approach to the Temple will eventually prevent approach to the community. In a *halakhah* which specifies the qualifications of witnesses we are told:

> No-one who has consciously transgressed anything of a precept is to be believed as a witness against his fellow, until he has been purified to return (CD X 2; DSST, 41).

The term used, «to return», is *šûb*, a technical term to denote union with the sect or reinstatement in it after a period of suspension[221]. It is normal that whoever has been set apart from the group on account of his transgressions will not be accepted as a witness against one of the members until he has been reinstated. What is more interesting, though, is that the procedure needed for this reinstatement should be considered as a purification.

Even clearer on this matter are two other *halakhot* which also deal with witnesses[222]. In them, both in the case where only two witnesses testify to the misdeed of a member in a capital lawsuit and in the case of a single witness in a lawsuit about property, the member acknowledged as guilty is «separated from the purity» (CD IX 19-23). The meaning of the phrase is, obviously, that the accused cannot share in the pure food of the sect. This implies that he is considered as impure and reduced to the status of a aspirant. However, the use of the expression «to separate from the purity» to indicate this expulsion from the group shows us the transfer of the idea of purity of the Temple sphere and of the community to be a fact. As Forkman has indicated[223], the punishment in this case acts as a means of protection against possible defilement of the holy community. The witness against the accused is not enough to declare him guilty according to the law, but it is enough to separate him, as a precaution, from the Temple which is the community.

This element, as well as other typical aspects of the Qumran concept of purity, are found fully developed in the texts which we will consider next.

## IV  Purity in 1QS VI 24- VII 25

The transfer of the requirements of purity, originally attached to the Temple, to the community conceived as its substitute occurs clearly developed in the section of the *Rule of the Community* labelled «Penal Code». This section belongs to the third redactional level of 1QS, according to J. Murphy-O'Connor's theory[224]. In any case, it exhibits an advanced and structured phase of the sect's existence[225].

This section (1QS VI 24- VII 25) occurs immediately after the description of the process of joining the sect (VI 13-23). The Code is presented as a list of offences, each followed by the penalty to be imposed on the guilty person. The list of offences is significant: false declaration of possessions, lack of respect towards the hierarchy of the sect, sins against the divine name, misdeeds in everyday relationships with other members or with the priests, lies, misuse of common possessions, complaining, coarse language, etc. There follows a list of possible transgressions during the session of the Many: interrupting someone speaking, falling asleep during the session, being absent or spitting in it. Next comes a series of offences against modesty: showing one's genitals, laughing thoughtlessly or raising the left hand for permission to speak. The list also mentions a series of offences against the sect or its members: cursing another member or the Many, rebelling («murmuring») against the sect or against another member. The Code ends with a discussion of the case of someone betraying the community: if the offender has been a member for only a short time he can still repent and start the admission process again. But if he has been a member for more than ten years his expulsion is final. This list of offences shows a withdrawn community, careful to avoid problems from its members living together. It is possible, as Schiffman suggests[226] that the Penal Code is simply a compilation from a longer text and that the choice of themes it presents is determined by its function of forming part of the last stage of the initiation rite. In any case, it is significant that among all the failings indicated, not even one refers to the domain of purity. What connects this Code with our topic is not the faults which are mentioned but the punishments it provides for each one of them. These punishments vary in extent between ten and thirty days, two, three or six months, one or two years and frequently include a twofold element. As an example we can cite the first law of the Code:

> If one is found among them who has lied *25* knowingly concerning goods, he shall be excluded from the pure food of the Many for a year and shall be sentenced to a quarter of his bread (1QS VI 24-25; DSST, 10).

The punishment imposed is twofold and clearly differentiated: separation from the «purity» of the sect for one year and being deprived of part of the food. The second element is easily understood. The first is understandable only in the light of the admission procedure of the sect, described in the same column of the *Rule of the Community*. The candidate begins by being examined by the superior, designated with the name *Paqid*. If he approves him, he brings him into the covenant and instructs him in all the statutes of the community. Afterwards, the Many examine him and one by one pronounce his fate. If he is admitted, he spends a year's trial and afterwards is again examined by the Many. If he passes this examination as well, the candidate must spend yet another whole year, followed by yet another examination, after which:

> And if *22* the lot results in him joining the Community, they shall enter him in the Rule according to his rank among his brothers for the law, for the judgment, for purity and for the placing of his possessions in common (1QS VI 22; DSST, 10).

Only at this moment is his membership of the sect complete as is his participation in the purity. What is most interesting is that this whole lengthy procedure is described as a process of progressive purification. Each stage allows the candidate to pass on to a level of purification, which each time allows him a fuller share in the purity of the sect. The text is precise:

> *16* If he is included in the Community council, he must not touch the pure food of *17* the *Rabbim* (the Many) while they test him about his spirit and about his deeds until he has completed a full year (1QS VI 16-17; DSST, 10).

Only after this year can he come into contact with the purity of the many. This purity is not «the special ritual acts of purification practised by the members of the community» as Moraldi supposes in his note[227], no doubt influenced by Josephus' description of the Essene «novitiate». Instead, it is the pure food of the sect, as Licht proved[228]. But, even after this first step, his level of purity is still not considered complete. It is enough for his possessions to be recorded in the Community ledger, but not for him to be considered sufficiently pure to be able to take part in the *mašqeh*, the drink of the Many:

> He must not touch the drink of the Many until *21* he completes a second year among the men of the Community (1QS VI 20-21; DSST, 10).

Only when the level of purity acquired by the candidate is enough to allow him to share the liquid food of the community is he considered a full member in respect of *ṭehorah*, purity.

This process of gradual membership enables us to understand the series of punishments imposed for the various transgressions in the Penal Code. «Separation from the purity of the Many» for a year means that the transgressor has been reduced back to the stage of purity of one whose presence would defile the community. In other words, he is relegated to the level of purity in which aspirants are found and needs to purify himself for a year before full reinstatement in the community.

An example taken from the end of the Penal Code proves to us, with no room for doubt, that this is the correct interpretation. It describes exactly this same process not as a process of introducing a new member but as the punishment imposed for a serious misdeed:

> The person whose spirit turns aside from the foundation of the Community to betray the truth 21 and walk in the stubbornness of his heart, if he repents, he shall be punished for two years; during the first year he shall not approach the pure food (*tohorah*) of the Many. And during the second he shall not approach the drink (*mašqeh*) of the Many and shall sit behind all the men of the Community. 23 When the days of the two years are complete the Many shall be questioned concerning his matter; if they admit him, he shall be enrolled according to his rank; and later he will be questioned in connection with judgment (1QS VII 20-23; DSST, 11-12).

In these halakhic texts we find all the typical elements of the Qumran solution to the problem of purity. The transfer of the requirements of purity from the Temple sphere to the community is complete. The punishments imposed have no other purpose than to guarantee the purity of the community. Separation from this community is atoning and acts as a substitute for the atonement of the Temple. Around the community, a series of levels of progressive purity is created, in parallel with the concentric levels of holiness and purity around the Holy of Holies.

Another fundamental element in these texts is that they completely equate what we distinguish into ritual impurity and moral impurity. In Qumran, the concept of impurity has been equated with the concept of sin. This innovation is considered by Neusner «entirely without parallel»[229]. The impurity contracted by anyone from the failings listed in the Code is considered to take effect and the guilty person must undergo a process of purification to be able to free himself from it and share again in the purity of the sect. The offences which initiate separation from the purity of the community are not only the transgressions which caused a ritual impurity but transgression of any precept. As Neusner says, in Qumran «The *yahad*'s laws treat committing a sin not as a metaphor for becoming unclean, but as an actual source of uncleanness... He is *actually* unclean and requires a rite of purification. So the uncleanness is not metaphorical but is treated as equivalent to the impurity imparted by a corpse or a menstrual woman». Just as in traditional *halakhah*, for example, the period of a woman's impurity is greater after giving birth to a girl than to a boy, so at Qumran the period of punishment is related to the seriousness of the offence. The period of separation from the purity of the community shows us the gravity of the fault committed and the gravity of the defilement which this fault assumes for the purity of the sect.

Until now, we have concentrated exclusively on the halakhic texts of the sect. Even though, perhaps, they are the least suitable to express a theology, they are the best suited to reflect the life of a group and to indicate to us the process of the sect's self-awareness. We cannot forget, in fact, that within the Judaism of the Second Temple the ideological differences are, ultimately, only of relative importance. It is in the *halakhah* governing the life of the group that its sectarian development is defined. We cannot leave our topic, however, without mentioning at least some of the texts with strong theological content. In these, the expression of thoughts about purity tells us what, perhaps, comprises the most radical element of the Qumran concept of purity. I refer to what Paolo Sacchi has defined as «the identification of man and impurity». This is to view the very structure of a human being as impure and to equate purification with justification.

At Qumran, in fact, man is considered as radically impure, «a structure of sin». Whoever does not belong to the sect is described as follows:

> He will not become clean by the acts of atonement, nor shall he be purified by the cleansing waters, nor shall he be made holy by the seas 5 or rivers, nor shall he be purified by all the water of the ablutions. Defiled, defiled shall he be... (1QS III 4-5; DSST, 5).

But this radical condition of impurity is not exclusive to non-members of the community. In the Hymn which concludes the *Rule of the Community*, the psalmist says explicitly:

> 9 However, I belong to evil humankind
> to the assembly of wicked flesh;
> my failings, my transgressions, my sins, {...}
> with the depravities of my heart,
> 10 belong to the assembly of worms
> and of those who walk in darkness (1QS XI 9-10; DSST, 18).

In this situation, which is that of every man, impurity, as Sacchi says «is not only a force which weakens man, it is evil itself»[230]. From this situation only God can save man, by justifying him – a justification which is a purification. The same Hymn of the *Rule* states:

in his plentiful goodness
he will always atone for all my sins;
in his justice he will cleanse me
from the uncleanness of the human being
*15* and from the sin of the sons of man (1QS XI 14-15; DSST, 19).

This justification, though, does not take place in the Temple sphere but is only obtained within the community, the new Temple in which the divine Spirit is active, which makes the sect the place of purification and justification:

> For, by the spirit of the true counsel concerning the paths of man all *7* his sins are atoned so that he can look at the light of life. And by the spirit of holiness which links him with his truth he is cleansed of all *8* his sins. And by the spirit of uprightness and of humility his sin is atoned. And by the compliance of his soul with all the laws of God his flesh *9* is cleansed by being sprinkled with cleansing waters and being made holy with the waters of repentance (1QS III 6-9; DSST, 5)[231].

The member of the sect purified in this way is situated at the level of purity of the angels. The texts describing the community of the end of times provide us with the sect's supreme ideal of purity: a community so pure that the angels themselves are to be found within it[232]. The *Rule of the Congregation* (1QSa II 3-11; DSST, 127) specifies precisely those who will be able to form part of the community of the end of times. As is foreseen, all those disqualified by any physical defect (according to Lv 13 and 21) from exercising priestly functions are also excluded from the Congregation. And not only those. «No man defiled by any of the impurities of a man» will be able to belong to this community. The reason given is «because the angels of holiness are among their congregation». The *War Scroll* offers us the same ideal. Excluded from the army of the sons of light are the same persons denied a part in the eschatological community (1QM VII 4-5). Neither they nor «any man suffering from uncleanness in his flesh, none of these will go out to war with them». Here as well the reason is: «for the holy angels are together with their armies» (1QM VII 6). These are the same angels who, according to 1QM XII 7-9, fight the final battle at the side of the sons of light against the sons of darkness and the armies of Belial, but, above all, the angels who officiate in the heavenly Temple and with whose liturgy the sectarians are associated.

To close I will summarise briefly the results of my study. In the Israel in search of its identity in the Second Temple period, the problem of purity was decisive in providing the Qumran group with its own identity. It also distinguished it from other Jewish groups which did not share the same ideals of purity and ended up being considered impure, with whom all contact was forbidden.

At Qumran, at the beginning, as in the rest of Israel, purity is a requirement of the Temple area and of the cult, and chiefly affects the priest. In the texts of the formative period we find that there is however, already a tendency to extend the requirements of Temple purity to the whole holy city. Also, not to restrict it to the priests but to extend it to all the faithful. At the same time, we have been able to establish an increase in the requirements of purity, a greater rigour, in agreement with the stance of the Sadducee group.

Once the break with the Temple had taken place, whose cult was considered profane and whose ministers are seen as impure, the community accommodates the rules of purity to its new situation. Its purpose is to safeguard the purity of the community. The community itself is seen as a substitute for the Temple. This implies a transfer of the requirements of purity to the sphere of the community. Study of the Penal Code and of the admission procedure has shown us that the concept of impurity ended with it being equated with the concept of sin. Faults of members demanded a separation from the purity of the community. The presence of a sinner makes the community impure, and every sin is a source of impurity. The theology of the sect even went as far as to reify the radical impurity of man and equate purification with justification. Lastly, the texts which describe for us the eschatological community set the purity of the sect on a par with the purity of the heavenly Temple. That purity permits communion with the angels and is the highest ideal and the ultimate requirement of Qumran purity.

# Messianic Hopes in the Qumran Writings[233]

## Florentino García Martínez

In the first twenty-five years which followed the discoveries and first publications of the texts from Qumran few topics were so widely discussed as that of «messianism»[234]. The reason for this interest is easy to understand. In most of the other Jewish writings of the Second Temple period, the figure of the Messiah either does not feature or plays a very secondary role. In contrast, the new texts expressed not only the hope of an eschatological salvation but introduced into this hope the figure (or the figures) of a Messiah using the technical terminology. Thus they promised to clarify the origins of the messianic hope which occupies such a central position within Christianity. The expectations of the first years of research were not fulfilled and the reaction was not long in coming. The interest in «Qumran messianism» moved rapidly to a secondary level on the agenda of Qumran studies[235].

In publications of the last few years a new interest in the topic of Qumran messianism is evident, not dependent on the messianic idea of the New Testament but as an object of study in its own right. New studies appear regularly and abundantly[236]. It would not be necessary, though, to deal with the topic again except that, in the course of 1992, several texts were published which throw new light on Qumran messianism[237] but have not as yet been incorporated into an overall view of the problem.

My intention is simply to present the messianic texts recovered, that is, *all* the texts from the Qumran library (published or unpublished) in which are found references to the figure of the Messiah using the technical term, or to various other messianic figures, agents of eschatological salvation who are not referred to with the actual term Messiah. Naturally, I will discuss in more detail the texts which until now have been studied less and much more briefly those of which the content has been analyzed at length in the past. Unlike the presentation of other scholars[238], I make no distinction between texts which can be considered sectarian and those whose character is more uncertain. This is because I am convinced that the simple fact of these texts being included in the sectarian library is enough to guarantee that their content was seen as in agreement with the basic thought of the group. Also these texts whose origin is difficult to determine reflect the development of biblical ideas prevalent in the period when the real sectarian texts were composed.

The picture that emerges is fragmentary and kaleidoscopic, like the texts themselves. We cannot forget that we find ourselves before an accumulation of texts produced during a period of not less than two hundred years. They can reflect perfectly well different perceptions, changes and transformations of a single idea. The library of Qumran is uniform but it is not one-dimensional or

monolithic. We cannot expect more uniformity in it than is found in the Hebrew Bible, the base text which forms the foundation of all later developments

In none of the 39 times where the Hebrew Bible uses the word «Messiah»
does this word have the precise technical meaning of the title of the eschatological figure whose coming will bring in the era of salvation[239]. The «Messiahs»
of the Old Testament are figures of the present, generally the king (in Is 54:1
it is Cyrus) and more rarely, priests, patriarchs or prophets. And in the two
cases when Daniel uses the word, they are two persons whose identity is difficult to determine, though certainly not «messianic» figures. Later tradition was
certainly to re-interpret some of these Old Testament allusions to the «Messiah» as «messianic» predictions. However, the roots of the ideas which later
would use the title of «Messiah» to denote the figures who would bring eschatological salvation, are found in other Old Testament texts which do not use the
word «Messiah». Texts such as the blessings of Jacob (Gn 49:10), Balaam's
oracle (Nm 24:7), Nathan's prophecy (2 Sm 7) and the royal psalms (such as Ps
2 and Ps 110) would be developed by Isaiah, Jeremiah and Ezekiel in the direction of hope in a future royal «Messiah», heir to the throne of David. The
promises of the restoration of the priesthood in texts such as Jr 33:14-26 (missing from the LXX) and the oracle about the high priest Joshua included in Zac 3,
were to act as a starting point for later hope in a priestly «Messiah». Similarly,
the double investiture of the «sons of oil», Zerubbabel and Joshua, in Zac 6:9-14
would be the starting point of the hope in a double «Messiah», reflecting a particular division of power already present since Moses and Aaron. In the same
way, the presence of the triple office: king, priest, prophet, combined with the
announcement of the future coming of a «prophet like Moses» of Dt 18:15.18
and with the real hope in the return of Elijah of Mal 3:23, would act as the
starting point for the development of a hope in the coming of an agent of eschatological salvation, whether called «Messiah» or not. Similarly, the presentation of the mysterious figure of the «Servant of YHWH» in chapters 40-55 of
Isaiah, as an alternative to traditional messianism in the perspective of the restoration, would result in the development of a hope in a «suffering Messiah».
Also, the announcement of Mal 3:1 that God was to send his «angel» as a messenger to prepare his coming would permit the development of hope in an
eschatological mediator of non-terrestrial origin.

This complex of such different «messianic» hopes, barely alluded to in the
Hebrew bible, are included and developed in the manuscripts from Qumran.
The exception, perhaps, is the figure of the «Son of Man», a figure derived
from Dn 7, who reaches his full messianic development in the *Book of the Parables of Enoch*. About him, however, the manuscripts from Qumran seem to
maintain a silence which does not fail to be surprising, given the influence of
Daniel on the Qumran writings and the presence among them of various
pseudo-Danielic compositions. All the other potentially messianic figures of the

Old Testament occur in the writings from Qumran, in various stages of development. Analysis of the texts containing these references permits us to outline the complex picture of the messianic hopes of the community.

We begin with those texts which actually mention a single messianic figure, either because he was the only one hoped for or because the chances of preservation have deprived us of the passages in which other messianic figures were mentioned. We end with those texts in which several messianic figures occur together.

## 1 Texts which Mention a Single Messianic Figure

### 1 Davidic Messianism

At Qumran we find a series of texts which contain the elaboration of the basic lines of royal and davidic messianism of Old Testament origin, exactly as expressed in texts such as Jr 23:5-6, Balaam's Oracle in Nm 24:17 and Ps 2. These texts prove to us that within the community, hope in a «Messiah-King» was very much alive. The move from allusion to an anointed-King to hope in an «Anointed One», who would come in the future as a King, is to be found in the following texts:

#### 1.1  4Q252(4QpGen[a])

This first text shows us that within the Qumran community the famous blessing of Judah by Jacob of Gn 49:8-12 was already interpreted in a clear messianic sense, so confirming the antiquity of the messianic interpretation of this text found in the Palestinian Targum[240]. The text in question comes from a discontinuous *pesher* on Genesis which has still not been published in full, but of which the messianic section has been known since 1956 as 4QPatriarchal Blessings[241]. This composition is preserved in three fragmentary copies (4Q252, *253* and *254*), of which 4Q252 is the longest. From what can be deduced from the fragments preserved, the work commented on selected excerpts from Genesis: the story of the flood, the curse on Canaan, the covenant with Abraham, the Sodom and Gomorrah episode, Esau's descendants and the blessings of Jacob. The commentary on these blessings, acknowledged as an independent unit[242], filled at least three columns of the text[243].

The literary form of the work is that of a discontinuous or thematic *pesher*. This is proved by the introductory formulas, «as it is written» (III 1), «as he said» (IV 2) or the resumptive use of pronouns (V 2,3) and by the actual use of the technical term *pesher* in IV 2. This itself shows us that it is an original composition from the Qumran community, a fact evident from the use of the expression «the men of the community» in V 5 and of the formula «as he said through Moses in respect of the last days» in IV 2. As a *pesher*, then, the text attempts to offer us the deeper meaning of the biblical text. For the community, Jacob's blessing of Judah contains the coming of the «Messiah» and actually refers to it. The text in question (4Q252 V 1-7) can be translated as follows:

> *1* A sovereign shall [not] be removed from the tribe of Judah. While Israel has the dominion, *2* there will [not] lack someone who sits on the throne of David. For «the staff» is the covenant of royalty, *3* [and the thou]sands of Israel are «the feet». *Blank* Until the messiah of justice comes, the branch *4* of David. For to him and to his descendants (to them) has been given the covenant of royalty over his people for all everlasting generations, which *5* he has observed [...] the Law with the men of the community, for *6* [...] it is the assembly of the men of [...] *7* [...] He gives (DSST, 215).

To the extent that the fragmentary nature of the text allows one to ascertain, each element of the biblical quotation has been supplied with its interpretation[244]. The Hebrew word *šebeṭ* has been interpreted in its double meaning of «sceptre» and «tribe». Further, sceptre has been understood as «sovereign», and while not going as far as the radical interpretation of the Palestinian Targum which translates explicitly as «king», has the same implications. «The staff» is understood as the covenant of royalty and not as the Interpreter of the Law as in CD VI 7. These expressions place the interpretation squarely in the perspective of the promise of dynastic succession, culminating, as the text states, in the coming of the «Messiah». The equation of «the feet» with the thousands of Israel highlights the military context of the promised royalty. PAM 41.708(FE 409) shows the existence of a *Blank* in the manuscript, and this fact explains why the expression «Messiah of justice» is presented as equivalent to the mysterious *šiloh* of the biblical text. The expression is unique in the texts from Qumran, but the parallel with the Teacher of Righteousness makes it clear that its meaning is none other than the true, lawful Messiah[245]. The clear dependence of the expression on Jr 23:5 and 33:15: «In those days I shall raise up for David a lawful shoot who will do what is right and just», also shows the polemical nature of the expression in the anti-Hasmonaean context of the community. It allows us, therefore, to set this development of a hope in a «messiah king» for the end of times, within an apocalyptic context. The most logical antecedent of the clause «which he has observed» seems to be «his people», but the break in the manuscript does not permit the meaning of «his people» to be determined. The union with the men of the community in the observance of (all the precepts of) the Law leads us to suppose that from the viewpoint of the text the kingdom of the «Messiah» is limited to the loyal people. This would mean the members of the Qumran community, but such a conclusion goes beyond the preserved evidence. The loss of the rest of the text also prevents us from knowing in what sense the reference to the peoples of the Genesis text was interpreted. The reconstruction of «to whom the peoples owe obedience» in the lacuna is no more than one of the reconstructions possible. It is suggested by the resump-tive pronoun, and *keneset* is only used one other time in all the texts (4QpNah III 7), in a negative sense, referring to the association of those seeking easy in-terpretations.

In spite of that, the general lines of the text are clear enough to assure us that in Qumran interpretation, Jacob's blessing of Judah was seen as a promise of the restoration of the davidic monarchy and of the perpetuity of his royal of-fice. And since the future representative of the dynasty is identified not only as the shoot of David, but also explicitly as the «true anointed», there remains no doubt about the «messianic» tone of the text. Unfortunately, the details which the text provides about this «Messiah» are not many. Besides his legiti-mate and davidic character, his inclusion in a perpetual dynasty and the mili-tary aspect of his kingdom, the text presents his coming in connection with the Qumran community and in dispute with the Hasmonaean usurpers. Unfortu-nately, the fragmentary nature of the text and the ambiguity of the pronouns used do not enable us to determine whether his perpetual royalty is exercised over all the people (of Israel) or only over his own people comprising those who observed the Law within the community. Nor can we determine in which sense the other «peoples» are placed in relation to his coming.

This first text, then, only reflects the traditional idea of the «Messiah», son of David. However, it is necessary to insist on one important proviso. 4Q252, in spite of being the most complete copy preserved of the work, is an extremely fragmentary manuscript. Therefore, it cannot be excluded that other messianic figures played a role in the other missing sections of the work. This proviso is not merely a methodological constraint, but is prompted by two surprising allusions found in the other two copies of the work, even more fragmentary and still unpublished. In one of the fragments of the lower part of a column of 4Q254[246] the following lines can be read clearly: «/[...] the two sons of the oil of anointing who [...] / [...] observed the precepts of God [...] / [...] because the men of the co[mmunity...]». The reference to Zac 4:14 leaves no doubt at all. Also, this text, as we will see further on, seems to have played an important part in the development of the two-headed messianism which we find in the writings from Qumran. In turn, the larger fragment, 4Q253[247], which preserves remains of two columns, includes a literal quotation of Mal 3:17-18. This text comes just before the promise of the return of Elijah, a promise which deter-mines the hope in the eschatological prophet of the community, whose messi-anic character we will indicate below. These two texts do not permit any con-clusion to be drawn, but they are a precious indication of the kind of material lost from our *pesher* on Genesis, and comprise a real invitation to prudence.

We will find the same hope in a shoot of David as future Messiah-King in other clearly sectarian texts. In spite of their fragmentary nature, these texts provide some more details which allow us to sketch the outlines of this figure.

## 1.2   4Q161 (4QpIsaᵃ)

The text in question belongs to a continuous *pesher* on Isaiah, of which three columns have been preserved and it provides us with the Qumran interpretation of the classic text Is 11:1-5[248]. After quoting in full the biblical text in question in lines 11-17 of column III, the text offers the Qumran interpretation:

> *18* [The interpretation of the word concerns the shoot] of David which will sprout [in the final days, since] *19* [with the breath of his lips he will exe-cute] his enemies and God will support him with [the spirit of] courage [...] *20* [...] throne of glory, [holy] crown and hemmed vestments *21* [...] in his hand. He will rule over all the peoples and Magog *22* [...] his sword will judge all the peoples. And as for what he says: «He will not *23* [judge by ap-pearances] or give verdicts on hearsay», its interpretation: *24* [...] according to what they teach him, he will judge, and upon his mouth *25* [...] with him will go out one of the priests of renown, holding clothes in his hand (DSST, 186).

The text does not use the technical term «anointed one» but simply speaks of the «shoot of David»; however, the apposition in the text cited previously of «Messiah of justice» with the «shoot of David» guarantees us that both expressions denote the same messianic person whose coming is awaited «in the final days». Just like the blessing in Gn 49:10, the passage Is 11:1-5 is interpreted within the Qumran community as a messianic prediction. It is clear that it is a «Messiah-King», from the dynastic connotations of the term used: «shoot of David». It is also clear from the allusions to the attributes of his royalty: the throne of glory, the crown and his embroidered clothes. Our text stresses the military character of the hoped for «Messiah», described to us as a victorious warrior. The destruction of his enemies and dominion over all the peoples, including the archetypal enemy Magog, are the results of his action. He also describes to us his judicial function; but although this will be extended to all the peoples, it is subject to the instruction and authority which he will receive. The lacuna has deprived us of express mention of these instructors and guides of this «Messiah», but in view of the subordination of the «Messiah of Israel» to the priests in 1QSa II 11-21, it is most probable that it was the priests who, with their instruction and with their authority, guided the judgments of the «Messiah».

   Once the messianic interpretation of Is 11:1-5 is established, the application of this text to a person who recurs with frequency in the Qumran writings and

who is called the «Prince of (all) the congregation»[249] allows us to understand
that this person is no other than the «shoot of David» and the «Messiah of justice». Two of the texts which apply the prophecy of Isaiah to the «Prince of the
congregation» are the following:

### 1.3   1Q28b (1QSb) V 20-29

*20 Blank* Of the Instructor. To bless the prince of the congregation, who [...]
*21* [...] And he will renew the covenant of the Community for him, to establish the kingdom of his people for ever, [to judge the poor with justice]
*22* to rebuke the humble of the earth with uprightness, to walk in perfection
before him on all his paths [...] *23* to establish the [holy] covenant [during]
the anguish of those seeking it. May the Lord raise you to an everlasting
height, like a fortified tower upon the raised rampart. *24* May [you strike
the peoples] with the power of your mouth. With your sceptre may you lay
waste *Blank* the earth. With the breath of your lips *25* may you kill the
wicked. [May he send upon you a spirit of] counsel and of everlasting forti-
tude, a spirit *Blank* of knowledge and of fear of God. May *26* your justice be
the belt of [your loins, and loyalty] the belt of your hips. May he place
upon you horns of iron and horseshoes of bronze. You will gore like a bull
[.. you will trample the peo]ples like mud of wheels. For God has established you as a sceptre. *28* Those who rule [... all the na]tions will serve
you. He will make you strong by his holy Name. *29* He will be like a li[on
...] the prey from you, with no-one to hunt it. Your steeds will scatter over
(DSST, 433).

This lovely blessing of the «Prince of the congregation» forms part of the *Collection of blessings* included in the same manuscript that originally contained the
*Rule of the Community* and the *Rule of the Congregation*[250]. The blessing collects
together the echoes from a whole series of texts which play an important role
in the development of later messianic ideas, such as Nm 24:17 and Gn 49:9-10.
But there is no doubt that Is 11:1-5 provides the author with most of his ideas
and expressions (Is 11:4 in lines 21-22 and 24-25; Is 1:2 in line 25; Is 11:5 in
line 26). The long introduction which precedes the blessing proper (lines 20-23)
where the figure of the «Prince of the congregation» is described as the instrument chosen by God to «establish the kingdom of his people for ever» shows
clearly that he is a traditional Messiah-King, although the technical term is not
used. A conclusion which the very content of the blessing confirms in full: the
twofold reference to the sceptre underlines its «royal» character and the references to Is 11:1-5 stresses its davidic origin; his military functions are to the
fore and stressed by the reference to Mic 4:13 in line 26 and all the nations end
by submitting to him. These elements agree with those we have found in the

preceding texts. The new contribution of this blessing consists in presenting us with the hoped for «Messiah» in function of the eschatological community. This detail appears in the actual title by which he is called, «Prince of the congregation», a title which places him in direct relationship with the community of the last times. It also appears in the first of the functions assigned to him: to renew the covenant of the community through him.

In the preserved text of 1Qsb there is no explicit mention of any other messianic figure. However, this could be due to the gaps in the text, so that from this fact no conclusion can be drawn. We possess remains of a blessing clearly intended for blessing «the priests, sons of Zadok» (III 22). It is also certainly possible, as the editor suggests, that the blessing partially preserved in II 1- III 21 was destined for the High Priest of the end of days, the Messiah of Aaron or priestly Messiah.

In 1Qsb, the identification of the «Prince of the congregation» as the «shoot of David» is implicit. Therefore, it could be disputed. Fortunately, this identification is explicit in the following text, a text still partly unpublished but which has received great publicity recently. It is fragment 5 of 4Q285.

The work from which this fragment comes has been preserved in two copies[251] and was known as *Berakhot Milhamah*. It is quite possible, though, that both copies come from the lost ending to the *War Scroll*, known through copies from Cave 1 and Cave 4. The general content of the preserved fragments, the reference in both to the destruction of the *Kittim*, the mention of the archangels Gabriel and Michael and the allusions to the «Prince of the congregation»[252], are so many indications in this direction. Whether or not the two compositions are identical, it is certain that fragment 5 of 4Q285 is of interest for our topic.

The fragment was presented by professors R. Eisenman and M. Wise in the press, in November 1991, as containing the death of the Messiah and so providing a perfect parallel to the Christian idea and to the later rabbinic concept of the Messiah, Joseph's son, who dies in an eschatological battle. A later article by G. Vermes[253] provided the first scholarly analysis of the text, to which J. D. Tabor replied later[254]. The text in question can be translated as follows:

### 1.4  4Q285 frag. 5

*1* [... as] the Prophet Isaiah [said] (10:34): «[The most massive of the] *2* [forest] shall be cut [with iron and Lebanon, with its magnificence,] will fall. A shoot will emerge from the stump of Jesse [...] *3* [...] the bud of David will go into battle with [...] *4* [...] and the Prince of the Congregation will kill him, the sh[oot of David ...] *5* [...] and with wounds. And a priest will command [...] *6* [...] the destruction of the Kittim [...] (DSST, 124).

The debate evidently centres on the interpretation of line 4 and is due both to the fragmentary nature of the text and to the very ambiguity of the Hebrew expression used. The *hiphil* form used can be vocalised as a third person plural (they will kill) or as a third person singular with a suffix (he will kill him). The use of a verb in the plural in line 3 could favour understanding the verb as a plural, assuming continuity between the two. However, the lacuna and the presence in line 5 of a verb in the singular lessen the force of this argument. On the other hand, the absence of the object marker (*'et* in Hebrew) before «Prince of the congregation» clearly counsels considering «Prince of the congregation» as the subject of the verb, although this is not a decisive argument either. Ultimately, only the context can assist us in deciding between the two grammatically possible interpretations. However, this context does not leave any doubt at all about the meaning of the clause.

In the text from Isaiah which the author quotes exactly, the death of the «shoot of David» is not announced. Rather, that it will be plainly he who will judge and kill the wicked. The Qumran interpretation of this biblical text in 4Q161, which we cited above, is even more important. There, the «Prince of the congregation» is mentioned in column II 15 and his victorious character is also stressed and «Lebanon» and «the most massive of the forest» are interpreted as meaning the *Kittim* who are placed in his hand (col. III 1-8). We have seen the same victorious exaltation of the «Prince of the congregation» in 1QSb, which also uses the text from Isaiah and it also appears in the other Qumran allusions to that person. In the same way, the reference to the destruction of the Kittim in line 6 places us clearly in the perspective of the *War Scroll* and of the final victory over the powers of evil. This indicates that the interpretation according to which it is the «Prince of the congregation» who kills his foe is the one which fits best the original biblical text and the other interpretations of this text in the Qumran writings. This best explains all the elements preserved and is supplied with convincing parallels in other related texts.

On the other hand, the idea of the death of this «Prince of the congregation» at the hands of his eschatological foe is not documented in any other Qumran text dealing with the davidic «Messiah», or in any other of the Qumran texts mentioning the «Prince of the congregation». The allusion to the death of the «Anointed» in Dan 9:25-26 or the allusions to the «Suffering Servant» of Is 40-45 play no role. Accordingly, we must conclude that the death of the «Messiah» is contextually alien to the tone of our text.

This new text supplies us in a simple and tangible way with the detail that the victory of the «Messiah son of David» will include the destruction of his eschatological foe in the war of the end of times. And the definite proof that in the Qumran texts the messianic figure of the «Prince of the congregation»[255] is the same as the «shoot of David», that is, the traditional «Messiah-king».

Another text which could refer to the same messianic figure has been published recently by E. Puech[256]. It is a fascinating text although its interpretation is not without problems. The manuscript had been described by J. Starcky in 1956: «Un beau texte mentionne le Messie, mais les bienfaits du salut eschato-logique, évoqués d'après Is xLss et Ps cxLvi, sont attribués directement à Ado-nai»[«A lovely text mentions the Messiah, but the benefits of eschatological salvation evoked, according to Is 40ff. and Ps 146, are attributed directly to Adonai»][257]. The reference to the «Messiah» appears in the best preserved fragment, frag. 2, col. ii:

### 1.5  4Q521 2 II

*1* [for the heav]ens and the earth will listen to his Messiah, *2* [and all] that is in them will not turn away from the holy precepts. *3* Be encouraged, you who are seeking the Lord in his service! *Blank 4* Will you not, perhaps, encounter the Lord in it, all those who hope in their heart? *5* For the Lord will observe the devout, and call the just by name, *6* and upon the poor he will place his spirit, and the faithful he will renew with his strength. *7* For he will honour the devout upon the throne of eternal royalty, *8* freeing prisoners, giving sight to the blind, straightening out the twisted. *9* Ever shall I cling to those who hope. In his mercy he will jud[ge,] *10* and from no-one shall the fruit [of] good [deeds] be delayed, *11* and the Lord will perform marvellous acts such as have not existed, just as he sa[id] *12* for he will heal the badly wounded and will make the dead live, he will proclaim good news to the meek *13* give lavishly [to the need]y, lead the exiled and enrich the hungry. *14* [...] and all [...] (DSST, 394).

The first problem which the text presents is that of determining whether the first line refers to one «Messiah» (as we have translated) or to several. The Hebrew text clearly reads *lemešiho*, but as the editor notes, in Qumran Hebrew the form could also be read as a plural (and in fact quite a number of scholars translate *lemešiho* of CD ii 12 «his anointed ones» in the plural without correcting to *lemešihy*), which is why Puech translates cautiously «His Messiah(s)». If I have opted conclusively for a translation in the singular, this is due to the presence of the same word in fragment 8,9, but in a form which is obviously plural[258] and seems to denote the prophets (or, according to Puech, the priests). Also because the parallel in line 6 «his spirit... with his strength» seems to favour clearly the interpretation of the word in the singular with the suffix clearly referring to God.

The text, then, deals here with a single «Messiah». It is not easy, though, to determine whether this person is the «Davidic Messiah» or another «messianic» figure, since the only thing the text tells us about him is that «the heavens and the earth will listen to him» and that in his era «all that is in them will not turn away from the precepts of the holy ones»[259]. A fragmentary reference to his «sceptre» in the next column (frag. 2 III 6) could point us towards the «royal Messiah». However, partly the reading is uncertain and partly there is no way of proving that this person is the same as the «Messiah» of II 1[260]. The only indication I find in the text to identify this «Messiah» with the «Prince of the congregation» is that the horizon of eschatological salvation which the Lord achieves during his age seems to be limited to the eschatological congregation, the assembly of the faithful in the last times. It is certain that nearly all the formulas used are rooted in the bible, but the whole set of promises is certainly limited to those who seek the Lord, hope in him and persevere in his service. In themselves these expressions can of course refer to all the faithful of Israel. However, there is a twofold mention of the «devout» (the *hasidim* who will be rewarded with the «throne of eternal royalty») which frames the references derived from Psalm 146. And, one of the actions of this messianic age is precisely the elimination of physical obstacles which hinder belonging to the Community. These two factors seem to indicate that the horizon of the eschatological salvation which the Lord achieves in the age of his «Messiah» is limited to the members of the eschatological congregation. This could indicate that in our text the simple title «Messiah» was used as a reference to the «davidic Messiah», the «Prince of the congregation», whom the 1QSb presents in strict relationship to the congregation.

The only study of this manuscript which has appeared so far[261] considers that our text does in fact speak of the davidic «Messiah». No other argument is adduced except the assertion (clearly false) that in Qumran (with the possible exception of 1QS) only one «Messiah» was hoped for. According to the authors of this study, the person described in 4Q521 would be the direct antecedent to the Christian concept of the «Messiah». Their argument is twofold. The supposition that 4Q521 presents the «Messiah» raising the dead. And the parallel to the expressions in line 12 of Mt 11:4-5 and Lk 7:22-23, the reply to the Baptist's embassy, in which are described the signs of the arrival of the «Messiah». This second statement is correct inasmuch as the combination in a single phrase of the resurrection of the dead with the announcement of good news to the ʿanawim, which comes from Is 6:1, was not previously documented outside the New Testament. But the first supposition, which sees the «Messiah» as an agent of the portentous actions of eschatological salvation, seems completely mistaken and is simply the result of reading the manuscript incorrectly.

In line 10 they read «and [in his good]ness [for ever. His] Holy [Messiah] will not delay [in coming]», supporting their reconstruction with the use of this same expression in 1Q30. However, both the readings «and in his goodness» and «Holy» are palaeographically impossible; the strokes purported to be there do not match the traces preserved. Just as false is their reading «his work» in line 11, which besides being syntactically odd, deprives the following verbs of a subject. With the editor, read «he will do».

Wise-Tabor feel obliged to accept that the Lord is the agent of the deeds announced in lines 5-9 (among which are found some of the elements that also appear in the New Testament texts, such as the cure of the blind men), but they suppose a change of subject starting from line 10. For that they insert a mention of the «Messiah»²⁶² in the lacuna of line 10. And in line 11 they insert an idea which not only does not appear in the text if read correctly, it is even contrary to the thought of the whole Hebrew Bible: the idea that there are won-derful actions (in the positive sense) which are not the work of the Lord. Wise-Tabor translate the lines in question as follows: «(10) a[nd in His] go[odness forever. His] holy [Messiah] will not be slow [in coming.] (11) And as for the wonders that were not the work of the Lord, when he (i.e. the Messiah) [come]s (12) then he will heal the sick, resurrect the dead, and to the poor announce glad tidings». However all these speculations are unnecessary if the text is read correctly. In it, the Messiah does not raise up the dead, nor are there wonderful deeds which are not the work of God. What the text teaches us is that in the final epoch, in the time of the «Messiah», God will perform wonderful deeds as he has promised and the resurrection of the dead (those who have been faith-ful, of course²⁶³) will be one of the wonderful deeds.

These texts are sufficient proof for us that the hope in a future «Messiah», heir to the davidic promises, which was to comprise the core of later rabbinic messianism, was very much present in the thought of the Qumran community. However, unlike later messianism, the messianic hopes of the community were not limited to this figure of the Messiah-King, but at the same time several of the other potentially messianic figures of the Old Testament were developed.

## 2 Priestly Messianism

Together with the King, the High Priest is one of the main individuals to re-ceive an «anointing» in the Hebrew Bible. There is nothing unusual, then, that within the Old Testament we already find indications of the possible develop-ment of these references to the High Priest as «anointed one»–in the course of hope in a priestly agent of salvation in the eschatological era–together with the «anointed one» of royal character. It is in this sense, I think, that the vision of Zac 3 and its development in Zac 6:9-14 must be interpreted. In the first text, the future messianic age is clearly dominated by the figure of the High Priest Joshua, while the «shoot» only appears in passing and in a subordinate role. Neither of these two characters therefore is explicitly called «Messiah», but both texts are open to such an interpretation. As we will see further on, this interpretation will be developed within the Qumran community into a two-headed messianism. However, a recently published text enables us to glimpse an independent development of the hope in the coming of the «priestly Messiah» as an agent of salvation at the end of times.

It is an Aramaic text, one of the copies of the *Testament of Levi*, recently published by E. Puech[264], which contains interesting parallels to chapter 19 of the Greek *Testament of Levi* included in the *Testaments of the XII Patriarchs*. From what can be deduced from the remains preserved, the protagonist of the work (probably the patriarch Levi, although it cannot be completely excluded that it is Jacob speaking to Levi) speaks to his descendants in a series of exhortations. He also relates to them some of the visions which have been revealed to him. In one of them, he tells them of the coming of a mysterious person. Although the text is hopelessly fragmentary it is of special interest since it seems to evoke the figure of a «priestly Messiah». This «Messiah» is described with the features of the Suffering Servant of Isaiah, as J. Starcky indicated in his first description of the manuscript[265]. The two longest and most important fragments of this new text can be translated as follows:

2.1  4Q541 frag. 9 col. I

*1* [...] the sons of the generation [...] *2* [...] his wisdom. And he will atone for all the children of his generation, and he will be sent to all the children of *3* his people. His word is like the word of the heavens, and his teaching, according to the will of God. His eternal sun will shine *4* and his fire will burn in all the ends of the earth; above the darkness his sun will shine. Then, darkness will vanish *5* from the earth, and gloom from the globe. They will utter many words against him, and an abundance of *6* lies; they will fabricate fables against him, and utter every kind of disparagement against him. His generation will change the evil, *7* and [...] established in deceit and in violence. The people will go astray in his days and they will be bewildered (DSST, 270).

The preserved text does not actually call this person «Messiah». In spite of that, and in spite of the fragmentary condition in which the text has reached us, there is no doubt that it is possible to recognise the person described as a messianic figure whose coming is announced in the future. That this future is the eschatological future is evident since it is described as the period of the kingdom of light. During it, darkness will vanish from the globe, but a section of the people will remain in error and directly oppose this emissary. The priestly character of this figure is indicated expressly by his atoning character: «And he will atone for all the children of his generation». This same person will clearly have to teach and will possess supreme wisdom since his «His word is like the word of the heavens».

The agreement of the person thus described with the «Messiah-priest» described in chapter 18 of the Greek *Testament of Levi* is surprising[266]. At least it shows us that the presence of this priestly figure in the *Testaments of the XII Patriarchs* should not simply be ascribed to interpolations or Christian influence. Rather, it is a development which exists already within Judaism. This text also shows us that the portrayal of this «Messiah-priest» with the features of the «Suffering Servant» of Deutero-Isaiah is not an innovation of purely Christian origin either, but the result of previous developments. Our text stresses that although he would be sent «to all the sons of his people», the opposition to this figure, «light of the nations» (Is 42:6) would be great: «They will utter many words against him, and an abundance of lies; they will fabricate fables against him, and utter every kind of disparagement against him» (compare Is 50:6-8; 53:2-10). What is more, according to the editor, it cannot be excluded that the Aramaic text even contained the idea of the violent death of this «Messiah-priest». In other words, this opposition would reach its ultimate outcome as in Is 53. His argument comes from the other fairly extensive fragment of the work, in which possible allusions to a violent death by crucifixion are found. However, to me this interpretation seems problematic. The fragment in question can be translated as follows:

2.2   4Q541 frag. 24 col. II

*2* Do not mourn for him [...] and do not [...] *3* And God will notice the failings [...] the uncovered failings [...] *4* Examine, ask and know what the dove has asked; do not punish one weakened because of exhaustion and from being uncertain a[ll ...] *5* do not bring the nail near him. And you will establish for your father a name of joy, and for your brothers you will make a tested foundation rise. *6* You will see it and rejoice in eternal light. And you will not be of the enemy. *Blank 7 Blank* (DSST, 270).

The first lines are very confused and lines 4 and 5 present problems both of reading and of interpretation. The reading we have translated as «being uncertain» and the editor as «being hanged» is not certain and the interpretation of the previously unknown Aramaic word, which we translate «nail», is not definite. In addition, it seems impossible to prove that both fragments refer to the same person. What really is clear is that both fragments are composed in a distinctive style and that the second is direct address. Its admonishing character, the formula used, and the fact that the *Blank* of line 6 is followed by a completely blank line suggests that this fragment has actually preserved the end of the work, or at least, the end of a large section. The exhortation not to mourn could be understood perfectly before the imminent death of the Patriarch, just as the final promise could refer to his descendant. Whatever might be the possible allusion to the death of the expected «Messiah-priest», the identification of this figure with the «Servant» of Isaiah seems confirmed by the parallels indicated in fragment 9. In any case, the idea that the eventual death of the «Messiah-priest» could have an atoning role, as Christian tradition attributes to the death of the «Servant», is excluded from our text, since the atonement he achieves (frag. 9 II 2) remains in the perspective of the cult.

As far as I know, this is the only text which in the preserved sections deals with the priestly «Messiah» alone. However, many other texts refer to this figure when speaking of a two-fold messianism. This is the two-headed messianism in which we are presented with the «davidic or royal Messiah» and the «levitical or priestly Messiah» together. They are called the «Messiahs of Israel and of Aaron» respectively. Before going on to consider compositions which mention several «Messiahs», however, we must present another text which refers to another type of «messianic» figure, a superhuman agent of eschatological salvation.

### 3 A Heavenly «Messiah»

The title of this paragraph could cause surprise and even seem contradictory. It is perfectly understandable that hope in a superhuman agent of eschatological salvation could have developed in the Judaism of the period. To consider this agent of eschatological salvation as a «Messiah» could appear to be not just an unacceptable broadening of the concept of «Messiah» but even a broadening which empties the concept of «Messiah» of its deepest characteristic, its human dimension. It is difficult enough to imagine the possibility of a superhuman person being considered as «anointed» (angels certainly did not receive an anointing). Even more, the human nature of the «Messiahs» which we have seen so far, should be strongly stressed both in the davidic descendance of the «Messiah-king» and in the cultic perspective in which the «Messiah-priest» performs his atonement. If, in addition, it is accepted that the technical term «anointed» does not occur in the text in question, the attempt to consider it as «messianic» could seem to be somewhat artificial, and the semantic widening of the term «Messiah» so implied as meaningless.

And yet it seems difficult to avoid using the adjective «messianic» to characterise the hero of this text, since the functions attributed to him really are «messianic» functions. Other Jewish writings, not from Qumran, describing a superhuman agent of eschatological salvation, use the technical term «Messiah» as one of the names for the saving figure which they describe. This proves that the widening of the semantic field of «Messiah» had already taken place in the Judaism of the period and forces us not to exclude these texts *a priori*, under pain of ignoring one of the possible developments of «messianic» hope reflected in the manuscripts preserved. The texts I am referring to are, of course, *The Parables of Enoch* and *IV Esdras*. The first occasionally uses the term «Messiah» (in 48:10 and 52:4) together with the more common titles of «Chosen One» and above all «Son of Man»[267] to denote an existing, transcendental figure of celestial origin. In the vision included in chapter 13 by the author of *IV Esdras*, a person «like a man», called «Messiah» in 7:28 and 12:32 and more often «son/servant of God», is clearly presented also as an existing, transcendental person of celestial origin[268]. Both figures are called «Messiah» in these texts, in spite of their superhuman nature and in spite of being described with images traditionally associated with the divinity. Accordingly, as Collins correctly observes[269], «the understanding of "messiah" is thereby qualified». These parallels in two compositions, of which the Jewish origin does not seem to be doubted, justifies our inclusion of the following text in our study.

A few lines of this text have been known for quite some time[270] and have been extensively studied[271]. However, the recent complete publication of the fragment[272] which informs us of the last five lines of column II allows a fuller analysis. It is the only fragment preserved of an Aramaic composition dated palaeographically to the first half of the 1st century. This fragment comes from the end of a leather leaf and preserves traces of sewing to the following sheet; in it is preserved a complete column of nine lines and approximately half of the preceding column. The text can be translated as follows:

4Q246 col. I

> *1* [...] settled upon him and he fell before the throne *2* [...] eternal king. You are angry and your years *3* [...] they will see you, and all shall come for ever. *4* [...] great, oppression will come upon the earth *5* [...] and great slaughter in the city *6* [...] king of Assyria and of Egypt *7* [...] and he will be great over the earth *8* [...] they will do, and all will serve *9* [...] great will he be called and he will be designated by his name (DSST, 138).

Col. II

> *1* He will be called son of God, and they will call him son of the Most High. Like the sparks *2* of a vision, so will their kingdom be; they will rule several years over *3* the earth and crush everything; a people will crush another people, and a city another city. *4* *Blank* Until the people of God arises and makes everyone rest from the sword. *5* His kingdom will be an eternal kingdom, and all his paths in truth and uprigh[tness]. *6* The earth (will be) in truth and all will make peace. The sword will cease in the earth, *7* and all the cities will pay him homage. He is a great God among the gods (?). *8* He will make war with him; he will place the peoples in his hand and cast away everyone before him. *9* His kingdom will be an eternal kingdom, and all the abysses (DSST, 138).

I described the contents of the text as known in 1983:

The text tells us that someone (a seer?) falls down in front of a king's throne and addresses him. He describes to him the evils to come, among which reference to Assyria and Egypt play an important role. Even more important will be the apparition of a mysterious person to whom will be given the titles of «son of God» and «son of the Most High», a person who «will be great upon the earth» and whom «all will serve». His appearance will be followed by tribulations, but these will be as fleeting as a spark and will only last «until the people of God arises». The outcome will be the end of war, an eternal kingdom in which all will make peace, cities will be conquered, because the great God will be with him (with his people?) and he will make all his enemies subject to him[273].

First I set out the interpretations of Milik (who identified the mysterious person as Alexander Balas), Fitzmyer (who applied the titles to a royal but non-messianic person, heir to David's throne) and Flusser (who saw a reference to Antichrist in this mysterious person) and the reasons why they seemed insufficient. I then proposed understanding the person to which the text refers as an «Eschatological liberator» of angelic, that is to say, non-human nature, a figure similar in functions to those which 11QMelch ascribes to Melchizedek or 1QM to the «Prince of Light» or to the archangel Michael. E. Puech, the editor of the whole text, thinks that the preserved text does not allow definitive resolution between an «historicizing» interpretation like Milik's and a «messianic» interpretation, towards which his preferences seem inclined. Puech seems to exclude my interpretation for two reasons. It is not certain that 4Q246 is a composition of Qumran origin and because, in his opinion, «the "heavenly" figures who are the mediators of salvation in ancient Judaism, Enoch, Elijah, Melkizedek or the Son of God have not, strictly speaking, received the title of "messiah"»[274]. However, as we have indicated, this statement is not completely correct. Also, the parallels I noted with ideas contained in other Qumran writings, may not be determinative in assigning a sectarian origin to the composition, but do at least make it completely compatible with the thought of the Qumran group.

I remain convinced, then, that my interpretation of the first fragmentary column and of the first four lines of column II continues to be the best to explain the elements preserved. My description of the person in question as «angelic» was based on the parallel with other non-human figures of the Qumran texts. Perhaps it would be more correct to denote this superhuman figure simply as «heavenly». And the new lines now available confirm and emphasise this conclusion, since they describe this figure with the features of Daniel's «Son of Man»[275]. The quotations from Dn 7 are especially striking. «His kingdom will be an eternal kingdom» of column II 5 comes from Dn 7:27 where it is applied to the «people of the holy ones of the Most High». «His kingdom will be an eternal kingdom» of column II 9 comes from Dn 7:14, where it is applied to the «Son of Man». In the biblical text, the parallelism of both expressions in the vision and in its explanation could favour the interpretation of the «Son of Man» as a collective figure. The author of our composition, however, seems to attribute both expressions to the mysterious protagonist of the narrative, whom he considers without any doubt whatever as an individual, so anticipating the clear interpretation as an individual we find in the *Book of Parables*.

The preserved text does not completely exclude the possibility that the third person pronominal suffixes it uses, beginning with column II 5, could refer to the people of God. In fact, biblical equivalents could be found for most of the expressions used, which refer sometimes to an individual person and some-times to a person representing the people, or to the people. In spite of this ambiguity, though, the lines published recently incline me to modify the position I had adopted in 1983, attributing these pronouns to the «people of God». I now adopt Puech's interpretation who refers them clearly to the protagonist mentioned at the end of column I and at the beginning of column II.

Puech notes that «may he raise» [«qu'il relève»] can be read in column II 4 instead of «may (the people of God) rise» [«que se (re)lève le peuple de Dieu»], and «may he make all rest» [«qu'il fasse tout reposer»] instead of «all will rest» [«tout reposera»]. This enables line 4 to be understood as the climax of the pe-riod of crisis described beforehand, enables the lofty titles given to the protago-nist to be understood, since the task he has to fulfil is to bring in the situation of eschatological peace, and it enables the particle used to be given its value of a limit[276]. This interpretation is strengthened by the use of «he will judge» in column II 5, and by the statement of the cosmic dimension of his kingdom in column II 9.

This reading of the text is strengthened by the way in which the sentence in question is set out in the manuscript. The *Blank* which comes before mention of the «people of God» seems intended to emphasise that this situation of es-chatological peace is precisely the conclusion of the situation described previ-ously and is due to the activity of the protagonist, to whom the lofty titles «son of God» and «son of the Most High» are given. The *Blank* which follows this expression on the same line removes the need to make a whole series of suffixes in the following lines refer to the nearest antecedent («the people of God», the object of the preceding phrase). They can refer to the subject of the phrase, the «son of God» and «son of the Most High».

Understood in this way, 4Q246 describes an eschatological liberator, a heav-enly being similar to the «Son of Man» of Dn 7, called «son of God» and «son of the Most High». He will be the agent to bring eschatological salvation, judge all the earth, conquer all the kings through God's power and rule over the whole universe.

This messianic interpretation of the «eschatological liberator» of 4Q246, which I proposed in 1983, agrees completely with the «messianic» interpretation proposed by Puech as an alternative to Milik's «historicising» interpretation (which he accepts as equally valid). Although Puech insists on the royal character and on the Davidic lineage of this person, he ends by considering this «Messiah» as a special divinised «Messiah», similar to the Melchizedek of 11QMelch and the heavenly Son of Man[277]. And this is precisely the element which has to be emphasised here. In Qumran, together with a «Messiah-king» and a «Messiah-priest», the coming of an agent of eschatological salvation was expected (who is not explicitly referred to as «Messiah» in the text) as exalted as the pre-existent «Son of Man» of the *Parables of Enoch* or like the «Messiah» of *IV Esdras*.

This same type of saviour figure of superhuman nature is found in another text (11QMelch), where the title «Messiah of the Spirit» has been partially preserved. However, this title seems to refer to the «messianic» figure of the eschatological prophet, mentioned together with the eschatological deliverer of heavenly nature who is Melchizedek. Therefore, this text must be considered among those which tell us of several messianic figures. We will discuss it briefly in what follows.

## II  Texts which Mention Several Messianic Figures

### 1  Two «Messiahs»: the «Messiahs of Aaron and Israel»

Perhaps the most studied and best known element of Qumran messianism is its two-headed messianism: the hope in a double «Messiah», «the Messiah of Aaron» and the «Messiah of Israel». The key text comes from the *Rule of the Community*[278]

#### 1.1  1QS IX 9–11

*9* They should not depart from any counsel of the law in order to walk *10* in complete stubbornness of their heart, but instead shall be ruled by the first directives which the men of the Community began to be taught *11* until the prophet comes, and the Messiahs of Aaron and Israel. *Blank* (DSST, 13-14).

The text is crystal clear and expresses without any doubt the hope, within the Qumran community, in the future coming of the two «anointed ones» (in the plural). The «Messiah of Aaron» and the «Messiah of Israel», two figures who apparently correspond to the «priestly Messiah» and the «royal Messiah» whom we came across as separate figures in the preceding texts. Together with them, and distinct from both «Messiahs», there was hope in the eschatological future for the coming of another person: a prophet. The only thing the text tells us about these three figures is the hope in their coming. It tells us nothing about their functions, about the biblical basis which allowed their hope to develop, their possible identification with other titles used in the texts to give these figures a name. The exception is the priestly character implied in the provenance «from Aaron» of one of them and of the non-priestly character of the other who comes «from Israel». In spite of its laconic nature, this text is fundamental since it allows us to clarify a whole series of expressions which mention the «anointed one» (in the singular) of Aaron and of Israel as referring not to a single «Messiah», priest and king at the same time, but to two «Messiahs»: a «Messiah-priest» and a «lay-Messiah».

There has been much discussion about the origin of this hope in a double «Messiah», who also appears in the *Testaments of the XII Patriarchs*[279], especially after it was known that in the oldest copy of the *Rule of the Community* (4QS$^e$) the passage in question does not occur[280]. In that manuscript, the text goes straight from VIII 15 to IX 12[281]. It is impossible, though, to know whether it is an accidental omission by the copyist of something that was there in the original work, or of a later addition inserted into the copy from Cave 1. In any case, the presence of this passage in the manuscript of 1QS is enough for our purpose. It proves that this hope in a double «Messiah» existed at Qumran and guarantees that the same hope is found reflected in the other texts which they use to express it less clearly.

The text does not allow us to determine whether the first figure it introduces – a prophet – does or does not have «messianic» features. Its contrast to the «Messiahs» seems rather to indicate the opposite. But other texts which we will see later enable us to determine that this expected prophet was also considered a «messianic» figure. Of the «messianic» nature of the «Messiahs of Aaron and Israel» there can be absolutely no doubt. This messianic character is even more obvious in the other texts in the *Damascus Document*[282] which mention these two figures, although in none of these references is the word «Messiah» used in the plural.

### 1.2  CD

*22 Blank* And this is the rule of the assembly *23* [of the ca]mps. Those who walk in them, in the time of wickedness until there arises the messiah of Aaron *1* and Israel, they shall be ten in number as a minimum to (form) thousands, hundreds, fifties *2* and tens (CD XII 22- XIII 2; DSST, 43).
*Blank* And this is the exact interpretation of the regulations by which [they shall be ruled] *19* [until there arises the messiah] of Aaron and Israel[283]. He shall atone for their sins [... pardon, and guilt] (CD XIV 18-19; DSST, 44).

These shall escape in the age of the visitation; but those that remain shall be delivered up to the sword when there comes the messiah *11* of Aaron and Israel (CD XIX 10-11; DSST, 45).
And thus, all the men who entered the new *34* covenant in the land of Damascus and turned and betrayed and departed from the well of living waters, *35* shall not be counted in the assembly of the people and shall not be inscribed in their [lis]ts, from the day of the session *1* of the unique Teacher until there arises the messiah of Aaron and Israel. *Blank* (CD XIX 33- XX 1; DSST, 46).

As we have indicated, these four texts use one somewhat ambiguous expression: «Messiah of Aaron and Israel» in CD XII 23[284], XIV 19 and XIX 10, and «Messiah of Aaron and of Israel» in CD XX 1, an expression which can be translated both by «Messiah of Aaron and of Israel» and by «Messiah of Aaron and (Messiah) of Israel». Although the second expression can be interpreted more easily as referring to two different persons[285], the possibility of interpreting both phrases as referring to a single person who comes from Aaron and Israel at the same time, is not only an actual possibility but it is also strengthened by the fact that in CD IX 19 the expression is followed by a verb in the singular. Accordingly, several scholars have made the «Messiah» the subject of the verb. And since the act is one of atonement, they have concluded that the figure indicated will be that of the «priestly Messiah» who will atone for the sins of the people[286]. But the text already cited, 1QS IX 11, resolves the ambiguity of the Hebrew expression. It proves that in all these cases the most likely interpretation is one which sees in these phrases a reference to the two «Messiahs» expected by the community[287].

In these four texts, the coming of these persons is expected for the «time of wickedness» and «the age of the visitation», two expressions which leave no doubt at all about the eschatological perspective in which the hope in their arrival is placed. The texts tell us hardly anything directly about the functions of these persons. The first and fourth references place his coming in relation to the structure and organization of the community in the eschatological period. The second reference relates it to the exact interpretation of the regulations; the third, to the different fates, salvation or damnation, which will befall the faithful or the unfaithful when they come. Finally, the fourth reference suggests that their coming is expected (shortly) after the disappearance of the «Unique Teacher», the historical figure we know as the «Teacher of Righteousness», and already a figure of the past at the time when this version of the *Damascus Document* was edited.

We can deduce more details about his functions from two texts from another of the manuscripts which seem to mention both figures together, the *Rule of the Congregation*[288].

1.3  1QSa

*11* This is the assembly of famous men, [those summoned to] the gathering
of the community council, when [God] begets *12* the Messiah with them.
[The] chief [priest] of the all the congregation of Israel shall enter, and all
*13* [his brothers, the sons] of Aaron, the priests [summoned] to the assembly, the famous men, and they shall sit *14* befo[re him, each one] according
to his dignity. After, [the Me]ssiah of Israel shall ent[er] and before him
shall sit the chiefs *15* [of the clans of Israel, each] one according to his dignity, according to their [positions] in their camps and in their marches
(1QSa II 11-14; DSST, 127).
*17* And [when] they gather at the table of community [or to drink] the new
wine, and the table of *18* community is prepared [and] the new wine [is
mixed] for drinking, [no-one should stretch out] his hand to the first-fruit
of the bread *19* and of the [new wine] before the priest, for [he is the one
who bl]esses the first-fruit of bread *20* and of the new wine [and stretches
out] his hand towards the bread before them. Afterwards, the Messiah of
Israel shall stretch out his hand *21* towards the bread. [And after, he shall]
bless all the congregation of the community, each [one according to] his
dignity. And in accordance with this regulation they shall act *22* at each
me[al, when] at least ten m[en are gat]hered. *Blank* (1QSa II 17-22; DSST, 127-
128).

These two fragments mention a «priest» and the «Messiah of Israel» as two
clearly distinct figures. About the «Messiah» it apparently tells us that God
«begets» him with them. The syntax is strange and the reading uncertain; but
the editor is reliable in as much as either «will beget» or «will cause to be born»
can be read in the manuscript[289]. This means that our text must include the
ideas of Ps 2:7, applying them to the «divine» origin of the «Messiah». Due to
a lacuna, it is not possible to know for certain whether it is a question of the
«anointed [priest]» (as Kuhn proposes, identifying him with the Messiah of
Aaron) or of an absolute use of the «Messiah» which could instead correspond
to the person which the following text denotes as «Messiah of Israel». The uncertainties of the text prevent us from attaching great weight to this person
about whom the opinions of scholars are so divided.

Fortunately, there is more agreement about the identity of the priest in question. Most of the researchers recognise in him the «High Priest» of the eschatological period, whom they identify with the «Messiah of Aaron». The eschatological period is involved, as shown by the text itself, indicating that they are
regulations «for the end of times» (col. I 1). The «priest» is the High Priest, as
is also evident in the text which defines him as «chief of the whole congregation
of Israel». This High Priest of the eschatological period is the same figure we

met in the preceding texts, called «Messiah of Aaron». That is a logical deduction based on his superiority over the «Messiah of Israel» who is mentioned next, a superiority already indicated in the very formula in which they both appear together: «Messiah of Aaron and of Israel»²⁹⁰. Our text emphasises the connection of this messianic figure with the congregation. It also emphasises his superior function both in relation to the other sons of Aaron, the priests, and especially the non-priestly members of the community, including the «Messiah of Israel». Both in the assemblies and in the banquet it is he who presides and occupies the most eminent position. Concerning the «Messiah of Israel» these texts emphasise his subordinate position to the priest and his military character, indicated in the terminology used which depends on Num and agrees with 1QM.

Another possible allusion to the functions of both «Messiahs» could be provided by 4Q375 and 4Q376, although the meaning of these two texts is ambiguous and problematic, and their interpretation is very uncertain.

Both manuscripts were published by J. Strugnell²⁹¹, who considers them to be two possible copies of a single composition. 4Q376 is certainly another copy of the work known from several fragments from Cave 1 (1Q29), and it seems reasonable to consider these three manuscripts as copies of the same composition. In addition, the editor presents certain arguments from style in favour of identifying the composition represented in these three texts with the Moses apocryphon known as *Words of Moses* (1Q22) which would provide the narrative framework of the composition. However, this seems too problematic and in any case is not important for our purpose. What could really be important is the reference in 4Q375 1 I 9 to «the anointed priest upon whose head the oil of anointing has been poured». Similarly, the mention in 4Q376 1 III 1 of «the Prince who is over the whole congregation» in a clear military context, and in connection with «the anointed priest» mentioned in the first column of this manuscript (4Q376 1 I 1).

If 4Q375 and 4Q376 really were two copies of the same composition; if the «Prince of the whole congregation» had the same meaning in this work as in *all* the other Qumran texts where the expression is used and where it *always* denotes the «davidic Messiah»; and if it could be shown that this person is located in an eschatological context, these fragments would be very interesting for this study on messianic ideas. This would allow an allusion both to the High Priest and to the «priestly Messiah» to be seen in the «anointed priest upon whose head the oil of anointing has been poured». And in the «Prophet» an allusion to the eschatological Prophet. Further, the complex procedure by which the High Priest determines whether the prophet is true or false by means of a sacrificial rite, the investigation of hidden precepts and the oracular use of the *Urim* could be interpreted as a process of verifying whether in fact the prophet is the eschatological Prophet or not and not merely whether the prophet is true or false.

However, to me it seems impossible to prove definitively the conditions upon which this interpretation rests[292]. There is no clear indication that both texts are located in an eschatological perspective. The texts can be explained perfectly as an apocryphon in which, in pure deuteronomistic language the High Priest judges a false prophet who has the backing of a whole tribe which considers him as a trustworthy prophet. The process used is different from what is prescribed in Dt 13 and 18, comprising an atonement ceremony, the investigation of the divine precepts which have been hidden from the people and the oracular use of the *Urim*. And «the Prince of the whole congregation» could only be a modification of the plural form «princes of the congregation» of Ex 16:22, Num 4:34, 16:2, 31:33, 32:2 and Josh 9:15.18. Accordingly, for the moment this fascinating text must remain outside the discussion of «messianism».

### 2  Two «Messiahs»: the «Prince of the Congregation» and the «Interpreter of the Law»

Together with texts which mention the two «Messiahs» of Aaron and of Israel we find others which also mention two messianic figures called by other names. We must try and establish their identity.

#### 2.1  CD VII 18–21[293]

*18 ... Blank* And the star is the Interpreter of the law, *19* who will come to Damascus, as is written: (Num 24:13) «A star moves out of Jacob, and a sceptre arises *20* out of Israel». The sceptre is the prince of the whole congregation and when he rises he will destroy *21* all the sons of Seth. *Blank* (DSST, 38).

The «Prince of the whole congregation» is familiar to us and, apart from 4Q376, where his character cannot be determined, always denotes a «messianic» figure. As in the previous texts, here he is equated with the sceptre. There is no doubt, therefore, about his identity with the «Messiah-king», the davidic «Messiah» of Jewish tradition and the «Messiah of Israel» of the other texts where the davidic character of such titles is muted. This text only tells us about the one who «will destroy all the sons of Seth», using the expression of Num 24:17, but without specifying its meaning (which in the original biblical text is not very clear either). But who is the «Interpreter of the Law» who here appears in parallel with him? Is he a figure from the past or from the future?

The ambiguity of the text is well known and, ultimately, everything depends on the value of past or future given to the participle used. The authors who are convinced that in this *Amos-Numbers Midrash* only one messianic figure is spoken about[294] consider the «Interpreter of the Law» as a figure from the past. Whereas, those who see in our text an allusion to two «messianic» figures see a figure of the future in this same «Interpreter of the Law», contemporary with the «Prince of the whole congregation»[295].

The strict parallelism between the two figures, the fact that both are interpreted starting from the same biblical text (to which later tradition was to give a clear messianic value) and, above all, the details which 4Q174 give us about this «Interpreter of the Law» who will come in the final times together with the «shoot of David», a figure whom 4Q174 explicitly identifies with the «Prince of the congregation», are enough, in my opinion, to resolve the ambiguity of the text in favour of the interpretation which sees reflected here hope in two messianic figures.

It seems more difficult to determine who this «Interpreter of the Law» is. Two interpretations have been suggested. Starcky[296] identified him with the expected eschatological prophet, although this identification starts from a false premise, the non-separation of the two «Messiahs» of Aaron and of Israel in CD. The more prevalent opinion, following van der Woude[297], identifies this «Interpreter of the Law» with the «Messiah of Aaron». I.e., the «priest-Messiah» who should be identified with the eschatological figure of Elijah. Van der Woude's reasoning essentially is as follows. The «Interpreter of the Law» of the passage is a person from the future and thus distinct from the «Interpreter of the Law» who occurs in CD VI 7 and is a person from the past. This person is found in parallel with the «Prince of the whole congregation», who is a messianic figure identical with the «Messiah of Israel», so that he must also be a messianic figure. The title given him, «Interpreter of the Law», is very general and can denote various figures, but the specification «who will come to Damascus» (meaning Qumran) is more significant. The clause comes from 1 Kg 19:15, where Elijah receives from God the order to go to Damascus to anoint the king of Syria, the king of Israel and the prophet Elisha. In later tradition (attested in Justin, *Dialog.* 49[298] and in the Karaite material collected by N. Wieder[299]) Elijah is portrayed as the eschatological High Priest who performs the anointing of the Messiah. In rabbinic tradition, Elijah is also portrayed as one who will resolve the halakhic problems the rabbis are unable to solve, when he returns at the end of times as a forerunner of the «Messiah». This permits van der Woude to conclude that the «Interpreter of the Law» denotes Elijah whose coming is expected at the end of times. This figure is seen as a «priestly Messiah» and thus is identical with the «Messiah of Aaron» of the other Qumran texts.

My problem with this reasoning is that the two texts which mention the eschatological figure of the «Interpreter of the Law» tell us absolutely nothing about his priestly character; the features of «prophet» seem more characteristic of Elijah than those of «priest». Accordingly, for very different reasons from those of Starcky, I feel more inclined to identify this messianic figure of the eschatological «Interpreter of the Law» with the messianic figure about whom we have not yet spoken. He is the «Prophet» expected at the end of times, whose identification with Elijah *redivivus* can be accepted without problems. The reasons for this inclination will be set out when dealing in more detail with this figure of the «eschatological Prophet».

### 2.2 4Q174 (4QFlorilegium)

The other text which mentions these same two «messianic» figures is known as *Florilegium*[300].

> *10* And «YHWH de[clares] to you that he will build you a house. I will raise up your seed after you and establish the throne of his kingdom *11* [for ev]er. I will be a father to him and he will be a son to me.» This (refers to the) «branch of David», who will arise with the Interpreter of the law who *12* [will rise up] in Zi[on in] the last days, as it is written: «I will raise up the hut of David which has fallen», This (refers to) «the hut of *13* David which has fallen», who will arise to save Israel. *Blank* (DSST, 136).

This text refers to the «Interpreter of the Law» by name. Together with him it speaks about the «branch of David», a familiar expression to denote the «Messiah-king», named «Prince of the whole congregation» in the preceding text. His identity with the «Messiah of Israel» presents no problem. Apart from their future coming, it tells us nothing about both figures. The requirement that this coming would take place in «the last days» remains important since it stresses his clear eschatological character.

### 3 Two «Messiahs»: the «Heavenly Messiah» and the «Eschatological Prophet»

Another of the Qumran fragments in which the figure of a heavenly «Messiah» appears is a midrash of eschatological content, in which a heavenly person, an *elohim*, called Melchizedek, is the divine instrument of salvation and executes justice. The central part of the fragment (col. II 6-19) can be translated as follows[301]:

> *6* He (Melchizedek) will proclaim liberty for them, to free them from [the debt] of all their iniquities. And this will [happen] *7* in the first week of the jubilee which follows the ni[ne] jubilees. And the day [of atonem]ent is the end of the tenth jubilee *8* in which atonement will be made for all the sons of [God] and for the men of the lot of Melchizedek. [And on the heights]

he will decla[re in their] favour according to their lots; for *9* it is the time
of the «year of grace» for Melchizedek, to exa[lt in the tri]al the holy ones
of God through the rule of judgment, as is written *10* about him in the
songs of David, who said: «Elohim will stand up in the assem[bly of God,]
in the midst of the gods he judges». And about him he said: «Above it
*11* return to the heights, God will judge the peoples». As for what he sa[id:
«How long will yo]u judge unjustly and show partiality to the wicked?
*Selah.*» *12* Its interpretation concerns Belial and the spirits of his lot, who
were rebels [all of them] turning aside from the commandments of God [to
commit evil.] *13* But, Melchizedek will carry out the vengeance of God's
judges [on this day, and they shall be freed from the hands] of Belial and
from the hands of all the sp[irits of his lot.] *14* To his aid (shall come) all
«the gods of [justice»; he] is the one who will prevail on this day over] all
the sons of God, and he will pre[side over] this [assembly.] *15* This is the
day of [peace about which God] spoke [of old through the words of Isa]iah
the prophet, who said: «How] beautiful *16* upon the mountains are the feet
of the messenger who announces peace, of the mess[enger of good who
announces salvation,] saying to Zion: "Your God [reigns"».] *17* Its interpretation: The mountains are the pro[phets ...] *18* And the messenger is [the
ano]inted of the spirit about whom Dan[iel] spoke [... and the messenger
of] *19* good who announces salv[ation is the one about whom it is written
that [...] (DSST, 139-140).

In spite of the uncertainty of the reconstructions, the broad lines of the content
seem clear enough and are well known. Here, therefore, we only need to note
the details which they give concerning the messianic figures to whom the text
refers. The weave of the text is formed by Lv 25:8-13 concerning the jubilee
year, Dt 15 concerning the year of release and Is 61. The author also applies to
Melchizedek, the protagonist, other texts from Isaiah, the Psalms and Daniel,
the interpretation of which allows him to develop his ideas. The eschatological
content is evident through the execution of justice and the deliverance from
Belial. It is also evident because the whole is set specifically in the first week of
the tenth jubilee, the final jubilee in his chronological system. In this context,
the author ascribes three fundamental functions to this exalted figure: to be an
avenging judge (with reference to Pss 82:1-2 and 7:1); to be a heavenly priest
who carries out atonement for his inheritance on the «day of atonement»; and
to be the ultimate saviour of «the men of his lot» who destroys the kingdom of
Belial and restores peace.

With the restoration of the day of peace, the text seems to introduce a new
person, identified as «the messenger» of Is 52:7, a text which the author combines with Is 61:2-3. It defines this person as «the anointed by the spirit»,
clearly in the singular. Unfortunately, neither the text of Daniel nor further

details have been preserved. All that we can assert about him, therefore, is that the text clearly distinguishes him from the prophets of the past, and seems to consider him as introducing the action of the «heavenly Messiah». His identification as the «eschatological Prophet», which we will study next, cannot be considered as completely proved, but is certainly the most probable[302].

### 4 Three «Messiahs»: the Eschatological Prophet

In commenting on the key text 1QS IX 11, we left in suspense the third figure who appeared there together with the «Messiahs of Aaron and of Israel» and is simply called «the Prophet»: «until the prophet comes and the Messiahs of Aaron and Israel». It is obvious from his juxtaposition to the two «Messiah» figures that this person is an eschatological person. It is less evident that he is a true «messianic» figure, since unlike the other two he is not termed «anointed» here. And yet I think that even so he must be considered as a true «messianic» figure.

In essence, my reasoning is as follows. 4QTestimonia, a collection of texts which the community interprets messianically, and corresponds to the three figures of 1QS IX 11, begins by quoting Dt 18:18-19 as the base text which is the foundation for hope in the «Prophet like Moses», «the Prophet» awaited at the end of time. Then comes Num 24:15-17, which is the foundation for the hope in the «Messiah-king». Then Dt 33:8-11, which is the foundation for hope in the «Messiah-priest». The three quotations are at the same level and in complete parallelism, and therefore must refer to similar figures. This figure of the «Prophet» is identical with the figures which the other texts denote as the «Interpreter of the Law», who «teaches justice at the end of times» and the «messenger»-figures which have a clear prophetic character and are considered as messianic figures. Like them, then, the «Prophet» must be considered as a «messianic» figure. About the last of these figures, «the messenger», we are told expressly in 11QMelch II 18 that he is «anointed by the spirit». In other words, the technical term which in 1QS IX 11 is applied to the other two «messianic» figures is applied to him, in the singular. Accordingly, it seems justifiable to consider this «Prophet», whose coming is expected at the same time as the «Messiahs of Aaron and of Israel», as a true «messianic» figure.

The first item in my argument is obvious and needs no explanation. Perhaps, though, it might be useful to note that «anointed» can be applied to the first of the three figures referred to by the biblical texts of this collection of *testimonia*, as well as to the other two. The choice of Dt 18:18-19 shows that the expected «Prophet» is a «Prophet like Moses». At Qumran, both Moses and the Prophets are called «anointed ones», a title which seems to be based on the parallel between «anointed ones» and «prophets» in Ps 105:15 and in the Old Testament allusions to the «anointing» of prophets. The parallel with «seers» and the function of announcing and teaching which is attributed to them in the following two texts make it clear that the «anointed ones» spoken about are none other than the prophets. 1QM XI 7 runs: «By the hand of your anointed ones, seers of decrees, you taught us the times of the wars of your hands». And CD II 12: «And he taught them by the hands of his anointed ones[303] through his holy spirit and through seers of the truth». This allows CD VI 1 to be interpreted in the same way, where those who lead Israel astray rise against Moses but also against «the holy anointed ones». And in a still unpublished fragment of a pseudo-Mosaic composition, to be published by D. Dimant, can be read «through the mouth of Moses, his anointed one»[304]. This seems to be nothing else than a description of Moses as a prophet.

It will be useful, perhaps, to quote the biblical text with which hope in his coming is justified, since it makes it clear that this expected prophet like Moses is portrayed in the biblical text as a true interpreter of the Law:

> *5* «I would raise up for them a prophet from among their brothers, like you, and place my words *6* in his mouth, and he would tell them all that I command them. And it will happen that the man *7* who does not listen to my words, that the prophet will speak in my name, I *8* shall require a reckoning from him.» *Blank* (4Q175 5–8; DSST, 137)[305].

The second element is the most complex and implies examining the texts in which these figures occur. We have already quoted CD VII 18-21 and 4QFlorilegium col. I 11-12, which portray the figure of the «Interpreter of the Law». But there is another text from the *Damascus Document* in which the same expression, «Interpreter of the Law», occurs again. It is CD VI 7, where the «staff» of Nm 21:18 is identified as the «Interpreter of the Law», to whom the text of Is 54:16 is applied. In this case, the wording and context of the text are sufficient proof that he is a person from the past. Most scholars identify him as the historical Teacher of Righteousness, also a person from the past[306]. One of the great merits of Van der Woude's work is his convincing proof that both epithets «Interpreter of the Law» and «Teacher of Righteousness» are used as titles in CD. They are used to denote a person from the past and also an eschatological person whose coming is expected in the future. This enabled him to resolve the problem posed by the reference to an «Interpreter of the Law» in CD VI 7 as a figure from the past. He was also able to solve the problem posed by the text immediately after (in CD VI 11) which mentions a clearly eschatological figure from the future, given a title identical to that of «Teacher of Righteousness»: «until there arises he who teaches justice at the end of days».

Van der Woude assembled the main arguments provided by the text proving that the historical figure referred to as «Teacher of Righteousness» and «Interpreter of the Law» was seen as a true «prophet». This allowed him to conclude that this historical figure had been perceived as a «Prophet like Moses», whose coming is expected in 1QS IX 11. In my view, this conclusion is wrong. A text such as CD XIX 35- XX 1 proves that the period of existence of the «unique Teacher» (or of the Teacher of the community) is seen as clearly different from the future coming of the «Messiahs» with whom the coming of the «Prophet» is associated[307]. However, his arguments to prove the prophetic character of the person are completely correct. And they prove that the figure called «Interpreter of the Law» or «he who teaches justice at the end of days» must be identified with this «Prophet», expected together with the «Messiahs of Aaron and of Israel». Precisely because the historical «Teacher of Righteousness» was perceived as a true prophet like Moses it was possible to use the titles «he who teaches justice» or «Interpreter of the Law» for this figure expected for the end of time and also described as a «Prophet» like Moses.

The fundamental difference between my way of seeing and Van der Woude's is that for him the «Prophet» is not a «messianic» figure, but a forerunner of the Messiahs. I, on the other hand, believe that the eschatological «Prophet» is a «messianic» figure. He can only be identified with a historical person from the past if this person is considered as *redivivus*. His character of «messianic» figure is not an obstacle to his character of «forerunner». This appears to be proved by the third figure: the «messenger» whom 11QMelch describes together with the heavenly «Messiah», whose coming is expected in the final jubilee of history, and in the manuscript is called not only prophet but also «anointed by the spirit».

To complete this presentation of the texts it is necessary to include three references, one published and the other two from still unpublished manuscripts, which mention one or more «anointed ones». Unfortunately, the phrases lack a context which would allow their meaning to be determined. Yet, everything indicates that the first two refer not to a «Messiah» but to one or more «prophets». The person to whom the third reference applies cannot be determined.

The first reference occurs in 1Q30 fragment 1,2[308] and the reading is very uncertain: «[an]ointed of holiness». The parallelism with the expression of CD VI 1 and the possible reference of line 4 to «the five books» suggest that it applies to a prophet.

The second reference is in the last line of a column, the only line preserved in fragment 10 of 4Q287[309]. The work from which it comes is a collection of blessings and curses of which several copies have been found and from which Milik had published a few lines[310]. According to the transcription of the line in question in the *Preliminary Concordance*, the phrase should be translated «the holy spirit [res]ted upon his anointed one». However, the reading is uncertain. In fact, the photograph allows reading the plural «his anointed ones», and the parallel in CD II 12 requires the translation: «upon the anointed ones of the spirit of holiness», i.e., the prophets.

We cannot conclude anything either from another recently published text in which the phrase «anointed with the oil of kingship»[311] occurs. This is because we do not know to whom it refers. In the fragment where it occurs (frag. 2 of 4Q458[312]) someone destroys someone else and devours the uncircumcised, so that the phrase could have been applied to the expected «king-Messiah». However, all that can be concluded is that it expresses the royal anointing of the person to whom it refers, whoever that person might be.

The simple presentation of the «messianic» texts has turned out to be too lengthy to allow us now to try and summarise the data they provide as a form of conclusion. In addition, I am not certain that a summary like J. Starcky's famous summary[313], in which he discovered four stages of development in the Qumran community, would be possible today. The famous omission of the messianic passage 1QS IX 11 from the oldest copy, palaeographically speaking, of the *Rule*, if not due to accidental causes, suggests a certain development. And the palaeographically late date (1st century CE) of the two texts which mention the heavenly «Messiah» could indicate that this form of messianic hope is a later development. However, these simple facts do not allow a summary to be attempted. Even, for example, a summary which, starting with the clear biblical antecedents of the idea of a davidic Messiah, and going on to a priestly Messiah, double messianism, the multiplication of expected messianic figures (whether called «Messiah» or not) culminates in the hope for a heavenly «Messiah».

I am not even convinced that it would be possible to fit all these texts into G. Scholem's scheme of a «restorative messianism» versus a «utopian messianism» as Talmon and Schiffman do[314]. This does not necessarily imply the conclusion that for the Qumran community «messianic» ideas were a private matter, in which different and even conflicting opinions could co-exist in harmony because ultimately they lack importance[315], or because in «messianology» consistency is impossible[316]. The large number of references inserted in every kind of literary context, including legal contexts, testifies to its importance for the Qumran community. And the hope in many and varied «messianic» figures cannot be considered as itself «inconsistent». Ultimately, in the 1st century the Jewish group whom we know through the New Testament was to merge the hope in a «Messiah king», a «Messiah-priest», a «Prophet like Moses», a «Suffering Servant» and even a «heavenly Messiah» into one historical person from the past whose return is expected in the eschatological future.

III *Qumran and the Origins of Christianity*

# The Dead Sea Scrolls, Jesus Christ and the Origins of Christianity[317]

## Florentino García Martínez

Forty years have passed since the day when a young bedouin shepherd of the Taᶜamireh tribe accidentally discovered in an inaccessible cave next to Wadi Qumran, on the shores of the Dead Sea, a set of ancient Hebrew and Aramaic manuscripts deposited in the bottom of some jars. This discovery and the almost storytale adventures which followed already belong to history and are so well known it is pointless summarising them here. (Archaeologists, businessmen and politicians were involved, not to mention the Jordanian army and the then recently formed State of Israel. Also, the accumulation of mistakes, the large quota of guesswork and the amount of collective effort invested).

The results of these discoveries are also known. From eleven caves thousands and thousands of fragments which come from more than 800 different manuscripts have been recovered. These manuscripts encompass the whole of the Hebrew Bible and the wide field of apocryphal writings (to which they add a large number of previously unknown works). Also, a great quantity of writings which reveal to us the organization, beliefs and religious aspirations of the ancient Jewish sect from whose library all these manuscripts come and whose centre has been discovered close to the caves.

One of the most sensational elements from this discovery was the antiquity of these texts. All the manuscripts are earlier than the catastrophe of 70 CE and a large part comes from the 1st and 2nd centuries BCE. Another of the fascinating elements is that now, for the first time, we possess a large quantity of religious works which have come down directly to us, absolutely free from any later interference. Free from the interference of Jewish censorship (which destroyed all previous religious literature not conforming to the new rabbinic orthodoxy). And free of Christian censorship (which would have accepted part of these works, adapting them however to their own needs).

However, this discovery has stimulated like no other both the imagination of scholars and that of non-specialists in this twentieth century (rich enough, on the other hand, in sensational discoveries). This is due to the manuscripts from Qumran throwing light on precisely that grey area between the Old and New Testaments: the period in which budding Christianity was constituted and in which rabbinic Judaism was formed.

To be able to understand correctly the numerous contributions of these ancient texts, however, it is first of all necessary to get rid of a series of misunderstandings. So as not to become lost in the maze of detailed contributions which 40 years of study have given us it is also helpful to be able to insert, to some extent, all these contributions within a complete and unifying perspective. This is the purpose of my lecture:

– on the one hand, to clear the ground of obstacles to a correct understanding of the significance of the Dead Sea Scrolls for a knowledge of Jesus Christ and of Christianity;

– on the other hand, to sketch the broad outlines in which to insert the numberless additional details produced by research on the manuscripts.

Each part of this lecture will be concerned with one of these functions.

I

1  The Conspiracy of Silence

The first misunderstanding which it is helpful to dispel is what can be called «the myth of the conspiracy of silence». This myth is found especially in popular publications of an esoteric kind, and rarely flourishes in academic publications. The content of this myth in its crudest form can be expressed as follows. Among the Dead Sea Scrolls there are many texts the publication of which would pose a great danger for the established religions, Judaism as well as Christianity. These alleged texts would allow the falsehood of both Christianity and Judaism as a religion to be demonstrated. For this reason, the religious authorities (Jewish and Christian alike) have prevented their publication until now. In another version of the myth, the religious authorities (the Great Rabbinate, the Vatican or the Council of Churches) are not involved. Instead, the actual research scholars responsible for publication (some of whom are priests or ministers) willingly censored certain texts which offended their religious sensibilities or delayed their publication to prevent the harm they could do to the faithful.

These accusations are so ridiculous they would not merit the trouble of paying attention to them if they had not gained a high level of publicity thanks to their frequent appearance in the newspapers. It will be enough to remember that the members of the international and interconfessional team for the publication of the texts include people as lacking in religious concern as John Allegro (the author of *The Sacred Mushroom* and of *The Dead Sea Scrolls and the Christian Myth*, for example). Also, since 1967 the control of all the manuscripts from Qumran is in the hands of the Department of Antiquities of the State of Israel. This Department (as the excavations in the burial area of the Ophel proved) is free from the control of the Rabbinate. However, as my first task is to remove obstacles, and since as editor of the texts from Cave 11, I feel personally alluded to in this myth, I would like to go into its foundations in some detail.

The myth of the conspiracy of silence is based on a real fact. After 40 years, not all the manuscripts found in the Qumran caves have been published yet.

This fact would not be so strange if one thinks, for example, that the material which comes from the Cairo Genizah, discovered last century, still remains unpublished to a large extent. Or if it is considered that in the huge mass of manuscripts, only one part of those from Cave 4 and some fragments from Cave 11 are still unpublished. However, as I say, the fact on which the myth is based is true. What is completely false is the explanation that is given for this fact (that is to say, that the publication of this material would suppose a danger for established religions). In fact, all the responsible research institutions in the world have a concordance available in which are noted *all the words* preserved in *all* the Qumran manuscripts, including those still unpublished. There is, then, no text which has been kept secret.

The real explanations for the delay in the publication of the texts are many and varied. The war, a tangled political situation and the premature death of the first two directors of the editorial project (Roland de Vaux and Pierre Benoit); also, several of the editors (Patrick Skehan, Yigael Yadin and Jean Starcky) died before finishing their work. These are some of the factors which have influenced the present situation. However, the most important factor is the actual condition of the still unpublished texts, hundreds of minute fragments, with pathetic remains of incomplete words.

When the texts in question have been preserved in relatively large fragments, the task of reading, translation and interpretation is not extremely complicated. Even texts previously unknown can be published with relative speed. However, even in such cases, the speed of publication can have disastrous results, as the publication of the first set of texts from Cave 4 proves. Their publication in the official series, under John Allegro[318], appeared with great speed in 1968. However, this hasty edition (of only 90 pages of text) is so flawed that it cannot be used without the corrections (over 100 pages) published in 1971 by the later director of the international team for the edition of the texts, John Strugnell, of the University of Harvard[319].

When all that has been preserved of the original texts are extremely minute fragments, with very little written text, the task of reconstructing this gigantic jigsaw with thousands of tiny pieces with no direct joins is hopeless. Not forgetting that the separate fragments allow of multiple interpretations which all have to be appraised before proceeding to publication.

I will end with an example of what *not* to do to speed up the publication of material still unpublished: the case of 4QTherapeia. This small fragment, almost triangular in shape, with remains of 11 apparently complete lines, was assigned to Joseph Milik for publication. Allegro thought that it was an extraordinarily important text, the publication of which had been kept secret because it could be used as the basis for a gnostic interpretation of Christian initiation by means of anointing with sperm (a rite to which Jesus would have submitted his disciples). So he published it in 1979 in an appendix of a book about the

Christian myth[320]. According to his interpretation, the Qumran fragment preserved, in a weird mixture of Greek, Hebrew and Aramaic, notes from visits
made by an Essene doctor. Also, the treatments which the aforesaid doctor
Ormiel had used on a certain Caiphas. Due to the scarcity of Jewish medical
texts of the pre-Christian period, a text of this kind would actually be very
important, irrespective of any symbolic interpretation. The text would be even
more spectacular if the prescription which doctor Ormiel recommends and
uses to cure Caiphas were, as Allegro surmises, the application of semen from
a goat. Unfortunately, however, the Qumran fragment has nothing to do either
with medicine or with the use of goat semen as a rite of mysterious initiation
(as Allegro supposes). Nor is it a simple remedy (as Charlesworth conjectures
in a monograph dedicated to this text in 1985[321]). The text (as Joseph Naveh
has proved[322] and as Charlesworth himself acknowledged in a public retraction)
is a simple writing exercise. It was executed by a scribe on a remnant of skin
to train his hand before beginning to copy his texts and contains nothing more
than a list of Hebrew names in alphabetic order. This huge mistake of interpretation is a sad example of the consequences resulting from persisting in the
myth of the conspiracy of silence to interpret the Qumran texts.

## 2 Esoteric Interpretation

Another of the most widespread misunderstandings must also be dispelled. It
is circulated by those who think that the true importance of the manuscripts
from Qumran for understanding Christianity can only be perceived by means
of an esoteric reading of the Qumran texts. Unlike the previous myth, this new
myth appears in serious publications which pretend to be academic. Its two
defenders, who have the highest academic credentials, are Barbara Thiering, of
the University of Sydney, in Australia, and Robert Eisenman, of the State
University of California. The former has published four books[323], the latter two
volumes[324]. It is a fact that there are significant differences of detail between
the works of both scholars. For the former, the Teacher of Righteousness was
John the Baptist and his rival Jesus Christ. For the latter, the Teacher of Righteousness was Saint James, and his rival, Paul. However, the methodological
elements they have in common allow us to include them under a single denom-
inator. Both start from the premise that the Dead Sea Scrolls and the New
Testament were written in code. The texts do not say what they say, but instead have a secret meaning which is hidden under the terse surface of the
words. They (Thiering and Eisenman) are the ones who for the first time have
deciphered the secret code and have been able to reveal this mystery hidden
throughout two thousand years. And there is more: both sets of writings are
two sides of the same coin. Both tell us the *same* story from different points of
view: the New Testament, from the viewpoint of Jesus and of Paul; the Dead

Sea Scrolls, from the viewpoint of John the Baptist and of St James.

As in the case of the previous myth, this new myth also starts from a genuine fact. A group of Qumran manuscripts, the *pesharim*, are in fact written in such a way that their meaning is only obvious to the initiated, that is to say, the members of the sect. This is something very different from considering such texts as a *roman-à-clef*. These texts, which are commentaries on the prophetical books and the Psalms, consider the biblical text as containing a mystery which has remained hidden even from its own authors, the Prophets, and has been revealed only to the Teacher of Righteousness. This mystery is that the real meaning of the biblical texts does not refer to the period of the Prophets but to the present of the Teacher of Righteousness and of his community, a present which is considered as «the end of times». However, this present, this reality of the end of the 2nd century before Christ is rarely actually named in these texts. Only one of them, the Nahum *pesher*, uses proper names: Demetrius and Antiochus. In the rest of the texts, the protagonists of this actuality are concealed under titles such as «Teacher of Righteousness», «the Wicked Priest», «the Liar», «the Angry Lion», the «seekers of easy interpretations», «the simple», «Ephraim and Manasseh», «the house of abomination», etc. These titles, which to the Qumran community must have been transparent, are not so to us, and to us these persons are mysterious. However, the historical framework in which they are located and act does not therefore cease to be clear and exact. It is Palestine from the close of the 2nd century before Christ up to the middle of the 1st century after Christ.

In the New Testament, too, we find the same hermeneutic principle, by means of which the words of the Prophets are related to the present reality of Jesus. Unlike the *pesharim*, though, in the New Testament this reality is not concealed under symbolic titles but is completely transparent.

This is an actual fact. The explanation proposed by those who suggest decoding the texts is utterly false and violates the plain meaning of both types of text. The events to which both series of texts allude are different realities and are separated by almost two centuries.

Independently of the content of the texts, archaeological excavation has proved definitely that the Qumran community existed and produced these texts between the close of the 2nd century before Christ and the moment when its buildings were destroyed by the Roman attack of 68 CE.

In the same way, and independently of the content of the texts, palaeography has proved that the copies of the Qumran texts which have reached us were made between the 3rd century BCE and the middle of the 1st century CE. No theory which explains the content of the texts can ignore or go against this external and independent evidence. And both Thiering and Eisenman feel obliged to deny this evidence. In both cases, they do not offer an hypothesis to explain the facts but distort the facts so that they can fit the hypotheses.

Allegro's interpretation is of a different kind. He has worked directly with the Qumran manuscripts and has learned to respect the chronological limits imposed by palaeography and archaeology. However, since he is convinced that the New Testament is written in a secret language, he has no misgivings about imposing the chronological and historical framework of the Qumran texts on the New Testament. The result is that Jesus Christ, who was the Teacher of Righteousness, must have lived in the mid-second century BCE! Whereas Thiering and Eisenman do not respect the data from archaeology and palaeography, Allegro forgets the most solid facts of history. Ultimately, all these attempts are not science but science fiction. And it is not worth wasting any more time with them.

We move on, now, to the second part of this lecture, in which I try to show where to find the real contributions contained in the Qumran manuscripts as an aid to knowledge of Jesus Christ and of Christianity.

II

The great contribution of the Qumran manuscripts is the following. They have revealed to us the Jewish background against which to draw, into which to insert and from which were developed the figure of Jesus Christ and of his message as well as early Christianity. In broad terms, I would say that the Dead Sea Scrolls do not explain Christianity to us but help us know the Judaism from which Christianity was born. It is a Judaism which is very different, much richer, and more varied and pluralistic than we could imagine from the image reflected in the rabbinic writings with which we are used to compare Christianity.

Perhaps it may seem strange, but the fact is that our ignorance about the historical period in which Christianity was born and in which Rabbinic Judaism was formed can only be compared to the very importance of this period. It is true that we have the New Testament, Flavius Josephus, Philo and some other items from the Roman historians. But for us the religious literature of the period, the ideological development, the halakhic disputes, the liturgy, the mystical speculations, etc., was an unknown world before the Qumran discoveries. It is enough to peruse the list of *Materials for the Historical Dictionary of the Hebrew Language*[325] which the Academy of Language of Israel is preparing – it is a collection of *all* extant Hebrew texts between 200 BCE and 300 CE – to verify that (apart from a few very short inscriptions or expressions written on coins) *all* the material collected comes from the Qumran finds. The awareness of our ignorance is only defined with the acquisition of new knowledge.

I do not think it an exaggeration to say that before the Qumran discoveries, the figure of Jesus Christ appeared like a magnificent and exotic fruit. Now we can see the tree, which has very different fruits, but also a common sap which each branch transforms in its own way. And it is precisely the Qumran texts which, like no other text, allow us to understand the roots of this tree and its different branches. We can also see how this common sap is transformed into very different fruits.

All this, however, can seem very abstract. I will illustrate this metaphor with some concrete examples, beginning at the purely literary level, proceeding through the *halakhah* and ending with theology.

## 1 4QBéat

No gospel composition is so well known or has been studied so much as the Beatitudes. Each and every one of its expressions has been examined in detail and all its Old Testament forerunners emphasised. Until now, however, no Jewish text was known which provided a really close literary parallel to the series of blessings of the text of Mark. However, a text from Cave 4, published recently[326], contains the following fragment:

> *1* [Blessed is the one who speaks the truth] with a pure heart,
> and does not slander with his tongue.
> Blessed are those who adhere to his laws,
> *2* and do not adhere to perverted paths.
> Blessed are those who rejoice in her.
> and do not explore insane paths.
> *3* Blessed are those who search for her with pure hands,
> and do not importune her with a treacherous heart.
> Blessed is the man who attains Wisdom,
> *4* and walks in the law of the Most High,
> and dedicates his heart to her ways,
> and is constrained by her discipline
> and always takes pleasure in her punishments;
> *5* and does not forsake her in the hardship of [his] wrongs,
> and in the time of anguish does not discard her,
> and does not forget her [in the days of] terror,
> *6* and in the distress of his soul does not loathe her (4Q525 II 1-6; DSST, 395).

As can be appreciated, it is in fact a pure wisdom text. Neither the programmatic character nor, especially, the eschatological dimension echoed in the Beatitudes is present. However, the actual literary form is identical and the series of blessings it contains are a marvellous portrayal of the literary form used for the composition of the Beatitudes. It also proves that the literary model circulated in the Jewish background revealed by the Qumran texts.

## 2 The Halakhah

If from the purely literary parallels we move on to the field of legal prescriptions, the importance of the Qumran manuscripts and their illuminating function appears even more clearly since, as is known, Judaism is and has always been more an «orthopraxis» than an «orthodoxy». Well, then, while rabbinic *halakhah* is well known, we knew very little about pre-Mishnaic *halakhah* or about *halakhah* from the pre-Christian period.

Let us take, for example, the juridical process of brotherly rebuke, expressed so clearly in Mt 18:15-17, which gives details on what to do about a member who has strayed from community practice. A juridical regulation of this kind simply does not exist in Rabbinic Judaism and its presence in the gospel of Matthew was baffling. Now, though, we have an excellent parallel in the juridical process of brotherly rebuke, current within the Qumran community. What I do not wish to say is that the Matthean process of rebuke is dependent on that of Qumran. It does prove, though, that the practice of a juridical process of rebuke of the faults committed by the members of a group was not something unusual within the pluralistic Judaism of the 1st century. It also accounts for the halakhic origin of this process which starts from the texts of the Old Testament[327].

At the same time, knowledge of the sectarian halakhic attitudes allows the enormous differences among the different groups to be shown. Going back to the metaphor of the tree and its branches, it shows how the same sap can produce different fruits. The best way to appreciate the differences among these fruits is to compare the programmatic expressions of the Sermon on the Mount with similar expressions of the text (4QMMT) which defines the reasons why the Qumran group separated from the rest of Judaism[328]. It deals with problems such as the ban on non-Jews to bring offerings to the temple; the ban on cooking offerings in copper vessels; the ban on accepting sacrifices from the gentiles; the ban on leaving certain offerings to be eaten on the following day; the law of the red heifer; the ban on bringing animal skins into the temple; the regulations concerning skins and bones of unclean animals; the impurity of those carrying the skin, bones or carcass of an unclean animal; the slaughter of pregnant animals; the exclusion of the blind and the deaf from the Sanctuary; the purity of flowing liquids (*nisoq*); the ban on bringing dogs into Jerusalem. Also, whether fruits from the fourth year belong to the priests; whether the tithes of the flocks belong to the priests; the regulations on the purification period for lepers; the impurity of human bones; the ban on marriage between priests and Israelites, etc. It is difficult to imagine a greater contrast between this programme and the programme which the Sermon on the Mount proposes to us.

## 3 Theology

The same illuminating function of the Dead Sea Scrolls appears especially whenever we move to the level of ideas and expressions with religious content, to theology.

The midrash on Melchizedek from Cave 11[329] provides a good example. It presents a certain person as an angelic figure and as a heavenly saviour, allows us to understand the developments involved and helps bridge the gap between the Melchizedek of Genesis and the Melchizedek of the epistle to the Hebrews.

The following text[330], which comes from the hymns ascribed to the Teacher of Righteousness, allows us to understand in a new way the Jewish roots of the Pauline formulas about justification.

> I know that there is hope, thanks to your kindness,
> and trust in the greatness of your strength.
> For no-one is just in your judgment,
> or innocent at your trial.
> Only through your goodness is man justified.

And since our main theme is the figure of Jesus Christ, I would like to conclude by translating an Aramaic text from the 1st century before Christ, recently published in full (4Q246)[331]. It uses a whole series of expressions which are familiar to us from Lk 2:32-35 and introduces a mysterious person of heavenly origin who appears at the end of history and unleashes the final phase of the eschatological battle which will be followed by lasting peace:

> Great will he be called and he will be designated by his name.
> *1* He will be called son of God, and they will call him son of the Most High. Like the sparks *2* of a vision, so will their kingdom be; they will rule several years over *3* the earth and crush everything; a people will crush another people, and a city another city *4* until the people of God arises and makes everyone rest from the sword (4Q246 I 9- II 1-4; DSST, 138).

It is not my task here to explain who this mysterious person is. However, his presence in a Qumran text from the 1st century BCE allows us to perceive the variety and richness of the Judaism which the Dead Sea Scrolls have revealed to us.

These examples represent only a very small proof of the significance of the Qumran manuscripts for a knowledge of Jesus Christ and of Christianity. I hope, however, that they will be enough to show the enormous importance which the discovery of these manuscripts has had in depicting for us this pluralistic Judaism in which the figure of Jesus has its roots, from which it feeds and of which it comprises its best fruit.

# The Qumran Texts and the New Testament

## Julio Trebolle Barrera

The publication of new manuscripts from Qumran in recent years and, occasionally, the suspicion that sensational material could still come to light has made topical the question of the relationship between the Christian writings of the New Testament and the Essene writings from Qumran.

E. Renan penned a sentence which achieved fame when the Dead Sea Scrolls had not yet been discovered: «Christianity is an Essenism which succeeded». When the texts from Qumran came to light, it seemed to be confirmed that they were, in fact, the writings of the ancient Essenes. Many scholars, therefore, saw in the manuscripts from Qumran the missing link connecting definitively the primitive Christians with the Essenes and Jesus of Nazareth with the so-called Teacher of Righteousness. The first reaction of scholars when they study new texts such as those which came to light in Qumran is to look for points of contact between the new material and what is already known. With the passage of time, when the approach of study is widened and there is greater distance in respect of matters of detail, the differences and the contrasts are more noticeable. Today we have a great deal of information which brings together the world of the early Jewish-Christians and the Jewish world of the period, especially the Essene world. At the same time, there clearly appear the differences which separate Christianity from Essenism or from what it is possible to know about it. It does not cease to be important that current research tends to relate the figure of Jesus more with a Pharisee than with that of an Essene, recognising moreover the original outline of the figure of Jesus, whose antecedents, if he has any, go back to the figures of the great biblical prophets. It is not possible to reduce the comparison between the New Testament and the Qumran texts to matters of detail. Comparison of these two collections, as a whole and not just of isolated verses taken from one and the other, brings out more the differences which separate them.

The certain fact is that the New Testament texts show many parallels and points of contact with the texts from Qumran. As the Essene writings are more ancient than the Christian writings it is logical to assume that the former could influence the latter. Undoubtedly, just as two parallel lines never actually meet, a Qumran text and a gospel text can run in parallel without it meaning that the first has influenced the second directly. Study of comparative literature and comparative religion has often fallen into «parallelomania» (Sandmel), which confuses parallels with tangents and similarities of form or content with direct contacts or influences. In this respect it is a really surprising fact that the gospel of Mark, the most ancient and most Semitic of the gospels, offers very few parallels with the texts from Qumran, whereas the gospels of Matthew and

John and the epistles of Paul provide, as we will see, many points of contact.

It is necessary to remember that the Qumran writings are earlier than the birth of Christianity. Accordingly, they provide no information at all on Christian origins. Two authors, Robert H. Eisenman, professor of the State University of California in Long Beach and Barbara Thiering of Australia think, instead, that some of the most important writings of those found at Qumran are of Jewish-Christian origin. R. Eisenman even identifies Saint James, the Lord's brother (Gal 1:19), with the «Teacher of Righteousness», and Paul with the «Man of Lies» (1QpHab 2:2). With similar presuppositions B. Thiering establishes very different identifications. John the Baptist was the «Teacher of Righteousness» and Jesus the «Wicked Priest». These opinions conflict with the facts and findings of archaeology, palaeography and analysis of the manuscripts with radiocarbon dating. Nor do they take into account the fact that the manuscripts were copied in a specific period which is much older than they suppose. Also, the writings of which these manuscripts are a copy go back to an even earlier period and in general after a lengthy and complex redaction of its text

Although they offer no direct evidence about Christian origins, the importance of the texts from Qumran for study of the New Testament is absolutely conclusive. They provide much rich and valuable information about the Judaism of the period and as a consequence allow us to know what has been called the Jewish matrix of Christianity (Käsemann).

Up to the moment of the Qumran discovery there was no other resort except to compare early Christian literature with contemporary Hellenistic literature or with rabbinic literature of a later period (Billerbeck). Today we have at our disposal material which comes from just before the Christian period or is strictly contemporary with the period of Jesus. This does not mean that the information from rabbinic literature cannot be used for the study of the early Christian writings. The fact that references from the rabbinic writings find a parallel in texts from Qumran or in the works of Philo and Flavius Josephus shows that, in one way or another, they go back to the 1st century CE or to an earlier period. They can be used, therefore, for comparative study with similar references in the texts of the New Testament

In what follows we present some of the most important points of contact between the texts from Qumran and the New Testament texts. The selection is far from exhaustive. Nor should it be forgotten that the interpretation of many of the passages to be considered is the subject of debate among scholars and for that reason it is not possible to establish conclusions that are too rigorous.

## 1 John the Baptist

The assertion that John the Baptist could have been in contact with the Essenes had already been made by H. Graetz in the previous century. It is easy to think that this was the case. John preached on the banks of the Jordan in a geographical area very close to that in which, according to classical sources, the Essenes lived. The Qumran texts have come to provide new material which encourages connecting John even more with the Essenes of Qumran. However, in spite of there being much more information available than there was a century ago, today no-one would dare to state, as Graetz was able to do in his time, that John was an Essene and that John's baptism was only a rite of entry into the Essene movement.

The Qumran texts do not mention John the Baptist at all. There would be nothing unusual if John had belonged to the Qumran community for a period. What is certain, though, is that there are no facts either to affirm or to deny this. Flavius Josephus says he himself spent some time among the Essenes (*Vita* 2 nn. 10-11). John the Baptist could have done the same. The fact that, according to the gospel of Luke (1:80), John lived «in the desert» until the time to begin his own mission, could refer to this. When alluding to the presence of John in the desert, the four evangelists quote the expression from Is 40:3: «the voice of one who cries in the desert» (Mk 1:3; Mt 3:3; Lk 3:3-6; Jn 1:23). It is significant that the *Rule of the Community* (1QS VIII 12-16) also makes use of this quotation from Isaiah to account for the presence of the Qumran community in the desert.

If John did belong to the Qumran community, he must have left it at a certain moment to follow his own path and dedicate himself to preaching a baptism of conversion to all the Jews without exception. Unlike the men from Qumran, John did not establish strict divisions between Jews.

John's baptism is also comparable to the baptismal rites of the Essenes. It differs, however, in being unique and unrepeatable. It also differs from them by being a baptism «of repentance for the forgiveness of sins» (Mk 1:4; Lk 3:3). The relation of baptism with sin is common to the baptism of John and of the Essenes:

> He should not go into the waters to share in the pure food of the men of holiness, for they have not been cleansed *14* unless they turn away from their wickedness (1QS V 13-14; DSST, 8).

The sentence of John the Baptist referring to the baptism of Jesus, «he will baptise with the holy spirit and with fire» (Lk 3:16) has to be placed in relation to the following passage from the *Rule of the Community*:

Then, God will refine, with his truth, all man's deeds, and will purify for himself the configuration of man, ripping out all spirit of injustice from the innermost part *21* of his flesh, and cleansing him with the spirit of holiness from every irreverent deed. He will sprinkle over him the spirit of truth like lustral water (1QS IV 20–21; DSST, 7).

The austere and ascetic figure of John, comparable to that of the Essenes from Qumran, is, however, very far from their closed and sectarian spirit. It is therefore difficult to think that John could have been at home in a community which had broken off all relations with the Jerusalem priesthood to which John's family belonged.

## II  Jesus of Nazareth

The Qumran writings do not mention Jesus of Nazareth either. G. Lankester Harding even went as far as to suggest that perhaps Jesus studied with the Essenes of Qumran. Anyone visiting the ruins of Qumran can wander the classrooms and corridors of the school in which Jesus studied. Scholars would do well not to draw attention to their discoveries in the style of the credulous mediaeval pilgrims who tried to locate each and every footstep of Jesus according to the geography of Palestine.

It is impossible to know whether Jesus had any connection with the Essenes of Qumran. The text of Mt 24:26 «If they say to you: "Look, the Messiah is in the desert" ... do not believe them», could provide an indication that such was the case. Still, there is no way in which it can be proved that these words refer to Qumran.

When it comes to sketching the historical figure of Jesus or what is discernible of it in the sources, it is necessary not to succumb to any bias of an apologetic or polemic character and still less to a craving for sensationalism. It is a pity that while there is an enormous academic bibliography on the figure of Jesus, what mostly reaches the general public is the result of sensationalism and of very biased and partisan views.

Before and after the Qumran discoveries, many and very different portraits of the figure of Jesus of Nazareth have been made. He was an apocalyptic messiah (A. Schweitzer), the great master of ethics, far removed from apocalyptic fancies (especially as visualised by those representing the theological liberalism of the 19th century), a rabbi or existential prophet (Bultmann), the prophet-messiah and «Suffering servant» according to the texts of the so-called Second Isaiah (W. Manson, V. Taylor, Dodd, Cullmann, Kümmel), an Essene (Flusser) or a Teacher of Righteousness in Essene guise (Allegro), a zealot or political revolutionary (Reimarus, Brandon, Carmichael), a zealot for whom the Kingdom would be established from on high by pure divine intervention (Bartsch), a pacifist (G. Edwards, A. Trocmé) or someone at all events far removed from zealot trends (F. Hahn), a magician in the style of other magicians known from the polemic sources and magical writings of the period (Morton Smith), a Galilaean charismatic who performed cures and taught the people, and at the same time, a «just man» or «saint» in the style of the *hasidim* and of figures such as Honi and Hanani ben Dosa (Vermes), etc.

There has been no lack of interpretations favourable to the figure of Jesus made from perspectives far removed in principle from religion, such as the Marxist and atheistic interpretation of Jesus by Machovec. Other interpretations, instead, have been malicious like Allegro's explanation of the name of «Jesus» as a cryptic reference to «Sacred mushroom», a hallucinogenic drug supposedly used by the early Christians (Allegro). It has also been possible to say that Jesus was actually married or had romantic relationships (Ben-Chorin, Kazantzakis). On the other hand, it has also been asserted that Jesus remained celibate, in conformity with the model of prophetic celibacy practised in Qumran (Vermes 1973).

Although the texts from Qumran contain no explicit information at all about Jesus, they do provide rich and very valuable information about the period in which he lived. Qumran has thus contributed in a positive way to a whole movement of «return to the historical Jesus». It is not surprising that a current trend of research should stress the continuity between the Jesus of history and later christology (Hengel) as against those who, since the time of Bousset, contrast the historical Jesus with the Christ of faith, or the historical figure of Jesus of Nazareth with the figure of Christ resurrected and enthroned on the right hand of God the Father.

The parallels which can be established between Jesus and Qumran concern aspects or isolated data. In what follows some of the most important parallels are indicated very simply.

1. Jesus' attitude towards wealth is comparable to that of the Essenes from Qumran. Jesus openly renounces every kind of private property and warns about the dangers which riches entail. The suggestion to the disciples not to carry money and to rely on the hospitality of the communities to which they go (Mt 10:9) corresponds to what was a common practice of the Essenes, according to the testimony of Flavius Josephus (*Wars* 2.8.4, nos. 142-146). There is no information that other groups knew this kind of practice which however has antecedents in the Old Testament, so that it is not necessary to think that Jesus came to know about it through the Essenes. Jesus himself and on his own initiative could have made a recommendation very much in agreement with the spirit of biblical tradition.

2. Jesus accompanied his cures and exorcisms with the laying of hands upon
the sick and possessed. Jewish texts of the period make no connection between
the laying on of hands and healing or exorcism. A passage from the *Genesis
Apocryphon*, though, makes this connection:

> He came to me and asked me to come and pray for the king, and lay my
> hands upon him so that he would live.... I prayed for [...] and laid my
> hands upon his head. The disease was removed from him... (1QGenesis
> Apocryphon XX 22.29; cf. DSST, 233 and 234).

Assyro-Babylonian magic literature knows this usage, which must have been
widespread in very different settings and not only among the Essenes, so that
it cannot be established with certainty that Jesus was directly in debt to the
Essenes on this point.

3. The teaching of Jesus with regard to the ban on divorce seems to have no
parallel at all in the Jewish world of the period. It is now possible to find a
similar doctrine in the *Temple Scroll*:

> He shall take no other wife apart from her *18* because only she will be with
> him all the days of her life. If she dies, he shall take *19* for himself another
> from his father's house, from his family (11QTemple Scroll LVII 17-19;
> DSST, 174).

Another text from the *Damascus Document* also bears comparison:

> They are caught twice in fornication: by taking *21* two wives in their lives,
> even though the principle of creation is (Gen 1:27) «male and female he
> created them» (*Damascus Document* IV 20-21; DSST, 36).

These texts imply that the Essene doctrine concerning divorce was certainly
known in the period prior to the creation of the Qumran community, although
in fact neither Philo nor Josephus provides information about it. The fact that
the passages from the New Testament alluding to divorce (Mk 10:6 and Mt
19:4) and the passage quoted from the *Damascus Document* base the ban on
divorce on the primitive order established at creation (Gen 1:27) does not cease
to be important.

4. At the start of Qumran research, A. Jaubert proposed that the last supper of
Jesus with his disciples took place on the evening of the Wednesday of the
Passover week and not on Friday night. Jesus followed the solar calendar of the
Essenes, attested in the book *Jubilees* and also indirectly in the *Damascus Docu-*

*ment* (VI 19). Some Christian groups still used this calendar a couple of centuries later in the patristic period. Later research (J. Blinzler), however, has cast doubt on the arguments put forward by A. Jaubert. She did not take enough account of the enormous complexity of the gospel data. On the other hand, she assumed that the last supper had a paschal character, which is far from having been proved conclusively. The gospels assume that the last supper took place as a mark of celebration of the Jewish Passover, but this description could correspond more to the desire to confer a theological and liturgical meaning on the last supper than to reality (Haag). What is certain is that the very aspects in which the last supper of Jesus seems to have no relation with the Jewish passover supper find, instead, analogies in the kind of meals which the Essene community celebrated.

In this, as in many other cases, research has become more cautious. Before stating that certain characteristics of Jesus' last supper have their origin in the meals of the Essenes, it is necessary to take into account that there must have been other kinds of celebrations also consistent with religious or ritual meals but different from what was practised by the Essenes of Qumran. A known example is that of the last meals celebrated in the «brotherhoods» or *haburoth* of the pharisees. The last supper of Jesus could have had aspects similar to any of these forms of celebration, all religious in character in some way, but at the same time was able to have its own original character.

5. Within a common monotheistic frame of reference, the concept of Good expressed in the New Testament is different from that of the Qumran texts. Jesus addresses God in a familiar way as *abba*, «father» or «dad» (Mk 14:36; Gal 4:6; Rom 8:15). In the Old Testament it is rare for an individual to address God using the title «Father» (cf. Sir 51:10). In the Qumran texts two examples are to be found: «My Father, my God, do not abandon me to the Gentiles» (4Q372 1 16 and «My father and my lord» (4Q460 V 6).

6. An exceptional field of comparative study between the New Testament and Qumran concerns the titles used for the person of Jesus: «Son of God», «Lord» (*Kyrios*), «Son of man» and Servant of Yahweh».

*a)* In the Old Testament the title «Son of God» has different uses and meanings. It is said of angels in a mythological sense, of the people of Israel as the chosen people, of the kings of the Davidic dynasty considered to be adopted sons of the deity and also of the «just» Israelite (Sir 4:10; Wisd 2:18). There have been attempts to ascribe a messianic meaning to the title «Son of God» which, however, it lacks both in the Old Testament (not even the text of Ps 2:7 is a valid example) and in pre-Christian Jewish literature. On the other hand, the emperor Augustus and many other Roman emperors vaunted the title «son of god» (*divi filius* or *theou huios*). It is reasonable to think that use of this title in the Graeco-Roman world carried weight for the early Christians when they were proclaiming that for them the «Son of God» was Jesus the Christ. However, the antecedents of the New Testament use of this title have to be sought in the biblical and Jewish world.

A text from Qumran was actually given the title 4QSon of God (now called 4QAramaic Apocalypse (4Q246) II, 1). In it the following passage can be read: «He will be called son of God, and they will call him son of the Most High.»

The title «Son of God» (*bereh dî 'el*) was known in Palestine in the 1st century BCE and the 1st century CE, for the manuscript which includes this text goes back to the Herodian period. The text cited uses the titles «son of God» and «son of the Most High» (*bar 'elyôn*), as well as the verb «he will be called son ...», which are used in the account of the annunciation in the gospel of Luke (Lk 1:32.35). The expression of Lk 2:14 *anthropoi eudokias* («men of [divine] favour», more traditionally, «men of good will») also has a parallel in Qumran.

*b)* Before the Qumran discoveries it was customary to state that the title *Kyrios*, «Lord», applied to Jesus, originated in the same title used for pagan gods in the Hellenistic world. This statement seemed to have support from texts such as 1 Cor 8:5-6:

> For, although there are some called gods, in heaven or on earth, (as in fact there are many «gods» and many «lords»), we however have a [single] God, the Father, from whom the Universe [proceeds] and to whom we [[are destined], and a [single] Lord, Jesus Christ, through whom the universe [exists], and we also through him.

According to Bultmann, it was not possible to apply the title «the Lord», to God and especially to Jesus unless it was accompanied by some kind of qualifier such as «Lord of heaven and earth» or «our Lord». Two texts from Qumran have shown that the use of «Lord» on its own was, in fact, possible in the Judaism of the period. The *Targum of Job* (11QtgJob XXIV 6-7) uses the term «Lord» (*mare'*) in parallelism with «God» (*'elaha'*). Similarly, in 4QEn[b] ar (4Q202) IV 5, there occurs the expression «[And to Gabriel] the Lord [said]: Go [to the bastards...]» (DSST, 249). The title «(the) Lord» was well known in Judaism. The Jewish Christians were able to apply it to the resurrected Jesus.

In conclusion, these two christological titles, «Son of God» and «Lord», can be explained in the context of the Jewish world without the need to refer to the pagan Greek world, although there is no doubt that, from the beginning, the use of these same titles in relation to pagan gods had an enormous influence on the meaning and development of the Christian titles.

*a)* The origin and meaning of the title «son of man» have prompted continual debate. In search of an explanation, recourse has been made to the Iranian world and even to the pre-biblical Canaanite world. According to Mowinckel, the image of the «son of man» belongs to Hellenistic Oriental syncretism and a clear distinction must be made between the mythical figure of the «son of man» and the national figure of a Jewish «messiah». Mowinckel considered these two terms as true titles. Today, of course, it is not accepted that the epithet «Son of man» comprises a true title. The idea of a heavenly saviour occurs frequently in the texts, in very different and also very muddled forms and images. In Daniel and in the *War Scroll* (1QM) the saviour is the archangel Michael; in 11QMelch it is Melchizedek; in the *Sibylline Oracles* (chap. 5), the man of heaven; in 4 Esdras, the man of the sea, etc. These texts comprise the background for the study of the New Testament figure of the «son of man» who comes upon the clouds with the angels («one like a son of man», in Dan 7 and «this son of man» in the Parables of 1 Enoch). The different formulations are not important compared with the idea of hope in a salvation brought by a heavenly saviour.

The expression «son of man» is known in the Qumran texts. The Greek version (*ho huios tou anthropou*) still remains unusual. Preceded by the article as «the son of man», it is common in the synoptic gospels (Mk 2:10; Mt 9:6; Lk 5:24; Mt 1:19; Lk 7:34). The expression without the article, «son of man» (Ap 1:13; 14:14; Heb 2:6; Jn 12:34) is less unusual. It could very well be a Semitism which translates the Hebrew expression *ben 'adam* or the corresponding Aramaic expression *bar 'enaš*, with the general meaning of «man», «human being» (Dan 7:13). The expression occurs in the texts from Qumran as in: «I will multiply your descendants like the dust of the earth which no-one (literally "which no son of man") can count» (1QapGen XXI 13, DSST, 234). It also occurs in the Targum of Job, in the translation of the passage Job 35:8: «Your sin (affects) [a man like you], your justice, a son of man» (11QTgJob XXVI 2-3, DSST, 148). These expressions were known in the Jewish world at the time of Jesus both in the indeterminate sense of «someone» and in the generic meaning of «man», «human being». No use of this expression as a title is ever found, though, as is the case in the New Testament, nor as a substitute for the pronoun of the first person singular «I», which occurs in the *targumim*. The New Testament use, therefore. continues to be original and unique in character.

*d)* The Qumran texts frequently apply the title «a servant» to Moses, David and the prophets. In prayers, the expression «your servant» is the equivalent of the simple pronominal referent «I». No Qumran text ever has the expression «servant of Yahweh», typical of biblical prophecies concerning the Suffering Servant (Is 40-53). It cannot be said that the motif of a «suffering Messiah» is in any way characteristic of the Old Testament nor is it likely to occur in any Qumran text. This motif occurs, instead, in the New Testament and only in

Lucan passages, both in the gospel and in the Acts of the Apostles (Lk 24:26; Acts 3:18; 26:23).

## III   The Gospel of Matthew and the Qumran Texts

As in the previous sections we will restrict ourselves to some of the most conspicuous parallels between the Qumran texts and the gospels, beginning with Matthew.

1. The Sermon on the Mount contains a collection of nine beatitudes (5:3-11). The literary form called «beatitude», marked by the expression «Blessed be he/ they who ...(for)», was well known in the Old Testament, particularly in wisdom literature (Ps 1:1; 2:12; Prov 3:13; 8:32.34; Qoh 10:17; Wisd 3:13). A recently published manuscript (4Q525) has provided a whole collection of Qumran beatitudes, quoted above, p. 199. The text surely refers to «Wisdom» or better perhaps to the «Law». Since Wisdom and Law are equivalent, the meaning of the composition does not change in any particular case. In any case it has a wisdom character. The beatitudes of the gospel of Matthew have a more marked eschatological character. Evidently, Jesus and the evangelists made use of a literary form, the «beatitude», singly or as a collection, which was well known in the Old Testament and in the Judaism of the period.

2. The doubts which Joseph displays before the birth of Mary's son have a kind of parallelism in the doubts of the ante-diluvian patriarch Lamech, expressed in the *Genesis Apocryphon*:

> *1* Behold, then, I thought in my heart that the conception was the work of the Watchers and pregnancy, of the Holy Ones, and it belonged to the Gian[ts, ...] *2* and my heart within me was upset on account of this boy. *Blank* [...] *3* Then I, Lamech, was frightened and turned to Bitenosh, my wife, [and said: ...]. *4* [Swear to me] by the Most High, by the Great Lord, by the King of the Uni[verse, ...] *5* [...] the sons of heaven, that you will in truth let me know everything (1QapGen ar II 1-6; DSST, 230).

The rest of the narrative makes it perfectly clear that the birth of Noah is the fruit of the union of his parents, but in the text the idea and the possibility that the conception could have taken place in a different way remain unresolved.

3. The wording of the expression «You have heard what has been said: "love your neighbour and hate your enemy"» (Mt 5:43) makes one think that Jesus is referring to a known biblical text. The two expressions «love your neighbour» and «hate your enemy» must occur in a passage from the Old Testament or in

a Jewish text from the period. In fact, the first occurs in Lev 19:18. The commandment to «hate the enemy», however, has no parallel at all except in two passages from the *Rule of the Community*:

> ... to love all the sons of light, each one according to his lot in God's plan, and to detest all the sons of darkness, each one in accordance with his blame in God's vindication (1QS I 9-10; DSST, 3); And these are the rules of behaviour for the Inspector. in these times, concerning his love and his hatred. Everlasting hatred for the men of the pit (1QS IX 21-22; DSST, 14).

4. Jesus' statement: «Be perfect as your heavenly Father is perfect» (Mt 5:48) could be compared with the Qumran expression «so as to be united in the counsel of God and walk in perfection in his sight» (1QS I 8; DSST, 3). God's title as «Heavenly Father» is, however, omitted.

5. The doctrine of two «ways» expressed in Mt 7:13-14 and later developed in the early Christian literature, has antecedents in a passage from the *Rule of the Community*, which has a marked dualistic emphasis:

> In the hand of the Prince of Lights is dominion over all the sons of justice; they walk on paths of light. *21* And in the hand of the Angel of Darkness is total dominion over the sons of deceit; they walk on paths of darkness (1QS III 20-21; DSST, 6).

6. Jesus' statement in respect of the building of the Church upon the «rock» which is «Peter», against which (the rock-the Church) the gates of hell will not prevail (Mt 16:16-19) has a certain similarity with a phrase from the *Rule of the Community* in which, however, the term *qahal*, corresponding to «Church», is missing, as is the reference to building the community upon a person (Peter):

> When these things exist in Israel, *5* the Community council shall be founded on truth, *Blank* like an everlasting plantation, a holy house for Israel and the foundation of the holy of *6* holies for Aaron, true witnesses for the judgment and chosen by the will (of God) to atone for the earth and to render *7* the wicked their retribution. *Blank* It will be the tested rampart, the precious cornerstone that does not *Blank 8* /whose foundations will not/ shake or tremble in their place (1QS VIII 4-8; DSST, 12).

7. The recommendations concerning brotherly rebuke collected in Mt 18:15-17 and placed in the mouth of Jesus also have certain points of contact with the regulations for living together in the Qumran community, particularly as regards the process of rebuke in three stages, as shown in the next chapter.

IV  The Gospel of John and Qumran Dualism

Critics differ in their suggestions, but there is no doubt that the gospel of John
was composed over a period of several years, at the time when a whole school
of Johannine thought was developing. This gospel collects and incorporates
elements of very different origins, from the Qumran texts, Jewish apocalyptic,
wisdom literature, rabbinic midrash, the mysticism of the *halakhot* and gnostic
texts. It is possible that this gospel stems from esoteric oral teaching, like that
of Plato's Academy. Judaism is dominant but Hellenistic Greek is not absent.

1. The ethical and eschatological dualism expressed in the gospel of John
through the opposition of light-darkness (Jn 1:4-5; 3:19; 12:35; 1 Jn 1:5-6) and
truth-deceit (Jn 3:21; 8:44; 1 Jn 2:21.27; 4:6) has better parallels in the ethical
dualism of Qumran than in Mandaic ideas or in the *Corpus hermeticum* adduced
as proof by R. Bultmann, C. H. Dodd and others.

In the *Rule of the Community* the following passage can be read: «He created
the spirits of light and of darkness and on them established all his deeds» (1QS
III 25). The Angel of light is also called «spirit of light» (1QS III 25), «spirit of
truth» (1QS IV 21.23; 1QM XIII 10), «holy spirit» (1QS IV 21; IX 3; 1QH VII 7, etc.).
The angel of darkness is called «spirit of iniquity» (1QS III 18-19; IV 20.23).
Other passages oppose «spirit of truth» and «spirit of injustice», «spirit of holiness» and «impure spirit» (1QS IV 20-23, DSST, 7). A text may be quoted at
length:

> From the source of light come the generations of truth, and from the
> source of darkness the generations of deceit. *20* In the hand of the Prince
> of Lights is dominion over all the sons of justice; they walk on paths of
> light. And in the hand of the Angel *21* of Darkness is total dominion over
> the sons of deceit; they walk on paths of darkness. Due to the Angel of
> Darkness *22* all the sons of justice stray, and all their sins, their iniquities,
> their failings and their mutinous deeds are under his dominion *23* in com-
> pliance with the mysteries of God, until his moment; and all their punish-
> ments and their periods of grief are caused by the dominion of his enmity;
> *24* and all the spirits of their lot cause the sons of light to fall. However, the
> God of Israel and the angel of his truth assist all *25* the sons of light. He
> created the spirits of light and of darkness and on them established all his
> deeds *26* [on their p]aths all his labours (1QS III 19-26; DSST, 6).

The gospel of John applies the Qumran adjectives of «angel, Prince of light» and «spirit of truth (who leads the sons of light)», to Jesus, light of the world and truth, and to the Paraclete, Spirit of truth. It should be noted, though, that the Christian community is based on faith in the person and in the mission of Jesus, truth incarnate; the Qumran community is based on the interpretation of the truth revealed in the Torah.

The expression «sons of» light or darkness is not found in the Old Testament or in rabbinic literature. This makes the parallel with Qumran more conspicuous. The gospel of John speaks of «the light which shines in the darkness» (1:5) and of «the light of the world» (8:12) and of a battle between light and darkness: «And the light shines in the darkness, and the darkness has not extinguished it» (1:5). The text of 12:35-36 provides this same opposition:

> A little while longer will the light be among you. Walk while you have the light so that the darkness does not overtake you. He who walks in darkness does not know where he goes. While you have the light, believe in the light, so that you become sons of the light.

The expression «sons of (the) light» also occurs in other passages of the New Testament such as 1 Thess 5:5 or Lk 16:8, but this not apply to the expression «sons of darkness» or to the opposition between them. This means that not all the New Testament writings use this terminology peculiar to Palestinian Judaism of the period.

2. The Prologue to the gospel of John presents other parallels with the Qumran texts which refer to the creator God and his wisdom displayed in creation: everything exists and happens because God in his wisdom has so commanded. A poetic passage from the *Rule of the Community* runs as follows:

> By his knowledge everything shall come into being,
> and all that does exist
> he establishes with his calculations
> and nothing is done outside of him.
>     (1QS XI 11; DSST, 18)

Other hymns express the same idea:

> 7 In your wisdom you es[tablished] eternal [...];
> before creating them you know all their deeds
> 8 for ever and ever. [...]
> [Without you] nothing is done,
> and nothing is known without your will.
>     (1QH XI 7-8; DSST, 325-326).

And in the wisdom of your knowledge
you have determined their course
before they came to exist.
*20* And with [your approval] everything happens,
and without you nothing occurs.
    (1QH XI 19-20; DSST, 326).

Yet another text in prose from the same *Rule* can be quoted:

From the God of knowledge stems all there is and all there shall be. Before
they existed he made all their plans *16* and when they came into being they
will execute all their works in compliance with his instructions, according
to his glorious design without altering anything. In his hand are *17* the laws
of all things and he supports them in all their needs. He created man to
rule *18* the world and placed within him two spirits so that he would walk
with them until the moment of his visitation: they are the spirits *19* of truth
and of deceit (1QS III 15-19; DSST, 6).

The similarity of these texts with expressions such as «All things were made
through him (the Logos) and without him nothing was made that was made»
from the gospel of John (1:3) hits you in the eye. The Qumran texts, though,
do not speak of a personified Logos nor do they hint even remotely at other
specifically Christian ideas.

### v  The Epistles of Paul and the Qumran Texts

The Pauline epistles show clear points of contact with the writings from Qumran, but this not mean to say that many of the ideas and expressions of Paul
must be due to Essene influence. It is more likely that disciples of Paul, members of the Pauline school such as those who composed the epistle to the Ephesians, had more direct contact with Essene trends or perhaps with Essene
groups converted to Christianity.

Very typical terms of the epistles of Paul have conspicuous analogies in the
texts from Qumran: mystery, flesh and spirit, power, perfect, truth, holy, etc.
Similarly, ideas considered to be unique and characteristic of Paul are already
to be found in the Judaism of the period (200 BCE-200 CE). Examples are man's
sinful nature (Rom 3:23; 1QH I 22); man's inability to gain God's pardon (Gal
2:16; 1QH IV 30) and the insistence on the importance of the Spirit. Also, such
ideas as the Law not being a sufficient means to attain justification before God,
that only God can make man just and that God predestined for salvation only
those whom he called. When it comes to establishing parallels between the
Pauline texts and the Qumran texts one should avoid picking out facts from

this text or that, with no critical method at all, making a jumble of texts which never were connected.

1. Right at the beginning of research on Qumran, K. G. Kuhn drew attention to a passage from the second epistle to the Corinthians (6:14-17) which has clear parallels with the texts from Qumran and the works of Philo of Alexandria. The text of Paul is the following:

> Do not be make an unmatched pair joined at the yoke with [the] unbelievers; for, what partnership [can] justice and iniquity [make]? Or what fellowship between [the] light and [the] darkness? And what harmony between Christ and Belial, or what part in common [has] the believer with [the] unbeliever? And what agreement between [the] sanctuary of God and [the] idols? For we are [the] sanctuary of the living God, as God said: «I will live and walk among them, and I will be their God, and they shall be my people; therefore, come out from among them and be separate, says [the] Lord, and touch [nothing] unclean; and I will welcome you and will be a father to you, and you shall be my sons and daughters», says [the] Lord Almighty. So then, dear brothers, keeping these promises, let us purify ourselves from every stain of [the] flesh and of [the] spirit, completing [our] purification in [the] fear of God.

This Pauline text has parallels in passages from the *Hymns* of the Qumran community which oppose justice and sin, light and darkness, flesh and spirit, and refer to purification and radical separation from the wicked ones of Belial. Some scholars suppose that in fact the Pauline text is due to direct Essene influence, though at the same time they consider the passage not to be original but an interpolation in the text of the letter. It is a baptismal exhortation similar to those contained in texts such as Acts 26:18 and Col 1:12-14.

The hypothesis has also been proposed that the passage 2Cor 6:14-7:1 reflects theological ideas of Paul's opponents, which suggests further that the «heresy» of the Colossians had Essene characteristics and roots. If this passage does actually have an Essene origin, its presence in the epistle of Paul could be connected with the deportation of two thousand Jewish families from Babylonia to Asia Minor in the time of Antiochus III, somewhat before the Qumran community came into being. It is also possible to fall back on the hypothesis according to which, after the destruction of the Qumran community some of its members and other Essenes fled to Asia Minor and there had an influence on groups whose ideas find expression in the Pauline passage quoted. The theology of this passage is, in any case, markedly dualistic and its origin certainly Judaeo-Christian. Today there is no easy answer to the question about the possible Essene origin of the baptismal instruction included in the Epistle to the

Corinthians. The same applies to the channel through which this instruction came to be inserted into the epistle of Paul. This is due to the complexity of the data involved and the lack of much other data about which no information has reached us.

2. The letter to the Ephesians seems to offer the best parallels with the Qumran texts both in respect of language and style and in terms of the ideas expressed. Very early on, Kuhn drew attention to the points of contact which exist between the passage Eph 5:5-11 and several texts from Qumran. The Pauline text is as follows:

> Be sure then, that no fornicator or impure person or miser (that is to say, idolater) will share in the inheritance of the kingdom of Christ and of God. Let no-one deceive you with empty words, for these things the wrath of God discharges upon the sons of disobedience. Therefore, do not be their accomplices; for in another time you were darkness, but now [you are] light in [the] Lord; walk like sons of [the] light – for the fruit of the light [consists] in all kinds of goodness, justice and truth –, knowing how to distinguish what it is that is pleasing to [the] Lord; and do not take part in the unfruitful works of darkness, before rebuking them openly.

The reader can judge for himself by comparing the text of Paul with the following passages from the Qumran texts:

> The corrupt spirit you have purified from the great sin so that he can take his place 22 with the host of the holy ones, and can enter in communion with the congregation of the sons of heaven (1QH XI 21-22). In the hand of the Prince of Lights is dominion over all the sons of justice; they walk on paths of light (1QS III 20). To achieve together truth and humility, 4 justice and uprightness, compassionate love and seemly behaviour in all their paths (1QS V 3-4). He should swear by the covenant to be segregated from all the men of sin who walk 11 along paths of irreverence (1QS V 10-11). Be accursed, without mercy, for the darkness of your deeds... (1QS II 7).

3. The Pauline idea of justification by faith has some parallels in texts from Qumran such as the closing hymn of the *Rule of the Community*:

> 9 However, I belong to evil humankind
> to the assembly of wicked flesh;
> my failings, my transgressions, my sins,
> with the depravities of my heart,
> 10 belong to the assembly of worms

and of those who walk in darkness.
For to man (does not belong) his path,
nor to a human being the steadying of his step;
since judgment belongs to God,
*11* and from his hand is the perfection of the path.
By his knowledge everything shall come into being,
and all that does exist
he establishes with his calculations
and nothing is done outside of him.
As for me, if I stumble,
*12* the mercies of God shall be my salvation always;
and if I fall in the sin of the flesh,
in the justice of God, which endures eternally, shall my
judgment be;
*13* if my grief commences,
he will free my soul from the pit
and make my steps steady on the path;
he will draw me near in his mercies,
and by his kindnesses set in motion my judgment;
*14* he will judge me in the justice of his truth,
and in his plentiful goodness
always atone for all my sins;
in his justice he will cleanse me
from the uncleanness of the human being
*15* and from the sin of the sons of man,
so that I can extol God for his justice
and The Most High for his majesty.
Blessed be you, my God,
who opens the heart of your servant to knowledge!
    (1QRule of the Community XI 9-15; DSST, 18-19).

The author of the *Hymns* acknowledges his sinful being. It is possible to find a parallel in the epistle to the Romans 3:23: «for all sin and fall short of God's glory». The Qumran text speaks of «the justice of God», just as Rom 1:17 does. The author of the *Hymns* believes that at God's judgment the grace of the same God will intervene: «and by his kindnesses he set in motion my judgment; he will judge me in the justice of his truth, and in his plentiful goodness». The Pauline idea of God's justice and of justification by grace finds in some way an antecedent in these texts: the sinner sees himself judged by God and at the same time set free by God's grace. Paul ascribes all this to Christ who frees the sinner before God's tribunal (Rom 4:24-25). On the other hand, justification is achieved by God's grace through faith.

It is necessary to avoid at all costs the temptation to read pauline ideas or terminology into texts from Qumran. It is easy to find parallels in the Qumran texts when they have first been «christianised», ascribing to them a meaning they did never had.

If only the points of contact between the New Testament texts and those from Qumran are noticed, a distorted view of them both results. It is important not to forget the points of disagreement, which we have not considered here but turn out to be more numerous and, in general, more significant. So, for example, the concepts of «Law» and «Covenant» are fundamental in the texts from Qumran. In the message of Jesus, however, the concept of «the Kingdom of God» is predominant, but is very marginal in the texts from Qumran. The sole exception is the *Songs of the Sabbath Sacrifice*: «And they will recount the splendour of his kingdom, according to their knowledge, and they will extol [his glory in all] the heavens of his kingdom» (Frag. 2:3-4).

In line with texts from the Old Testament, especially the prophet Ezekiel, the writings from Qumran stress divine transcendence and present the figure of a God who unleashes his wrath against successive generations of men. In each generation, God does not allow more than a small remnant to remain (*Damascus Document* III 13). These texts comprise a link between the Old Testament and the Pauline doctrine of Rom 9-11, but on the other hand they offer a strong contrast with gospel texts which speak of God the Father, «who makes his sun rise upon evil and good and rains over just and unjust» (Mt 5:45), or of the Father who orders the fatted calf to be killed on the return of the prodigal son (Lk 15:23). Ultimately, the overall image of the message and figure of Jesus presented in the gospel texts contrasts with the extremely rigoristic attitudes expressed in the texts of the Qumran sect.

Brotherly Rebuke in Qumran and Mt 18:15-17[332]

Florentino García Martínez

In the first translation of the *Rule of the Community*, W. H. Brownlee[333] had already indicated the reciprocal relationships between 1QS V 26- VI 1 and Mt 18:15-17, distancing himself from the interpretation which M. Burrows and S. Iwry had proposed for the passage in question[334]. It is not surprising, then, that in the first decade of Qumran research the procedure of brotherly rebuke at Qumran was often cited as one of the parallels which can explain the same procedure reflected in the text of Matthew[335]. The views of the various authors who have studied the topic in that decade can be grouped into two categories: those who maintain the dependence of the gospel text on the Qumran texts[336]; those who see both texts as parallel developments from a single biblical foundation, but independent of each other[337]. Both, however, start from the supposition that both procedures of brotherly rebuke reflect the same reality, a reality which eventually ends up being represented in a slightly different practice. It is this supposition which we wish to examine in some detail. This is because in studies made in the first ten years of Qumran research, instead of a deep analysis there were fleeting allusions to the problem and because later studies accepted this supposition as something already definitively proved[338]. It does not seem out of place, then, to consider anew the data provided by the Qumran texts to determine the elements which can help in a better understanding of the New Testament text. All the more so, now the Qumran procedure of brotherly rebuke is better known today thanks to the studies by L. Schiffman who has analyzed it and compared it with rabbinic *hatra'ah*[339], and by G. Forkman, who has compared it with rabbinic *nidduy*[340].

1 Qumranic Rebuke

The Qumran law of rebuke is expressly formulated in the text already cited, 1QS V 24- VI 1, and in CD IC 2-8[341]. It is helpful to analyse these texts in some detail, in order to understand the motives and the concrete form which the law of rebuke acquires in them and to understand better other isolated allusions to it within the Qumran writings.

CD IX 2-8[342]

> *2* And as for what it says: «Do not avenge yourself or bear resentment against the sons of your people» (Lv 19:18): every man of those who entered *3* the covenant who brings an accusation [lit., word] against his fellow, unless it is with rebuke (*bhwkḥ*) before witnesses, *4* and who brings it when

he is angry, or he tells it to his elders so that they despise him, he is «the one who avenges himself and bears resentment». *5* Is it not perhaps written that only «He avenges himself on his foes and bears resentment against his enemies» (Nah 1:2)? *6* If he kept silent about him from one day to the other, or accused him of a capital offence, *7* his fault is upon himself[343], for he did not fulfil the commandment of God which tells him: «You shall *8* rebuke your fellow so as not to incur sin because of him» (Lv 19:17) (DSST, 40).

This text shows us clearly that the Qumran *halakhah* has arrived at the formulation of the need for rebuke before witnesses by means of exegesis of Lv 19:17-18. It also shows that it is a *halakhah* peculiar to the members of the sect since the formulation only concerns all those «who entered the covenant»[344]. And it shows that in the Qumran writings, the term *ḥwkḥ* is used only as a technical term to denote the Qumran understanding of the biblical *ḥwkḥ*, that is, rebuke «before witnesses».

The text is divided into two parts, separated by the quotation from Nahum 1:2 and framed by the quotations from Lv 19:18 and Lv 19:17. The *halakhah* of the first part apparently contains three separate elements: an accusation without rebuke before witnesses; an accusation when one is angry; an accusation to provoke contempt. However, a close examination of the wording allows the conclusion that the last two elements are only an explanation of the first, with which they are in parallel. That is to say, every accusation which is not a rebuke before witnesses is considered as motivated either by anger or by the desire to disparage one's fellow. As such, it is considered a violation of the precept of Lv 19:18. Whoever commits such an act is defined, in a paraphrase of the biblical text, as «the one who avenges himself and bears resentment», and the text from Nahum is used to prove that this is something forbidden to all men and reserved exclusively to God. The only accusation permitted the members of the sect, when they have been witnesses to a fault, is rebuke before witnesses. In that case, the rebuke before witnesses is obligatory, as the second part of the text proves.

In this second part we are presented with a twofold concrete example of the precept of rebuking one's fellow of Lv 19:17: in the case where the witness of a failing does not rebuke him in front of witnesses and in the case where the accusation is made in anger. In both cases, the law of rebuke is transgressed, by disobeying a commandment and by incurring the blame of the transgressor. The starting point is understanding the commandment of rebuking one's fellow as an obligation to rebuke before witnesses[345]. Schiffman has proved[346] that the obligation of rebuke has been deduced by analogy with the law of annulment of a woman's vow by her husband in Nm 30:15, a text reflected in the wording «from one day to the next».

This obligation occurs clearly in a text from the *Rule of the Community* forming part of the «Penitential code»:

1QS VII 10-11[347]

> And whoever feels animosity towards his fellow for no cause will be pun-
> ished for {six months} /a year/. And likewise for anyone retaliating for any
> reason (DSST, 11).

The use of the verbs «feel animosity» and «retaliate» evidently refers back to Lv
19:18. And the requirement that whoever does not fulfil the law (*lw' bmšpṭ*),
according to which he must not feel animosity and take his revenge, will be
punished, shows clearly that the interpretation of this biblical text given in CD
IX 2-8 is considered to be an obligatory *halakhah*, the transgression of which
brings with it a specific punishment. Since the text of the *Damascus Document*
specifies clearly that whoever does not fulfil the law of rebuke is «he who takes
revenge and feels animosity», the conclusion that the punishment indicated
here is intended for whoever transgresses this law of rebuke must be accepted.
In other words, that withholding a part of the food ration for six months (or for
a year[348]) is intended for those members who have been present at the failings
of others and have not complied with the precept of rebuking them in front of
witnesses.

This obligation occurs just as clearly in the *Damascus Document*. There is a
list of such typical precepts as «not entering the Temple», abstaining from unjust wealth, keeping the sabbath or the regulations of purity, etc. These precepts, if fulfilled, permit the distinction between «those who have entered the
Covenant» and «the sons of the pit». Among them we find the following:

CD VII 1-3

> To refrain from fornication *2* in accordance with the regulation; for each to
> rebuke his brother in accordance with the precept, and not to bear resent-
> ment *3* from one day to the next; to keep apart from every uncleanness ac-
> cording to their regulations (DSST, 37).

In this text, which forms part of what Murphy-O'Connor calls the «Memorandum»[349], the obligation of brotherly rebuke is combined with that of two other
precepts. Like rebuke, they have an obvious biblical foundation, but like it,
they have evolved within the community in a particular direction. Within the
community, the ban on fornication (*hzwnwt*) has been understood to include
the ban on polygamy (CD IV 21- V 1) and the regulations for separating the pure
from the impure have been considerably extended[350]. Both precepts must have
been kept according to the legal developments typical of the sect, as the stipula-
tion «according to their laws» (*kmšpṭm*) shows. If in the case of rebuke our text
uses *kmṣwh*, it is undoubtedly to stress the connection of the precept with the
complete wording of the *halakhah* in CD IX 2-8, where *mṣwt* occurs.

The specification «of a capital offence» (lit., "a matter of death") in the second part of this text from the *Damascus Document* (CD IX 6-8) puts into practice³⁵¹, the somewhat generic wording of the first part (CD IX 2-5). It applies the principles of the law of brotherly rebuke to the concrete case of offences punished by the death penalty. This does not imply that rebuke is not considered obligatory in the other cases, but that the seriousness of capital offences justifies their being treated separately and more rigorously. A famous text of the law concerning witnesses seems to offer the proof of this separate treatment of different offences. This text also provides us with concrete information about the way in which rebuke was carried out within the community:

CD IX 17-23

Any matter in which a man sins *17* against the law, and his fellow sees him and he is alone; if it is a capital matter, he (the witness) shall denounce him *18* in his (the transgressor's) presence, with rebuke (*bhwkyḥ*), to the *Mebaqqer*, and the *Mebaqqer* shall write with his own hand until he (the transgressor) commits it *19* again in the presence of someone alone, and he denounces him to the *Mebaqqer*; if he returns and is surprised [for a third time] in the presence *20* of someone alone, his judgment is complete; but if they are [only] two who testify about a matter³⁵², the guilty person is only to be excluded from the pure food on condition that *22* they are trustworthy, and that on the same day on which he saw him, he denounces him to the *Mebaqqer*. And concerning riches, they shall accept two *23* trustworthy witnesses, and only one, to exclude from the holy food (DSST, 40-41).

This text, heatedly discussed for the solution it gives to the problem of the single witness³⁵³ (a radically different from the soution of rabbinic tradition), establishes a clear distinction between two types of crime: those which result in death, and crimes of a financial nature. For someone guilty of the first to be convicted, the testimony of three witnesses is required. To condemn someone guilty of monetary crimes, the testimony of two witnesses is enough. In both cases the lower number of witnesses (two successive testimonies or a single one, respectively) is enough to keep the guilty person apart from the pure food of the sect, that is, to reduce him to the status of an applicant. This distinction confirms the proposed interpretation of the law of rebuke. The first part contains wording of a general kind and the second part, a more restrained wording for capital offences. Within the community, the only accusation allowed of any fault committed by a member is «rebuke» in the required form. If it is a matter of faults which carry the death penalty, the accuser must proceed that very day and without anger, under pain of incurring the guilt of the accused person.

CD IX 17-23 also indicates the way in which the rebuke must be carried out.

For successive accusations by a single witness to be valid and take effect, they must be «rebukees» (*hwkyh*). In other words, accusations in the required form made in front of the *Mebaqqer* of the community in the presence of the offender, with witnesses, and duly recorded by the *Mebaqqer*. The use of the term *rebuke* and the requirement that the accusation has to be made *on the very day* the fault was committed, without keeping silent from one day to the next, are a clear indication that the text refers to the law of rebuke mentioned previously in CD IX 2-8. Also, that the requirements in respect of the procedure for these accusations were normal within the community.

The other key text for understanding the Qumran procedure for rebuke is 1QS V 24- VI 1[354]

> A man should rebuke (*lhwkyh*) *25* his fellow in truth, in meekness and in compassionate love for the man. No-one should speak to his brother in anger or muttering, *26* or with a hard [neck or with passionate] spiteful intent and he should not detest him [in the stubbornness] of his heart, but instead rebuke him (*ywkyhnw*) that very day so as not *1* to incur a sin for his fault. And in addition, no-one should raise a matter against his fellow in front of the Many unless it is with rebuke (*btwkht*) in the presence of witnesses (DSST, 9).

This text provides an excellent parallel to CD IX 2-8 and proves that the law of rebuke was in force in the Qumran community in the more restricted sense at an advanced stage of its existence. Most of the text is devoted to specifying the moral attitudes with which the rebuke had to be made between the members of the community. However, our text also makes clear that the obligation of rebuke is not a mere moral obligation but rather a strictly juridical obligation. This is indicated by the closing requirement that every rebuke within the community had to be made *before witnesses* and that every accusation before the *Rabbim* had to be preceded by the rebuke. *Rabbim*, «the Many», is a term which denotes the community assembly. It is a more precise technical term in Qumran literature than that of «elders» used in the parallel text from CD. An accusation before the *Rabbim* is, without doubt, a juridical procedure within the community. With these specifications, our text dispels any doubt at all about the nature of rebuke at Qumran. This rebuke, which of course must contain all the requisites of a moral nature that the text mentions, is not to be reduced to a simple brotherly warning. Instead, it forms part of a precise and specific juridical procedure. Within the community, the only rebuke permitted is the rebuke made before witnesses. This element had appeared already in CD and makes clear that it is a question of a juridical obligation which must be fulfilled according to specific regulations. In addition, however, this text from 1QS adds that every accusation made before the *Rabbim* must have been preceded by a rebuke. This means that within the juridical process of accusation of a member before the council, the rebuke comprises the first step, a stage without which it is impossible to proceed further. The fact that within Qumran legislation the *Mebaqqer* had to note down the rebukees made with the purpose of an eventual condemnation of the guilty person later, certainly facilitated the verification of the fulfilment of this condition in the accusations made before the *Rabbim*[355].

Another text from the *Damascus Document* can help to clarify this twofold element, rebuke first and then sentence by the assembly:

CD XX 4-8

> In accordance with his misdeed, all the men *5* of knowledge shall rebuke him (*ywkhwhw*), until the day when he returns to take his place in the session of the men of perfect holiness. But when his deeds are evident, according to the exact interpretation of the law in which *7* the men of perfect holiness walked, no-one should associate with him in wealth or work, *8* for all the holy ones of the Most High have cursed him (DSST, 46).

This text deals with the temporary expulsion of unfaithful members and is generally considered as an interpolation in CD, which reveals the practice of a later community[356]. What interests us here in this text is the clear distinction between the rebuke made for «the men of knowledge» and the later judgment before the assembly. Only when the guilty person is condemned in this judgment, in which his misdeeds are judged in the light of the sectarian *halakhah* («the exact interpretation of the law in which the men of perfect holiness walked»), does his expulsion from the community take place. However, this judgment is not possible without the previous rebuke before witnesses.

It is true that the text of 1QS VI 1 uses *twkht*[357] instead of *hwkyh*, but both terms are synonymous. Although *twkht* is used in 1QH with a different meaning (divine rebuke[358]) one of the two uses in the Habakkuk pesher (1QpHab V 10) provides a good example of Qumran rebuke. In this case it is the rebuke by the Teacher of Righteousness of the Man of Lies within the community to which both belong[359].

In 1QS V 24- VI 1, together with the obligation of rebuke and with the proviso that this must be made «on the (same) day», we find the reason for this obligation. The members of the community must rebuke the guilty person to *avoid incurring the guilt witnessed*. Leaney translates the sentence: «but on the same day he shall rebuke him and not heap iniquity upon him» and expressly denies the interpretation we propose here[360]. He prefers to interpret the text as a commandment whose purpose is to prevent the transgressor falling into the power of Belial, the prince of darkness, when darkness follows day. The interpretation of «on the day» as denoting not a period of twenty-four hours but the period up to sunset is the most probable. But his understanding of the rest of the sentence seems forced: it requires giving to the *qal* form of the verb *naśa'* the force of a *hiphil* and disregards the influence that Lv 19:19 has on the wording of the law of Qumran rebuke. The idea that the witness who fails to rebuke a fault incurs the fault witnessed by him is one of the basic elements of Qumran rebuke. It is derived from the exegesis of Lv 19:17-18 given in CD IX 2-8.

The last of the typical elements of the law of Qumran rebuke is that this law only applies to the members of the sect. This limitation could come, as Schiffman supposes, from the fact that the rest of the Judaism of the period ignored this juridical process of rebuke[361]. Or, as seems more probable, it could result from the isolationist attitude of the sect which leads it to consider all non-members as excluded from the «new covenant». In any case, this limitation is clearly expressed in one of the laws which regulate the behaviour of the *Maśkil*:

1QS IX 16-18

> He should not rebuke (*lhwkyh*) or argue with the men of the pit, *17* but instead hide the counsel of the law in the midst of the men of sin. He should rebuke (*wlhwkyh*) (with) truthful knowledge and (with) just judgment those who choose *18* the path (DSST, 14)[362].

So then, we can summarise the procedure of rebuke at Qumran as a specific juridical process deduced from exegesis of Lv 19:16-18 and only applicable to members of the sect. Every member who witnesses a fault committed by another member is obliged to rebuke him before witnesses the very day on which the offence has been committed and in the presence of the *Mebaqqer*, who notes down the fact, under pain of his incurring the guilt of the fault committed. This rebuke before witnesses is, in addition, an indispensable condition for the later judgment of the transgressor before the assembly.

## II Rebuke in Mt 18:15-17

All the commentators agree that Mt 18:15-17 describes a form of legislation concerning brotherly rebuke which is *unique* in the New Testament[363]. Here, therefore, we can dispense with the other allusions to rebuke which occur in the NT. This includes those expressed by means of *noutheteô-nouthesía* or by *epitimaô*, and those in which the key terms *elenchô-elenchos*[364] (the terms preferred by the LXX to translate *ykh* and *twkht*). And it includes the references, so frequent in the pastoral epistles, to the obligation those with authority within the community[365] are under to rebuke those who stray. All the commentators agree that these allusions to brotherly rebuke indicate only a moral or pastoral obligation which is essentially different from the juridical process outlined in Mt 18:15-17.

The commentators are also agreed that vv. 15-17 form a separate and self-contained unit, in terms of both form and content. Also, that this unit has been incorporated without great changes into the present context provided by chapter 18 of Matthew. The changes in meaning which this new context brings to the content of the unit considered in isolation have been extensively and knowledgeably studied[366]. Accordingly, we do not need to spend time on the meaning which the text acquires once it is read in the context of chapter 18 and generally in the present gospel of Matthew. We are only interested in the meaning which the pericope offers as an isolated unit. The reason is that only at that level is it possible to establish a comparison with the procedure of rebuke at Qumran, outlined above, to see if the supposed influences are real or not.

As for the origins of this independent and autonomous unit, the opinions of the commentators are less in agreement. However, in one form or another they all connect it with Lk 17:3. Brooks considers the unit as an expansion of one the Q sayings, preserved in its more original form in Lk 17:3, due to the redactor of the gospel of Matthew which reflects in it the discipline of his own age[367]. Most of them, however, while retaining its dependence on Lk 17:3, consider that this older form of the *logion* had already been transformed into a regulation of ecclesiastical discipline in a Judaeo-Christian community[368]. It is from there that Matthew takes it.

None of these solutions, however, explains the texts correctly. Mt 18:15-17 does not appear to be an expansion of a *logion* reflected better in Lk 17:3. The penitential discipline reflected in the text of Matthew does not seem to be a development of the Lucan prescription.

Matthew knows the series of sayings collected in Lk 17:1-4 as is evident from the correspondence between Lk 17:1-2 ‖ Mt 18:6-7, Lk 17:3 ‖ Mt 18:15-17 and Lk 17:4 ‖ Mt 18:21-22. However, if we compare the wording of Lk 17:3 with that of Mt 18:15-17 it is difficult to see in Luke any indication of priority or establish a dependence in the wording of Matthew on that of Luke. The text of Matthew retains some more markedly Semitic overtones than the text of Luke. Although it is certain that, in general, the language of Matthew reflects a more popular and less stylistic Greek than that of Luke, in this case it is Luke who uses much commoner verbs than Matthew to express the meaning of «to obey»[369]. In addition, and this reason is the most important, Mt 18:15-17 depends directly on Lv 19:17 and Dt 19:15 (LXX). These texts have no influence on Lk 17:3 but they determine the wording and content of Mt 18:15-17. The conclusion which seems inevitable is that Matthew, who knows the series of *logia* preserved in Lk 17:1-4 (and in the same order) has taken advantage of the presence of the *logion* about brotherly correction to insert his (own) law about rebuke (related in theme) replacing the *logion* which we know through Lk 17:3. Our text, then, is not a development of Lk 17:3 but a *replacement* for it, and its original meaning can perfectly well have been different from that of Lk 17:3.

Nor does it seem obvious that the Church discipline reflected in Mt 18:15-17 evolved from the *logion* of Lk 17:3. Although the wording of Lk 17:3 is generic: «if your brother sins», the meaning seems to refer to offences between brothers, as the fact that it is the brother who forgives clearly indicates and as the «against him» of 17:4 specifies[370]. Certainly, some Greek manuscripts include «against him» in Mt 18:15. This element, though, is generally recognised as a later corruption of manuscript tradition, under the influence of Luke and of Mt 18:21, and critical editions generally relegate it to the apparatus as an addition[371]. In the *logion* preserved in Lk 17:3, then, it is a matter of a correction limited to offences which one brother has committed against another. In Mt 18:15-17, on the other hand, it is a matter of any offence and not only offences committed against brothers. Certainly it is perfectly feasible that a prescription limited to correction between brothers has been expanded later and accorded general scope and in fact Gal 6:1 points to exactly this development. However, that a moral or pastoral obligation has been changed into a juridical process is more problematic[372]. And the problem is that Lk 17:3 evidently remains in the range of moral obligation. In this sense, there is no difference at all between the Lucan text and all the other New Testament allusions to brotherly rebuke. Certainly, the text seems to remain at a purely personal level. However, the legal style in which the pericope is couched, the influence of Lv 19:7 and above all the quotation of Dt 19:15[373] leave no doubt at all that it is a question of a juridical process of which the final outcome is the expulsion of the sinner from the community.

The inevitable conclusion seems to be that we must consider Mt 18:15-17 as a text independent of Lk 17:3. It is a text which describes a specific juridical process of brotherly correction which has been arrived at through an exegesis of Lv 19:7 and of Dt 19:15, incorporated by the redactor of Matthew into his gospel to replace the *logion* recorded by Luke.

Separated from its context in the gospel of Mark, the pericope provides exact legislation about the way to behave with a member who strays from the community norms. The pericope is tightly structured and is couched in a series of conditional clauses in a clear Old Testament style, corresponding to each other and marking a clear progression: rebuke in private, before witnesses, before the community. The first rebuke in private is considered as part of the juridical process, as is clear from the match between the expressions used: «if he listens to you ‖ if he does not listen to you ‖ if he does not wish to listen to them». This shows that the correction is in the first instance intended to gain the brother who strays. Yet, at the same time it is the beginning of a procedure which, unless it gives the desired result, ends with the expulsion of the sinner from the community.

This *halakhah* presents rebuke as an obligation on each member. The first stage is rebuke in private, with the clear intention of attracting the transgressor to the good path. If this strictly individual rebuke does not obtain the desired result, the one making the rebuke is obliged to proceed to a new rebuke in the presence of one or two witnesses. Although the text does not specify, the function of the witnesses (witnesses of the misdeed or witnesses of the rebuke?) seems to be not only to give the correction greater force but to testify that the correction has been made and that the condition which precedes the third phase has been carried out. This third phase is rebuke before the community, the Church, evidently made by the same accuser (and in the presence of the aforementioned witnesses?). If this rebuke does not obtain the desired result either, the transgressor is considered like someone who, in effect, has put himself outside the community.

As a description of a juridical procedure and in spite of the clarity of wording, the pericope does not specify a series of important elements. It does not specify the way in which the rebuker learns of the offence nor does it require him to have been an eyewitness of the accused person's misdeed. Nor does it specify when the rebuke has to be made or make explicit the motivation for the obligation to rebuke. It does not indicate whether the total number of witnesses (two or three) is related to the type of offence. The general wording of the *halakhah* implies that the rebuke is obligatory in every type of offence. It leads one to suppose that expulsion from the community as a consequence of the procedure of rebuke is definitive, etc.

The origin of this practice of brotherly rebuke is impossible to determine. It seems clear that it was a practice originally developed in a Jewish group or with deep Jewish roots. This appears from the use made of the biblical texts and from the terminology used for the person who does not accept the rebuke made within the community («gentile», «tax-collector»). On the basis of the use of the LXX and the references to Lv 19:17 and Dt 19:15-16, it could be argued that it was a group in which the main language was Greek. However, this indication is not decisive since it cannot be excluded that this influence of the LXX was introduced by the final redactor who incorporated the block into the gospel. And since this procedure of rebuke is not mentioned either in the New Testament or in later rabbinic literature it is impossible to know in which group it originated[374].

### III  Conclusions

This summary discussion of the original meaning of the pericope included in Mt 18:15-17 and the description of the procedure of rebuke it contains, is enough to establish a comparison with the Qumran procedure of rebuke. And it shows that the statements of those who established its origins, directly or indirectly, in Qumran practice, lack foundation.

1) In Mt 18:15-17 the first stage of the procedure of rebuke is private rebuke. Qumran does not know this private rebuke intended to gain the transgressor.

2) In Mt 18:15-17 this private rebuke is mandatory in every case, as can be deduced from the generic nature of the wording. In Qumran, any private rebuke is strictly forbidden and is compared to a rebuke motivated by anger or by the desire to disparage one's fellow.

3) The common element in both juridical procedures of rebuke is the rebuke before witnesses. Even in this case, though, the differences between Qumran and Mt 18:15-17 are considerable. In Qumran there is provision for the requirement by the *Mebaqqer* to note down the rebuke before witnesses. Also, this noting down permits both the addition of witnesses and the use of a previous rebuke in a procedure before the community. In Qumran, a distinction is also established between misdeeds which result in death and misdeeds concerning money, as well as the number of witnesses necessary in each case. In Qumran, it is specified that one must be an eyewitness of a misdeed to be able to rebuke the transgressor and that the rebuke must be carried out on that day. None of these elements is reflected in the New Testament rebuke before witnesses.

4) in Mt 18:15-17 the motivation for the necessity of this rebuke is indirectly explained as the desire to «gain» the brother. At Qumran the express motivation for the necessity is to avoid incurring the misdeed witnessed.

5) There is no exact match, either, in the result of both procedures. In Mt 18:15-17, which does not know different degrees of belonging to the community, the result of the procedure of rebuke not resulting in repentance is permanent expulsion of the sinful member. At Qumran this is not necessarily the case. Relegation of the transgressor to one or other of the stages of previous membership is provided for, or exclusion for a time or permanent exclusion depending on the case.

Summarising, both the law of rebuke at Qumran and the law contained in Mt 18:15-17 are juridical procedures of rebuke. In both it is required that this rebuke must be made before witnesses. Here, though, the similarities between the two end. The differences, on the other hand, seem sufficiently striking and important to suggest that the law of rebuke at Qumran could not have acted as a model or antecedent and even less as the origin of the law of rebuke of Mt 18:15-17. And if one considers that the oldest law (the Qumran law) is more complete and at the same time more complex, this suggestion becomes a reasonable certainty. To equate both juridical procedures of rebuke, as was prevalent in the first decade of Qumran studies, seems like a hasty conclusion. The more moderate conclusions of later studies[375] must be refined even further.

This conclusion, though, does not cancel interest in the law of rebuke at Qumran for understanding Mt 18:15-17 better, both in its original form and in its gospel context. Its very existence proves that the practice of a juridical procedure of rebuke of faults committed by the members of a group is not something unusual within the pluralistic Judaism of the first century. At Qumran it is easier to perceive the exegetical foundations which led to the formulation of the law of rebuke and to understand its halakhic derivation from Scripture. At Qumran, too, the sociological conditions which prompted the formulation of the law of rebuke are easily seen. This element leads to the supposition that the law of rebuke included in Mt 18:15-17 also originated and originally thrived within a group with more or less sectarian features and that the law, in any case, was born as the result of exegetical activity.

In spite of the silence of rabbinical sources on the subject, both juridical procedures of rebuke, parallel but different, prove one thing. In the pluralistic Judaism of the first century the practice of brotherly rebuke, understood as a legal obligation deduced from the biblical text, was something completely normal and current within different kinds of sectarian groups. It is in this varied practice and not in a development from Lk 17:3 or in influence from the Qumran community that the origins of Mt 18:15-17 must be sought.

*Notes*

# Notes

1 Written at the request of Rosario Bofill and published in *El Ciervo* 490 (1992) 6-14.
2 The reader can find a clear account of the discoveries in J. C. VanderKam, *The Dead Sea Scrolls Today*, Grand Rapids 1994. They are presented in greater detail in the next chapter.
3 Like the other characters in this story, Sukenik has given us his own version of events in the introduction to his *The Dead Sea Scrolls of the Hebrew University*, Jerusalem 1953, 13-17, a work which contains the official publication of the three manuscripts he acquired.
4 A. Y. Samuel, *Treasures of Qumran. My Story of the Dead Sea Scrolls*, London 1968, 141-201.
5 J. C. Trever has also published his version of events in *The Dead Sea Scrolls. A Personal Account*, Grand Rapids 1977, a corrected and expanded version of his *The Untold Story of Qumran*, published in 1965. The three manuscripts were published by M. Burrows, J. C. Trever and W. H. Brownlee, *The Dead Sea Scrolls of St. Mark's Monastery*, Volume I, New Haven 1950 (1QIsa$^a$ and 1QpHab), and Volume II, New Haven, 1951 (1QS). The archimandrite did not authorise opening the fourth manuscript which was in a very bad condition, so that its partial publication was only effected later.
6 Y. Yadin, *The Message of the Scrolls*, London 1957. The official edition of the first three manuscripts, prepared by E. L. Sukenik appeared after his death: *The Dead Sea Scrolls of the Hebrew University*, Jerusalem 1955; 1QapGen was later published by N. Avigad and Y. Yadin, *A Genesis Apocryphon. A Scroll from the Wilderness of Judaea*, Jerusalem 1956.
7 In the periodicals *Bulletin of the American Schools of Oriental Research* and *The Biblical Archaeologist* of 1948 and 1949.
8 The results of the excavation were published as the first part of the volume which contains the publication of the fragments acquired or recovered: *Discoveries in the Judaean Desert I: Qumrân Cave 1*, Oxford 1955.
9 All the material found in these caves, called «small caves», was published by M. Baillet, J. T. Milik and R. de Vaux in *Discoveries in the Judaean Desert of Jordan III: Les «Petites» Grottes de Qumrân*, Oxford 1962.
10 The reader can find a short description of each of these collections of manuscripts and of their publication in the «Introduction» to DSST, XXXII-XXXV.
11 The reader can find a very brief description of each of the manuscripts found as well as publication details in the «List of Manuscripts from Qumran» included in DSST, 465-513.
12 Some doubt could remain after the analyses made by the method of carbon 14 dating in the fifties, due to the existing margin of error and the fact that it had been applied to textiles and wood and not directly to the manuscripts so as not

to destroy them. However, these doubts have ben completely eliminated through new analyses made in 1990 directly on the manuscripts, thanks to the use of a new technique which considerably reduces the amount of material needed for the analysis. Carbon 14 dating of the texts which underwent analysis agrees completely with the palaeographic dating proposed; see G. Bonani, M. Broshi, I. Carmi, S. Ivy, J. Strugnell, W. Wölfi, «Radiocarbon Dating of the Dead Sea Scrolls», *Atiqot* 20 (1991) 27-32.

13 Published by R. de Vaux, *Archaeology and the Dead Sea Scrolls*, London 1979.

14 G. Vermes, *The Dead Sea Scrolls. Qumran in Perspective*, London 1977, 10.

15 The main results gained in this field are given in more detail in the chapters «The Bible and Biblical Interpretation in Qumran» and «Biblical Borderlines» pp. 99-138.

16 *30 Giorni*, July 1992, 12.

17 J. O'Callaghan, «Papiros neotestamentarios en la cueva 7 de Qumrân?», *Biblica* 53 (1972) 91-100. O'Callaghan provided a longer and more detailed presentation in his book *Los papiros griegos de la cueva 7 de Qumrân*, Madrid 1974. The most recent presentation of his hypothesis is to be found in his article «Sobre el papiro de Marcos en Qumrân», *Filología Neotestamentaria* 5 (1992) 191-198.

18 Translated by W. L. Holladay, «New Testament Papyri in Qumrân Cave 7?», Supplement to *JBL* 91/2 (1972) 1-14.

19 J. A. Fitzmyer, *The Dead Sea Scrolls. Major Publications and Tools for Study*. Missoula 1975, 119-123.

20 C. P. Thiede, *Die älteste Evangelium-Handschrift? Das Markus-Fragment von Qumran und die Anfänge der schriftlichen Überlieferung des Neuen Testaments*, Wuppertal, 1986.

21 In the Catholic university of Eichstätt, from 18th to 20th October 1991. The lectures have been published in the book edited by the organiser of the congress, B. Mayer. *Christen und Christliches in Qumran?*, Regensburg 1992.

22 M. Baillet, the editor of the texts from Cave 7, replied to O'Callaghan in two long articles: «Les manuscrits de la grotte 7 de Qumrân et le Nouveau Testament», *Biblica* 53 (1972) 508-516 and 54 (1973) 340-350.

23 Baillet has accepted without difficulty the identification of 3Q5 as remains of the *Book of Jubilees* or the identification of 6Q8 as remains of the *Book of Giants*, in spite of having previously identified the corresponding fragments as parts of other apocryphal compositions.

24 7Q5 has been identified with various works of classical Greek literature, with various texts of the Greek Old Testament and with works of apocryphal literature which have survived in Greek, such as the *Book of Enoch*.

25 See G. W. Nebe, «7Q4 Möglichkeit und Grenze einer Identifikation», *Revue de Qumrân* 13 (1988) 629-633.

26 For further detail see the chapter «The Dead Sea Scrolls, Jesus Christ and the Origins of Christianity», pp. 193-202.

27 The reader can find more detailed information in the following introductions to the Scrolls: J. Allegro, *The Dead Sea Scrolls: A Reappraisal*, London, 1964; F. M. Cross, *The Ancient Library of Qumran and Modern Biblical Studies: Revised Edition*, Grand Rapids, MI, 1980; M. Delcor-F. García Martínez, *Introducción a la literatura esenia de Qumrán*, Madrid, 1982; R. de Vaux, *Archaeology and the Dead Sea Scrolls*, London, 1973; A. Dupont-Sommer, *The Essene Writings from Qumran*, Oxford, 1961; J. A. Fitzmyer, *The Dead Sea Scrolls: Major Publications and Tools for Study, Revised Edition*, Atlanta, GA, 1990; *Responses to 101 Questions on the Dead Sea Scrolls*, New York, 1992; N. S. Fujita, *A Crack in the Jar: What Ancient Jewish Documents Tell Us about the New Testament*, New York-Mahwah, NJ, 1986; A. González Lamadrid, *Los descubrimientos del Mar Muerto*, Madrid, 1971; E.-M. Laperrousaz, *Qoumrân: L'Etablissement essénien des bords de la Mer Morte. Histoire et archéologie du site*, Paris, 1976; J. T. Milik, *Ten Years of Discovery in the Wilderness of Judaea*, London, 1959; G. Vermes, *The Dead Sea Scrolls. Qumran in Perspective*, Philadelphia, 1981; Y. Yadin, *The Message of the Scrolls*, New York, 1992.

28 M. Burrows, *The Dead Sea Scrolls of St Mark's Monastery*, vol. 1, New Haven, 1950.

29 E. L. Sukenik, *The Dead Sea Scrolls of the Hebrew University*, Jerusalem, 1955.

30 Y. Yadin and N. Avigad, *A Genesis Apocryphon: A Scroll from the Wilderness of Judaea*, Jerusalem, 1956.

31 In G. E. Wright, ed., *The Bible and the Ancient Near East*, Garden City, NY. 1958, 133-202.

32 D. Barthélemy, *Les Devanciers d'Aquila*, Leiden, 1963.

33 *Qumrân Cave 4 II. I. Archéologie II. Tefillin, Mezuzot et Targums* (4Q128-157), Oxford, 1977.

34 D. N. Freedman and K. A. Mathews, 11QpaleoLev$^a$, *The Paleo-Hebrew Leviticus Scroll*, Winona Lake, 1985.

35 G. Vermes, *The Dead Sea Scrolls. Qumran in Perspective*, London 1977, 24.

36 H. Stegemann, «The Qumran Essenes – Local Members of the Main Jewish Union in Late Second Temple Times», *The Qumran Madrid Congress*, Leiden-Madrid, 1992, I, 96.

37 DSST, XXIV.

38 P. W. Skehan, E. Ulrich, J. Sanderson, *Qumran Cave 4. IV: Palaeo-Hebrew and Greek Biblical Manuscripts*, DJD IX, Oxford, 1992.

39 Cf. *Folia orientalia* 26 (1989) 229-230; *Qumran Chronicle* 1 (1990) 10-11.

40 Lecture read in the Salón de Actos de la Cámara de Comercio e Industria de Madrid on the 22nd April 1993, on the occasion of the presentation of the work *Textos de Qumrán*, Trotta, Madrid, $^4$1993.

41 For a description of these cemeteries see R. de Vaux, *Archaeology and the Dead Sea Scrolls*, London 1973, 45-48 and 57-58.

42 The text was published by J. Strugnell-D. Dimant, «4QSecond Ezekiel» in F.

García Martínez-E. Puech (eds.), *Mémorial Jean Carmignac*, Paris 1988, 45-58. For a detailed study of this text, my article «4QSecond Ezekiel y las tradiciones apocalípticas» in *III Simposio Bíblico Español*, Valencia 1991, 477-488 can be seen.

43 A translation of the text reconstructed by E. Qimron and J. Strugnell is to be found in DSST, 77-79. For an overall study of 4QMMT see L. H. Schiffman, «The New Halakhic Letter (4QMMT) and the Origins of the Dead Sea Sect», *Biblical Archaeologist* 55 (1990) 64-73.

44 Hebrew text in M. Burrows (ed.), *The Dead Sea Scrolls of St Mark's Monastery. II/2: The Manual of Discipline*, New Haven 1951.

45 Hebrew text in M. Broshi (ed.), *The Damascus Document Reconsidered*, Jerusalem 1992.

46 I translate column III of fragment 1 and column I of fragment 2 of 4Q186, a text published by J. Allegro, *Discoveries in the Judaean Desert of Jordan V*, Oxford 1968. It is a Hebrew text, although written out in reverse sometimes using Greek and palaeo-Hebrew letters as well as some from one of the cryptic alphabets. 4Q581, which seems to be the source of 4Q186 and partially overlaps it, has not been published yet.

47 Hebrew text published by D. Barthélemy in *Discoveries in the Judaean Desert I*, Oxford 1955.

48 Aramaic text published by J. T. Milik, «4QVisions de ᶜAmram et une citation d'Origène», *Revue Biblique* 79 (1972) 77-99.

49 According to the expression of 4Q405, the «Songs of the Sabbath Sacrifice».

50 Hebrew text published by M. Baillet, *Discoveries in the Judaean Desert VII*, Oxford 1982.

51 Hebrew text published by E. L. Sukenik, *The Dead Sea Scrolls of the Hebrew University*, Jerusalem 1955. My translation follows the reconstruction of the manuscript proposed by E. Puech, «Quelques aspects de la restauration du Rouleau des Hymnes (1QH)», *JJS* 39 (1988) 38-55.

52 Hebrew text published by E. L. Sukenik, *The Dead Sea Scrolls of the Hebrew University*, Jerusalem 1955.

53 Hebrew text published by E. Puech, «Une apocalypse messianique (4Q521)», *Revue de Qumrân* 15/60 (1992) 475-522.

54 This brotherly correction is discussed in greater detail in the chapter «Brotherly Rebuke at Qumran and Mt 18:15-17», below pp. 221-232.

55 The three fragments which make up the text can be found reproduced, together with fragments from other manuscripts, in the following photographs: PAM 40.622, 41.208, 41.707 and 41.894. The photographs PAM 42.937 and 43.562 show the three main fragments which comprise the text, already grouped in two consecutive columns. The first of these columns has only preserved the ends of four lines.

56 See pp. 193-202 of this volume.

57 The reader can find more detailed information in the following works: J. M. Baumgarten, «Some Remarks on the Qumran Law and the identification of the Community», in *Qumran Cave IV and MMT: Special Report*, ed., Z. J. Kapera, Cracow, 1991, 115-117; T. S. Beall, *Josephus' Description of the Essenes Illustrated by the Dead Sea Scrolls*, Cambridge, 1988; J. J. Collins, *The Apocalyptic Imagination in Ancient Judaism*, New York, 1984; J. J. Collins, (ed.), *Apocalypse. The Morphology of a Genre*, Missoula, MT, 1979; H. E. Del Medico, *Deux manuscrits hébreux de la Mer Morte*, Paris, 1951; A.-M. Denis, «Evolution de structures dans la secte de Qumrân», in *Aux origines de l'Eglise*, Bruges, 1964, 23-49; R. Donceel-P. Donceel, «Reprise des travaux de publication des fouilles au Khirbet-Qumran», *RB* 99 (1992), 557-573; J. Dumaime, «L'instruction sur les deux esprits et les interpolations dualistes à Qumrân», *RB* 84 (1977), 566-594; N. Golb, «The Problem of Origin and Identification of the Dead Sea Scrolls», *Proceedings of the American Philosophical Society* 124/1 (1980), 1-24; F. García Martínez, *Qumran and Apocalyptic*, Leiden, 1992; P. D. Hanson, *The Dawn of Apocalyptic*, Philadelphia, 1975; G. Klinzing, *Die Umdeutung des Kultus in der Qumran Gemeinde und im Neuen Testament*, Göttingen, 1971; A. R. C. Leaney, *The Rule of Qumran and Its Meaning*, London, 1958; J. Murphy-O'Connor, «La genèse littéraire de la Règle de la Communauté», *RB* 76 (1969), 528-549; Peter von der Osten-Sacken, *Gott und Belial: Traditionsgeschichtliche Untersuchungen zum Dualismus in den Texten aus Qumran*, Göttingen, 1969; H. Stegemann, «The Qumran Essenes – Local Members of the Main Jewish Union in Late Second Temple Times», in *The Madrid Qumran Congress. Actas del Congreso Internacional sobre los Manoscritos del Mar Muerto (Madrid, 18-21 de marzo de 1991)*, Madrid, 1992, 83-165; Y. Sussmann, «The History of *Halakha* and the Dead Sea Scrolls – Preliminary Observations on *Miqṣat Maʿaśe Ha-Torah* (4QMMT)», *Tarbiz* 49 (1989-1990), 11-76; J. C. VanderKam, «The People of the Dead Sea Scrolls: Essenes or Sadducees?», *Bible Review* 7 (1991), 42-47; G. Vermes, *The Essenes according to Classical Sources*, Sheffield, 1989.

58 See the chapter «The Origins of the Essene Movement and of the Qumran Sect», pp. 77-96.

59 See the chapter «The Problem of Purity. The Qumran Solution», pp. 139-157.

60 See the chapter «Messianic Hopes in the Qumran Writings», pp. 159-189.

61 Lecture given during the II Spanish Biblical Symposium held in Cordoba from 15th to 18th September 1985 and published in the proceedings of the Congress, edited by V. Collado Bertomeu and V. Vilar Hueso, *II Simposio Bíblico Español*, Valencia-Cordoba 1987, 527-556.

62 These two approaches represent the sediment and the consensus reached after calmer study has allowed the conflicting theories put forward in the first years following the discovery of the manuscripts to be sifted and rejected. For a survey of these opinions see M. Delcor-F. García Martínez, *Introducción a la literatura esenia de Qumrán*, Madrid 1982, 28-35. We do not include in this

presentation the two latest theories published, that of B. E. Thiering, *Redating the Teacher of Righteousness* (Sydney 1979), *The Gospels and Qumran* (Sydney 1981), *The Qumran Origins and the Christian Church* (Sydney 1983) and *Jesus the Man. A new interpretation of the Dead Sea Scrolls* (New York 1992) and that of R. Eisenman, *Maccabees, Zadokites, Christians and Qumran* (Leiden 1983) and *James the Just in the Habakkuk Pesher* (Leiden 1986). They are such preposterous and subjective hypotheses that to discuss them would only serve to distract us from the real problems. On R. Eisenman's hypothesis see F. García Martínez, *Journal for the Study of Judaism* 14 (1983) 189-194; on Thiering's hypothesis see F. García Martínez, *Journal for the Study of Judaism* 14 (1983) 98-99 and 15 (1984) 210-211. Norman Golb's thesis, set out repeatedly since his article «The Problem of Origin and Identification of the Dead Sea Scrolls», *Proceedings of the American Philosophical Society* 124 (1980) 1-24, denies the relationship between the manuscripts and the ruins of Qumran and the Essene origin of the Qumran manuscripts, and postulates that they all come from Jerusalem and were hidden in the different caves by the defenders of the city in the period of the fight against Rome (68-70 CE). It does not respect the archaeological evidence nor does it explain the uniform content of the manuscripts, unless one supposes that they all come from the library of a similar group located in Jerusalem. If so, the objections he flourishes against the usual explanation are turned back on his own hypothesis. A detailed rebuttal is to be found in F. García Martínez-A. S. van der Woude, «A «Groningen» Hypothesis of Qumran Origins and Early History», *Revue de Qumrân* 14 (1990) 521-544.

63 Although the actual reconstructions of the Qumran origins provided by various authors are rather less uniform. Compare, for example, the reconstruction of the summary article by J. H. Charlesworth, «The Origin and Subsequent History of the Authors of the Dead Sea Scrolls. Four Transitional Phases among the Qumran Essenes», *Revue de Qumrân* 10 (1979-81) 167-233, with those of J. Carmignac, «Les Textes de Qumrân traduits et annotés», *Revue de Qumrân* 11 (1963) 48-56, of A. Dupont-Sommer, *Les Ecrits Esséniens découverts près de la Mer Morte*, ⁴1983, 349-368 and with the classic reconstruction by J. T. Milik, *Ten Years of Discovery in the Wilderness of Judaea*, ²1963, 80-98, to mention some of the typical reconstructions which starting from the same presuppositions arrive at completely different results. A good presentation of the problematic elements of these reconstructions can be found in the book by P. R. Callaway, *The History of the Qumran Community. An Investigation (JSPS 3)* 1988.

64 H. Stegemann, *Die Entstehung der Qumrangemeinde*, 1971.

65 In several of his publications, from his thesis in 1953, *Les Manuscrits du Désert de Juda*. The most recent presentations of his summary are those included in his *The Dead Sea Scrolls: Qumran in Perspective*, 1977, 137-162 and *The History of the Jewish People in the Age of Jesus Christ* (the new Schüler), vol. II, 1979, 585-590 as well as his article «The Essenes and History», *Journal of Jewish*

*Studies* 32 (1981) 18-31.

66 Stegemann, *Die Entstehung*, 210-232.

67 This information is conveniently assembled in A. Adam C. Buchard, *Antike Berichte über die Essener*, ²1972, where not only are the classic texts from Josephus, Philo and Pliny to be found but also a whole series of lesser information, often dependent on the foregoing, taken from Synesius, Hegesippus, Hippolytus, Epiphanius, the *Apostolic Constitutions*, Jerome, Filastrius, Nilus, Isidore of Seville, Michael of Antioch and Solinus, and even Jospon and Albert the Great. The most important of these witnesses are also assembled in G. Vermes-M. D. Goodman, *The Essenes According to Classical Sources*, 1989, from which the English translations are taken.

68 These are the arguments already used by A. Dupont-Sommer, *Ecrits Esséniens*, 80-81, the first to defend identifying the Qumran sect as Essene, and repeated by other scholars.

69 Which they reckon to number about 4,000, see Philo, *Quod omnis probus*, 75 and Josephus, *Antiq.* XVIII 21.

70 Josephus, *War* II 124. Philo contradicts himself in this regard, since, whereas the fragment of his *Hypothetica* preserved in the *Praeparatio evangelica* by Eusebius, states that they live in many of the cities of Judah, in *Quod omnis probus*, 76, he shows them living in the villages and avoiding the cities on account of the immorality of the inhabitants.

71 Josephus, *Life.* 10.

72 *War* I 78-80 and *Ant.* XIII 311-313; *Ant* XV 373-378; *Ant* XVII 345-348 and *War* II 567 and *War* III 11.19 respectively.

73 See the arguments of halakhic agreement recently brought by J. M. Baumgarten, «The Disqualification of Priests in 4Q Fragments of the "Damascus Document, a Specimen of the Recovery of pre-Rabbinic Halakha"», in *The Madrid Qumran Congress*, vol. II, 1992, 504-505. The identification by Pliny, *Natural History*, V, 15/73 of the Qumran establishment as the residence of the Essenes is an argument that cannot be dismissed lightly. See in the same vein J. C. VanderKam, «Implications for the History of Judaism and Christianity» in *The Dead Sea Scrolls after Forty Years*, 1992, 22-25. T. S. Beall, *Josephus' description of the Essenes illustrated by the Dead Sea Scrolls* (SNTMS 58) 1988, has studied all these elements in great detail, but see the reservations expressed in *Journal for the Study of Judaism* 20 (1989) 83-88.

74 *War* II 160-161.

75 As a literal interpretation of the text requires, which implies that the Antiochus in question is the last Seleucid king to occupy Jerusalem. The short reign of Antiochus V (164-162 BCE), a nine-year old boy, is marked precisely by the campaign which he and Lysias, his general (the one who effectively took control) undertook against Judas Maccabaeus (1 Mac 6:28-54; 2 Mac 13:1-2; *Ant.* XII 366-383) and in which, in spite of an agreement with Judas, he penetrated

the Temple and destroyed the walls before withdrawing.

76 G. Vermes, *Qumran in Perspective*, 147-150; «The Essenes and History», 26.

77 G. Jeremias, *Der Lehrer der Gerechtigkeit* (SUNT 2) 1962, 159-162.

78 1QH frag. 1.5 and 4Q166 I 12.

79 A fact noted in the earliest commentaries on CD and is very noticeable in the stichometric layout by Jeremias, *Die Lehrer*, 151-152; see R. A. Soloff, «Toward Uncovering Original Texts in the Zadokite Fragments», *New Testament Studies* 5 (1958-59) 62-67, and P. R. Davies, *The Damascus Document* (JSOTSS 25) 1982, 61-65.

80 For a good discussion of the various opinions and a defence of the literal interpretation, see P. Sacchi, «Il problema degli anni 390 nel Documento di Damasco I, 5-6», *Revue de Qumran* 5 (1964-66) 89-96.

81 For an analysis of 1QS see J. Murphy-O'Connor, «La genèse littéraire de la Règle de la Communauté», *Revue Biblique* 76 (1969) 538-549. This analysis was developed and slightly modified by J. Pouilly, *La Règle de la Communauté de Qumrân: son évolution littéraire* 1976. Although it has not been unanimously accepted [see the reviews by E. Puech in *Revue de Qumrân* 10 (1979-81) 103-111 and P. A. Mantovani in *Henoch* 5 (1983) 69-91] its influence on the study of 1QS has been decisive. The same can be said for his series of articles devoted to the study of the various redactional levels of CD published in *Revue Biblique*: J. Murphy-O'Connor, «An Essene Missionary Document? CD II, 14-VI, 1», *RB* 77 (1970) 201-229; «A Literary Analysis of Damascus Document VI,2-VIII, 3», *RB* 78 (1971) 210-232; «The Translation of Damascus Document VI, 11-14», *RQ* 7 (1969-71) 553-556; «The Original Text of CD 7:9-8:2 = 19:5-14», *Harvard Theological Review* 64 (1971) 379-386; «The Critique of the Princes of Judah (CD VIII, 3-19)». *RB* 79 (1972) 200-216; «A Literary Analysis of Damascus Document XIX,33-XX,34», *RB* 79 (1972) 544-564.

82 J. Murphy-O'Connor, «The Essenes and their History», *RB* 81 (1974) 215-244 and «The Essenes in Palestine», *Biblical Archaeologist* 40 (1977) 100-124.

83 J. Murphy-O'Connor, «The Essenes and their History», 220. Later, Murphy-O'Connor gave up this interpretation of CD VI 5 and has accepted the translation «the converts of Israel»; see his «The *Damascus Document* Revisited», *RB* 92 (1985) 223-246 (on pp. 232-233), although for CD XIX 33-34 he maintains the meaning «who returned (to Judaea)»; he has also given up his date of 165-160 BCE for the return and suggests that the return could have been prompted «on the basis of some esoteric computation in the anticipation of an eschatological event» at a date he does not specify.

84 J. Murphy-O'Connor, «An Essene Missionary Document?», 211-212.

85 J. Murphy-O'Connor, «The Critique of the Princes of Judah», 211.

86 See the detailed investigation by H. J. Fabry, *Der Wurzel ŠWB in der Qumran-literatur*, 1975.

87 M. A. Knibb, «Exile in the Damascus Document», *Journal for the Study of the*

*Old Testament* 25 (1983) 98-117.

88 Which Murphy-O'Connor takes from W. F. Albright, *From the Stone Age to Christianity*, ²1957, 376.

89 Which Murphy-O'Connor derives from S. Iwry, «Was there a Migration to Damascus?», *Eretz Israel* 9 (1969) 80-88.

90 L. H. Schiffman, «Legislation Concerning Relations with Non-Jews in the Zadokite Fragments and in Tannaitic Literature», *RQ* 11 (1982-84) 379-389; *Sectarian Law in the Dead Sea Scrolls*, 1983.

91 R. de Vaux, *Archaeology and the Dead Sea Scrolls*, 1973, 5 and 116-117.

92 In his previous publications; see his reports in *Revue Biblique* 61 (1954) 231; 63 (1956) 538 and 565; 66 (1959) 102.

93 These arguments are: the remains of its occupation are so meagre that *it is certain* that the occupation was *for a short time*; the absence of coins prevents dating this period of occupation directly; the pottery remains are identical to those of the following period which indicates continuity of occupation between periods ꞮA and ꞮB. Period ꞮB begins during the high priesthood of Alexander Jannaeus and since «the modest nature of the buildings and the scarcity of archaeological material attest the fact that this first installation was of short duration», to extend it up to the high priesthood of Jonathan, about 50 years, is uncalled for and without foundation.

94 Milik identifies the Wicked Priest as Jonathan, *Ten Years*, 84-87; Cross identifies him as Simon, see his book *The Ancient Library of Qumran and Modern Biblical Studies*, 1958, 107-115.

95 R. de Vaux, *Archaeology and the Dead Sea Scrolls*, 116-117.

96 F. M. Cross, *The Ancient Library of Qumran*, 43-44.

97 See Y. Meshorer, *Jewish Coins of the Second Temple Period*, 1967, 41-52 and «The Beginning of the Hasmonaean Coinage», *Israel Exploration Journal* 24 (1974) 59-61.

98 E.-M. Laperroussaz, who has analysed critically the archaeological arguments of de Vaux reaching a different conclusion in respect of the end of period ꞮB, admits that it is impossible to date precisely the beginning of the Qumran buildings, period ꞮA, *Qoumrân. L'établissement Essénien des bords de la Mer Morte. Histoire et archéologie du site*, 1976, 33.

99 A. S. van der Woude, «Wicked Priest or Wicked Priests? Reflections on the Identification of the Wicked Priest in the Habakkuk Commentary», *Journal of Jewish Studies* 23 (1982) 349-359. Several Wicked Priests had been postulated by W. H. Brownlee, «The Historical Allusions of the Dead Sea Habakkuk Midrash», *BASOR* 126 (1950) 10-20, and even earlier, by B. Reicke, «Die Ta'amire-Schriften und die Damaskus Fragmenten», *Studia Theologica* 2 (1949) 60, but without receiving any reaction. Van der Woude has provided the hypothesis with the requisite methodological foundations and has recast it as the key to understanding the *pesharim*. The most difficult element of the hypothe-

sis, the possibility of the High Priest being Judas Maccabaeus, has been confirmed by my study «Judas Macabeo. ¿Sacerdote Impío? Notas al margen de 1QpHab VII, 8-13», in *Mélanges bibliques et orientaux en l'honneur de M. Mathias Delcor* (AOAT 15) 1985, 169-181.

100 J. Murphy-O'Connor, «The Essenes and History», 224-225.

101 In his article «The *Damascus Document* Revisited», *RB* 92 (1985) 240, Murphy-O'Connor makes an important remark which apparently contradicts this assumption: this literature would belong to the prehistory of the Teacher of Righteousness but not to the prehistory of the Essene movement before and independent of him. However, since this figure is determinative in the formation of Qumran thought, as Murphy-O'Connor himself accepts, his «prehistory» can be considered as the prehistory of the sect which he began.

102 Mentioned in CD XX 14.

103 D. Dimant also, in her contribution «Qumran Sectarian Literature», in *Jewish Writing of the Second Temple Period* (Compendia Rerum Iudaicarum ad Novum Testamentum, II, 2) 1994, 483-550, concludes her presentation of the history of the sect by distinguishing between the origins of the sectarian doctrines, which she dates to an unspecified movement in the 3rd and 2nd centuries BCE, and the historical and political circumstances, which she does not specify, and which lead to the actual creation of the sect. Although her conclusion rightly disassociates the ideological origins of the sect from the antiochene crisis and places these origins in Palestine in an earlier period, she does not succeed in identifying the actual terrain in which the sectarian doctrines arise («a wider trend existing in Judaism») and above all she maintains the identity between the Essene movement and the sectarian group, so undermining her historical reconstruction.

104 Ant. XIII 171-172.

105 See the references in L. H. Feldman, *Josephus and Modern Scholarship, 1937-1980*, 1984, 590-592.

106 Hippolytus, with clear apologetic intent, will reverse the terms and make Pythagoras and the Stoics depend on the Essenes: «For the discipline of these men in regard to the Divinity is of greater antiquity than that of all nations. So it is that the proof is at hand that all those who have ventured to make assertions concerning God, or concerning the creation of existing things, derived their principles from no other source than from Jewish legislation. Among these, Pythagoras and the Stoics among the Egyptians derived their principles after becoming disciples of these men», *Refutatio* IX 27.

107 M. Hengel, *Judentum und Hellenismus*, ²1973, 445-453.

108 As noted by Feldman, *Josephus and Modern Scholarship*, 564-594.

109 Compare CD XII 1-2 with 11QTemple XLV 11-12, for example.

110 CD XI 17-21.

111 R. Beckwith, «The Significance of the Calendar for Interpreting Essene Chro-

nology and Eschatology», *RQ* 10 (1979-81) 167-202; «The Earliest Enoch Literature and its Calendar», *RQ* 10 (1979-81) 365-403; «The Pre-History and Relationship of the Pharisees, Sadducees and Essenes. A Tentative Reconstruction», *RQ* 11 (1982-84) 3-46.

112 D. Dimant, «Jerusalem and the Temple in the Apocalypse of the Animals (1 Enoch. 85-90) in the light of the thought of the Dead Sea Scrolls», *Shnaton* 5/6 (1981-82) 177-183 [in Hebrew]; «History according to the Apocalypse of the Animals», *MYMY* 2 (1982) 18-37 [in Hebrew]; «Qumran Sectarian Literature», 544-545.

113 Its date of composition is generally put between 165 and 160 BCE, which would allow it to be considered as a work from the formative period; but, in spite of the relationships with Qumran literature emphasised by D. Dimant, its pre-Maccabaean stance seems to imply a non-sectarian origin. At Qumran, four copies of the work have been found: 4QEn$^g$ is from the third quarter of the 2nd century BCE; 4QEn$^e$ was written in the first half of the 1st century BCE and 4QEn$^{c,d}$ in the last third of the 1st century BCE; see J. Milik, *The Books of Enoch* (1976) 5.178.225 and 224.

114 A similar argument can be constructed from *Jub.* 23:26: «And in those days, children will begin to search the law, and to search the commandments, and to return to way of righteousness». *Jubilees* is also a work connected with sectarian thought and quite a few copies of it have turned up in Qumran – written in the first half of the 2nd century BCE; it cannot be considered a Qumranic work either, see J. C. VanderKam, *Textual and Historical Studies in the Book of Jubilees*, 1977, 258-283.

115 *Ant.* XIII 172: «The race of the Essenes, by contrast, makes Fate mistress of all and says that nothing comes to pass for humans unless Fate has so voted»; see also *Ant.* XVIII 18.

116 See most recently H. Lichtenberger, *Studien zum Menschenbild in Texten der Qumrangemeinde*, 1980, 184-200 and the earlier monograph of E. M. Merrill, *Qumran and Predestination*, 1975, which focuses on 1QH.

117 P. Sacchi, «Riflessioni sull'essenza apocalittica: Peccato d'origine e libertà dell'uomo», *Henoch* 5 (1983) 31-61; see also his previous study, «Il Libro dei Vigilanti e l'Apocalittica», *Henoch* 1 (1979) 42-78.

118 An obstacle which prevents Sacchi deriving the origins of Essene determinism from apocalyptic tradition, «Riflessioni», 61.

119 J. Blenkinsopp, «Interpretation and the Tendency to Sectarianism: An Aspect of Second Temple History», in *Jewish and Christian Self-Definition*, vol. II, 1981, 1-26.

120 This aspect is emphasised by O. Betz, *Offenbarung und Schriftforschung in der Qumransekte*, 1960.

121 See F. García Martínez, «Las Tablas Celestes en el *Libro de los Jubileos*», in *Palabra y Vida. Homenaje a José Alonso Díez*, 1984, 333-349, where the depen-

dence of *Jubilees* is emphasised in connection with *1 Enoch* in this respect.

122 See F. Nöttscher, «Himmlische Bücher und Schicksalglaube in Qumran», *RQ* 3 (1958-59) 405-411.

123 C. Rowland, *The Open Heaven*, 1982, 113 sees in it the very essence of apocalyptic.

124 Rowland insists on the permanent nature of this Qumranic communion with the heavenly world, which differentiates it from the temporal nature which it presents in apocalyptic: *The Open Heaven*, 120. According to him this change is due to the community having replaced the Temple as the meeting-place with heavenly beings.

125 I have developed this element at great length in «Essenisme Qumranien: Origines, caractéristiques, héritage», in *Correnti culturali e movimenti religiosi del Giudaismo*, 1987, 37-57 and in «La Nueva Jerusalén y el Templo Futuro de los MSS de Qumrân» in *Salvación en la Palabra. En Memoria de Alejandro Díez Macho*, 1986, 563-590.

126 R. G. Hammerton-Kelly, «The Temple and the Origins of Jewish Apocalyptic», *Vetus Testamentum* 20 (1970) 1-15.

127 Equally categorical is 4Q171 III 15-17: «Its prediction refers to the Priest. the Teacher of Righteousness,whom God chose to stand in front of him, for he installed him to found the congregation of his chosen ones for him, and straightened out his path, in truth».

128 The only other use of the verb *drk* in CD occurs in the quotation of Nm 24:17 in CD VIII 19, where it specifies that this star is the Interpreter of the Law.

129 The most recent attempt to trace this development is that of P. R. Davies, «Eschatology at Qumran», *Journal of Biblical Literature* 104 (1985) 39-55. Davies supposes that the eschatology of *Jubilees*, CD and 4QDibHam represents Essene eschatology as distinct from Qumran eschatology and defines the Qumran group as a schismatic group which affects to have accomplished Essene expectations.

130 This development has been emphasized by J. Duhaime, «La Règle de la Guerre de Qumrân et l'Apocalyptique», *Science et Esprit* 36 (1984) 67-88, who explains the transformation of eschatological hope within the Qumran community in terms of the priestly origins of the sect which made apocalyptic thought its own.

131 See M. Delcor-F. García Martínez, *Introducción*, 187-206 and B. Z. Wacholder, *The Dawn of Qumran*, 1983, 206.

132 See E. Qimron-J. Strugnell, «An Unpublished Halakhic Letter from Qumran», *Biblical Archaeology Today* 1985, 401.

133 See L. Schiffman, «Miqṣat Maʿaśeh Ha-Torah and the Temple Scroll», *RQ* 14/55 (1990) 435-457.

134 *Halakhoth* 1 to 7 of the published list: 1) ban on accepting sacrifices from the gentiles; 2) slaughter of pregnant animals (11QTemple LII 5); 3) those forbidden

to enter the assembly (1QSa II 5-9; 1QM VII 3-6; 4Q491 1-3,6); 4) the law of the red heifer (11QTemple LXIII 1-8); 5) exclusion of the blind and the deaf from the Sanctuary (11QTemple XLV 12-13); 6) purity of flowing liquids; 7) ban on bringing dogs into Jerusalem (11QTemple XLVII 1-14): see E. Qimron-J. Strugnell, «An Unpublished Halakhic Letter», 401-402.

135 *Halakhoth* 8-12 of the published list: 8) the fruits of the fourth year, for the priests; 9) the tithe of the flock, for the priests (11QTemple LX 1-5); 10) regulations on the purification period of the leper (11QTemple XLV 17ff.); 11) uncleanness of human bones (11QTemple I 5-9; LI 4-6); 12) ban on marriage between priests and Israelites (11QTemple LXV-LXVI). According to Qimron-Strugnell, 402, the work probably included other marriage *halakhoth* in the text which followed this last *halakhah*.

136 It is interesting to note that this element does not appear either in the summary of CD VI 11-VII 4, which provides a good parallel in respect of the content of the two elements indicated here as characteristic, presented as prescriptions for those who have been admitted into the Covenant: calendar and feasts (VI 18-19); prescriptions relating to the Temple (VI 15-16), the cult (VI 10), impurity (VI 17-18); tithes (VI 20). The summary adds other prescriptions which presume the community to be already established (VI 14-15; VII 1-4).

137 It suffices to refer to the classic article by S. Talmon, «The Calendar Reckoning of the Sect from the Judaean Desert», *Scripta Hierosolymitana* IV (²1965) 162-199.

138 The correction of the text proposed already by S. Schechter, *Documents of Jewish Sectaries*, 1910, XXXIX, to read KMṢWT «according to the precepts» instead of KMṢ'T of the manuscript and which has been accepted by Talmon, 166 and A. Dupont-Sommer, *Les écrits esséniens*, 147, among others, does not seem necessary. The expression, which is parallel to PRSWH, used in line 18 to mean the correct interpretation of the *sabbath*, and in line 20 for the correct interpretation of «the holy things» (tithes) underlines by itself the special character of the festival calendar of the group.

139 With (possibly) the sole exception of the addition which the Slav translator of Josephus has preserved in *War* II 147, which specifies that as well as keeping the *sabbath*, they also keep «the seventh week, the seventh month and the seventh year», a detail which would relate them with the system of reckoning we know through the *Book of Jubilees*, see M. Philonenko. «La notice de Josèphe slave sur les Esséniens», *Semitica* 6 (1956) 69-73. However, the evaluation of Slavic Josephus is a much discussed question and its reliability questionable.

140 Philo, *De vita contemplativa*, 65. On the underlying calendar see the commentary by P. Goeltrian, «Le *Traité de la vie contemplative* de Philon d'Alexandrie. Introduction, traduction et notes», *Semitica* 10 (1960) 1-66, on pp. 24-25 as well as A. Jaubert, *La notion d'alliance dans le Judaïsme*, 1963, 477-479 and J. van Goudoever, *Fêtes et Calendriers Bibliques*, ³1967. See also the article by J. Baum-

garten, «4QHalakah^a 5, the Law of Hadah and the Pentecostal Calendar», *JJS* 27 (1976) 39-42. On the Essene character of the Therapeutae group see G. Vermes, «Essenes and Therapeutai», *RQ* 3 (1962) 594-604 and *The History of the Jewish People*, vol. II, 591-597.

141 A. Jaubert, «Le Calendrier des Jubilés et la secte de Qumrân. Ses Origines bibliques», *Vetus Testamentum* 3 (1953) 250-264; *La date de la Cène*, 1957; «Fiches de Calendrier», in *Qumrân. Sa piété, sa théologie et son milieu*, 1978, 305-311. Jaubert's hypothesis has been defended by J. C. VanderKam, «The Origin, Character and Early History of the 364-day Calendar. A Reassessment of Jaubert's Hypothesis», *Catholic Biblical Quarterly* 41 (1979) 390-411, who has even attempted to establish that this ancient calendar was used in the Temple cult until 167 BCE, the date when it was replaced by a Seleucid luni-solar calendar, see «2 Maccabees 6. 7a and the calendrical change in Jerusalem», *Journal for the Study of Judaism* 12 (1981) 51-74, but has been refuted by P. R. Davies,, «Calendrical Change and Qumran Origins: An Assessment of VanderKam's Theory», *CBQ* 45 (1983) 80-89.

142 See the articles cited in note 111.

143 R. E. Brown, «The Pre-Christian Semitic Concept of Mystery», *CBQ* 20 (1958) 417-443 had already indicated some time ago that Qumran literature is the only literature to use the category of mystery in speaking of the interpretation of Scripture.

144 These texts refer to the movement to which both the Teacher of Righteousness and his followers and their enemies belong with the nickname «House of Abaddon» (1QpHab V 9-12); the members of the movement who do not accept the Teacher of Righteousness as "Scoffers" (CD XX 10-13; 4Q162 II 6.10) and «Traitors» (1QpHab II 1-3); and the chief of the movement which opposes the Teacher of Righteousness as «Scoffer» (CD I 13-17; XX 11-12) and especially «The Man of Lies» (CD I 15; IV 19; VIII 13; XX 15; 1QpHab II 1-3; V 9-12; X 9-13; 4Q171 I 18- II 1; IV 14-15).

145 This is how Murphy-O'Connor defines the oldest stage of the *Rule of the Community* which to some extent outlines the programme of the future sect and comes from its formative period.

146 One possible route to determine some of these circumstances comprises the different position of the authorities in relation to the Essene movement and the Qumran sect. Philo assures us, in his description of the Essenes (*Quod omnis probus*, 89-91) «But none of them (the rulers of Palestine up to his period), neither the most cruel, the most unprincipled and false, was ever able to lay a charge against the society known as Essaeans, or Saints; on the contrary, they were all defeated by virtue of these men. They could only treat them as independent individuals, free by nature». And in his *Hypothetica*, 18, he relates that «even the great kings were surprised at them and were pleased to give homage to their venerable character and to load them with favours and honours».

This is understandable given that Josephus describes them as subject to all authority, even to the extent of including loyalty for those who hold political power in the oath of admission, «for authority never falls to a man without the will of God» (*Bell.* II 140). The Qumran writings, on the other hand, provide a different picture. In the *pesharim*, particularly, the sect is in constant conflict with the established authority, the Hasmonaean High Priest. Two of these High Priests, designated as Wicked Priests, come into direct conflict with the Teacher of Righteousness. Hyrcanus persecutes him, once the schism was complete and the community was established in Qumran (1QpHab XI 4-8). The punishment suffered by Jonathan at the hands of Tryphon is attributed specifically to his sin against the Teacher of Righteousness (1QpHab IX 9-12). The possible influence on this hostility against the political power of the demands reflected in the «Torah of the King» of 11QTemple presented as a programme against the sovereignty of the Hasmonaean dynasty, is an as yet undetermined factor, but certainly relevant. Another possible field is the study of *halakhoth* in relation to (or in dispute with) known or presumed historical facts. Examples are the clause which in 11QTemple XLVII 7-8 forbids the hides of unclean animals to be brought into Jerusalem and the parallel decree of Antiochus III concerning the Temple (see *Ant.* XII 146); or the parallels with the *halakhoth* attributed to Hyrcanus (*m.M.Sh.* V 15) or Jonathan (*m.Par.* III 5) in rabbinic texts.

147 The reader can find more detailed information in the following works: M. Burrows, *The Dead Sea Scrolls of St. Mark's Monastery*, I: *The Isaiah Manuscript and the Habakkuk-Commentary*, New Haven, 1950; G. J. Brooke, *Exegesis at Qumran: 4QFlorilegium in its Jewish Context*, Sheffield, 1985; F. M. Cross, «The Old Testament at Qumrân», in *The Ancient Library of Qumrân and Modern Biblical Studies*, Grand Rapids, MI, 1980, 161-194; D. Dimant, «Qumran Sectarian Literature», in M. E. Stone (ed.), *Jewish Writings of the Second Temple Period*, Assen-Philadelphia, 1984, 483-550; A. Dupont-Sommer, *Les Ecrits esséniens découverts près de la mer Morte*, Paris, 1964³; M. Fishbane, *Biblical Interpretation in Ancient Israel*, Oxford, 1985; D. N. Freedman-K. A. Mathews, *The Palaeo-hebrew Leviticus Scroll* (11QpaleoLev), Winona Lake, IN, 1985; J. A. Sanders, *The Dead Sea Psalms Scroll*, Ithaca, NY, 1967; P. W. Skehan, «Qumran. IV, Littérature de Qumran – A. Textes bibliques», *DBS* 9, Paris, 1979, cols. 805-822; K. Stendahl, *The School of St. Matthew and Its Use of the Old Testament*, Philadelphia, 1968; E. L. Sukenik, *The Dead Sea Scrolls of the Hebrew University*, Jerusalem, 1955; cf. the publication of manuscripts in the series *Discoveries in the Judaean Desert*, Oxford 1955; J. Trebolle Barrera, *Biblia judía y Biblia cristiana. Introducción a la historia de la Biblia*, Madrid, 1993³; E. Tov, «Hebrew Biblical Manuscripts from the Judaean Desert: Their Contribution to Textual Criticism», *JJSt* 39 (1988), 5-37; G. Vermes, «Bible and Midrash: Early Old Testament Exegesis», in *The Cambridge History of the Bible*, vol. 1, Cambridge, 1970, 199-231.

148 The reader can find the bibliographical references to the editio princeps or the preliminary editions of all these manuscripts in the «List of Manuscripts from Qumran», DSST, 467-513.

149 Conference delivered on the 13th June 1991 in the Faculty of Theology of the University of Navarra and published in *Scripta Theologica* 23 (1991) 759-784.

150 The proceedings of the Congress have been published recently in two volumes by J. Trebolle Barrera-L. Vegas Montaner, *The Madrid Qumran Congress. Proceedings of the International Congress on the Dead Sea Scrolls, Madrid 18-21 March 1991* (STDJ 11), Madrid-Leiden, 1992. An extensive critical summary of all the material presented can be found in F. García Martínez, «Resultados y Tendencias. Congreso Internacional sobre los Manoscritos del Mar Muerto», *Sefarad* 51 (1991) 417-435.

151 For a presentation of all the biblical manuscripts which come from Qumran published until 1989 see F. García Martínez, «Estudios Qumránicos. Panorama crítico VI», *Estudios Bíblicos* 47 (1989) 225-266, or A. S. van der Woude, «Fünfzehn Jahre Qumranforschung (1974-1988) (Fortsetzung)», *Theologische Rundschau* 55 (1990) 274-307. For a complete list of the biblical manuscripts from Cave 4 which are still unpublished see E. Ulrich, «The Biblical Scrolls from Qumran Cave 4: A Progress Report of their Publication», in F. García Martínez (ed.), *The Texts of Qumran and the History of the Community*, vol. I, Paris 1989, 207-228.

152 All the manuscripts of Jeremiah from Cave 4 have been published by E. Tov, «The Jeremiah Scroll from Cave 4», in *The Texts of Qumran and the History of the Community*, vol. I, 189-206.

153 Cross has set out his theory in many publications. Perhaps the most important on this aspect are his articles «The Oldest Manuscripts from Qumran», *JBL* 74 (1955) 147-172; «The History of the Biblical Text in the Light of the Discoveries of the Judean Desert», *HTR* 57 (1964) 281-299, and «The Evolution of a Theory of Local Texts» in F. M. Cross and S. Talmon (eds.), *Qumran and the History of the Biblical Text*, Cambridge 1975, 306-320.

154 It is most characteristic element of the theory of S. Talmon, «The Textual Study of the Bible-A New Outlook», in F. M. Cross-S. Talmon (eds.), *Qumran and the History of the Biblical Text*, 321-400.

155 Some of the variants of this text were known already from 1974 [see D. N. Freedman, «Variant Readings in the Leviticus Scroll from Qumran Cave 11», *CBQ* 36 (1974) 525-534], but the complete manuscript was published in 1985: D. N. Freedman-K. A. Mathews, with the collaboration of R. S. Hanson, *The Paleo-Hebrew Leviticus Scroll* (11QpaleoLev), Winona Lake, 1985. The textual character of the manuscript has been studied by E. Tov, «The Textual Character of the Leviticus Scroll from Qumran Cave 11», *Shnaton* 3 (1978-79) 238-244 (in Hebrew) and by K. A. Mathews, «The Leviticus Scroll (11QpaleoLev) and the Text of the Hebrew Bible», *CBQ* 48 (1986) 171-207.

156 Carried out by J. Sanderson as a doctoral thesis: «An Exodus Scroll from Qumran. The Textual Character of 4QpaleoExod$^m$, Scribal Practice, and the Samaritan Tradition», and published with the title *An Exodus Scroll from Qumran. 4QpaleoExod$^m$ and the Samaritan Tradition* (Harvard Semitic Studies, 30), Atlanta, 1986. Sanderson has also refined her conclusions in a later article, «The Contribution of 4QpaleoEx$^m$ to Textual Criticism», in *Mémorial Jean Carmignac*, Paris 1988, 547-560.

157 Prepared by N. Jastram, «The Text of 4QNum», in *The Madrid Qumran Congress*, 177-198.

158 E. Tov, «A modern Textual Outlook Based on the Qumran Scrolls», *HUCA* 53 (1982) 11-27. The editor, K. A. Mathews, reaches a very similar conclusion: *CBQ* 48 (1986) 198.

159 Among the many publications in which Tov has set out his hypothesis perhaps the most important and influential has been the article mentioned, «A Modern Textual Outlook Based on the Qumran Scrolls», *HUCA* 53 (1982) 11-27 and his summary article «Hebrew Biblical Manuscripts from the Judaean Desert: Their Contribution to Textual Criticism», *JJS* 39 (1988) 5-37.

160 E. Tov, «Hebrew Biblical Manuscripts», 35.

161 J. E. Sanderson, «The Contribution», 553.

162 A factor underlined in exemplary fashion in the study of Bruno Chiesa, «Textual History and Textual Criticism of the Hebrew Old Testament», in *The Madrid Qumran Congress*, 257-272.

163 J. Duncan, *A Critical Edition of Deuteronomy Manuscripts from Qumran Cave IV* (Diss. Harvard University, 1989) 89-114.

164 J. Duncan, «A Consideration of the Text of 4QDt$^i$ in Light of the 'All Souls Deuteronomy' and Cave 4 Phylactery texts», in *The Madrid Qumran Congress*, 199-216.

165 S. A. White, *A Critical Edition of Seven Deuteronomy Manuscripts* (Diss. Harvard University, 1988).

166 S. A. White, «4QDt$^n$: Biblical Manuscripts or Excerpted text?», in H. Attridge, J. J. Collins, T. H. Tobin (eds.), *Of Scribes and Scrolls. Studies on the Hebrew Bible, Intertestamental Judaism, and Christian Origins* (Resources in Religion 5) Lanham, 1990, 13-20.

167 Published by Y. Yadin, *Megillat ham-Miqdash – The Temple Scroll*, 3 vols. and a suppl. Jerusalem, 1977 (in Hebrew); 1983, English edition with supplements.

168 Published by C. A. Newsom, «The 'Psalms of Joshua' from Qumran Cave 4», *JJS* 39 (1988) 56-73.

169 Published by J. Strugnell-D. Dimant, «4Q Second Ezekiel», in *Mémorial Jean Carmignac*, Paris 1988, 46-58; «The Merkabah Vision in Second Ezekiel», in F. García Martínez (ed.), *The Texts of Qumran and the History of the Community*, Vol. II, Paris, 1990, 331-348.

170 Published by J. Strugnell, «Moses-Pseudepigrapha at Qumran. 4Q375, 4Q376,

and Similar Works», in L. H. Schiffman (ed.), *Archaeology and History in the Dead Sea Scrolls* (JSP 8), Sheffield 1990, 221-247.

171 By J. M. Allegro in *Discoveries in the Judaean Desert of Jordan* V, Oxford 1968.

172 Known previously as 4QPP [=4QP(araphrase of the) P(entateuch)] and is still so designated in the publications by Toy and White to be mentioned below.

173 Y. Yadin, *Megillat ham-Miqdash*, Supplementary Plates, Pls.. 38,5 and 40,1-2.

174 Communicated in a personal letter which I published in «La Nueva Jerusalén y el Templo Futuro de los mss. de Qumrán» in *Salvación en la Palabra. Targum-Derash-Berith. En memoria del profesor Alejandro Díez-Macho*, Madrid 1986, 363-364.

175 E. Tov, «The Textual Status of 4Q364-367[4QPP]» in *The Madrid Qumran Congress*, 43-52.

176 In his lecture to the Madrid Congress. In the published version in the proceedings of the Congress, the sentence in question as well as the transcription and analysis of column II of fragment 28 have not been included. See S. A. White, «4Q364 & 365: A Preliminary Report» in *The Madrid Qumran Congress*, 217-228.

177 J. Starcky, «Le travail d'édition des fragments manuscrits de Qumrân», *Revue Biblique* 63 (1956) 66.

178 J. T. Milik, «Les modèles araméens du livre d'Esther dans la Grotte 4 de Qumrân» in E. Puech-F. García Martínez (eds.), *Mémorial Jean Starcky* II, Paris 1992, 321-406, quoted on p. 321.

179 «L'analyse du contenu des manuscrits *proto-Esther* de 4Q, confrontée aux textes des cinq versions du livre d'*Esther*, nous a conduit à postuler, à titre d'hypothèse, l'existence des trois écrits esthériens anciens distincts: *a-c, d* et *f, e*. Ces compositions successives se caractérisent par l'enrichissement progressif des thèmes, intrigues, trames», «Les modèles», 384-385.

180 Although Milik himself accepts that the argument from palaeography used to ascribe the different fragments to separate manuscripts is not completely conclusive owing to the similarity of the scripts used, «Les modèles», 384.

181 J. T. Milik, «Les modèles», 399.

182 *Ibid.*, 324-325 (Aramaic text); 325-331 (analysis and commentary.

183 *Ibid.*, 331 (Aramaic text); 332-333 (analysis and commentary).

184 *Ibid.*, 333 (Aramaic text); 334-336 (analysis and commentary).

185 *Ibid.*, 365-366 summarises the content of the three manuscripts as follows: Of the three fragments which belong to the same Aramaic story, the first, *a*, formed part of the opening section of the work, while fragments *b* and *c* come towards the end of the scroll. The fictional account developed two motifs of the tale, both linked to courtly life. The first dealt with the theme of service rendered to the prince, rescued from the oblivion into which he had fallen and rewarded with generosity. The second concerned the rivalry between two officials at court, one important and the other unimportant, but is the winner in the end. I do not think, in view of the size of the scroll, that there could have

been room for a third popular motif: the foreign beauty who succeeds in becoming queen.

186 *Ibid.*, 375-376, summarises their content as follows: The text preserved in 4QprEsthar$^d$ places us in the familiar area of a literary intrigue in which two motifs from court tales are intertwined: the meteoric rise of a foreign favourite in the court of the Great Persian King, and the career and rivalries of another foreign official. The novel feature of the author of the Aramaic text is that of transferring en bloc a complex literary and historical theme, of neighbours' disputes betwen two brother-peoples, Jews and Samaritans, who lived in an obscure part of the world, right to the splendid centre of the capital of the great Empire.

187 *Ibid.*, 336-337 (Aramaic text), 338-347 (analysis and commentary).

188 *Ibid.*, 347 (Aramaic text), 348-351 (analysis and commentary).

189 *Ibid.*, 351-352 (Aramaic text), 352-358 (analysis and commentary).

190 A parallel analysed in detail by Milik. The reader can find a good edition and translation of this work in J. Lindenberger, *The Aramaic Proverbs of Ahiqar*, Baltimore, 1983. A new edition of the Aramaic fragments differently arranged can be found in B. Porten-A. Yordeni, *Textbook of Aramaic Documents from Ancient Egypt*, 3, Jerusalem 1993, 24-52.

191 Lecture given at the Associazione Biblica Italiana at Bressanone, from the 7th to 9th September, 1987 and published in Italian in the proceedings of the congress edited by G. L. Prato, *Israele alla ricerca di identità tra il II sec. a.C. e il I sec. d.C.* (RSB 1), Bologna 1989, 169-191.

192 J. Neusner, *The Idea of Purity in Ancient Judaism* (Studies in Judaism in Late Antiquity 1), Leiden 1973, p. x.

193 Y. Yadin, *Megillat ha-Miqdaš – The Temple Scroll*, Jerusalem 1977, 3 vols. [in Hebrew]; English translation, Jeusalem 1983.

194 E. Qimron-J. Strugnell, «An Unpublished Halakhic Letter from Qumran», in *Biblical Archaeology Today*, Jerusalem 1985, 400-407.

195 J. Neusner, *A History of the Mishnaic Law of Purities* (SJLA 6) Leiden 1974-1977.

196 Which can be found conveniently collected in recent monographs: R. P. Both, *Jesus and the Laws of Purity: Tradition History in Mark 7* (Journal for the Study of the New Testament Supplement Series 13) Sheffield 1986, and N. Newton, *The Concept of Purity at Qumran and in the Letters of Paul* (Society for New Testament Studies Monograph Series 53) Cambridge 1985.

197 Studies on the problem of purity at Qumran in the first years of Qumran research were many and varied. As typical examples of works devoted specifically to the topic the following can be noted: G. W. Buchanan, «The Role of Purity in the Structure of the Essene Sect», *Revue de Qumrân* 4 (1963-64) 397-406; A. Dupont-Sommer, «Culpabilité et rites de purification dans la secte juive de Qoumran», *Semitica* 15 (1965) 61-70; S. B. Hoenig, «Qumran Rules of Impuri-

ties», *Revue de Qumrân* 6 (1967-69) 559-568; H. W. Huppenbauer, «THR und THRH in der Sektenregel (1QS) von Qumran», *Theologische Zeitschrift* 13 (1957) 350-351. For a summary of these works and of the material then available the thesis of L. Rosso, *La purità legale a Qumran*, Turin 1973, can be consulted. In recent years there have been fewer studies on the topic. B. Sharvit, «Purity and impurity according to the Sect of the Desert of Judah», *Bet Miqra'* 26 (1980/81) 18-27 [in Hebrew]; B. Janowski-H. Lichtenberger, «Enderwartung und Reinheitsidee. Zur eschatologischen Deutung von Reinheit und Sühne in der Qumrangemeinde», *Journal of Jewish Studies* 34 (1983) 31-62 and L. H. Schiffman, «Purity and Perfection: Exclusion from the Council of the Community in the Serekh Ha-Edah» in *Biblical Archaeology Today*, Jerusalem 1985, 373-389 appear to be the most important.

198 P. Sacchi, «Omnia munda mundis, Tito 1.15: il puro e l'impuro nel pensiero ebraico», in *Il pensiero di Paolo nel cristianesimo antico*, Genova 1984, 29-555; «Il puro e l'impuro nella Bibbia. Antropologia e storia», *Henoch* 6 (1984) 65-80. For studies of the vocabulary of purity see W. Paschen, *Rein und Unrein. Untersuchung zur biblischen Wortgeschichte* (Studien zum Alten und Neuen Testament 2), Munich 1970 and A. Vivian, *I campi lessicali della separazione nell'ebraico biblico, di Qumran e della Mishna* (Quaderni di Semitistica 4) Florence 1978.

199 Both statements are justified in F. García Martínez, «Essenisme Qumrânien: Origines, caractéristiques, héritage», in B. Chiesa (ed.), *Correnti culturali e movimenti religiosi del giudaismo*, Rome 1987, 37-57; «Qumran Origins and Early History: A Groningen Hypothesis», *Folia Orientalia* 25 (1988) 113-136. See the study «Origins of the Essene movement and of the Qumran sect» in this volume pp. 77-96.

200 E. Lupieri, «La purità impura. Giuseppe Flavio e le purificazioni degli Esseni», *Henoch* 7 (1985) 15-43.

201 *Ant.* XIII 171-173; *War* II 119-166.

202 See J. M. Baumgarten, «The Pharisaic-Sadducean Controversies about Purity and the Qumran Texts», *Journal of Jewish Studies* 31 (1980) 157-170 and the studies by G. Alon collected in the volume *Jews, Judaism and the Classical World*, Jerusalem 1977.

203 As noted by R. de Vaux, *Ancient Israel. Its Life and Institutions*, London, 1965, 258.

204 M. Smith, «The Dead Sea Sect in Relation to Ancient Judaism», *New Testament Studies* 7 (1960) 352; J. Neusner, *The Idea of Purity*, 28.

205 The relevant texts are collected conveniently in A. F. J. Klijn-G. J. Reinink, *Patristic Evidence for Jewish-Christian Sects* (Supplements to Novum Testamentum 36) Leiden 1973; see, for example, Origen, *In Matth.* XI 12 (p. 128), Epiphanius, *Panarion* 30,2.3-6 (p. 176); 30, 15.3 (p. 182).

206 As I think I have proved elsewhere, see F. García Martínez, «Sources et rédaction du Rouleau du Temple», *Henoch* 13 (1991) 219-232.

207 For further details see F. García Martínez, «El Rollo del Templo y la Halaká sectaria», in *Simposio Bíblico Español*, Madrid 1984, 611-622.

208 As noted by Yadin, *Megillat ha-Miqdaš*, vol. I, 224-225 who also noted that in 1QSa I 25-26 a three-day purification is required for taking part in the assembly of the future community.

209 J. Milgrom, «Studies in the Temple Scroll», *Journal of Biblical Literature* 97 (1978) 501-523.

210 In the decree of Antiochus III concerning the Temple of Jerusalem, Flavius Josephus, *Ant. Bibl.* XII 146, includes a clause forbidding the introduction into Jerusalem of the hides of unclean animals, a clause so foreign to Jewish tradition that it was used as an argument to deny the historicity of the decree. For a defence of its historicity cf. E. Bickermann, «La charte Séleucide de Jérusalem», *Revue des Etudes Juives* 100 (1935) 4-35, reprinted in vol. II of his *Studies in Jewish and Christian History*, Leiden 1981. 11QTemple is much more rigorous than the decree of Antiochus III since it even forbids bringing the hides of clean animals into Jerusalem and considers as lawful only the transport of merchandise in the hides of clean animals sacrificed in the Temple.

211 This implies that the latrines described in 11QTemple XLVI 13-16 were beyond the distance one could walk during the sabbath. The unavoidable consequence is that the members of the sect had to refrain from defaecation on the sabbath, as Flavius Josephus states the Essenes did, *Jew. War* II 147-149; see the discussion by Y. Yadin, *Megillat ha-Miqdaš*, vol. I, 228-229.

212 CD XV 15-17, completed from the 4QD$^b$ copy according to J. T. Milik, *Ten Years of Discovery in the Wilderness of Judaea*, London 1959, 114; 1QSa II 5; 1QM VII 3-6; 4Q491 1-3,6.

213 See the similar *halakhah* of CD XII 16-18 and its parallel in Targum Jonathan *Num* 19:14.

214 Targum Jonathan *Num* 19:16 does not even consider the person to be defiled: «Whoever touches in the field – and not, therefore, in the case of a dead person found in the his mother's womb – someone who has been stabbed...».

215 Six fragmentary copies of this work have been preserved inn Cave 4 (4Q394-399). The work, to the extent that it can be reconstructed by joining the different fragments together, seems to be composed of the following sections: Introduction (which has not been preserved), Calendar (partially preserved), list of *halakhah* peculiar to the sect, Epilogue (containing some theological principles of Qumran with a discussion of the reasons why the sect separated from the rest of the people, encouraging the opponents to return to the correct path). See E. Qimron-J. Strugnell, «An Unpublished Halakhic Letter from Qumran». The text has now been published as DJD X (Oxford 1994).

216 In his contribution «Da Qohelet al tempo di Gesù», in *Aufstieg und Niedergang der Römischen Welt*, II, Principat 19.1, Berlin-New York 1979, 3-32.

217 The relevant rabbinic texts are collected and commented on in the article J. M. Baumgarten, «The Pharisaic-Sadducean Controversies about Purity and the

Qumran Term», cited already.

218 As it is considered to be by C. Rabin, *The Zadokite Documents. I. The Admoni-tions. II. The Laws*, Oxford 1958, who in his translations adds: «Thus far» (p. 63). Others prefer to consider the text as the beginning of a new section of which the contents have been lost; thus, E. Cothenet in *Les Textes de Qumran traduits et annotés*, Paris 1963, vol. 2, 198.

219 Hebrew text in M. Broshi (ed.), *The Damascus Document Reconsidered*, Jerusalem 1992.

220 J. T. Milik, *Ten Years*, 152.

221 See the monograph by H. J. Fabry, *Die Wurzel ŠWB in der Qumran-Literatur* (Bonner Biblische Beiträge 46) Köln-Bonn 1975.

222 Studied by L. H. Schiffman. *Sectarian Law in the Dead Sea Scrolls* (Brown Judaic Studies 33) Chico 1983, 55-88.

223 G. Forkman, *The Limits of the Religious Community* (Coniectanea Biblica. New Testament Series 5) Lund 1972, 65.

224 J. Murphy-O'Connor, «La genèse littéraire de la Règle de la Communauté», *Revue Biblique* 76 (1969) 528-549, and J. Pouilly, *La Règle de la Communauté de Qumran. Son évolution littéraire* (Cahiers de la Revue Biblique 17) Paris 1976; «L'évolution de la législation pénale dans la Communauté de Qumrân»: *Revue Biblique* 82 (1975) 522-551.

225 «Tradition B» of P. Arata Mantovani, in «La stratificazione letteraria della Regola della Communità: a proposito di uno studio recente», *Henoch* 5 (1983) 69-91; or the «second level» of E. Puech, in his review of Pouilly's book in *Revue de Qumrân* 10 (1979-81) 103-111.

226 L. Schiffman, *Sectarian Law*, 157.161.173.

227 L. Moraldi, *I manoscritti di Qumran*, Turin 1970, 153.

228 J. Licht, *Megillat ha-Serakim*, Jerusalem 1965, 294-303 [in Hebrew] and already previously, S. Liberman, «The Discipline of the so-called Dead Sea Manual of Discipline», *Journal of Biblical Literature* 71 (1952) 199-206.

229 J. Neusner, *The Idea of Purity*, 54.

230 P. Sacchi, «Da Qohelet al tempo di Gesù», 26-27.

231 This translation of 1QS III 6-7 follows the explanation of the text by Janowski-Lichtenberger, «Enderwartung und Reinheitsidee», 49-50, and H. Lichtenberger, *Studien zum Menschenbild in Texten der Qumrangemeinde* (Studien zur Umwelt des Neuen Testaments 15) Tübingen 1980, 120, note 8.

232 The topic of purity in 1QSa has been studied adequately by L. H. Schiffman in his article «Purity and Perfection», cited above.

233 Written at the request of Professor Günter Sternberger and published in German in the *Jahrbuch für Biblische Theologie* 8 (1993).

234 From the basic work by A. S. van der Woude, *Die messianische Vorstellungen der Gemeinde von Qumran* (Studia Semitica Neerlandica 3) Assen 1957. A bibliography of the most important works from these twenty-five years is to be found

in J. A. Fitzmyer, *The Dead Sea Scrolls. Major Publications and Tools for Study* (SBL Resources for Biblical Study 4) Missoula 1975, 114-118.

235 It is significant that in the 1991 edition of his *The Dead Sea Scrolls. Major Publications and Tools for Study* (SBL Resources for Biblical Study 20, Atlanta 1991, 164-167 adds only six titles to the list published in 1975.

236 Among the studies published recently see G. J. Brooke, «The Messiah of Aaron in the Damascus Document», *RQ* 15/57-58 (1991) 215-230; A. Chester, «Jewish Messianic Expectations and Mediatorial Figures and Pauline Christology», in M. Hengel-U. Heckel (eds.), *Paulus und das antike Judentum*, Tübingen 1992, 17-89; M. A. Knibb, «The Teacher of Righteousness – A Messianic Title?», in P. R. Davies-R. T. White (eds.), *A Tribute to Geza Vermes* (JSOT 100) Sheffield 1990, 51-65; M. A. Knibb, «The Interpretation of *Damascus Document* VII, 9b-VIII, 2a and XIX, 5b-14», *RQ* 15/57-58 (1991) 243-251; P. Sacchi, «Esquisse du développement du messianisme juif à la lumière du texte qumrânien 11Q Melch», *ZAW* 100 (Supplement) (1988) 202-214; F. M. Schweitzer, «The Teacher of Righteousness», in Z. J. Kapera (ed.), *Mogilany 1989. Papers on the Dead Sea Scrolls*, Volume 2 (Qumranica Mogilanensia 3), Kraków 1991, 53-97; L. E. Schiffman, «Messianic Figures and Ideas in the Qumran Scrolls», in J. H. Charlesworth (ed.), *The Messiah. Developments in Early Judaism and Christianity*, Minneapolis 1992, 116-129; S. Talmon, «Waiting for the Messiah-The Conceptual Universe of the Qumran Covenanters», in S. Talmon (ed.), *The World of Qumran from Within. Collected Studies*, Jerusalem/Leiden 1989, 273-300 (= J. Neusner-W. S. Green-E. Frerichs (eds.), *Judaisms and Their Messiahs at the Turn of the Christian Era*, Cambridge 1987, 111-137); S. Talmon, «The Concept of Māšîaḥ and Messianism in Early Judaism», in J. H. Charlesworth (ed.), *The Messiah*, 79-115; J. C. VanderKam, «Jubilees and the Priestly Messiah of Qumran», *RQ* 13/49-52 (1988) 353-365.

237 They are the *editio princeps* of three Aramaic texts completed by E. Puech, «Fragment d'une apocalypse en araméen (4Q246 = pseudo-Dan) et le 'Royaume de Dieu'», *RB* 99 (1992) 98-131; «Une apocalypse messianique (4Q521)», *RQ* 15/60 (1992) 475-522; «Fragments d'un apocryphe de Lévi et le personnage eschatologique. 4QTestLévi^{a-d}(?) et 4QAJ», in J. Trebolle-Barrera-L. Vegas Montaner (eds.), *The Madrid Qumran Congress* (STDJ 11) Leiden 1992, 449-501, pls. 16-22; and of a Hebrew fragment published by G. Vermes, «The Oxford Forum for Qumran Research: Seminar on the Rule of War from Cave 4 (4Q285)», *JJS* 43 (1992) 85-94.

238 For example, L. H. Schiffman in «Messianic Figures and Ideas in the Qumran Scrolls» (cited in note 236).

239 In Hesse's words, «Keine der Messias-Stellen des Alten Testaments kann messianisch gedeutet werden», *TWNT* IX, 494.

240 In which the Blessing of Jacob comprises one of the key texts for the expression of messianic hope. See the detailed study by M. Pérez Fernández, *Tradiciones mesiánicas en el Targum Palestinense*, Jerusalem-Valencia 1981, 112-144,

especially pp. 123-135 on Gn 49:10.

241 The messianic passage was published by J. M. Allegro, «Further Messianic References in Qumran Literature», *JBL* 75 (1956) 174-184; the first two preserved columns of the manuscript have been published recently by T. H. Lim, «The Chronology of the Flood Story in a Qumran Text (4Q252)», *JJS* 43 (1992) 288-298. The photographs of all the fragments preserved is to be found in PAM 43.253 and 43.381, reproduced in plates 1289 and 1375 of R. H. Eisenman-J. M. Robinson (eds.), *A Facsimile Edition of the Dead Sea Scrolls*, Biblical Archaeological Society, Washington 1991 (= *FE*).

242 Separated by a *Blank* in the foregoing text and with the heading «Jacob's Blessings» in 4Q252 IV 3.

243 Column IV 3-7 contains remains of the blessing of Reuben, V 1-7, part of the blessing of Judah and the remains of column VI correspond to the blessing of Naphtali.

244 The actual quotation has not been preserved and its is impossible to know whether a literal quotation from Gn 49:10 preceded the commentary of this column V. The evidence of the preceding columns is ambiguous in this regard; the blessing of Reuben begins with the literal quotation followed by its *pesher*, but the interpretation, for example, of the story of the flood is incorporated into the additions, changes and omissions of the actual account.

245 As Van der Woude had already proved (op. cit. in note 234) 171-172.

246 4Q254 (4QpGen^c): PAM, 43.233, *FE* 1270.

247 4Q253 (4QpGen^b): PAM 43.258, *FE* 1294.

248 Text in J. M. Allegro, *Discoveries in the Judaean Desert of Jordan* V, Oxford 1968, 11-15, plates 4-5, with the corrections by J. Strugnell, «Notes en marge du volume V des 'Discoveries in the Judaean Desert of Jordan'», *RQ* 7 (1969-71) 183-186.

249 A title which, in itself, seems to identify its bearer as the davidic «Messiah» in so far as it obviously derives from the «Prince» of Ezekiel 40-48, the chief of the future community, of which Ezk 34:24 and 37:25 says precisely «and my servant David will be his prince for ever».

250 Published by J. T. Milik in *Discoveries in the Judaean Desert* I, Oxford 1955, 118-130, pls. 25-29.

251 4Q285 and the copy which comes from Cave 11, published by A. S. van der Woude with the title 11QBerakhot, «Ein neuer Segensspruch aus Qumran», in *Bibel und Qumran* (Festschrift H. Bardtke), Berlin 1968, 253-258, which matches fragments 3 and 4 of 4Q285. This match was noticed by J. T. Milik, «Milkî-ṣedeq and Milkî-reša^c dans les anciens écrits juifs et chrétiens», *JJS* 23 (1972) 143, who was also the first to suggest that both manuscripts come from the lost ending to the *War Rule*.

252 Besides fragment 5,4 there are references to the «Prince of the congregation» in fragments 4.2 and 6,2; unfortunately, though, they are references which are

too fragmentary to provide us with any useful elements.

253 G. Vermes, «The Oxford Forum for Qumran Research: Seminar or the Rule of War from Cave 4(4Q285)» (cited in note 237).

254 J. D. Tabor, «A Pierced or Piercing Messiah? – The Verdict is Still Out», *BAR* 18/6 (1992) 58-59.

255 Besides the texts quoted, the «Prince of the congregation» occurs in 1QM v 1, where only tells us the inscription he will bear on his sceptre, and in CD 7,20 and 4Q376, two texts we will study below.

256 E. Puech, «Une apocalypse messianique» (cited in note 237).

257 J. Starcky, in «Le travail d'édition des manuscrits de Qumrân», *RB* 63 (1956) 66.

258 In fragment 9,3 the word «Messiah» is incomplete, so that it cannot be used.

259 A unique expression and difficult to explain, given that in the other writings it is always a matter of God's «precepts» and in most cases God is explicitly mentioned. In the Qumran texts, as in the Hebrew Bible, «Holy Ones» could evidently denote the angels. Accordingly, the phrase could mean the union of the «Messiah» with the «Holy Ones» and indicate that in the messianic age all creation will keep the angelic precepts. However, «the holy ones» is also used (especially in texts of eschatological content, such as 1QM and 1QSb) to denote the members of the community, so that the expression could be understood as alluding to the divine precepts exactly as they are interpreted by the members of the community. Or is it merely an objective adjective for these precepts as holy precepts?

260 In fact, the reference to «all Israel» in III 5 could imply a different context since the author appears to restrict his horizon to the faithful members of the community in the description of the messianic age of column II. In the allusion to the sceptre a reference to the «Messiah of Israel», and in the allusions to the priesthood of fragments 8-9, Puech accepts a possible reference to the «priestly Messiah», but prudently concludes that the condition of the manuscript does not permit any definitive conclusion.

261 M. O. Wise-J. D. Tabor, «The Messiah at Qumran», *BAR* 18/6 (1992) 60-65.

262 Although they accept that it is a purely speculative reconstruction.

263 As specified in fragment 7+5 II 5-6: «like these, the accursed; and they shall be for death [when] (6) [he makes] the dead of his people [ri]se».

264 E. Puech, «Fragments d'un apocryphe de Lévi et le personnage eschatologique. 4QTestLévi^{a-d}(?) et 4QAJ» (cited in note 237).

265 J. Starcky, «Les quatre étapes du messianisme à Qumran», *RB* 70 (1963) 492.

266 «And after vengeance on them will have come from the Lord, the priesthood will fail. Then the Lord will raise up a new priest, to whom all the words of the Lord will be revealed; and he will execute a judgment of truth upon the earth in course of time. And his star will arise in heaven, as a king, lighting up the light of knowledge as by the sun of the day; and he will be magnified in the world until his assumption. He will shine as the sun on the earth and will re-

move all darkness from under heaven, and there will be peace on all the earth»,
TestLev 18:1-4, as translated by H. W. Hollander-M. de Jonge, *The Testaments
of the Twelve Patriarchs* (Studia in Veteris Testamenti Pseudepigrapha 8) Leiden
1985, 177.

267 See recently J. C. VanDerKam, «Righteous One, Messiah, Chosen One, and
Son of Man in I Enoch 3-71» in J. H. Charlesworth (ed.), *The Messiah* (cited in
note 236) 169-191, with references to previous studies.

268 M. Stone, «The Question of the Messiah in 4 Ezra», in M. Stone, *Selected Stud-
ies in Pseudepigrapha & Apocrypha* (SVTP 9) 317-322(= J. Neusner-W. S. Green-
E. Frerich [eds.], *Judaism and Their Messiahs at the Turn of the Christian Era*,
Cambridge 1987, 209-224) and «Excursus on the Redeemer Figure», in M.
Stone, *Fourth Ezra* (Hermeneia), Minneapolis 1990, 207-213.

269 In an excellent article in which he stresses how both figures represent a particular «messianic» interpretation of Dan 7, «The Son of Man in First-Century
Judaism», *NTS* 38 (1992) 448-466. Collins suggests (p. 466 note 78) that 4Q246
could contain a similar messianic interpretation of the Daniel figure, an intu-
ition which seems absolutely correct and matches my own understanding of the
text.

270 The text was presented by J. T. Milik in a lecture given at Harvard University
in 1972 and was made known by J. A. Fitzmyer in his study «The Contribution
of Qumran Aramaic to the Study of the New Testament», *NTS* 20 (1972-74)
382-407 and reprinted with an important supplement in J. A. Fitzmyer, *A Wandering Aramean. Collected Aramaic Essays* (SBL Monograph Series 25), Chico
1979, 85-107.

271 See D. Flusser, «The Hubris of the Antichrist in a Fragment from Qumran»,
*Immanuel* 10 (1980) 31-37, and F. García Martínez, «The eschatological figure
of 4Q246» in F. García Martínez, *Qumran and Apocalyptic* (STDJ 9) Leiden 1992,
162-179. G. Kuhn, «Röm 1,3 f und der davidische Messias als Gottessohn in
den Qumrantexten», in Ch. Burchard-G. Thiessen (eds.), *Lese-Zeichen für
Annelies Findreiß zum 65. Geburtstag am 15. März 1984*, Heidelberg 1984, 103-
113.

272 E. Puech, «Fragment d'une apocalypse en araméen (4Q246 = pseudo-Dan^d) et
le 'Royaume de Dieu'» (cited above, note 237).

273 F. García Martínez, «The eschatological figure of 4Q246» (note 271).

274 E. Puech, 124-125 and 102, note 14.

275 On the interpretation of the «Son of Man» of Dan 7 as an individual with an
angelic nature see J. J. Collins, *The Apocalyptic Vision of the Book of Daniel* (HSM
16) Ann Arbor 1977, 144-147.

276 See E. Puech, 116-117.

277 *Ibid.* 129.

278 Edition and plates in *The Dead Sea Scrolls of St. Mark's Monastery*, Vol. II, New
Haven 1951. Colour photographs by J. C. Trever in *Scrolls from Qumran Cave*

*1*, Jerusalem 1972. I have also been able to use a new critical edition prepared by E. Qimron which includes the parallels from the copies from other caves, to be published shortly.

279 For a general view of the messianism of this work see A. S. van der Woude, *Die messianische Vorstellungen* (cited in note 234) 190-216.

280 A detail made known by J. T. Milik, *Ten Years of Discovery in the Wilderness of Judaea*, London 1959, 123-124 and in *RB* 67 (1960) 413 and exploited by J. Starcky in his famous article «Les quatres étapes du messianisme à Qumrân» (cited in note 265).

281 4Q259 col. III 6; see PAM 43.263, *FE* 1299.

282 I use the critical edition prepared by E. Qimron and included in M. Broshi (ed.), *The Damascus Document Reconsidered*, Jerusalem 1992, which is accompanied by photographs of excellent quality and contains parallels to the copies found in Qumran.

283 The phrase occurs in the oldest copy of CD from Cave 4, 4Q266 (4QDo.11a) frag. 18 III 12, which proves that it is an original reading and not a correction by a mediaeval copyist; see PAM 43.276, *FE* 1312.

284 The manuscript reads *meshuach*, an obvious mistake as all scholars accept.

285 Although the copy 4QD^b frag. 18 III 1 (PAM 43.270, *FE* 1306) reads «Messiah of Aaron and Israel».

286 See most recently the article by G. Brooke cited in note 236.

287 F. M. Cross, «Some Notes on a Generation of Qumran Studies», in *The Madrid Qumran Congress*, (STDJ XI/1) Leiden 1992, 14 frames this trenchant conclusion: «The putative single messiah is a phantom of bad philology».

288 Edition and plates in DJD I, Oxford 1955, 108-118, pls. 23-24. The only monograph devoted entirely to this manuscript is L. H. Schiffman, *The Eschatological Community of the Dead Sea Scrolls* (SBLMS 38) Atlanta 1989.

289 DJD I, 117. See also P. Skehan, «Two Books on Qumran Studies», *CBQ* 21 (1959) 74. For other readings and interpretations see K. G. Kuhn, «The Two Messiahs of Aaron and Israel», in K. Stendahl, *The Scrolls and the New Testament*, London 1958, 56 or L. H. Schiffman, *op. cit.* (previous note) 54, who follows the readings and reconstructions of J. Licht.

290 See, for example, A. S. van der Woude (*op. cit.* note 234) 101-104 and L. H. Schiffman (*op. cit.* note 288) 55-56. This conclusion forces this same messianic figure to be acknowledged in the «Chief Priest» or «High Priest» of 1QM II 1; XV 4 and XVI 13, as van der Woude already has, against what L. Schiffman explicitly states on p. 123 of the article cited in note 236. Even more than in 4Q285, which apparently comes from the end of the same composition, the «Prince of the congregation» plays an important role and as we have seen above, this name is one of the titles of the «davidic Messiah». Discussion of these texts, however, must be reserved for another occasion.

291 J. Strugnell, «Moses-Pseudepigrapha at Qumran: 4Q375, 4Q376, and Similar

Works», in L. H. Schiffman (ed.), *Archaeology and History in the Dead Sea Scrolls*, The New York Conference in Memory of Yigael Yadin (JSP 8) Sheffield 1990, 221-256.

292 The two most characteristic allusions in terms of vocabulary to indicate a Qumran origin of the composition, «hidden things» and «fathers of the congregation», are partly reconstructions by the editor.

293 The text is found in part in the copy 4QD$^b$ (4Q267) frag. 3 col. IV 9-10 (PAM 43.270, *FE* 1306) and possibly in 4Q271, 4QD$^f$ frag. 5 (PAM 43.300, *FE* 1335) although this is very uncertain.

294 As, for example, A. Caquot, «Le messianisme qumrânien» in M. Delcor (ed.), *Qumrân: Sa piété, sa théologie et son milieu* (BETL 46) Louvain 1978, 241-242.

295 For example, G. Brooke, «The Amos-Numbers Midrash (CD 7,13b-8) and Messianic Expectation», *ZAW* 92 (1980) 397-404. See most recently the detailed study of the passage by M. Knibb in *RQ* 15/57-58 (1991) 248-251 (cited in note 236).

296 J. Starcky, «Les quatres étapes» (cited in note 265), 497.

297 In the work cited in note 234, 43-61 and in his contribution to the IX$^{es}$ Journées Bibliques de Louvain, «Le Maître de Justice et les deux messies de la communauté de Qumrân» in *La secte de Qumrân et les origines chrétiennes* (RechBibl 4) Bruges 1969, 123-134.

298 See most recently P. Pilhofer, «Wer salbt den Messias? Zum Streit um die Chronologie im ersten Jahrhundert des jüdisch-christlichen Dialogs», in D.-A. Koch-H. Lichtenberger (eds.), *Begegnungen zwischen Christentum und Judentum in Antike und Mittelalter* (Festschrift für H. Schrekenberg), Göttingen 1993, 335-345.

299 N. Wieder, «The Doctrine of the Two Messiahs among the Karaites», *JJS* 6 (1953) 14-23.

300 Text and plates in DJD V, Oxford 1968, 53-57, pls. 19-20.

301 The manuscript was published by A. S. van der Woude, «Melchisedek als himmlische Erlösergestalt in den neugefundenen eschatologischen Midraschim aus Qumran Höhle XI», *Oudtestamentische Studien* 14 (1965) 354-373, 2. pls., and has been extensively studied. My translation incorporates most of the readings and reconstructions proposed by E. Puech, «Notes sur le manuscrit de 11QMelkisédeq», *RQ* 12/48 (1987) 483-513.

302 As the editor explained in an joint article with M. de Jonge, «11QMelchizedek and the New Testament», *NTS* 12 (1966) 307.

303 The correction of the text from «his anointed one» to «anointed ones» is generally accepted.

304 4Q377 2 II 5 *FE* 497, a central fragment with remains of two columns. Unfortunately, this photograph, the only one available to me, is of such bad quality that the fragment remains virtually unreadable. The manuscript is labelled Sl 12 in the *Preliminary Concordance to the Hebrew and Aramaic Fragments from Qumrân*

*Caves II-X*, where the phrase in question is transcribed.

305 Text and plates in DJD v, Oxford 1968, 57-60, pl. 21.

306 See the arguments adduced by Van der Woude in the works cited in note 299. This figure occurs frequently in 1QpHab and in CD, where he is called «Teacher of Righteousness», «Unique Teacher», «he who teaches justice» or «the unique teacher» interchangeably.

307 A fact which Van der Woude accepts, but resolves by supposing that the text of 1QS IX 11, which witnesses the hope in the «Prophet» is earlier than the appearance of the Teacher of Righteousness, his acceptance? as prophet and his death; see *Die messianische Vorstellungen*, 84-85 and 187.

308 Text and plates in DJD I, 132-133, pl. 30.

309 PAM 43,400; *FE* 1394.

310 J. T. Milik, «Milki-ṣedeq et Milki-rešaᶜ» (cited in note 251) 130-131.

311 (See DSST, 228ff.). The phrase is cited by Strugnell (article cited in note 291) as parallel to the expression «oil of anointing» in 4Q375 1 8, and to «oil of his priestly anointing» in 1QM IX 8, and as coming from 4Q453 2 II 6. The work has now been given the siglum 4Q458.

312 PAM 43.544; *FE* 1493.

313 In his article «Les quatre étapes du messianisme à Qumrân» (cited in note 265).

314 In the studies cited in note 236.

315 As M. Smith, «What is implied in the variety of messianic figures», *JBL* 78 (1959) 66-72 seems to suggest.

316 As J. H. Charlesworth, «From Messianology to Christology. Problems and Prospects», in *The Messiah*, 28, concludes.

317 Lecture given as part of a round table with professors H. Stegemann and E. Cothenet on the «Significance of the Dead Sea Scrolls for the knowledge of Jesus Christ and of Christianity» held during the Summer Course «Jesus Christ today», organized by the Universidad Complutense in the Escorial from 3rd to 7th July, 1989 and published in the collective volume *Jesucristo hoy*, Madrid 1990, 239-250.

318 J. M. Allegro, *Qumrân Cave 4. I* (4Q158-4Q186) (Discoveries in the Judaean Desert of Jordan v), Clarendon Press, Oxford 1968.

319 J. Strugnell, «Notes en marge du volume v des "Discoveries in the Judaean Desert of Jordan"», *Revue de Qumrân* 7 (1969-1971) 163-276.

320 L. Allegro, *The Dead Sea Scrolls and the Christian Myth*, London 1979.

321 J. H. Charlesworth, *The Discovery of a Dead Sea Scroll (4QTherapeia). Its Importance in the History of Medicine and Jesus Research*, Labbeck 1985.

322 J. Naveh, «A Medical Document or a Writing Exercise? The So-called 4QTherapeia», *Israel Exploration Journal* 36 (1986) 52-55.

323 Barbara E. Thiering, *Redating the Teacher of Righteousness* (Australian & New Zealand Studies in Theology and Religion) Sydney 1979; *The Gospels and Qumran. A New Hypothesis* (Australian & New Zealand Studies in Theology

and Religion) Sydney 1981; *The Qumran Origins of the Christian Church* (Australian & New Zealand Studies in Theology and Religion) Sydney 1983 and *Jesus the Man. A new interpretation from the Dead Sea Scrolls*, New York 1992.

324 R. Eisenman, *Maccabees, Zadokites, Christians and Qumran* (Studia Post-Biblica 34) Leiden 1983 and *James the Just in the Habakkuk Pesher* (Studia Post-Biblica 35) Leiden 1986.

325 *Materials for the Dictionary Series* I, Academy of the Hebrew Language. Historical Dictionary of the Hebrew Language, Jerusalem 1988. Distributed in an edition of 105 microfiches with over 21,000 pages of text.

326 E. Puech, «Un Hymne essénien en partie retrouvé et les Béatitudes. 1QH V 12-VI 18 (= col. XIII-XIV 7) et 4QBéat», in F. García Martínez-E. Puech (eds.), *Mémorial Jean Carmignac*, Paris 1988, 59-88 and «4Q525 et les péricopes des béatitudes en Ben Sira et Matthieu», *Revue Biblique* 98 (1991) 80-106.

327 On this subject see the chapter «Brotherly Rebuke in Qumran and Mt 18:15-17», pp. 221-232.

328 It is a letter (six copies of which have been preserved) sent by the chief of the Qumran community shortly after the separation of his group from the rest of Judaism, made known by E. Qimron and J. Strugnell, «An Unpublished Halakhic Letter from Qumran» in *Biblical Archaeology Today*, Jerusalem 1985, 400-407, discussed in more detail in the chapter «Origins of the Essene Movement and of the Qumran Sect» pp. 77-96

329 Published by A. S. van der Woude, «Melchisedek als himmlische Erlösergestalt in den neugefundenen eschatologischen Midraschin aus Qumran Höhle XI», *Oudtestamentische Studien* 14 (1965) 354-373.

330 Which comes from the collection of Hymns from Cave 1, 1QH IX 14-15.

331 This text is discussed in more detail in the chapter «Messianic Hopes in the Qumran Writings» pp. 159-189.

332 Written at the request of Professor Jesús Peláez and published in the periodical *Filología Neotestamentaria* 2 (1989) 23-40.

333 W. H. Brownlee, *The Dead Sea Manual of Discipline. Translation and Notes*, in BASOR Supplementary Studies 10-12, New Haven 1951.

334 Brownlee translates: «Indeed, a man shall not bring accusation against his fellow in the presence of the Many who has not been subject to [previous] reproof before witnesses» (p. 22) and adds in note 23: «The teaching of Jesus in Matt. 18:15-17 gives us the clue for interpreting the passage: Jesus specifies three stages for dealing with an erring brother: (1) personal reproof, v. 15; (2) reproof before witnesses, v. 16; (3) reproof before the Church, v. 17. The first of these corresponds with DJD V, 5f.; the second, with the "reproof before witnesses" of VI,1; the third with the "accusation ... in the presence of the Many" VI,1. M.B. and S.J. dissent from this position and would translate here "accusation ... which is without proof". But cf. col. VII, notes 18 and 23».

335 H. Braun, «Qumran und das Neue Testament. Ein Bericht über 10 Jahre

Forschung (1950-1959)», *Theologische Rundschau* 28 (1962) 134-136 offers an excellent survey of the various studies on the topic. See also his *Qumran und das Neue Testament* I, Tübingen 1966, 338-340.

336 As, for example, J. Braun, *Spätjüdisch-häretischer und frühchristlicher Radikalismus.* II, Tübingen 1957, 26 and J. Schmitt, «Contribution à l'étude de la discipline pénitentielle dans l'Église primitive à la lumière des textes de Qumrân» in *Les Manuscrits de la Mer Morte. Colloque de Strasbourg 25-27 mai 1955*, Paris 1957, 99-100.

337 So, for example, J. Carmignac, *Le Docteur de Justice et Jésus Christ*, Paris 1957, 80.

338 These studies have been made from a New Testamental viewpoint and focus on the text of Matthew. Those worth mentioning (in chronological order): J. Gnilka, «Die Kirche des Matthäus und die Gemeinde von Qumrân», *Biblische Zeitschrift* N. F. 7 (1963) 43-63; W. D. Davies, *The Setting of the Sermon on the Mount*, Cambridge 1963, 220-224; W. Thompson, *Matthew's Advice to a Divided Community. Mt 17,22-18,35*, Rome 1970; G. Bornkamm, «Die Binde- und Lösegewalt in der Kirche des Matthäus» in *Geschichte und Glaube* II, Munich 1971, 37-50; H. Frankemölle, *Jahwebund und Kirche Christi. Studien zur Form- und Traditionsgeschichte des "Evangeliums" nach Matthäus*, Münster 1973, 226-232; G. Künzel, *Studien zur Gemeindeverständnis des Matthäus-Evangeliums*, Stuttgart 1978, 194ff.; G. Barth, «Auseindandersetzungen um die Kirchenzucht im Umkreis des Matthäusevangeliums», *ZNW* 69 (1978) 158-177; S. H. Brooks, *Matthew's Community. The evidence of his special sayings material*, Sheffield 1983, 99-107; J. Gnilka, *Das Matthäusevangelium.* II (Herders Theologischer Kommentar zum Neuen Testament), Freiburg-Basel-Vienna 1988, 134-142.

339 L. H. Schiffman, *Sectarian Law in the Dead Sea Scrolls. Courts, Testimony and the Penal Code* (Brown Judaic Studies 33) Chico 1983, 89-109. Also «Reproof as a Requisite for Punishment in the Law of the Dead Sea Scrolls» in B. S. Jackson (ed.), *Jewish Law Association Studies* II, Atlanta 1986, 59-74.

340 G. Forkman, *The Limits of the Religious Community*, Lund 1972.

341 Here we can ignore the problem of whether both texts legislate for the same or different communities since both legislations are in agreement.

342 For our translation we use the facsimile of CD published by E. Qimron in M. Broshi (ed.), *The Damascus Document Reconsidered*, Jerusalem 1992, which contains the variants from the copies found in Cave 4 of Qumran, and the edition by C. Rabin, *The Zadokite Documents*, Oxford ²1958.

343 Following the correction of ʿnh hw to ʿwnw hw. This correction was proposed by Schechter and is accepted by Schiffman; it is supported by the use in Num 30:16 of ʿwnh and by the presence of ʿwwn in the parallel text 1QS VI 1. The literal translation of the text preserved from the genizah: «he has testified against him», seems tautological and the translators who adopt it are unable to explain the relationship of the phrase with the foregoing text; in fact, and to

avoid this difficulty, the most recently published translations, while keeping the reading ʿnh hw, give it a reflexive meaning: «he has testified against himself», arriving at a meaning similar to the one we adopt (for example, G. Vermes, *The Dead Sea Scrolls in English*, Sheffield ¹³1988, 93; A. Dupont Sommer in *La Bible. Ecrits Intertestamentaires*, Paris 1987, 168. I. Robinson, «A Note on Damascus Document IX,7», *Revue de Qumrân* 9 (1977-78) 237ff., suggests translating the sentence: «[God] has decreed against him», but his solution (to give ʿnh the meaning of «decree against» and to consider God as the subject) seems forced. The meaning suggested has no more support than a use in Ruth 1:21 (a text which the versions have understood as ʿinnah, «to humble») and the omission of the subject cannot be explained. With or without correction of the text, these three interpretations agree in considering the sentence as the apodosis of the two preceding conditional phrases which explains the result for the sinner of the actions mentioned. Our opting for a correction of the text has been influenced by the fact that the text from the genizah is defective in these lines as is proved by the repetition of hw after ʾpw of the preceding line and the fact that the Qumran copies of 4Q and 5Q have a different text.

344 Or to all the «members» of the covenant if the reading and interpretation of Rabin are adopted. In any case, it is clearly denotes the members of the sect.

345 Strangely, the Vulgate translates this text: «ne oderis fratrem tuum in corde tuo sed *publice* argue eum ne habeas super illo peccatum».

346 L. Schiffman, *Sectarian Law*, 90-91; «Reproof», 64-65.

347 We are using the edition by M. Burrows, *The Dead Sea Scrolls of St Mark's Monastery* II/2, New Haven 1951. Among the older commentaries on 1QS, those by P. Wernberg-Möller, *The Manual of Discipline*, Leiden 1957; J. Licht, *The Roll of the Rule* (in Hebrew) and A. R. C. Leaney, *The Rule of Qumran and Its Meaning*, London 1966 are still useful.

348 The phrase «one year» has been added above the line, although the phrase «six months» has not been erased, which seems to indicate a change in community practice and an increase in the punishment expected.

349 J. Murphy-O'Connor, «A Literary Analysis of Damascus Document VI,2-VIII,2», *Revue Biblique* 78 (1971) 210-232. According to P. Davies, the list contains «Main points of the community's halachah», see his *The Damascus Document* (JSOTSS 25) Sheffield 1983, 125-132 and for M. Knibb, *The Qumran Community* (CCWJCW 2) Cambridge 1987, 51-54 it is «A summary of the duties of members».

350 See the chapter above, pp. 139-157 and the study «Les limites de la communauté: pureté et impureté à Qumrân et dans le Nouveau Testament», in *Text and Testimony. Essays in honour of A. F. J. Klijn*, Kampen 1988, 111-122.

351 Unlike Schiffman, 66, who prefers to consider the specification as metaphorical.

352 In the script of the manuscript, the *daleth* and the *resh* are almost indistinguish-

able, so that the reading *'ḥd*, followed here, and the reading *'ḥr*, preferred by a good many commentators (among them the latest translations by G. Vermes and A. Dupont-Sommer) are possible. In that case it would involve two witnesses of two different offences and their combined testimony would be enough to exclude the guilty party from the «purity» of the sect.

353 See the series of articles on the topic which have appeared in the *Revue de Qumrân* 8 (1973-75): B. A. Levine, «Damascus Document IX, 17-22: A New Translation and Commentary», 195-196; J. Neusner, «By the Testimony of Two Witnesses in the Damascus Document IX, 17-22 and in Pharisaic-Rabbinic Law», 197-217; L. H. Schiffman, «The Qumran Law of Testimony», 603-612, and *Revue de Qumrân* 9 (1976-78): N. L. Rabinovitch, «Damascus Document IX, 17-22 and Rabbinic Parallels», 113-116; J. Neusner, «Damascus Document IX, 17-22 and Irrelevant Parallels», 441-444; B. S. Jackson, «Damascus Document IX, 16-23 and Parallels», 445-450.

354 J. Pouilly, *La Règle de la Communauté de Qumrân. Son évolution littéraire* (Cahiers de la Revue Biblique 17) Paris 1976, 45-50 considers the text to be part of an interpolation inserted at the third stage of the composition of 1QS. In our translation of line 25 we have taken into account the restorations of 4QS$^d$ suggested by J. T. Milik in *Revue Biblique* 67 (1960) 412.

355 The possibility of splitting the Qumran process of rebuke in two stages: a (private) rebuke before witnesses and a later (public) rebuke before the *Rabbim*, (a rebuke which could be the same as the rebuke before the *Mebaqqer*, one of the *Rabbim*, which acts as a basis for the eventual sentencing of the guilty person) in my view seems excluded by the same wording in that a *wgm* clearly separates both parts of the text and from the insistence on the rebuke before witnesses and the accusation before the *Mebaqqer* must be made the same day on which the fault has been witnessed, which is not required for the accusations before the *Rabbim*. The opinion of M. Knibb, *The Qumran Community*, 115, who thinks he can discern three stages in the Qumran rebuke seems even less likely to me.

356 See J. Murphy-O'Connor, «A Literary Analysis of Damascus Document XIX,33-XX,34», *Revue Biblique* 79 (1972) 544-564; P. Davies, *The Damascus Covenant*, 181-192 and M. Knibb, *The Qumran Community*, 72.

357 See the studies by H. Burgman, «ΤΨΚḤΤ in 1QpHab V,10. Ein Schlüsselwort mit verhängnisvollen historischen Konsequenzen», *Revue de Qumrân* 10 (1979-81) 293-300.

358 See 1QH VII 29; IX 33; XII 21.31; compare 1QH 9.24. The same manuscript also uses the verb *ykḥ* with a slightly different meaning and does not imply brotherly rebuke in the strict sense, see 1QH I 25; VI 4; IX 23; XII 28; compare XVIII 12.

359 It is a text which describes the founding schism of the community: the Man of Lies is presented as transgressing the law, the Teacher of Righteousness as

exercising his right of rebuke, and the council remaining silent without supporting the Teacher of Righteousness in this rebuke of the Man of Lies. The
result will be the split within the group to which both the Teacher of
Righteousness and the Man of Lies belong, and the installation in the desert
of the partisans of the Teacher of Righteousness.

360 A. R. C. Leaney, *The Rule of Qumran*, 179.

361 *Sectarian Law*, 96; «Reproof», 72.

362 One of the copies from Cave 4, 4QS$^d$, instead of «those who choose the path»
has «the chosen of the path». In both cases it denotes the members of the sect,
see CD I 13-16 and II 15-16.

363 See the studies cited in note 338 and the bibliography given in the most recently published commentary on Matthew: J. Gnilka, *Das Matthäusevangelium*,
142.

364 References in *TWNT* and Bauer-Aland, *Griechisch-deutsches Wörterbuch* (Berlin
1988) under the respective words.

365 1 Tim 5:20; 2 Tim 4:2; Tit 1:9.13; 2:15.

366 Especially by Bornkamm, «Die Binde- und Lösegewalt», 40-45; G. Forkman,
*The Limits*, 129-132 and G. Barth, «Kirchenzucht», 174-175.

367 *Matthew's Community*, 99-103.

368 Already R. Bultmann, *Die Geschichte der synoptischen Tradition*, Göttingen
$^7$1964, 151; see, for example, G. Bornkamm, «Die Binde- und Lösegewalt», 38-
39; G. Barth, «Kirchenzucht», 168-169; and J. Gnilka, *Das Matthäusevangelium*,
135. Bornkamm proposes the most arguments for identifying this community
as Judaeo-Christian. Gnilka ascribes the *halakhah* of vv. 15-17 to the school of
Matthew.

369 Reasons why W. G. Thompson, *Matthew's Advice to a Divided Community*, 234,
supposes that both Matthew and Luke transformed earlier tradition and that
in this case Matthew preserved better the primitive wording.

370 Which a certain number of manuscripts, both Latin and Greek, have even
added to 17:3.

371 See G. Barth, «Kirchenzucht», 168; J. Gnilka, *Das Matthäusevangelium*, 136.

372 The difficulty faced by those defending a development starting from Lk 17:3
to bridge the gap between the *logion* of Luke and the practice defined in Mt
18:15-17 is superbly reflected in G. Barth, «Kirchenzucht», 169-170.

373 S. H. Brooks, *Matthew's Community*, 101-102 has proved, against Barth and
Thompson, that the reference to Dt 19:15 (which also occurs in 2 Cor 13:1 and
1 Tim 5:19) is not a later addition but forms an intrinsic part of the pericope
in its primitive form.

374 The reason why this process of rebuke, in spite of its precise juridical structure, happened to be completely sterile and had no influence at all in the early
Church is a very interesting problem but it lies beyond the perspective of this
paper. See the references in this regard by G. Barth, «Kirchenzucht», 177 and

J. Gnilka, *Das Matthäusevangelium*, 141-142. It is interesting to observe that this process of rebuke developed only within monastic communities and others of the same type, since this fact shows us that sociological factors play a possibly decisive role in the exegetical activity which leads to the expression of the law of rebuke.

375 For example, G. Forkman, *The Limits*, 128: «But even if no literary dependence is to be found it is clear that factually Matt. 18:15-17 must have been influenced by either Qumran or some other similar community». J. Gnilka, *Das Matthäusevangelium*, 139: «Qumran provides the closest analogy. Dependence cannot yet be proved, but neither is it to be excluded completely».

Published by

E. J. Brill, Plantijnstraat 2, PO Box 9000, 2300 PA Leiden, the Netherlands
E. J. Brill (USA) Inc, 24 Hudson Street, Kinderhook, NY 12106, USA

Cover Design: Roland van Helden
Typographical Design: Alje Olthof
This book was set in Ehrhardt typeface by Perfect Service, Schoonhoven,
the Netherlands and printed by the Sigma Press, Zoetermeer, the Netherlands

The paper in this book meets the guidelines for performance and durability of the
Committee on Production Guidelines for Book Longevity of the Council on Library
Resources